For Pat —
For persistence + dedica
+ restocking + friendship —
Carol

Rude Awakenings

Rude Awakenings

An American Historian's Encounters with Nazism, Communism, and McCarthyism

Carol Sicherman

NEW ACADEMIA
PUBLISHING

Washington, DC

New Academia Publishing, 2012

Printed in the United States of America

Library of Congress Control Number: 2011939247
ISBN 978-0-9836899-8-0 paperback (alk. paper)

New Academia Publishing
PO Box 27420, Washington, DC 20038-7420
info@newacademia.com - www.newacademia.com

For Harry's further descendants
Miriam Sicherman
Noemi Sicherman
Una Yoorim Sicherman Rose

Contents

Acknowledgments

A number of people have been vital to my work on this book, which originates in the papers of Harry J. Marks, my father. The family of Ernest Engelberg, an age-mate and friend in Harry's Berlin days, has been generous with hospitality and information. A visit in 2005 to Engelberg, then ninety-six years old, his son (Achim), and wife (Waltraut) gave powerful impetus to the research. Achim later made a gift of his book about German refugee intellectuals who returned to Germany. Engelberg's biographer, Mario Kessler, also provided useful information. Relatives and friends of other people whom Harry knew in Berlin have also been generous with their knowledge. Dorothee Gottschalk–the widow of Lutz (Ludwig) Gottschalk, whom Harry had known in Berlin–contributed her knowledge of the Gottschalk family and some of their friends. Michael Freyhan contributed knowledge of the Freyhan family. David Sanford and Irene Hirschbach gave information on the Hirschbach family, and Irene sent two unpublished biographical essays by her late husband, Ernest Hirschbach. As time went on, I came to know (electronically) Peter-Thomas Walther of Humboldt University, Gottfried Niedhart of Mannheim University, and Daniel Becker, all of whom have shared their learning.

Other people have been generous in giving me information. Harry's late cousins, Margaret Marks and Hannah Bildersee, sent me family history twenty-five years before I dreamed of this project. Cousins of my generation, Mary Misrahi Rancatore and Julienne Misrahi Barnett, supplied additional information. When I interviewed my mother's oldest surviving sibling, Vida Castaline, in the mid-1970s, I had no idea that I would later rely on her remarkably detailed recall of life in Russia and, later, in Boston. Sidney

Lipshires, who had been a Communist official in Massachusetts and, later, Harry's doctoral student, knew valuable details about Harry's Communist past. Curt Beck, whose long career at the University of Connecticut (UConn) overlapped Harry's, offered additional information about the 1950s. Emanuel Margolis, a victim of McCarthyism at UConn, was kind enough to recall those painful days with a frankness that took my breath away. Bruce Stave, also of UConn, had just finished his excellent history of the university when I began my work and helpfully answered questions. Ellen Schrecker sent the spare but illuminating notes that she made when she interviewed Harry in 1979 for *No Ivory Tower: McCarthyism and the Universities*. Miriam Schneir gave invaluable advice at the end of the process and suggested the title. Lily Munford, Peter Schaefer, and Waltraut Engelberg helped transliterate the old German script in which most of Grete Meyer's letters and some of the other Berlin letters were written, as well as short notes written in German by my maternal grandmother's family. Lily, in addition to doing the lion's share of transliteration, undertook the considerable task of translating the Meyer letters. At the very beginning, Ingrid Finnan translated three of Engelberg's letters and insisted that I could do the other three, thus giving me an incentive to revive my college German; at the very end, she provided essential expertise in preparing the photographs for publication. Except for the Meyer letters and those that Ingrid translated, translations of letters from the Berlin friends are my own, as are any otherwise unascribed translations. Michiel Nijhoff helped with Dutch. Members of H-German, the H-Net discussion group on German history, advised a trespasser in their realm.

Librarians and archivists have given essential help. These include Betsy Pittman at the Thomas R. Dodd Center at UConn; Hermann Teifer at the Leo Baeck Institute in New York and other colleagues there; staff at the Harvard University Archives; and Sydney Van Nort at the archives of City College, City University of New York. In recompense, I have donated Harry's Berlin-related papers to the Leo Baeck Institute and the professional papers of Louis Marks, Harry's father, to City College (Harry's papers connected with his service at UConn are in the Dodd Center there). Two interlibrary-loan librarians–Suzanne Haber at the Mount Pleasant

Public Library and Eugene Laper at Lehman College–efficiently provided innumerable books and microfilms. Noemi Sicherman patiently solved word-processing problems and later proofread; together with Soji, she gave much comfort. Doris Irons read the page proofs. Long before I dreamed of this book, my daughter Miriam Sicherman, curious about her grandfather's past, obtained and sent a copy of his congressional testimony, which until then I had thought was secret.

The photographs come mainly from the Marks family archive. Achim Engelberg sent the photograph of the Engelberg family in Geneva in 1938, and Renate Engelberg Rauer explained the background circumstances. Harry took all other photographs of his Berlin friends. He also took the photographs of sites in Germany, with two exceptions–Mommsenstrasse 57, which I took in 2005; and the memorial to Kurt Singer, taken from Wikipedia Commons and published under the terms of its GNU Free Documentation License; Wikipedia Commons is also the source of the map of Germany, published under the same terms. The dates given in captions, some of which quote Harry, are either supplied by the photographers or inferred from other information. All of the illustrations were prepared for publication by Ingrid Finnan with enviable patience and persistence, particularly when she modified the map to include Heidelberg.

My greatest debts are to my husband, Marvin Sicherman, and to Volker Berghahn, professor of German history at Columbia University. It was Marvin who advised me to contact Volker, for he knew his reputation as a kind and erudite scholar. Volker's immediate response to the merest hint of the materials in my possession was to say: "Write something." When, in December 2005, I returned from visiting the Engelbergs in Berlin, he said plainly: "Either you give these materials to the Leo Baeck Institute and someone else will write them up, or write them up yourself." I have chosen both to write them up myself and to donate them so that others may use them in their research. Without Marvin's initial shove and Volker's boost, I doubt I would have written this book. Volker's advice as the book evolved put me in his debt. The mistakes that remain are my responsibility alone.

Abbreviations

AAUP	American Association of University Professors
AEW	Albert E. Waugh Papers, Dodd Research Center, University of Connecticut
BT	*Berliner Tageblatt*
CPUSA	Communist Party of the United States
DNVP	Deutschnational Volkspartei (German National People's Party)
DRC	Thomas J. Dodd Research Center, University of Connecticut, Storrs, CT
EEL	Ernst Engelberg letter to Harry Marks
FZ	*Frankfurter Allgemeine Zeitung*
Gestapo	Geheimnis Staatspolizei (Secret State Police)
GML	Grete Meyer letter to Harry Marks
HJM	Harry J. Marks
HJMD	Harry J. Marks diary
HJML	Harry J. Marks letter (to Louis and Sophie Marks, unless otherwise ascribed)
HUAC	House Un-American Activities Committee
Kostufra	Kommunistische Studentenfraktion (Communist Student Fraction)

KPD	Kommunistische Partei Deutschlands (Communist Party of Germany)
MIT	Massachusetts Institute of Technology
NCC	National Coordinating Committee for Aid to Refugees and Emigrants Coming from Germany
NSBO	Nationalsozialistische Betriebszellen Organization (National Socialist Factory Cell Organization)
NSDAP	Nationalsozialistische Deutsche Arbeiterpartei (National Socialist German Workers Party--Nazi Party)
NSDStB	Nationalsozialistischer Deutscher Studentenbund (National Socialist German Students' League)
NSL	National Student League
P.G.	Paul Gottschalk
RM	Reichsmark (literally, "Reich's mark" or sign; the German currency)
S.A.	Sturmabteilung (Storm Troop—brown shirts; Nazi paramilitary)
SLID	Student League for Industrial Democracy
SPD	Sozialdemokratische Partei Deutschlands (Social Democratic Party of Germany)
S.S.	Schutzstaffel (Protection Squad—political police formed in 1933 as Hitler's personal guard; later, under Heinrich Himmler, mass army supporting Nazis)
UConn	University of Connecticut
YCL	Young Communist League

VB	*Völkischer Beobachter* (People's Observer; Nazi newspaper)
Voss	*Vossische Zeitung* (liberal Berlin newspaper; the name derives from an eighteenth-century publisher, C.F. Voss)
WPA	Works Progress Administration

Rude Awakenings

An American Historian's Encounters
with Nazism, Communism,
and McCarthyism

1

Prologue

In this book I refer to my father, Harry J. Marks, as "Harry," a
name I never used to his face, as a way of distancing him from the
"Daddy" I knew, a way of helping me be an honest chronicler.
The book originates in a collection of family papers that I inherited when Harry died in 1988. These papers fall into two categories.
One group–family memorabilia and photographs–illustrates the
assimilation into mainstream American society of immigrant German Jews of modest background. Another set of documents–the literal and figurative center of this book–relates to Harry's postgradu-
ate studies in Berlin in 1931-33: some two hundred letters home
and the diaries he kept during that period, as well as related letters
in the following years; several dozen letters written in 1934-45 by
people he had known in Germany; and photographs that he took
shortly before leaving Germany in September 1933. My purpose is
not that of a memoirist, although this book has some memoiristic
features. It is, rather, to show the impact on an American intellectual of three movements: the rise of Nazism in Germany; Communism as a world phenomenon and, more particularly, its presence
in the United States; and the reaction to Communism known in the
United States as McCarthyism.

Harry's diaries and letters from Berlin constitute an eyewitness
response to the catastrophe unfolding in Germany, a response un-
mediated by the kind of retrospective analysis one finds in memoirs.[1] His friends' letters speak of the thunderstorm unleashed over
their heads and their efforts to find shelter. While often plain and
analytical in style, Harry's letters and, particularly, his diaries rise
at times to lyrical beauty and at others are marred by the precious

self-consciousness of a lingering adolescence. Although he traveled elsewhere in Germany and made study trips to other European countries, Harry's diaries and letters focus on Berlin, ground zero of the Nazi "revolution." In 1933, his writings increased in volume to accommodate the momentous events unrolling before his eyes. His letters (but not his diaries) became more circumspect both because he did not want to alarm his parents and because he feared confiscation and censorship. As one would expect, he omitted significant events; however, when he focused on a particular event, the detail often surpasses what even the most attentive historian might present.

In addition to conveying Harry's experiences, this book touches on the lives of more than thirty Germans with whom he was friendly during his two years in Berlin. These thirty include a group of people allied through family connections, including ties with Harry's family in New York; a fellow graduate student named Ernst Engelberg; and several professors who were forced out of Germany shortly after Hitler came to power. Of all of these people, only one had no Jewish connection by either descent or marriage: this was Engelberg, who was in peril because he was a Communist. These friends and relatives shared an atypical fate: all escaped from Germany, and all survived the war.

Harry's time in Germany, the subject of chapters 3 and 4, is the fulcrum of this book. The preceding chapters examine how his prior personal history shaped him for those two years, while the succeeding chapters depict how the Berlin years affected the rest of his life and the lives of his friends. As a budding historian, he felt fortunate to witness an unfolding cataclysm. "Even the dullest student at the University of Berlin during those years," wrote another neophyte American historian, "could not but have been aware of the fact, that there were sources of historical knowledge beyond the confines of the Historical Seminar," the department at the university encompassing modern history.[2] As Harry sailed home in September 1933, he envisioned a future as both a historian and a socialist; within months, he was a Communist. His future turned out less rosy than he had expected. He had a number of strikes against him, some not of his own making: the Depression and his Jewishness combined to foil his initial efforts to land an academic job, and for some years he taught high school. After World War II, he managed to achieve much of the academic career of which he dreamed, despite his painful experience of McCarthyism. His professional life at the University of Connecticut (UConn) coexisted with the evolution of a land-grant university from a "cow college" to a major research university. His yearning to belong to a community, manifested through his Communist activities in the 1930s, was fulfilled by his contributions to this academic community.

Harry's was an academic life well lived, but also one with a shameful secret. It has been unpleasant to investigate his early uncritical enthusiasm for Communism and dismaying to observe his later infection with anti-Communism, an infection that made him eager to inform on those who he believed were Communists. "Some of their descendants might wish this not to be true," writes Alice Munro about her own ancestors, "but there is not much to be done about the politics of our relatives, living or dead."[3] She speaks for me.

The nature of the evidence

Harry's Berlin letters are not, for the most part, especially private. Knowing that his parents would save the letters, he rarely repeated himself in his diary. He confided his most intimate thoughts in the diaries, which in other respects were similar in scope to the letters. Forty-eight years later, he used his diaries for a talk before the UConn History Club that he called "The Rise of the Nazis–A Kind of Personal Memoir." He seems to have used them the previous year to prepare for an interview for a UConn oral history project documenting the university. Some years earlier, he consulted the diaries when writing about the Dutch historian Jan Romein (see Chapter 8).

In order to highlight an apprentice historian's direct encounter with history in the making, I have ignored nearly all the passages in Harry's letters and diaries referring to family matters, as well as his (frankly boring) disquisitions on economics, lists of books he had read (or meant to read), opinions of opera singers, and so on. The letters that he received from German friends, in contrast, contain very little extraneous to my purpose. Almost all of them illustrate the writers' experiences of unspooling repression; some contain requests to make certain information known to others who might help save people at risk in Europe. I cannot believe that the writers, if alive, would reprehend me for quoting their words or for trying to uncover additional information about their escape from Nazism. Those of their descendants whom I have met or contacted have been pleased, without exception, that their ancestors' experiences will come to light.

Diarists and letter-writers

The centrality of Harry's diaries and letters in this book makes it necessary to establish their relationship to other such writings devoted to Germany in the 1930s. Uncounted diaries were written by Germans and other Europeans in 1933-45, some published and more unpublished (or lost), many of them concerning the war period and thus beyond the scope of this book. Of those focusing on the 1930s and published, only one diary raises the possibility of comparison with Harry's. In manuscript until an edited version appeared in 2009, *An American in Hitler's Berlin: Abraham Plotkin's Diary, 1932-33* covers the period of four and a half months when Plotkin, a forty-year-old trade unionist, lived in Berlin while undertaking an intensive study of unions and labor conditions in Germany. Differences in their ages, personalities, and purposes, as well as Harry's far longer stay and his immersion in a large Jewish social circle, make Plotkin's and Harry's diaries complementary rather than duplicative. While, for example, Harry felt safer if he avoided demonstrations and read about them in the newspapers, Plotkin sought them out and described them vividly. Harry's stance as a historian-in-training contrasts with Plotkin's thin knowledge of current and past German history: Plotkin's allusion to "anti-Semitic riots in the University of Breslau...against Prof. Cohn" (otherwise unexplained) is complemented by Harry's detailed analysis of Ernst Cohn's travails. Harry wrote his diary for himself, with the intimacy that such a reader implies; Plotkin, envisaging publication, wrote reportage for future public use and did indeed publish an article on his return. Plotkin's advantage over Harry lay in his long analytical interviews with union leaders, some of whom escorted him to meet the kinds of slum-dwellers about whom Harry only read. Overall, Harry's intensive reading of newspapers and his discussions with friends gave him a considerable advantage in assessing the dizzying developments of the early Nazi period; he understood immediately the consequences of Hitler's seizure of power. Plotkin was not so certain: while anticipating some kind of dictatorship, he thought that Alfred Hugenberg, leader of the German National People's Party, might well prevail over Hitler.[4]

Other published diaries and letters differ more markedly from Harry's than does Plotkin's diary. The diary and letters of the artist Oskar Schlemmer, for example, who moved to Berlin in 1932, focus on Nazi oppression of artists. The diaries of Count Harry Kessler, who was in Berlin for much of the 1920s and early 1930s, have nothing in common with Harry Marks's except left-wing sympathies and a revulsion against the Nazis. None of the (relatively fewer) volumes of published letters of the period are comparable; one can hardly put Thomas Mann's letters and Harry's in the same category. Harry's diary and letters are distinguished by his foreignness, his youth and inexperience, the intensity of his gaze, and—most notably—his self-education as a historian.

Memoirs and oral histories give another kind of witness to the times than do diaries and letters. Memoirists or interviewees who have sought verification may sometimes be more reliable than on-the-spot reporters, but they lack the immediacy of diaries and letters, with their fluctuating moods, their errors, and their self-correction. Memoirs and oral histories are, furthermore, selective, sometimes deliberately so. Harry's own oral history (1980), for example, omits his own leadership role among Harvard's student Communists.[5]

The most famous example today of a German diarist is Victor Klemperer, a professor of Romance literatures at Dresden Technical University who was determined to "bear witness." His anticipation of arrest or death at any moment—which did not come—fueled his efforts. Klemperer's feelings were far more intense than those of a temporary resident like Harry: fear, "disgust and shame" at the ready capitulation of so many Germans, and "shame for Germany."[6] Because Klemperer was so keen an observer, his diary for the 1930s contains information and observations that complement some of the letters that form the basis of my fifth chapter. He was also close in background to the members of Harry's circle: like Harry's teacher Gustav Mayer, he was an academic and a Jew; like Harry's Uncle Alfred Hirschbach's nephews, he was a Jew who had been baptized a Protestant. Klemperer also shared some commonalities with Harry, notwithstanding differences in temperament and age. Like Harry, he was awkward in social settings yet confident within academia; like Harry, he was indifferent to religion; like Harry, he was given to grandiose dreams of his future accomplishments.[7] In Klemperer's case, his dreams were fulfilled partly while he was alive, but most remarkably long after his death, when the publication of his diaries created a sensation in Germany.

In contrast with Harry's and Klemperer's diaries, those kept by the German journalist Bella Fromm and by three Americans–the journalist William L. Shirer, and the diplomats James G. McDonald and William E. Dodd–cover much more, and very different, ground. These diarists' professions brought them in frequent contact with power-brokers, which was hardly the case for either Harry or Klemperer. Fromm had access to the highest echelons of Berlin political society, about which she wrote in self-censored columns in the *Vossische Zeitung* and the *Berliner Tageblatt* (among Harry's favorite papers until ruined by Nazi controls). Meanwhile she kept a secret diary trenchantly expressing her real (and often prescient) views. Although Jewish, she was exempt for some years from anti-Semitic restrictions because the Nazis feared adverse publicity from the diplomatic corps, with which she was well connected. McDonald, High Commissioner for Refugees from Germany under the League of Nations, dictated his minutely detailed diary as a historical record and for the information of his co-workers. Dodd, the American ambassador to Germany, used his diary as a historical record; his children edited it for publication shortly after his death. Shirer, who reported for three years from Berlin (in 1934-37), "watched with increasing fascinating and horror" as Europe "plunge[d] madly down the road to Armageddon."[8]

Klemperer, Fromm, Dodd, McDonald, and Shirer wrote their diaries from a moral compulsion; they all felt an imperative to "bear witness." Harry's impulse was different, although also informed by morality. As a foreigner on a short-term assignment, he lacked the immersion of journalists like Shirer and two other American

journalists whose books on contemporary Germany he greatly admired–Edgar Ansel Mowrer (*Germany Sets the Clock Back*) and H. R.
Knickerbocker (*The German Crisis*). Seeing himself as a future historian of Germany, he wanted to understand the evil that was thrust
in front of him. As the tempo of the crisis increased, so did his drive
to learn contemporary history. With the truths of events obscured
by Nazi rant and lies, he meant to be a vigilant witness, to verify
what he could and to expose falsity whenever possible.

2

Harry's Home, Harry's Harvard

Part 1. Harry's Home

The old country was fairly near in psychological terms during the childhood of Harry's parents, Louis Marks and Sophie Levison Marks. Louis's parents were both born in East Prussia, as were Sophie's father and maternal grandparents. Louis's father, Julius (born in 1834), traveled to America twice in the mid-nineteenth century, the second time as an immigrant. The California Gold Rush lured his two older brothers; Julius, age fourteen, soon followed, traveling by mule across Panama and sailing north to San Francisco. His brothers remained in California and prospered; Julius, however, returned to Germany. When he emigrated some years later, he settled on the Lower East Side of Manhattan in an area so teeming with German immigrants that it was known as *Kleindeutschland* (Little Germany). In New York, he transmuted his teenage spirit of adventure into entrepreneurship: he ran a small department store and invested in real estate. His "more or less arranged marriage" (in 1865) to a shoemaker's daughter named Esther Buck, fourteen years his junior, followed a pattern then "common in middle-class Jewish families."[1] Among their six children, two sons–Harry (born in 1875) and Louis (born in 1876)–are significant for our purposes. When Julius Marks died in 1887, he left Esther well off and eager to rise in German-American Jewish society. In 1890, she married the cantor of their synagogue, Herman Goldstein. The Goldsteins lived far from the slums of the Lower East Side in a brownstone on East 68th Street on the elegant Upper East Side, where the synagogue also moved.[2] Esther had her portrait painted in oil. They had arrived.

Harry's maternal ancestors fit the same broad pattern. Sophie's grandparents, Caroline and Solomon Katz, emigrated in the later 1840s and married in the early 1850s; the oldest of their six children, Sarah, married a Prussian immigrant named Aaron Harry Levison, known as Harry (who became an American citizen in 1880). (Because of the proliferation of men named Harry among the Levison and Marks families, in this chapter I sometimes refer to my main subject as "Harry Julian.") The Levisons settled in the small upstate New York town of Goshen, where Harry established a tailoring business–"Merchant Tailor" is his occupation in the 1880 Federal Census–and participated in civic life, joining the Goshen Lodge of the Free and Accepted Masons in 1896; thanks to him, the Levison family plot in Mt. Carmel Cemetery in New York bears the Masonic emblem. Harry and Sarah had five children–a son, Leo; and four daughters, one of whom died in infancy. Deborah married Alfred H. Hirschbach, an American-born investment banker who had grown up in Germany and who, later on, introduced Harry Julian to his friends and relatives in Berlin.[3] The two other surviving daughters, Hannah Violetta and Sophie, trained as teachers and married two Marks brothers, Louis and Harry. In 1907, Harry Levison met a newsworthy end. A report in a Goshen newspaper–"Suddenly Stricken: Apoplexy Causes Death of Former Goshen Man on Elevated Train"–recounted how "a gentleman sat reading a newspaper" and

> remained motionless so long that the attention of the passengers was attracted and one of them, a physician, went to him, felt of his pulse, and then informed the guard that the man was dead, sitting upright in his seat and his newspaper still clasped in his stiffening fingers.

The gentleman was "A. H. Levison, for many years a well-known and highly respected resident of this village, where he conducted a clothing and custom tailoring establishment."[4] He, too, had arrived.

The Levinson–and probably the Marks–family had connections further east than Prussia. Some evidence appears in the will of

Harry Levison's brother Barnett (born about 1835), who emigrated about 1864. When his will was probated in 1910, the Surrogate's Court published the necessary legal notice (in English) in a Yiddish-language newspaper; it included a long list of possible "heirs and next of kin." Besides seventeen potential heirs in New York and nearby American states, there were thirteen others in Germany, Poland, and Russia. What happened to the thirteen? How many emigrated? How many, or how many of their descendants, perished in the Holocaust or, for that matter, beforehand in World War I or the Russian Revolution? The answers to these questions would keep a legion of genealogists busy.

For a generation or two, the Levison and Marks families were at least partly German in their language use, and one can assume that the relatives left behind in Europe were also German-speaking, no matter where they lived (there is some evidence that the Levisons knew some Yiddish). The language practice of Harry Julian's maternal ancestors appears in four brief messages to the seventeen-year-old Sarah Katz after she went to visit family and friends in Germany in the summer of 1872. Her parents, Caroline and Solomon Katz, wrote to her in fairly uneducated German, while her younger sisters, Francisca and Emily, wrote in English. For a whole hour after Sarah left, her mother reported, "die kleine Emily" ("little Emily," age seven) kept saying: "Schie schut kom bëk." This sentence defies comprehension until recognized as English written with a German accent: "She should come back."[5] As often happens in immigrant families, the younger generation understood the parents' mother tongue but used English, which the older generation understood but did not write. The younger generation did not pass such German as they knew down to their own children.

A similar language practice apparently prevailed in the Marks household. Louis, who studied German in college, could converse on cultural topics with his German-speaking stepfather. Cantor Goldstein, an ardent admirer of German culture, advised him to read Shakespeare in the beautiful "original," by which he meant the Schlegel-Tieck German version.[6] Louis later used German during a study trip to Berlin in 1907, when he was an elementary-school teacher about to become a principal. The Royal Prussian authorities granted him "permission to visit certain schools" in Berlin, including a technical school for bookbinders and printers.[7] His interest in applied subjects remained: a decade later, he fostered vocational education as principal of a large elementary school. He retained enough German to write a letter to his son in German in the summer of 1931, when Harry Julian was studying the language in Heidelberg. "Perhaps there are many errors," Louis wrote, "and for that reason you shouldn't show it to your professor."

The three children of Herman Goldstein, a widower, were living with his sister in Vienna when he and Esther married and, Esther assured her children, would remain there. Instead, however, they followed their father and became part of Esther's household. The remarriage alienated Esther's two oldest sons, Isidore and Harry, who refused to accept money from her to attend college and went to work for silk-and-ribbon merchants. Impressed with Louis's intelligence, they gave him spending money so that he could go to City College, which was entirely free.[8] The trajectory of the Marks family went in one generation from small tradesmen to successful businessmen and, in the next generation, to a top administrator in the New York City school system–the apex of the family until Harry Julian ascended yet higher with a Harvard PhD.[9]

Louis Marks in the private sphere

Graduating from City College in 1896, Louis began his career as a public-school teacher and ten years later received his principal's license. The year 1908 was momentous. He was appointed principal of Public School 43 in the Bronx, where he interviewed Sophie Levison for a position as a kindergarten teacher. After he hired her, he reportedly said: "She can hang her coat in my closet anytime." She did. In July, Rabbi Stephen S. Wise of the Free Synagogue officiated at their wedding and signed the gilt-edged Torah that commemorated the occasion.[10] The choice of the Free Synagogue–founded only a year earlier as a "pewless and dueless" institution committed to social justice–was in keeping with the progressive outlook that marked Louis's career.[11] The couple's honeymoon in Europe showed that in one generation Europe could become a foreign continent: a place to visit, not to come from. In keeping with custom, Sophie did not return to work after marrying. She gave birth to Harry the next year.[12]

The Marks and Levison families blended well, enjoying good times together and supporting one another in bad. Deborah and Alfred Hirschbach joined Sophie and Louis in celebrating the marriage of Leo Levison in 1912. For this occasion Deborah and Alfred composed (and had formally printed) doggerel songs, including a "beautiful quartet" in which "the other Schwiegermutter" (mother-in-law), Sarah Katz Levison, yearns: "If only with my Hannah some day I'll also have this joy." Her wish was fulfilled two years later, when Hannah married Louis's brother Harry, a widower.[13] For that event, the same forces presented a "Musical Photoplay" consisting of more doggerel set to popular tunes. When Hannah died after giving birth in 1915, Harry's family joined Louis and Sophie's household, his two daughters becoming Harry Julian's quasi-siblings.

Through energetic cultivation of his talents and his stock portfolio, Louis Marks became sufficiently prosperous to see his son through private school and send him to Harvard for his bachelor's and doctoral degrees (and, in between, to the University of Berlin). He also sent him on a high school trip to Europe in 1926, which Harry recorded in the first of his extant diaries. Louis and Sophie made at least four foreign trips after their honeymoon. Their travels in North Africa in 1932 yielded a somewhat surprising photograph of Sophie, grown pleasingly plump, smiling bravely atop a horse, en route to the oasis at Tozeur, Tunisia.

Louis Marks in the public sphere

When Louis attended City College, it occupied a grand ivy-covered building at Lexington Avenue and 23rd Street designed by James Renwick, Jr., one of the premier practitioners of the Gothic Revival. City College was–in the words of Supreme Court Justice Felix Frankfurter, who graduated six years after Louis–a "great institution for the acquisition of disciplined habits of work."[14] The young men (there were no women) were the sons of "petty tradesmen, clerks, and professional people"; they were "'new men,' without name, wealth, or family tradition," whose "moderate bourgeois circumstances" precluded their attending any other kind of college.[15] Within a few years, thanks to the enormous immigration that populated the Lower East Side, the student body was 80-90% Jewish.[16]

At a time when the only other postsecondary institutions in New York City–Columbia University and the University of the City of New York (later renamed New York University)–were expensive and private, ambitious young men like Louis were drawn to "the people's college," alias "the people's Harvard."

Students at City followed either the "classical" or the "scientific" course, neither of which gave much room for choice. Enrolled in the scientific course, Louis studied chemistry, physics, mathematics, biology, English, philosophy, history, drawing, and modern languages (French and German). He steadily improved his performance, in his first year ranking 152 out of 303 (labeled "Good") on the Merit Roll and in his last year ranking 29 out of 74 ("High").[17] In calculating student rank, "demerits" (awarded for such infractions as missing a class) were subtracted from grades. Someone wrote on the Registrar's records for 1895-96: "What a humbug is this Merit Roll!" But Louis and his brothers would not have regarded his success as "humbug."

City College resembled the Ivy League architecturally, but whereas the Ivy League aimed to reproduce the middle class, City had a transformative role in the lives of "proud sons of immigrant parents."[18] The solemnity of its purpose appears in Louis's class photograph. Seated in the front row are the president and the ten professors, bewhiskered or bearded or both, gold watch chains glinting here and there.[19] Seventy-two serious young men, nearly the entire class, stand on bleachers in six rows. Four of the graduates sport mustaches, and one has a beard that may hint at aspirations to join the faculty. Louis is in the center of the third row, his hair slicked down, his head tilted slightly to his right. The students' attire indicates their claim to middle-class status; despite the tight grouping, an occasional watch chain is visible, and some (like Louis) have a white handkerchief in the jacket pocket. When the graduation ceremony of Louis's class took place–at Carnegie Hall, no less–the students' appearance disturbed Robert Maclay, who as President of the Board of Trustees had just signed their diplomas. In a newspaper interview, Maclay deplored the "exceedingly imperfect" physical condition of the "narrow-chested, round-shouldered, stooped" young men.[20] He wanted City College to institute physical training. Louis's later emphasis on the "whole child" implies that he came to agree with Maclay.

Engraved on vellum, the diplomas that Maclay signed in 1896 were magnificently large: two feet high and seventeen inches wide. Embellished with calligraphic decorations, each diploma was stamped in red with the City College seal–a tripartite female figure facing past, present, and future–and signed not only by Maclay but by President Alexander Webb and the ten professors. The graduate's name and degree, as well as the date, were hand-lettered in big, bold Gothic script. At the top was engraved the City College coat of arms, an allegorical representation combining elements of the seals of the City and State of New York. Four figures represent the colonial heritage and ideals of City College: the male figures of an Indian and a colonial sailor on the left, and the female figures of Alma Mater and Discipline on the right. The Indian wears a feathered headdress and carries a bow and quiver, while the sailor holds a sextant and a shield depicting a Dutch windmill, two beavers, and two flour barrels. Alma Mater bears a Phrygian cap, symbolizing Liberty, and holds a spindle with the thread of life. Discipline, holding a sword in one hand and a scourge and balance in the other (the balance, like the sword, associated with Justice), is "waiting to accompany the Graduate and to prepare him for the Battle of Life with the Scourge for himself and the Sword for others."[21] Thus the male figures represent historical continuities while the female figures connote the fundamental American ideals of Liberty and Justice. Beneath the four figures the motto EXCELSIOR is writ large above a cornucopia, the abundance of fruits and vegetables signifying colonial diligence and the rewards of Liberty and Discipline. City College may have been free, say these symbols, but it was not cheap.

With his background in science, Louis dreamed of becoming a doctor and did indeed attend Columbia College of Physicians and Surgeons for a year. The prospect of more years of study, which would have kept him financially dependent on his brothers, persuaded him to drop out and get a job. He worked initially as an eighth-grade teacher but quickly moved into administration. At that moment in history, a career in education made sense. A huge expansion of public schools was under way, driven by an enormous influx of Eastern European Jews as well as other immigrant groups.[22] A college degree was the only qualification necessary to teach, but Louis had greater ambitions and enrolled in graduate programs in education. He earned a Master's in Pedagogy from New York University (NYU) in 1903; in 1905, he earned both a Master's Diploma in Pedagogy from Columbia Teachers College and an MA from Columbia University. In 1934, he completed a doctorate in education at NYU. He himself became a teacher of teachers, for several years lecturing part-time in the Department of Education at his alma mater.[23]

In 1917, Louis succeeded the founding principal of Public School 64 on the Lower East Side, where he made his most distinctive contribution to public education. The 3,000 children of P.S. 64 were housed in an innovative building designed by Charles B.J. Snyder, the school system's remarkable chief architect. P.S. 64 was (and is) a grand structure emulating a French Renaissance palace. Maximizing light and air in a neighborhood mostly devoid of both, the building showed the local slum-dwellers that their children were worthy of the most beautiful and elegant edifice.[24] There they would be educated to rise above the poverty surrounding them.

P.S. 64, which enrolled only boys except in the kindergarten and gifted classes, catered to the "whole child"–his health, his social welfare, his vocational orientation, and his academic training. It was the site of two "experiments." The shorter was a nineteen-week study conducted in 1918 by a Boston physician specializing in childhood malnutrition.[25] The other, a multi-year collaboration between Louis and his colleague Elizabeth Irwin, was designed to create "an environment in which the child himself could feel that he belonged."[26] Irwin, a psychologist at the school from 1912 to 1921, defined the central tenet of the experiment: the pioneering use of intelligence tests to assess each child's native ability. The tests, considered hallmarks of progressive education, classified the pupils under five broad headings: "gifted," "bright," "average," "dull normal," and "defective."[27] Each child was placed in a group of his intellectual peers. Because their IQ was the sole trait shared by children in any given group, the experimenters hypothesized that teachers would be able to observe and understand each child's "personal tendencies and endowments" and hence to individualize instruction; because the school valued "all kinds...of intelligence," it could direct every pupil toward "a life of personal effectiveness and social usefulness."[28] Devoting particular energy to vocational education for the "dull normal," Principal Marks provided "remarkable equipment" for teaching them "carpentry, metal working, plumbing, and electrical wiring." Equally interested in students at the top of the spectrum, he chaired Section 14, "Bright Children," of the New York Society for the Experimental Study of Education and contributed to the group's monthly *Bulletin*.[29]

Irwin and Marks described the successes (and failures) of their work in *Fitting the School to the Child: An Experiment in Public Education*, published in 1924 and favorably reviewed.[30] Writing in a friendly, accessible style that conveyed their passion and excitement, they hoped to encourage others to replicate the successes. Their task was formidable. Eighty percent of the children in P.S. 64 were born on the Lower East Side; the same percentage was born to Yiddish-speaking immigrants from Russia and Eastern Europe. Since most of the other children had Italian-born parents, nearly all of them were bilingual and many had parents with minimal or nonexistent English. In this neighborhood of "hopeful striving such as we should expect of a vigorous immigrant population,"[31] families united to foster the education of children thought to be particularly gifted, just as Louis's brothers had done for him. Among the many successful graduates was the sociologist Lewis Feuer, who appears in a different guise in Chapter 6. When I was introduced to Feuer in the mid-1960s in Toronto, he asked if I was Harry Marks's daughter. "I know him," Feuer said, "he's a decent guy but his father, he was a great man. He was the principal of the school I went to." And then Feuer began singing the P.S. 64 school song.[32]

Having had a good start under its first principal, P.S. 64 succeeded remarkably under its second. In a city in which only 61.7% of children passed from eighth grade into high school, 84% of the graduates of P.S. 64 did so.[33] Louis became well known as a champion of "progressive methods of teaching" that had been previously thought to be the province of private schools. These methods, according to his obituary, were only then "winning general acceptance"; indeed, he modeled P.S. 64 on "some of the best private schools," among them the Fieldston School, attended by his son.[34] The experiment ended at P.S. 64 in 1922, but not because Louis left that year. Rather, the building was requisitioned for a junior high school, and the elementary children were moved to other schools. Irwin transferred the experiment a few blocks away to an annex of P.S. 61 known descriptively as the Little Red School House; now located in Greenwich Village in lower Manhattan, the institution survives as a socially inclusive private school.[35]

Himself a child of the Lower East Side, Louis had given back to his neighborhood; after four years as principal, he was ready to move on. He was also keen to improve his financial situation, since inflation had reduced the once-considerable buying power of his principal's salary. Late in 1921, he ranked third on the examination for the Board of Examiners and was elected a member of that body, which was charged with establishing criteria for hiring and promoting teachers and principals, as well as standards for subject matter and grade levels. A member of the P.S. 64 staff wrote to congratulate him: "Someone has said that the two happiest things in life are a friendly marriage and work that we love: as you have been so absolutely blessed in both respects you are indeed a fortunate voyager." Rising to president of the Board of Examiners in 1938, he drew on his work there in his doctoral dissertation. Even though he earned a superintendent's certificate in 1937, he continued as an examiner.

Besides his paid work, Louis contributed to his profession in other ways. A handsome gavel with an inscription engraved in silver testifies to his presidency in 1940 of the Schoolmasters' Club, an important organization of educators.[36] He was also president of the Emile Fraternity, another professional association. After his death of colon cancer–he merited a sixteen-inch obituary in the *New York Times* complete with his photograph–his Emile colleagues produced a hand-lettered, illuminated testimonial celebrating the personal qualities that were inextricably connected to his professional success: "Genial in social contacts, kindly, gentle, and understanding in the discharge of his difficult duties, ever forward-looking in his approach to educational problems, he contributed mightily...to the advancement of education." Louis gave his expertise as well to the School Committee of Temple Rodeph Sholem, which presented him with an elegant silver-plated fruit bowl in 1919, "in appreciation of faithful service." Rabbi Stephen Wise, by then nationally prominent, officiated at his funeral as he had done at Louis's wedding thirty-five years earlier. Among the five hundred in attendance was one of his City College classmates, John E. Wade, Superintendent of Schools in New York City.[37] EXCELSIOR, indeed!

"Darling Harry" at Fieldston–the route to Harvard

From the very moment of his birth in 1909, Harry was destined for great things by his adoring parents. An early–perhaps his first–letter to his parents says it all: "Dear Mamma and Papa. I am a Good boy. Lots of Love and I am saving Kisses–Darling Harry." When his father detected favoritism at the local public school because he was a principal's son, he sent him to the Ethical Culture school later known as Fieldston. The school, founded by the philosopher Felix Adler, imparted excellent intellectual training and a liberal sociopolitical formation to the children of the Jewish elite, although it was not explicitly Jewish.[38] A roster of graduates published to commemorate the school's seventy-fifth anniversary lists forty of the approximately sixty members of Harry's class and gives a sense of their place in the world.[39] Four of the twelve men who responded had gone to Harvard, as had Harry's good friends Joseph Doob (Fieldston '26) and Edwin Popper (Fieldston '28). While it may seem impressive that a third of the boys went to Harvard, this is proportionately much less than the eighteen out of twenty-two Groton graduates who entered Harvard's class of 1900, among them Franklin Delano Roosevelt.[40] Such establishments were Harvard's main feeder schools, and their graduates set a tone quite alien to Fieldston alumni. Roosevelt and his ilk were WASPs–White Anglo-Saxon Protestants–and formed the dominant social group at the most prestitious universities.

Harry graduated from Fieldston in 1927 as valedictorian and president of his class.[41] Despite having traveled in France, Switzerland, and Italy on a closely chaperoned school study trip the previous summer, he entered Harvard a sheltered and unworldly young man.[42] To get there, he had hardly lifted a finger: he applied nowhere else, not out of bravado but out of ignorance. His only conception of what a college education might mean was derived from the biochemist hero of Sinclair Lewis's novel *Arrowsmith*, which won the Pulitzer Prize in 1926; he wanted to be like Arrowsmith.

As the fall semester approached, the newly appointed Dean of Harvard College, A. Chester Hanford, requested each father of an incoming freshman "to write about him...as fully as you are willing to do," promising that any "deficiencies in his earlier education or weaknesses of character would be kept confidential." Sophie kept Louis's draft because, she explained in a note, she wanted Harry to "see, some day,...what your darling 'Pop' thought of you–and how well he understood you." There were four headings: Physical, Intellectual, Moral, and Social. Under the first, Louis described Harry as "a big healthy young man weighing about 170 pounds" (he was somewhat overweight much of his life), whose "personal appearance is a little above the ordinary." He was "not proficient in any special athletic activity," but–Louis reassured sports-obsessed Harvard–"he has the vigor and the stamina to succeed in any line of this sort which may interest him." None ever did; however, as his father noted, his "unusual muscular coordination" at least made him "skillful with tools from his earliest years."

The headings "Intellectual" and "Moral" show, as one might expect, some inclinations that characterized the adult Harry and some that did not. Having learned to read before entering school, he had a "vigorous appetite for independent reading"; a carefully posed photo shows Louis and Harry (age eight) reading together. His intellectual interests were mainly "scientific, mechanical, mathematical and philosophical...rather than artistic or linguistic." By the time he graduated from Harvard, he had shed his former preference for "the Museum of Natural History or an automobile exhibit" (reported by Louis) and had developed strong interests in art history, music, and languages. At Fieldston, Louis wrote, he had enjoyed debating about ethics and economics–a pleasure that appears throughout his Berlin diary–and had "never missed a meeting" of the Saturday night discussion club of which he was secretary. Under "Moral," Louis observed his "fine sense of right and wrong"; everyone who knew him appreciated "his strong sense of duty and responsibility." One of his teachers had summed him up, Louis recalled, by saying that "Harry has ideas and ideals."

Under the final heading, "Social," Louis observed that until recently Harry had shown no interest in girls but had lately "formed an attachment for one of his former girl classmates."[43] He was afflicted with a painful shyness "in the company of strangers," which was "one of his greatest weaknesses." His compensating strength was an ability to form strong friendships. As a teenager he had been with Ed Popper and Joe Doob at school and at summer camps in Maine, and he overlapped with them at Harvard; they figure again and again in his Berlin diary.[44] The last social characteristic Louis described was endearing: "Altho usually serious in all he does... Harry has a quick and keen sense of humor, and a smile which will be a great asset throughout his life." And so it was.

Part 2. Harry's Harvard: Professing Inclusion, Practicing Exclusion

Undergraduate studies

Harry's plan to emulate Sinclair Lewis's bicochemist hero vanished when he earned a C in analytical chemistry. What to do? Before signing up for courses in his sophomore year, he asked his adviser, a physicist, whether a history major would be a good idea. The answer–"Why not?"–sufficed for him to enroll in a course taught by a new instructor, William L. Langer. As a freshman Harry had taken History 1 to fulfill a distribution requirement; he had done "tolerably well" and had been deeply impressed when Langer guest-lectured in the course for two weeks. Regarding American history as too easy because it didn't require mastery of foreign languages, he decided to concentrate on European history even though he earned a D in second-year German. Despite this unpromising start, by the time he graduated he had arrived at a focus, an intellectual passion, and much better German. He had also forged two professional relationships that were to be important throughout the 1930s. Langer, who was later to supervise his doctoral dissertation, had "ignited" his desire to become a historian. The other relationship, illustrated in Chapter 3, was with Langer's sabbatical replacement in Harry's senior year, a visiting professor from Oberlin College named Frederick B. Artz. No doubt he took History 42, Problems in the History of Continental Europe from 1870 to 1914, a graduate course open to senior Honors students, which was normally taught by Langer but that year by Artz. Meanwhile, a term paper on the German

Social Democratic Party (SPD), written for the economic historian Edwin F. Gay in his sophomore year, set his scholarly direction for the next decade.[45] His 112-page undergraduate thesis on the SPD, presumably supervised by Artz, showed that he was reasonably comfortable reading and translating German; it also demonstrated a lucid, self-conscious, and sometimes witty style that could carry the weight of his characteristic questioning. His topic was suitable for further development because, as he noted in introducing his bibliographical notes, there were "no good histories of the party in any language which cover its development completely in the period 1890-1914."[46] His doctoral dissertation, built on the foundation of his Honors thesis, did not completely fill this gap, for it stopped at 1903, only a brief epilogue extending it to 1914.

Jews are "better off at Harvard"

Harvard, Yale, and Princeton–"the Big Three"–were conventionally anti-Semitic WASP institutions, but they differed somewhat in their attitudes toward Jews. More Jews applied to Harvard than to the other two, President Charles W. Eliot explained approvingly, because they knew they would be "better off at Harvard than at any other American college." During Eliot's long presidency (1869-1909), Harvard offered more scholarships than any other university and awarded them on the basis of academic talent rather than pedigree. When it replaced its own examinations with those administered by the College Entrance Examination Board, it chose a national standard less susceptible to manipulation.[47] These policies had serious consequences for WASP hegemony: Jewish enrollment rose.

Eliot's successor, A. Lawrence Lowell–another Boston blue blood–sided with those alarmed by Harvard's unprecedentedly heterogeneous student body. Although he claimed to advocate mixing students "together so thoroughly that the friendships they form are based on natural affinities, rather than similarity of origin," in actuality Lowell sought "a homogeneous mass of gentlemen" of his own caste.[48] As vice-president of the Immigration Restriction League, he iterated the view common in his social class that the mainly Catholic and Jewish immigrants flooding in from Southern and Eastern Europe were endangering WASP control of America. "Nordics" were superior; Jews, Africans, and Eastern and Southern Europeans were inferior.[49]

The Immigration Acts passed in 1921 and 1924, enthusiastically backed by Lowell's League, inspired him to reverse the Jewish tide at Harvard. In force until 1965, these acts effectively stemmed the influx of Polish and Russian Jews, who, besides their other supposedly undesirable characteristics, were "the primary carriers of the un-American ideology of socialism."[50] When Felix Frankfurter entered Harvard Law School in 1902, a classmate told him that the only Jews he had previously met were "unclean" peddlers, and he was glad to meet a "clean" and well-mannered Jew.[51] Like Frankfurter, Harry was a "clean" German Jew and therefore capable of being "absorbed into the social pattern."[52] The rough-edged Jewish students who commuted to Harvard from their Eastern European immigrant parents' homes were assumed to lack that ability; their "naturally repulsive and repugnant"[53] manners and their socialist politics were alien to Harvard's culture. But they were there. The increasing numbers of Jewish students of both German and Eastern European origin made them the first minority group to threaten Protestant hegemony. There were few Catholics (many saw Harvard as a den of apostasy), and hardly any African Americans.[54] The latter, naturally, were prohibited from living in dormitories with white students.

Despite his superior pedigree, Harry shared certain Eastern European Jewish qualities offensive to WASPs: he harbored political sympathies like theirs; he lacked social polish; and he studied hard. As rational as Nazis, WASPs excluded Jews from most extracurricular activities yet condemned them for not participating widely in campus life. When Harry was enrolled in Harvard Graduate School, the very same Dean Hanford who had asked Louis Marks for his frank opinions of his son sneeringly told President James B. Conant that Harry and nearly all his Communist colleagues belonged to the "chosen race."[55] That "particular race and religion," Hanford informed Conant, also dominated the predominantly Jewish Harvard Commuters' Association. The commuters, those offensive sons of immigrants, had just been allotted Dudley Hall as a place to congregate, and "the others"–for once, Christians were Others–felt that they must "stay away" from Dudley Hall, when all they "want is a place to eat their lunch."[56] That was all the commuters wanted; unlike residential students, they brought brown-bag lunches from home. The WASPs and the Jewish commuters *were* different. Whereas the commuters debated current events over lunch, their gentlemanly colleagues were apolitical and sports-minded, sometimes to the point of violence, displaying their "high spirits" in riots usually connected with sports.[57]

In 1909, Eliot's last year as president and the year of Harry's birth, Harvard's enrollment was 9.8% Jewish; nine years later, as a consequence of Eliot's policies, it was 20% and rising.[58] The increase was alarming–to WASPs. Would Harvard go the way of Columbia, where Jews had constituted 40% of the student body in the late nineteenth century? By 1921, even though Jews had fallen to 22% of the Columbia student body, some people feared the damage was irreparable; one observer assumed that all grubbily unattractive students were Jews, who "lower[ed] the communal easy handsomeness."[59] Unlike the concerned Columbia alumnus, a Harvard faculty committee found photographs useless in identifying Jews. Agreeing that a "Jewish invasion" such as had occurred at Columbia would discourage boys of good family from applying, the leaders of the Big Three searched for ways to repel the assault. Under the guidance of its anti-Semitic president, Nicholas Murray Butler (in office 1902-45), Columbia instituted "mental alertness tests" suitable to the social experience of "the average native American boy," who was WASP by definition.[60]

Determined to avert a Columbia-style catastrophe, Lowell claimed to "revere the democratic ideal while never relaxing his faith in the destiny of his own kind."[61] When Harvard alumni protested in 1922 that too many Jews were enrolled, an abashed Lowell recommended to the Committee on Admission that "Hebrew" transfer applicants be "investigated with the nicest care"; he also proposed that "Hebrews" be awarded scholarships strictly according to their proportion in the student body, even though academic merit and need were the official criteria.[62] Public controversy erupted when Harvard made public the necessity for a "limitation of enrollment" to relieve a purported strain on the capacity of dormitories and classrooms. It was "natural," read the Harvard statement, to solve overcrowding by reducing "the proportion of Jews at the college."[63] The idea, Lowell explained in a commencement address, was to "sift" students so as to preserve the "homogeneous American type" threatened by "huge numbers of strangers." In a breathtaking confession of its intent, the Committee on Admission proclaimed that it did not wish to "practice discrimination without the knowledge and consent of the Faculty." Hence it called for an ad-hoc committee to be appointed, the purpose of which (in Lowell's words) was to avoid clashes among undergraduates caused by "particular temperaments."[64] The nature of this peacemaking effort would be plain to anyone who knew about the particular temperament that WASPs attributed to Jews. At its first meeting, the committee chair stated that the "proportion of Jewish students at the university is greater than that of any other race"; the only other "races" he mentioned were Chinese and Japanese, as if the default Caucasian "race" did not exist.[65] He said it was "astounding" that "a number of Jews, coming from poor districts,…enter Harvard and become remarkable students." "Sifting" students could not fully solve "this problem of the Jew," but it could reduce its severity, even at the cost of fewer "astounding" students.

Lowell initially advocated an explicit Jewish quota of 12% but settled for 15%, under a cloak of secrecy so as not to disturb the facade of egalitarianism.[66] As the controversy developed, five members of a Jewish student group, the Menorah Society, met with five Gentile counterparts for a constructive discussion of the attitudes of Gentile students concerned about *"too many Jews,…the 'City College' fear."*[67] What a Jewish alumnus called the "latent prejudices which wake to life at the lightest touch" were now on full display, and Jewish students and alumni weighed in on both sides: some thought it unseemly that any Jew would make a public protest, while others felt that anti-Semitism must be brought to public attention.[68] The illustrious journalist Walter Lippmann (Harvard '10), who had himself suffered anti-Semitism at Harvard, advised Lowell's committee against "too great a concentration" of Jews or any other "minority that brings with it some striking cultural peculiarity"; anything more than 15% would "produce a segregation of cultures rather than a fusion."[69] Thus kept in check, Jews and Catholics with suitable "character" might absorb WASP virtues.[70]

"Character" was a code word for qualities thought to be exclusively WASP: "'fair play,' 'public spirit,' 'interest in fellows,' and 'leadership.'"[71] Interviews could yield "a personal estimate of character" and, as Lowell privately admitted, "prevent a dangerous increase in the proportion of Jews."[72] When a highly qualified Jewish applicant was rejected, a Harvard official said that "no personal discrimination against him was involved."[73] He wasn't personally to blame for being Jewish, after all.

Lowell's ad-hoc committee fashioned various strategies to cope with the "Jewish problem." Beginning in 1923, the admissions form asked questions designed to identify Jewish applicants who lacked obviously "Jewish" names: "For the first time in Harvard's history an applicant was asked about his race and color. Other questions were 'Maiden Name of Mother,' 'Birth Place of Father,' and 'What change, if any, has been made since birth in your own name or that of your father? (Explain fully.)'"[74] If a candidate named Brown had a father originally named Brownstein or a mother born Cohen, the inference was obvious. The committee commissioned a statistical analysis that showed rising Jewish enrollment, as expected, but inconveniently proved that Jewish students achieved academic success at far higher rates than Gentiles.[75] Jews weren't really smart, though; as a student explained in 1922, they were like parrots: "They memorize their books!"[76]

The committee advised "discretion" in making a wise "discrimination" to ensure that students would benefit the college and the "community"—a code word signifying the WASP establishment.[77] Another device, greater geographical distribution, had dramatically lowered Jewish enrollment at Columbia and, the planners thought, would work at Harvard as long as students were recruited from regions with small Jewish populations.[78] Another new tactic was to admit students in the top seventh of their high school class without examination.[79] These plans backfired badly. In 1925, a shocking 27.1% of the student body was Jewish.[80] The next year, when five of the eight juniors elected to Phi Beta Kappa were Jewish, the student magazine the *Lampoon* published an article entitled "No Religious Discrimination at Harvard–Three Gentiles Elected to Phi Beta Kappa."[81] Harvard's Dean of Admission, in a brilliant stroke, proposed reducing the "25% Hebrew total to 15% or less by simply rejecting without detailed explanation."[82] That approach was effective. In the 1930s, during Harry's years as a graduate student, the percentage of Jewish students sank to between 12% and 14%.[83]

When Conant took over as president, he asked for statistics, some of which could be tortured to serve his purpose. Jewish students, the statistics showed, were "more prone to dishonesty and sexual offenses," although less likely to be drunkards or "to 'do something for Harvard'" in athletics; they were shamefully unrepresented–surprise!–in the most exclusive Harvard clubs.[84] The reduction of Jewish enrollment, while helping to sustain the primacy of WASP-dominated social and athletic activities, had one unexpected and unwelcome corollary: an increased number of WASPs were content to earn a "gentleman's C." An analysis of freshman academic achievement in 1933-42 showed an inverse relationship between social prestige and academic standing. Jewish freshmen garnered 31.9% of the top academic ranks despite a total enrollment of 19.3% while only 7.3% were "unsatisfactory"; the prestigious WASP private schools Andover and Exeter produced 13.9% of the top-ranked freshmen but 18.2% of those labeled "unsatisfactory."[85] Conant endorsed Lowell's plan for geographical distribution, explicitly seeking students from regions with relatively few Jews. He hired a Dean of Admissions who admired Harvard's wise and intelligent management of "the Jew problem."[86] In such an atmosphere, Harry's antagonism to all religion was irrelevant. One of his undergraduate teachers, Sidney B. Fay, told him plainly that being Jewish would harm him in the job market.[87] The prediction came true when he finished his doctorate (see Chapter 8).

Harry was admitted to Harvard just as Lowell's final solution to its Jewish problem was being effected. Two years earlier, in 1925, an alumnus wrote to Lowell to complain that Jews, "the skunks of the human race," had taken over Harvard; Lowell politely thanked him for his observations.[88] Was Harry aware that he, Joe Doob, and Ed Popper were skunks? Their common background helped sustain them in an unwelcoming atmosphere; no wonder they stuck together. A Harvard anthropology student who studied his fellow Jews in Harry's time found that the majority had "casual non-Jewish acquaintances but were widely regarded–and treated accordingly–as Jews."[89]

Sarah Katz Levison and Aaron Harry Levison, ca. 1898

Harry with his parents before
his trip to Europe,
12 June 1926

Sophie Marks in Tozeur, Tunisia, 1932

Harry at Harvard, 1928

3

A New Young Scholar in the (Old) World

Part 1. Summer in Heidelberg, 1931

The voyage out, aboard the St. Louis, gave Harry plenty of time to study German grammar. This "beautiful tongue," he rhapsodized, "now unravels its complexities for my straining-to-absorb wits (note the Germanic influence)"; grammatical rules were "as entrancing as ocean transportation is not."[1] Shipboard life made him acutely conscious of his social insufficiencies. In his diary he analyzed "an elemental loneliness, which comes over me at times," becoming sometimes "morbid, but not seriously." Even when lonely, though, he could feel uplifting emotions. A solitary walk on deck could be thrilling:

> Moonlight from the fresh icy crescent [moon], and a last saffron veil in the west, and the rushing waters colored blue-black-green, hissing as they foam past. The air had flavor, it tasted of cleanness that is originally pure, not scrubbed but born clean–deep draughts you drink, and grow intoxicated.... And so this air, these waters with their wind-whipped stipplings, this moon, and the steamless steel-hearted throbbing of the ship.[2]

Opera performances and German literature soon afforded similar experiences of intense aesthetic joy.

From Cuxhaven, where the ship docked, Harry made his way by train to Heidelberg. Buying the *Vossische Zeitung* at the Cuxhaven station, he read "laboriously" about President Herbert Hoover's proposal of "a general moratorium on both reparations paid from Germany to the Allies and war debts owed by the Allies to the US."[3] The moratorium, a response to deep German resentment of penalties imposed after the war, came too late to help forestall the bank crisis that Harry was to witness less than a month later.

One of 800 Americans studying in German universities,[4] Harry spent six weeks in Heidelberg improving his knowledge of German. Knowledge of Germany came more slowly, for students in Heidelberg's Vacation Courses for Foreigners had no contact with the heavily Nazi and anti-Semitic student body of Germany's oldest university.[5] Harry lodged with his teacher, Prof. Dr. Wilhelm Josef Dorn, "a large, friendly, middle-aged man who teaches in the [Helmholtz] *Gymnasium*–German literature, English, and history."[6] He took private lessons with Dorn and faithfully attended his class in intermediate German. The heterogeneous enrollment–Americans, Italians, Scandinavians, a Czech, and a Swiss–required it to be conducted entirely in German: "All except about 3 can speak much better German than I, but Dorn says I shouldn't worry–in a week or ten days I'll be all right."[7] A "revelatory" private lesson on the subjunctive persuaded him "that a benevolent providence guided me into his hands. He has the inestimable advantage of knowing English perfectly, knowing the difficulties which lie in German for English-speaking people, experience in teaching German, and the expository talent."[8] Prof. Dorn taught with humor, inventing the term "Gemixtes Pickles" to describe intermixed languages. A year later, arriving in Würzberg, an exhausted Harry illustrated "Gemixtes Pickles" when he asked for an "einfaches [simple] Room."[9]

The Dorns introduced Harry not just to the German language but to Heidelberg. Frau Dorn–much younger than her husband, a common disparity explained by the decimation of young men during World War I–led him to the university office, enrolled him in her husband's class, and took him to the market. He hit it off with the Dorns' little girl, Guga, later sending her presents. Dorn showed him the famous Heidelberg Castle ruins, played the harmonium for him, and took him to a beer hall.[10] A child of Prohibition, Harry thought beer "tasted like vegetables gone sour" and wondered whether "wine and strong beverages are as enchanting as beer." A few months later, he had "drunk my first coffee." He found it "mildly unpleasant" but less awful than beer: "I can understand that some people would like it."[11] Lemonade was his drink.

Once settled in, Harry paid attention to current events: "In Vienna, Munich, Berlin, & now Cologne, National Socialists have tried to raise hell with the universities.... Hitlerite agitators and student organizations go round demonstrating, walloping opposing students, university officials, and the police." He had a solution for immunizing the police force against "walloping." German policemen, "no bigger than the average small citizen," were outfitted in fancy uniforms to impress the citizenry, but this was a mere facade. Harry advocated importing "a dozen...six-and-a-half foot red-faced Irishmen," such as he had seen controlling the "democratic Freshman vs. Sophomore combats" at Harvard. In Germany, the combat was between Nazis and their enemies–Communists, Socialists, and Jewish student organizations.[12]

German social and economic problems were no laughing matter. A bank crisis came to a head in mid-July, when one bank failed and several others were temporarily shut down. In Heidelberg, violence erupted: "In my room I heard the sounds of rioting."[13] Harry read the leading liberal papers: all "three editions of the *Frankfurter Allgemeiner Zeitung*, and the *Berliner Tageblatt* & *Vossische Zeitung*."[14] With the university closed, he "saw in the market place a crowd of people with umbrellas" gathered around the Municipal Savings Bank in the darkening afternoon. He went to the Deutsche Bank to cash a check, found it closed, and photographed its imposing entrance. Police officers were much in evidence, and the "crowd was quiet. I was puzzled." He kept his distance, for the Dorns had told him of a demonstration a few months earlier when the police clubbed innocent bystanders, including an American who explained that "he was only passing by, was a foreigner and had nothing to do with the demonstration." A year earlier, Harry had seen similar crowds in New York when the Broadway Central Bank was liquidated, and he "understood those men and women in the gray rain." Despite this "bank 'holiday,'" daily life went on; "people who on Monday night found their purses empty and intended to draw cash from the bank this morning must either borrow from more fortunate friends" or buy on credit.[15]

Harry maintained a cool, ironic tone in writing of such events.

When certain newspapers were banned, he observed that there was no "German Civil Liberties League"; indeed, there were "apparently no German civil liberties." Giving a foretaste of the political tumult that dominated his last year in Germany, store windows already displayed "Swastikas and photos and sketches of Hitler," or "pictures of the German Heroes, and placards" showing "how Germany's...oppression has always been caused...by the Catholics, the Jews, and the Freemasons." Alert to such documentation, he later photographed such window displays. In Heidelberg, he photographed the entrance of a brand-new building at the university that bore a statue of Pallas Athena and an inscription later effaced by the Nazis. Suggested by a Jewish professor of German studies at Heidelberg, Friedrich Gandolf (1880-1931), the inscription read, in Thomas Mann's later translation, "To the living spirit."[16]

As he was about to leave Heidelberg to join his family on their European vacation, Harry reflected on his progress to date. Not only had his German improved, but he could not "have had a finer introduction to Germany than through the Dorns." Dorn replied warmly to his postcard, urging him to visit en route to Berlin.[17] Several months later, the Dorns invited him for Christmas. Knowing that Dorn's pay had been cut, he feared that he might "be an extra weight on them"; he declined and sent a present.[18] They "bemoaned my absence, thanked me for the books, and sent me a box of home-made Xmas cookies." He visited the Dorns in April and July of 1932; in July, their spare rooms were full, but they insisted that he take all his meals with them and treated him like a son. Frau Dorn and her friend came to the station to see him off, waving "as the train went past. I stood in the doorway and felt pangs at pulling out again, this having no roots, I thought, was not always so sweet a joy, and having friends a sweeter one."[19] After the Nazi takeover, the Dorns represented not just German friendship but Gentile decency. When a card came "inviting me down there again," Harry–too busy preparing to return home to accept–was "glad they haven't become anti-Semites." Indeed, Dorn spent the war years translating a book by Hyman Levy, a Scottish mathematician and philosopher who had grown up in an Orthodox Jewish home.[20]

Part 2. Harry's social environment in Berlin

Starting in Berlin

Harry had a room of his own in the apartment of Grete and Ernst Meyer in a handsome building at Mommsenstrasse 57, in the comfortably bourgeois Charlottenburg district.[21] Striding through the vast park of the Tiergarten, a young man with good shoes and energy could walk between the university on Unter den Linden to Mommsenstrasse; if tired or pressed for time, he could take the Stadtbahn, the municipal railway. A "suitable address for a would-be historian," the street commemorated Theodor Mommsen (1817-1903), a historian in the liberal tradition that the Nazis would soon crush. When Harry next went to Europe, in 1976, he was pleased to find Mommsenstrasse 57 "still standing–though all the other side of the street had been bombed out and was rebuilt with characterless modern housing warrens."[22]

In his first few months, Harry's still imperfect German, as well as his social insecurities, made adjustment difficult. The Meyers expected him talk during dinner, but his German was "wretched and always getting balled up."[23] This deficiency was soon remedied. A year after his arrival, his linguistic proficiency yielded the peculiar pleasure of being mistaken for a variety of foreigners (never for an American), and twice for a German. Traveling in Switzerland, he "talked a bit with a professor of geography–who asked me if I weren't a Russian. Delavaud [in Paris] first asked me if I were Italian. The Americans I translated to…in Nuremberg were surprised to learn I was an American. What can a poor Harvard man do?" In Italy, a "stout German woman" took him for a Scandinavian. In Germany, his dentist's nurse took him for Swiss. The most pleasing mistakes of all occurred in Italy: "Have finally been mistaken for a German by the Münchner landlady of this Pension" in Mirano, a supposition shared by his Italian hosts in Rome.[24] In the summer of 1932 his Harvard mentor, Frederick B. Artz, living in Heidelberg, seemed to think "that my preference for German conversation was vanity or something of the sort–in truth I couldn't get into the feel of English until we talked in a Konditorei a couple of hours after supper."[25]

In Berlin, Harry was fortunate to step into a ready-made social circle revolving around the Meyers and a genial rare-book dealer, Paul Gottschalk. Grete Meyer and Paul Gottschalk served in loco parentis. Paul was Harry's relative by marriage: Paul's cousin Rose had married Martin Hirschbach, Uncle Alfred Hirschbach's brother. No doubt either Paul or Martin arranged for Harry to board with their friends the Meyers. Paul's brother and sister Julia were doctors who shared a waiting room at 5 Neuekantstrasse in Charlottenburg. Julia Gottschalk appears rarely in Harry's diary or letters, but Ernst Gottschalk and his family were prominent in Harry's Berlin life: his wife, Laura, a rabbi's daughter; his sons, Heinz and Ludwig (known as Lutz); and his daughter, Betty, who was married to Walter Elberfeld, a surgeon (and a Gentile). Harry already knew Paul, for he always visited the Markses and Hirschbachs during his annual business trips to America.[26] He humorously accused the Markses of "feed[ing] him past endurance," a charge that Heinz supported "with tales of endless potatoes..., so that an evening at your mercy sounds here as if it were a gourmand's orgy." Harry suggested serving Paul "oatmeal and graham crackers just once"– but, he warned, "Don't put onions in the oatmeal." Years later, my mother, doubting the reality of Paul's famed antipathy to onions, secretly included some in a dish. He never knew.

The Meyers were sociable. Their four children's friends dropped by, as did various relatives–Grete's mother, Frau Juda; her brother, who lived in Paris; her nephew, who worked in the economics section of the *Berliner Tageblatt;*[27] friends visiting from out of town. Every two or three weeks Rudy Meyer, a medical student, or Heinz Gottschalk would accompany Harry on a Sunday excursion. Of Harry's age mates in Berlin, Heinz–who had lived in Cambridge when Harry was at Harvard–was the most insistently friendly; he was someone with whom, in the early days, Harry could talk English.[28] Once, after a big Sunday dinner at Paul's home that was followed all too soon by tea, "Heinz & I fled (before they called another meal) to Neubabelsberg, where we tramped through pine or fir woods and the well-known Markisch Sand until it was dark and murky."[29] Otherwise, his social life was limited to occasional refreshments with a classmate or invitations from a professor. He had nothing to do with a foreign-students society at the university, through which another American graduate student just a year older, Shepard Stone, met Raymond Aron. Harry himself met Aron at the home of Gustav Mayer, one of his professors and Paul Gott-schalk's cousin.[30] Mayer and his wife, Flora, came occasionally to Paul's parties.

The other central members of the group were the Hirschbachs and the Freyhans, both families being related to Paul. Rose Hirsch-bach, as just mentioned, was Paul's cousin, and Clara Freyhan was his sister. Martin and Rose Hirschbach, their oldest son (Ernst), and Martin's sister (Hedwig) attended Paul Gottschalk's parties; Hed-wig in profile looked strikingly like her brother Alfred, and "when Martin talked I thought I might have been hearing Alf himself."[31] The Freyhans were also regulars at Paul's: Clara; her husband, Max, a lawyer and notary; their sons, Fritz (a medical student) and Hans (studying music); and their daughter, Eva (a high school student).[32] Harry often argued with Max, who had published several books on modern German drama. When Harry became heated, Dr. Freyhan remained "quiet and patient, and in general unvehement," pitching his ideas in language "suitable to a poor foreigner, and remarkably quick to grasp the ideas which I stumblingly try to express."[33]

"Everyone tries to make me sociable," Harry complained: "Mr. G. tried, Heinz tried, now Professor Mayer tries." Mayer's weapon was his son Ulrich, "a good egg," who became a friend. Mayer's kindness released in him a capacity for social pleasure that he rare-ly felt. After a Sunday afternoon at Mayer's home, he wrote: "It is strange that a visit almost invariably stimulates me, and yet I enjoy thinking of myself as unsocial, if not antisocial."[34] Two days later, he added: "I've been in a state of exultant turmoil since Sunday."

Frau Meyer was in cahoots with Paul Gottschalk. One evening, "for my delectation, partly," she invited a number of people to sup-per. Harry's report illustrates both the social dynamics of the group and his own mixture of self-satisfaction, contempt, and regret at his own discomfort. Among the guests were Heinz Gottschalk and Raymond Goldschmidt,[35] the latter having recently returned from a year's study in the United States. Harry ungratefully complained that he had never "heard so many unfounded confident generaliza-tions in one evening before, probably because Heinz can talk faster in German, besides having support from the others in the exceptional moments between brilliant ideas."[36] It was just as well that Harry, who struggled to keep up with the intense conversation, "simply sat there and listened." It was a typical gathering of the Meyer/Gottschalk circle, which valued above all else an engaged intellect. Her mother's most notable quality, Grete Meyer wrote after her death, was "her vigorous, expansive mind."[37]

Within this circle, generational differences chiefly concerned women's higher education, which was taken for granted by the younger women but was unusual among their elders. Clara Freyhan was a highly cultivated woman without a profession, as was Grete Meyer. Clara's sister Julia Gottschalk, however, belonged to the pioneering generation of university-educated women. Freiburg, where Julia took her first medical examination (in 1913), had been among the first German universities to permit women to matriculate; the University of Berlin, where she passed the last examination (in 1916), granted women that right only in 1909.[38] In one respect, though, Julia was not unusual: a disproportionate number of the relatively few women doctors of her generation were Jewish.[39] This trend continued in the next generation, represented by the Meyers' daughter Lisel and Julia's niece, Betty Elberfeld, both studying medicine in the early 1930s. By then, 29% of German Jewish university students were women, as compared with 16% of Gentile students.[40] Jewish support of women's education was in keeping with the *Bildung* so treasured by German Jews: "a ceaseless quest for the good, the true, and the beautiful" that was conducted "through a study of literature and philosophy, and the refinement of one's aesthetic sensibilities through the arts and music."[41]

The values of Harry's social circle

Most of Harry's friends were typical German Jews of the educated stratum–students, lawyers, doctors, businessmen, and antiquarians who relished books, classical music, and intellectual debate. In politics, except for the ardent Communists Walter and Betty Elberfeld, they sympathized with the SPD. Political interests extended to the children. The youngest Hirschbach, Franz, recalled playing "Reichstag" as a boy in the early 1930s–performing speeches reported in the *Berliner Tageblatt* to the "applause and jeering" of his elders.[42]

Most members of the circle were moderate assimilationists. The Central Union of German Citizens of the Jewish Faith, the largest German Jewish organization, argued (in 1931) that Jews "must place the highest value on humanity as a whole, while at the same time loving the German people and our specific Jewishness."[43] This assimilationist ideal soon proved to be a pipe dream. Stung by the Nazi takeover, the Central Union declared on 23 March 1933: "No body can rob us of our German fatherland…. In that we fight this battle, we carry out a German, not a selfish-Jewish, fight."[44] This was the predominant view of liberal Jews. Peter Gay's family in Nazi Berlin, for example, thought that "the gangsters who had taken control of the country were not Germany–we were."[45]

Individuals in the Gottschalk/Meyer circle varied in their relationship to Judaism. Ernst and Laura Gottschalk kept kosher until World War I made observance difficult, and they did not resume after the war; they sent their sons to religious school and had them bar-mitzvahed, and they observed the Jewish holidays.[46] The Freyhans also practiced their religion, to Harry's disgust, for he had a visceral distaste for any religious observation. Harry described Hans Freyhan as "pretty thick and exceedingly pious, which are doubtless not unconnected,…so godfearing that when he came home from a holiday recently on a Saturday, he had his brother go to the station for him to carry his suitcase home."[47] Harry's ignorance left unremarked Hans's impious willingness to have someone else violate the prohibition against carrying anything on the Sabbath. Ernst Meyer's sons were bar-mitzvahed, but only because bar mitzvahs were the norm in his circle; he did not object when Rudy declared himself opposed to all religious observance.[48] Like Rudy, after his own bar mitzvah Gustav Mayer rejected the Jewish practice in which he had been raised. The Meyers observed Hanukkah in some fashion. When Grete gave Harry a present, she wrote a note: "So that you notice it's Hanukkah!"[49] In 1933, one or two of the younger generation became Zionists. From then on, Zionists and Nazis agreed in one goal: German Jews should move to Israel.

At the far end of the assimilationist spectrum were Rose Hirschbach, her siblings, and her husband, who would have nothing to do with Judaism. Rose and Martin had their four sons baptized Lutheran, and confirmed as well. Rose and Martin wanted their sons to merge totally into "German culture and civilization," for which Martin had fought in World War I; their Protestant identity "eliminated a major difference between us and our schoolmates."[50] To Hitler, though, "non-Aryan Christians" like the Hirschbachs were Jews.

Despite their mostly casual relation to Judaism, members of the circle had–Harry charged–an "absurd" tendency to view "things from a strictly Jewish center, a sort of Hebraico-Centric theory of the universe."[51] They had company. When, in 1932, the Jewish New Year "happened to coincide with [President Paul von] Hindenburg's birthday,...all the Berlin Jewish congregations sen[t] hearty congratulations, doubtless not wholly unmindful of the near possibility of having to have Hitler for President."[52] The accelerating tempo of anti-Semitic acts during the year preceding Hitler's accession to power made the Meyers "apprehensive.... As Herr Meyer one day remarked–'These are exciting times, would that they were less exciting.'"[53] As Chapters 4 and 5 will show, Harry's friends' hard-headed realization of the implications of Hitler's rise to power, coupled with their educational background, saved their lives.

Paul Gottschalk, alias P.G.

Paul Gottschalk's family and friends felt universal "admiration and love" for him.[54] To the young people in his family and his office he was a solicitous but stern mentor; they called him "P.G.," the abbreviation summing up the half-intimate, half-formal nature of many of his personal relationships. They were "fascinated by his unique and glamorous business"–visits to America were a rarity at the time–and appreciated him as "a cultured and friendly person with many stories about his friends and contacts on both continents."[55] With Paul as the generous host, the family gathered annually to celebrate his birthday; twenty guests attended his fifty-third, in 1933. Harry was grateful for P.G.'s self-assigned role as "guide and confessor."[56] Perhaps Paul recognized a kindred spirit, for as a youth he too had been so shy outside his family that he appeared to be "stupid or mute."[57] Harry could pop in to P.G.'s office at 3a Unter den Linden, just down the street from the university, and get advice or cash, pick up a book, or discuss politics.[58]

At the end of Paul's very long life, he was persuaded to write his memoirs.[59] He began with a reminiscence of his mother, from whom he "inherited a capacity for vivid fantasy, a quick wit, and perhaps also a great interest in people and their concerns, and if I may say so, the natural gift for gaining the confidence and winning the friendship of people." This gift was apparent in his relations with librarians and collectors, which were at once professional and social. His formal education ended in 1899, when he passed the *Abitur*. With a scholarly bent, he chose the antiquarian trade over academia because of the greater chance of success, for most Jewish academics were relegated to the lower ranks.[60] For the most part, he acquired on his own the "all-encompassing knowledge" that he thought essential for his chosen profession.[61] He was "at heart a pedagogue, with a need to teach all the bright, young, loyal workers he had the knack of finding."[62] In his New York office, even a part-time packer had to read French and German–"somewhat unusual requirements," recalled Arthur H. Minters, an assistant who became an antiquarian book dealer himself. P.G. lectured his assistants "about the book trade in Europe before both world wars"; subjecting them to a monthly quiz, "he would scold us or box our ears if we answered stupidly. 'A grown-up must do it!' he'd say if we called on him for help." One of his daily habits was looking in the *New York Times* obits for recently dead collectors whose heirs might be eager to sell.[63]

During the self-designed study tour to Italy in 1906 that launched his career, P.G. visited museums, libraries, antiquarians, and private collectors. Although only twenty-six, he so enchanted the specialists with whom he talked that they gave him good deals. In Rome the advice of an antiquarian to do business in the United States "struck me like lightening and was decisive for my business and for my life." On his first American trip later that year, he made cold calls on custodians of major research libraries, persuading them that he could find the rare and out-of-print books that they had hitherto sought in vain. He could, and he did. Beginning in 1907, he issued catalogues listing incunabula and other rare books, runs of European scientific journals, and unpublished manuscripts ranging from holograph scores by famous European composers to Americana by such figures as Franklin and Washington.[64] Copiously illustrated, accompanied by scholarly texts, and published privately in limited editions, these catalogues are now themselves antiquarian items. He was well connected throughout Europe. When the philosopher Karl Jaspers traveled in Italy in 1922, P.G.– who knew him through Gustav Mayer, Jaspers's brother-in-law– arranged for him to meet with the famous philosopher Benedetto Croce.[65] He also introduced Harry to Jaspers in Heidelberg. "Too naive to talk to one of Germany's two leading philosophers," Harry at least retained "a sort of photo image in my mind."[66]

Although P.G.'s life was affected by wars, economic downturns, and the like, his talent for making the best of things gave him success or serenity (and, at times, both). When World War I broke out, three American university libraries asked him to collect war-related materials, which he did even after being drafted; at the end of the war, he sent them collections of historical importance.[67] He had no qualifications whatsoever for soldiering. His poor eyesight relegated him first to chopping wood and digging ditches; a 1915 photograph shows him looking incongruously plebeian in his uniform as a *Schipper*–a man who uses a shovel.[68] The authorities soon made better use of his gifts, which included facility in languages; he liked to say that he spoke five languages *"fliessend und falsch"* (fluently and incorrectly). His military supervisor had him censor correspondence and foreign-language printed matter and later assigned him to appraise an Air Force library.[69] Reading German newspapers aloud to his fellow shovelers "gave me an excellent opportunity of becoming acquainted with the psychology of classes with which I had rarely come into contact." As Harry was later to do, he learned from the foreign newspapers what was being suppressed in the German press.

After World War I, P.G.'s astute decision to conduct business only in dollars shielded him from the economic afflictions of the 1920s, including the disastrous German crash in 1923, and enabled him to buy important collections from destitute collectors. Obtaining a visa to the United States right after World War I was extremely difficult, but not for him: a friend in Washington helped. Because the two countries were still technically at war, American reporters sought him for interviews that, when published, contained "almost nothing I had said!" His business was not seriously depleted by the

Depression; friends and relatives continued to invest in it, confident that his reliance on dollars would be protective.[70] World War II badly affected his pocketbook, but not his spirit (see Chapter 5).

The idea of "Germany"

For Harry, who never set foot in Berlin's renowned cabarets and bars, the city was another kind of paradise–a paradise of book shops, opera houses, and newspapers. The bookstores, with their enormous stocks, carried the "danger...that I can buy them faster than I can read them."[71] In the periodical room of the *Staatsbibliothek* (state library), which also served the university, he felt "the pulse of the world" stirring in the "thousands on thousands of periodicals on all subjects."[72] In Berlin, the center of a "Germany" that felt like an idealized home, he became an adult. Traveling in Europe as well as elsewhere in Germany tested and affirmed his self-sufficiency and, for a while, his love of Germany. If homesick while in other countries, he longed not for America but for Germany. In Rome, the sight of the imperial eagle at the Germany railway office and "the brass plaque on the gatepost" of the German Embassy cheered him up, as did any opportunity to speak German. Living in Germany meant "living in the present instead of scuttling around ruins," as he did dutifully in Rome.[73] It meant "the Reformation and the beginning of living mentally in this world, the antithesis to this church-infested capital of superstition." It meant moving briskly in "a cold northern exposure where the light is sharp and clear...instead of a hazy swaying in sultry day dreams." When his parents reproved him for his hostility to Rome, he expressed his disgust with the omnipresent Church. He admitted that "however regrettable in an aspirant historian, the sight of hoodoo in actual practice fills me with loathing and contempt."[74] Yet his "sharp and clear" Germanic intellect was at odds with the dreamy emotions that he confided in his diary. By the time he returned to America, in September 1933, he had begun to reconcile his intellect and his emotions.

Part 3. Harry's intellectual environment

The University of Berlin

The History Seminar (Department) of the University of Berlin, the epicenter of modern historical scholarship in Germany, was at a significant moment in its own history, for most of the older generation had either retired or were on the verge of retirement, and bright young recruits were emerging on a scene that was about to change dramatically. In his first semester Harry heard "the last series of public lecturers by Friedrich Meinecke, the dean of German historians."[75] His recollection fifty years later of Meinecke's "sensitive and carefully nuanced refined mind" belies the sharper impression in his diary of the great man's final lecture, attended not only by students but by colleagues distinguished by their "bald heads, beards, and a professional gravity." As he was about to begin, Meinecke was presented with "yellow tulips and a red rose bush–it looked like a wedding." Meinecke "was surprised and touched." The lecture displeased Harry, who thought Meinecke "mishandled the American revolution in an obsolete manner."[76] Another old-timer, Werner Sombart, "a celebrated economic and social historian, proved to be over the hill and on the way to foolishness."[77] The most important of the middle generation for Harry was Gustav Mayer, but the young fellows were more exciting. Because Harry's academic experiences in 1932-33 were of a piece with those in 1931-32, I discuss here Harry's second as well as his first year.

Assessing the instructors

German historians had a "patriotic duty" to devote themselves to studying the fatherland: so said Hermann Oncken, one of Harry's teachers, in the year that Hitler took power.[78] Harry deplored their "very unpleasant habit of writing *Weltgeschichte* [world history] which turns out to be the history of Germany with a few comments on the rest of the world."[79] From this nationalist focus it was a short step to Nazi history glorifying the Fatherland. In the meantime, though, there was plenty to learn. In his first semester, Harry "tasted" ten lecture courses, mainly in history, and attended six of them sometimes. In addition, he signed up for two seminars, the signature pedagogical innovation of German universities–one on the modern period, and the other on the Middle Ages.[80] Most of the lecturers were "the competent, conscientious, unassuming members which are the uninspiring core of every profession."[81] One lecturer he found easy to understand–a benefit while he was perfecting his German–but the lecture was

> Grade 7B stuff, which most of the class faithfully copied, word for word. At home only the girls are this way. Meinecke I cannot judge because I couldn't understand him. Sometimes he stutters over a word, all the time he speaks into the desk, and I could only catch the higher parts of the waves of his ascending intonation.[82]

Attendance requirements were minimal. In order to obtain the instructor's signature in their *Studienbuch* (study book), students had to attend a class once at the beginning and once at the end of the semester; the rest didn't matter. They paid a fee for each course, the source of income for most teachers, including the *Privatdozenten* (lecturers), who formed the majority of the teaching staff.[83] In Harry's first semester, he brought his *Studienbuch* to the medievalist Martin Weinbaum, who provided some adventitious amusement. They spoke German until Weinbaum, noting some hesitancy or a slight accent, asked whether he was German. Harry answered:

> Ich [I]. Ich bin Amerikaner.
> Er [He]. Well, why don't you speak English?
> Ich. ![84]

Weinbaum continued in unaccented English, and Harry attended most of his lectures. The "singsong" of another medievalist, Erich Caspar, nearly put him to sleep. He dragged himself to the final lecture to get Caspar's signature, but he "scuttled out of the room like a rabbit and walloped down the hall so that I will have to waste another hour on Saturday. A shameless ingrate, when I'd paid him $1.50 just to sign my book" at the beginning of the semester."[85] Harry's *Studienbuch*, signed by eminences like Sombart, would "serve as window dressing back at Cambridge [Harvard] where they probably don't know what a completely unendurable person Sombart is." "I've never heard such a big fraud," Harry told his parents (in German, to show off his skills): he was full of gas, just like Harvard professors, and he "looks like a billy goat but speaks like a donkey."[86]

Harry gave no quarter to anyone, no matter how distinguished. In one class Oncken, a leading light of German historiography, disputed the view of two Marxist students that "economic forces were the leading cause of the American revolution." Deducing that "Oncken's knowledge of the Am. Rev. did not form the basis of his professorship," Harry advised the Marxists to bolster their position by "read[ing] Beard & Schlesinger," and he resolved to "read a few books myself and see what we can do to overcome Oncken's insufferable complacency."[87] Only the prospect of disproving Oncken spurred him to continue in the seminar, which he scorned as "a high school class in history"—an echo of the opinion of his Harvard mentor, William L. Langer, that German seminars were "kindergarten stuff." The American Revolution was forgotten in the next class: "Instead Oncken asked me about the motives of Gustavus Adolphus. My dislike of the seminar system is growing."

The one professor whose classes Harry faithfully attended, although often complaining, was Gustav Mayer. Mayer's expertise was exactly what he needed for his proposed Harvard dissertation on the Social Democratic Party. In his first semester, he took Mayer's seminar on the early history of Marxist philosophy and his lecture course on German political parties. Assured by Mayer that there was room in the historical literature for his research, he began collecting the "protocols" of the SPD–the records of the proceedings of meetings that would be his "fundamental source"; soon he had acquired a complete set from 1887 to 1917.[88] Mayer introduced him to the director of the archive of the SPD newspaper, the *Vorwärts*.[89] He was thrilled by the SPD "library of 40,000 books on the socialist movement and history, economics, and sociology." A few months later, experiencing the common fumbling of the neophyte scholar, he was suffering from an embarrassment of riches: there was "too much material and the copying of it takes so much time"; he was looking for "a way out."[90] The SPD protocols presented another Everest, but eventually he realized that it was unnecessary to take notes on "everything these quibblers say in their repetitious hairsplitterei" (the German suffix *-erei*, substituting for the English "-ing," was an example of Dorn's "Gemixte Pickles").[91] He was learning to be a scholar.

On Harry's first visit to his home, Mayer generously offered me guidance and any kind of assistance on my thesis."[92] He "spent a grand couple of hours" in Mayer's "glorious library hearing how he dug up the [Ferdinand] Lassalle documents" for his book on that German socialist thinker. Mayer described his experiences as a reporter for the *Frankfurter Allgemeine Zeitung* in Belgium during the war. He talked, too, "about writing to a certain Ulyanov before the war–so that he is now the possessor of an interesting letter from Lenin–the later name of Ulyanov." Valuable as his personal connection with Mayer was, it carried with it "a certain disadvantage": he felt obliged "not to fall asleep" in class.[93] He "detest[ed] Mayer's classes, his lectures are not to be endured but his seminar is aggressively unbearable. To hell with *Geistesgeschichte!*"[94] Later on, though, *Geistesgeschichte*–the history of ideas, which was pioneered at the University of Berlin–became a central theme of his teaching and writing. A few days later, Mayer's lecture was "better... than usual" and even rose to "fairly interesting." But complaints resumed: "I had to listen to two hours of dry rot in Mayer's Seminar in an intolerable suffocation–all around me people were slouching, reading, or even (at the beginning) eating.... Result: nil."[95] The next lecture, though, was "not very intolerable."

Why did he find Mayer so disappointing as a teacher? The most obvious explanation, supported by the students' rude behavior, is that Mayer had no gift for teaching. Students came out of ideological sympathy: sixteen of the eighteen seminar students were Communists; the rest were "one SPD, and me."[96] Harry wanted teachers to connect past and present, as the previously despised Oncken did: "This afternoon Oncken...cited gleefully the Action Française of ca. 1924 to show that French desires for a disunited Germany didn't end with the 18th century."[97] The adverb "gleefully" suggests that Oncken lectured with feeling. Gerhard Masur made a good impression for a similar reason. "Very sensible and pleasant," he began his seminar by detailing "a dozen or more illuminating problems of

the Reformation, passing present-day matters not timidly but tastefully…. Most of the time we sat there silent, but there are more live
ones than in [Dietrich] Gerhard's troupe of last semester."[98] What
pleased Harry, then, was a combination of two factors. He required
a teacher who, unlike most German professors, connected the past
with "present-day matters," and did so "not timidly but tastefully."
And he demanded enough lively students to stir up discussion, as
happened from time to time.

Reaping the benefits

For all his grumbling, Harry found a good deal of stimulation in
Mayer's seminars. Early in 1932, when Mayer assigned him to report on two early papers by Engels, he indulged his "natural bent"
to nitpick, "avidly seeking Engels' errors."[99] This was not hard: Engels "was at the time of writing only a year and a half older than I
am now." He found "a certain agreeable peril in discussing Engels
before <u>the</u> Engels authority." He enjoyed Marx's *German Ideology*
"because it is so vigorously and spicily written"; Marx and Engels
"tear into theory…with such gusto and vim and malice that you
read it with pleasure."[100] An unanticipated payoff came some years
later, when Harry taught "Scientific Socialism of Marx and Lenin"
for the Communist student organization of which he was president
(see Chapter 6).

In the same semester that he was reading Marx and Engels,
Harry took Dietrich Gerhard's seminar on the British Empire, his
paper for which formed the basis of his sole published book. Gerhard assigned two students–Harry and a certain Fräulein Brose–
to study the transfer of power in Singapore from the Dutch to the
English. Harry was well equipped intellectually. In Paris he had
bought a Dutch grammar and dictionary because he wanted to read
a Dutch newspaper; "a misleading language" because of its likeness to German, Dutch nonetheless posed little difficulty. He mined
the amazing *Staatsbibliothek*, which held all the "early 19th century
things on Singapore…–practically everything in print that is not of
purely local Malayan interest." Gerhard "showed so much interest
in the discussion" that other topics had to be postponed.[101] Harry
was exhilarated to be writing history, not just reading it, for the
"Dutch side" of the subject had previously been neglected.

By the end of 1932, Harry's social skills allowed him to talk with Fräulein Brose, who had just returned from studying in the United States, "about Europe, America, and what not–for three hours." Eventually they "agreed to swap German and English conversation." His sociability spread. When a neighbor asked Frau Meyer if she knew anyone who could use a student ticket to the opera, he accepted–even though his fellow opera-goer would be a woman.[102] He laughed to think that "after how many years I suddenly in one month make the acquaintance of not one but two girls." Before long Fräulein Brose and Harry were "doing *Hamlet*" together. Another session on *Hamlet* made him exclaim: "My God I'm getting sociable." One evening Harry accompanied a woman named Eva Sinauer, apparently a guest of the Meyers, to hear the famous diva Fritzi Massary in Oscar Straus's new operetta *Eine Frau, die weiss was sie will* ("A Woman Who Knows What She Wants"). His judgment– "perfectly foul"–was not shared by the rest of the audience: the operetta was "one of the last glittering theatrical events that Berlin would ever see" before the Nazi takeover, which forced Massary, a "non-Aryan Christian," to flee to London.[103] Some weeks later, he walked Fräulein Brose home through the Tiergarten from a lecture, grilling her on her political views. It was possible to be friends with a woman, even one like Fräulein Brose with conservative politics.[104]

On the last day of 1932, Harry summed up his current academic situation in his diary: he had acquired 965 books and pamphlets and had completed his paper on Singapore. Ever self-critical, he castigated his paper as "repetitious, stylistically grotesque, and not properly spatially distributed" but felt confident that Gerhard would be unable "to contradict the ostensible facts." In the seminar, Fräulein Brose read her piece first; Harry was not impressed. The next week it was his turn: "Read Singapore this afternoon and got hoarse. Gerhard thinks I asked the right questions & gave the wrong answers."[105] He appreciated the value Gerhard put on "the right questions."

Sometimes Harry attended lectures in other fields. In his last semester, Hans Kauffmann's lectures on Dutch painting in the seventeenth century fed his love of Rembrandt and Vermeer. Like most art historians in Harry's view, Kauffmann was "a pleasant lecturer, slow and daintily speaking." Harry's initial praise of Kauffmann's "penetrating" discourse gave way to complaints of seven weeks "wasted...on Rubens." He enjoyed the lecture on Vermeer but wondered impatiently: "When is he coming to Rembrandt?" Finally Kauffmann delivered "a very fine lecture, full of understanding and feeling," about Rembrandt as a painter of "the dialectic of life": he painted the prodigal son when his own son died, and Bathsheba when his beloved Hendrikje Stoffels died. Harry was overcome with emotion by a slide of a self-portrait and another of Jacob blessing his grandchildren. He struggled to describe his feeling:

> It is not that ecstasy I feel when I hear [Sigrid] Onegin's voice—it may be what Spinoza meant with his intellectual love of god. It is less sensual, more appreciative than being dissolved into exquisite sensations by that heavenly voice. I love that man.... Learning to meet Rembrandt is maybe the most important result of these two years.

In Rembrandt, he saw an image of the man he hoped to become: faithful to his ideals and "independent...of his Mitmenschen," his fellow human beings.[106]

Extracurricular activities

Aside from colleagues in seminars, Harry had no direct contact with garden-variety students at the university—65% of whom, in his first semester, expressed support of the National Socialist German Student League.[107] He took part in no organized extracurricular activities, instead making up his own. The lack of specific requirements at the university made it easy for him to indulge his intellectual curiosity—occasionally, as with Kauffmann's lectures, at the university but more often outside of academia. As the next section will show, his travels during academic vacations were almost entirely educational in intent. He wanted to be able to read major European sources, and by the time he returned to America, he had six languages at his disposal: English, German, French, Italian, Dutch, and Spanish. Besides going to France and Italy to improve his knowledge of French and Italian, he found he could read Dutch and Spanish with the help of a dictionary. Armed with a Spanish dictionary, he read José Ortega y Gasset's *Revolt of the Masses* in the original: "I tried the first few paragraphs and found it easy."[108] Self-study included reading books by such authors as Karl Jaspers, to whom he had been too shy to talk in Heidelberg. Together with the Nazis, but for different reasons, he admired a new book by Jaspers, *The Spiritual Situation of the Age*. Harry liked Jaspers's concise exposition; the Nazis admired its apparent exaltation of emotion over reason.[109] The reviewer in Goebbel's paper *Der Angriff* (*The Attack*) would have been surprised to learn that Jaspers's wife, Gertrud, was Jewish–Gustav Mayer's sister.

Harry devoted important time to his long-standing interest in literature. The book that made the deepest impression on him was not a historical treatise but a novel, Thomas Mann's *The Magic Mountain*, which his parents had brought to him from Europe in 1928. Having read it off and on for years, in 1932 he "read thru the remainder in spurts that were at times feverish": "The last hundred pages I read with rising anguish mixed with impatient drive, troubled at the realization that it would last only a few more hours and anxious to know how it would end." It was "no ordinary story where everything is neatly tied up and labeled at the end…yet there is a fine sense of form, [it is] musically built, it has symphonic proportions, resonances, depths, colorings, melodies, counterpoint, it flows directly into your consciousness without the intermediary hindrance of words."[110] Mann's other great novel, *Buddenbrooks*, was "not a book but an experience."[111] Harry speculated that its great success among German-speakers–"more than 900,000 copies…sold"–would not extend in translation, because it was "too localized." Immediately upon Hitler's seizure of power, Mann became an exile, a "notorious liberalistic author" whose name was verboten in the press.[112]

Mann's novels spoke to Harry as Goethe's *Faust* did not. With *The Magic Mountain* he had felt "an imperious not-to-be-postponed urge to force my way thru," but not with *Faust*.[113] Still, when both parts of *Faust* were performed at the Berlin State Theater, he went. Part II, which he saw first, was "in spots very fine, in general minced into pieces, a collection of scenes without unity. Not much better in this respect than reading the text." Part I, though, was "a great event…. Towering. Miles above II." The theater, he realized, can make you "forget the proscenium and the footlights. You can be swung away."[114]

This repressed young man sought to "be swung away" by film, theater, opera, books, paintings, and even people. It happened occasionally. One evening in Munich, he was "doubly brightened." by the simple sight of "the glow on a woman's face that came when she saw her husband" and by an essay in the *Frankfurter Allgemeine Zeitung* about Mont St. Michel. The article gave him a "feeling of being brought out of [him]self, brought into the ideas of the words printed there, brought into a dreamy harmony." The final sentence– "Thrust in your sword, Michael, thrust it in"–made him dream that night that he was "swinging buoyantly one of those great shining two-handed swords" that he had seen recently in Nuremberg and Munich, and he felt "insuperable and gay."[115] He had similar experiences from time to time at the opera, rejoicing in the "marvelous voice" of Gertrud Bindernagel, "the moving mountain," and "the heavenly" Sigrid Onegin, who were "pretty nearly the only people who could sing in Götterdämmerung." Listening ecstatically to Onegin, he felt (echoing Hamlet) that he "could shuffle off this mortal coil painlessly." He imagined that "opium eaters faintly sense the same sort of exultation" as he felt listening to Onegin sing Schubert lieder and an aria from Glück's *Orfeo*.[116]

What good was all this pleasure, though? Was he any more than a dilettante? Exaggerating his lack of "patience and persistence," he bemoaned the "wide divergence between [his] ambitions and accomplishments." His indolence, he speculated, came from his Levison ancestors; he wished that "the Marks characteristics–except surliness, of which I already have an abundance–would come out more decisively." "Presently I'll be 23, and no wiser," he complained, his self-indictment echoing John Milton's sonnet:

> How soon hath Time, the subtle thief of youth,
> Stol'n on his wing my three and twentieth year!
> My hasting days fly on with full career,
> But my late spring no bud or blossom shew'th.

In his own "late spring," Harry, resolutely areligious, could not follow Milton's example and resolve his doubts by submitting to "the will of Heav'n." He could only indict himself for laziness. When he listed the books in English, French, and German that he had read in the year since he sailed from New York, the tally–by no means negligible–did not still his self-recrimination. A kinder judge would have said that he had studied reasonably hard.[117]

Travels in Europe

Earlier in 1932, Harry's undergraduate mentor Frederick Artz had weighed in with some unsolicited advice. Harry's "wideranging"– his extracurricular activities–"will unfit you for doing a thesis and getting your degree" at Harvard; if he wanted that degree, Artz advised, he should return immediately, even though his chances of an academic job would be "infinitesimal." Harry wondered how he could "collect the material for a thesis without being here," and he doubted that "getting my eyes opened" would "unfit" him for Harvard.[118] Indeed, a major part of Harry's education took place during vacations. In 1932 he traveled for language study to Paris in the spring, and to Rome in the summer for Italian (with stops en route in Germany, Switzerland, other Italian cities, Vienna, and Prague). In spring 1933, he roamed around Germany to find out how Hitler was received outside of the capital (see Chapter 4).

Five weeks in Paris, lodging with a family and working with a tutor, sufficed to improve Harry's French. He took no interest in Paris: "I live in a dream, I walk the streets of this city and am not there, I think of Germany, of Berlin, as from the distance of years, and calmly inquire how much tickets are to Mainz, steamers to Cologne, trains to Berlin." By the time he left, he understood spoken French (when "the daughter of the house told me her troubles with the Serb who has proposed marriage to her"); he owned seventy French books; and he could translate an article in the *Frankfurter Allgemeiner Zeitung* into French. As usual, he read the newspapers, an activity that gave rise to a "horrific sensation...of living in a twilight, and in the half dusk I make out huge forms writhing and wrestling in the mist, but what they are exactly is not clear to the excited crowd of commentators who write us dispatches." He thought of the comment attributed to Edward Gray, the British Foreign Secretary: "'The lamps are going out all over Europe,' said Gray one late afternoon toward the end of July 1914, "'we shall not see them lit again in our lifetime.'" If the period 1904-1914 was "the era of the armed peace," Harry wondered, "what will they call 1919-? It is armed but is it peace?" The nightmare he imagined would not "be dispersed by daylight," which only showed it "growing heavier, more frightful." What was happening? What was a "fact"? To judge "a new fact or pretended fact," a historian had to see how "it fits into the rest of 'facts.'... It is the sum total of changing knowledge which is the touchstone for any one of the member facts." Developing his theory of historiography, he continued:

> Thus the whole of knowledge and all experience are woven together into a web–at any one point vulnerable, perhaps, evolving as we regard it, supported by nothing but other similarly weak grains of "knowledge" but which twisted together, interlaced, intertwined, entangled, spun and woven, offer a net of elastic, indeed often fragile material upon which civilization and culture in all aspects bounces and floats.[119]

From France, where he felt "hotter and hotter for things German," he made straight for Heidelberg. Professor Dorn met his train and took him home, where the Dorns' servant, Gertrud, "stood at the head of the stairs with a friendly grin.... And in the hallway stood Guga & then Frau Dorn. It was very nice to be welcomed to a place instead of asking for a room." He had brought a toy elephant for Guga, who "later showed how well she had studied the book I sent her at Christmas." With her parents, he "talked and talked." Aware of his "Berlinish attempt at an accent," he found the Dorns' southern accent "friendlier, maybe, than the northern, at least less sharp, more gentle." After much talk, "we ate–what a relief after French meals!"[120]

On Harry's next trip, on the eve of the Reichstag election in July 1932, he proceeded to Rome very indirectly. His luggage consisted mainly of "seven Baedekers, assorted dictionaries, a camera, and other junk (pliers)."[121] The Germanic thoroughness of the famed Baedeker guidebooks, which suited Harry, later gave rise to a legend that after the British bombed the historic city of Lübeck, Hitler–Baedeker in hand–ranted in a Reichstag speech that Germany would return the favor; "Baedeker raids" did in fact take place on five British cathedral cities.[122] As Harry prepared for his trip, P.G. dispensed travel advice above and beyond the Baedekers, and Heinz told him "how to pat children on the head to create a sympathetic atmosphere in the [train] compartment." From Frankfurt, where he observed the election, he proceeded to Heidelberg. The Dorns were "more favorable to the left & center than I expected" in the election, in which the right received 45% of the vote.[123] Artz was in Heidelberg, studying German with Dorn and working on his book *Reaction and Revolution 1814-1832*. Conceding that another year in Germany "would be all right," Artz warned that "it would take two years of residence at Harvard afterwards to land the degree." That prospect was fine with Harry, "if my parents don't mind supporting their son for a little while longer." They didn't mind; he remained in Cambridge until 1939.

Artz had earlier sent Harry the outline for his book and asked for comments. Harry was flattered that Artz "sacrificed research time which he earnestly devoted, ordinarily, to study, to gab with me." He boldly suggested that Artz "give the book a statistical background: population, vital, trade, manufacturing, social statistics, such as history books never are furnished with but which would take some of the vague flabbiness out of them."[124] Artz "had no flair for that sort of thing," and so–in a classic use of free labor from a graduate student–he asked Harry to gather the statistics and promised to "put my name in the book."[125] Throwing himself into this project, Harry discovered so many statistical subjects for Artz's appendix that there was danger of appendicitis or worse: "perhaps the appendix might even burst & spill over into the rest of the book: acute peritonitis."[126] He worried over the statistics for the rest of his time in Germany.

From Heidelberg, Harry proceeded to southern Germany, Austria, and Switzerland. His object in Germany and Austria was to integrate new knowledge with old. In Rothenburg, he noted that the present inhabitants' "gardens, chickens, cats, their fruit trees, their sheds and haymows" looked much as they had in the Middle Ages, an impression further supported when "someone dumped a pot of urine" into the alley through which he was walking, luckily missing him. The most wonderful discovery was the Deutsches Museum in Munich: "This confoundedly colossal assemblage of universal objects is worth a dozen–a gross–of libraries. I can learn more history here in a week than from a whole history faculty in a semester." In Switzerland, reached via Innsbruck in Austria, his purpose was different. P.G. had persuaded him that he needed a rest and should go to the Alpine resort of Pontresina; Harry admitted that "it would be a great pleasure to relax, to not be solemn and heavy and scowling and full of hopes that tomorrow I'll begin to work." Resolutely solitary, he spent ten days reading intensely and walking in the mountains ruminating about himself and his future. Once he cast "a meditative eye on a girl in brown pants, a yellow polo shirt, and a beret, who is motorcycling by." He scolded himself: "You think a great deal more about girls and marriage than you talk or write about them, a great deal more than you imagine you ought to." When the proprietor of his pension commented that he talked to no one, he was defiant: "I shall preserve my isolation, cost what it may." But he admitted privately the social discomfort and embarrassment that caused him to "try to avoid even chance conversations."[127] His progress toward sociability was hardly a straight line.

The goal of the journey was Rome, his purpose to teach himself Italian: "The language...doesn't look too perplexing–just the usual painful drudging until a necessary amount of stuff is stored up in the memory, that treacherous lumber room of uncertain vagaries." He had a grammar, a dictionary, Frau Meyer's *1000 Worte italienisch* (A Thousand Italian Words), and a comic novel in English and in Italian translation. Avoiding a teacher was part of his plan for isolation. Nonetheless, one aspect of his surroundings pleased him: he "saw people smiling–imagine a Prussian caught smiling out of doors!" This good humor was vanquished by armies of bedbugs (later joined by fleas) and by the omnipresent Catholic Church. Counting his bites each morning, he attacked the bugs ineffectively with Flit and wished he could annihilate the Church. The bugs descended the moment he entered Italy. In Verona, he kept a "scorecard" of "mosquitoes killed" and "Bedbug Bites"–fourteen of the former, seventeen of the latter. When he "made the terrible discovery of 25 bed bug bites" a year later in Berlin, he got rid of them successfully.[128]

In Rome, Harry spent his mornings on Baedeker-guided tourism and his afternoons learning Italian through P.G. Wodehouse's novel *Carry On, Jeeves* (*Avanti! Jeeves*), reading the Italian along with the English original: "In this way I have plunged thru sixty pages of Italian in two afternoons–and with the greatest of pleasure." By the end of a month he was "able to read the *Messagero* [a Roman daily newspaper] without difficulty." He witnessed war games: sirens, airplanes, increased police presence, and many Black Shirts; neither the police nor the Black Shirts bothered Harry or the Romans, who instead of "ducking into doorways, [were] boldly parading thru the streets just as if nothing were going on."[129] From Rome he took his Baedekers to Siena, Florence, Ravenna, Padua, and Venice. But he kept his mind trained on Germany.

No sooner had Harry left Italy than the bedbugs and fleas that had set up residence in his clothing decamped. He was back in German-speaking cities–Vienna, Prague, and Dresden–blissfully speaking and hearing German. In Vienna, he saw the renowned actress Elisabeth Bergner in a new film: she "acts with such shivering honesty that you are overwhelmed, crushed, and exalted." Not all was well elsewhere in the city: "The University [of Vienna], to make me feel at home here, has been closed the last three days because of rioting"; clashes between Social Democrats and Nazis that left two Nazis and a policeman dead had been followed by attacks on Jewish students and the closure of the university. Moving on to Prague, he felt ill at ease. At the famous Altneu Synagogue, the janitor asked "if I was a Česky [Czech] or understood German; I said German. He asked me if I was a Jew and I said yes. Well, then, said he, you'd better put your hat on. Haven't any, I said." The janitor offered a yarmulke, but Harry "wasn't going to associate with other people's fleas." He refused on different grounds to put his handkerchief on his head, as a quasi-hat:

But you've got to wear a hat, you're a Jew, he complained. Oh hell, I said, I'm not religious, consider me a heathen.... Look here, said [a] bystander, you've got to do what the ritual requires. Yes, went on the janitor, see, there's a Christian and he wears his hat. I won't wear a hat, I answered. The bystander said–Look here, I'm a Jew and this peeves me (ich bin gekränkt). Sorry, I said. Well then, will you be good enough to leave? asked the janitor. Goodbye I said, and boiled away.[130]

Why should he accede to Jewish practice when he had "never been thrown out of a Catholic church for not crossing myself or kneeling before the altar"?

In Czechoslovakia and Austria, Harry was so pleased to be traveling in German-speaking countries that, when not afflicted by his own surliness, he dropped his reserve: "I remarked to a prosperous, well-fed and well-spatted fellow-traveller that the only really amiable frontier officials were the Austrians. He, being a Prussian, called them schlapp [spineless], I called them liebenswürdig [deserving love]."[131] The Prussian said that the Austrians "had been rotten allies in the war," but agreed that if the war had been fought with Austrian pastries–"Apfelstrudel, Kaiserschmarr[e]n, or whipped cream (Schlagobers)"–they would have triumphed.

Three days later, Harry was in Berlin, "back at the old stand and open for business." He was enraptured by the familiar scene:

> It is pleasant to see the yellow and brown & blue & brown Stadtbahn cars, the Zeitungsfahrer [newspaper distributor], the peddlers in boots, to hear street singing out of tune,…to see SA uniforms (they stand on street corners with red tin boxes with slots in them, jingling them for campaign contributions!)…

How could it possibly be "pleasant" to see S.A. men? Surely the writer of these puerile words knew that the S.A. and the S.S. had been banned on 15 April and unbanned two months later, and that Nazis in S.S. uniforms had attended the first meeting of the Reichstag on 30 August. He seems to have turned a blind eye to these ominous developments, so thrilled was he "to eat bean soup with wurst, to be told at the PO on asking for some registered packages I sent from Italy: '*Eengeschriebene Pakete? Aber so wat jibs nich.*'"[132] The packages weren't there, the clerk told him in the Berlin dialect that Harry cherished. He equally enjoyed a visit to Paul Gottschalk's, where Heinz joked and P.G. scolded him for not climbing the Alps.

Paying attention to current events

Harry's Germanophilia, which turned S.A. men soliciting funds into part of a "pleasant" scene, was a triumph of wishful thinking. Already in March 1932, as Bella Fromm noted in her diary, "the brown plague" of S.A. Brown Shirts was spreading, with "gangs of roughnecks...painting swastikas and 'we want Hitler' signs on the streets and buildings."[133] Until events forced him to pay attention, Harry was less insistently aware of such details than Fromm, as shown in his responses to May Day, when demonstrations were always rife. His diary for May Day 1932 mentions an expedition with friends to Potsdam but not the demonstrations. On his second May Day, however, he went to Unter den Linden and photographed Nazi banners (at 5 pm, the crowds had thinned); that evening, he listened to Hitler's speech on the radio. During his first year and a half in Germany, his diary and letters sometimes exhibit a self-involvement that dulled his response to what was going on before his own eyes. In November 1932, he failed to see the significance of a Berlin municipal transport strike during which a "united front of Red and Brown" caused chaos for several days at the time of the Reichstag election on 6 November (the alliance of Red Communists and Brown S.A. was not unusual).[134] He did observe that the government-operated *Stadtbahn* was "unusually crowded," because the rest of the system was shut down by the strike; but he wrote nothing about the strike as such.[135] That the strike was not supported by labor unions and was indeed intended to break them and their SPD allies at the moment of the election, that there was considerable violence including several deaths, that the sponors of the strike were radicals on the left and the right: all that went without comment in Harry's diary and letters. That evening he saw three *Schupos*–police officers–standing "dark blue and substantial in the dim light of the lamp" at the corner near the Meyers' building.[136] It was the aesthetic qualities of the *Schupos* that struck him, not their possible connection with the strike.

What matters for our purposes, of course, is not what Harry omitted from his diary and letters but what he included. From the beginning, he took verbal snapshots of the politico-social atmosphere, finding significance in seemingly small details. He explained why students had to show their university ID to get in each of the three university gates: "to keep political agitators who are not students out of the place." He noticed streets full of beggars and hardly a block "without moving vans, and no house without a for-rent sign," concluding: "Anybody looking for the end of an epoch could find material in Berlin." In the Meyers' building, three of the seventeen or eighteen apartments were vacant. Lutz Gottschalk, an idealistic teenager, was so eager to give money to the poor when the government curtailed unemployment relief that his father refused to give him any. The 603,000 unemployed people in Berlin in 1932 constituted over 10% of the national total.[137]

News sources are a constant subject of Harry's diaries and letters. German newspapers, his major source of (mis)information, were ill informed and full of errors and misinterpretations. He considered only three German papers reliable for European news: the *Vossische Zeitung*; the august *Frankfurter Allgemeine Zeitung*; and the *Berliner Tageblatt*.[138] To obtain breadth of coverage, he read–at first occasionally, and later obsessively–English and Continental papers. He liked the ironic toughness of a French columnist who went by the name of Pertinax, who "hoped Hitler would take the helm in Germany because then it would show the world how much of Germany's pretended peacefulness was real." As an American, he was interested in coverage of the United States. When Calvin Coolidge died, he read obituaries in three German papers and the Milan paper the *Corriere della Sera*: "The *Corriere* struck a far better note than the others–less self-conscious, less foreign." Perhaps Italians were "more bound to the U.S.,…because in the waves of immigration, the last great surge came in great measure from Italy, thus creating personal ties and new sympathies." For accuracy, he turned to two American news magazines, the *Nation* and the *New Republic*. They gave him "a feeling of pride," for they were "critical, independent of parties, well written, and with wide interests." One day, he went to the office of the *Manchester Guardian*, hoping to speak with their correspondent, Hermann Framm, who was out.[139]

Newspapers enabled Harry to construct an extensive account of a political crisis in the last two weeks of May 1932: "Today was not devoted to history–the history of a generation ago or centuries ago–but to the history of yesterday and the short time before that."[140]

That history was complicated by the problem of sources. Getting "a coherent idea of a situation" from newspapers, he later wrote, was "like estimating the length of a sausage while it is coming link by link from the machine."[141] But it was all he had. Because "the German ones are notoriously partisan, or taciturn, or full of gaps," he found information by reading twenty-one foreign papers as well as German ones: "papers of all parties in Germany, papers from Switzerland, England, and France. (And of course the Paris Herald, which can be called American)." By scouring the foreign press and "read[ing] between the lines" of the German papers, he inferred "the names of the people most German papers avoid naming" and pieced together what had happened. The issue was an emergency decree being constructed by the cabinet for the signature of President Hindenburg, who had never been "a brilliant intellect" and now, at eighty-five, was increasingly feeble. What interested Harry was the way Hindenburg was manipulated. By the time the political crisis was over, Chancellor Heinrich Brüning had resigned, along with the entire cabinet. General Wilhelm Groener, the Minister of the Interior and Defense, who had banned demonstrations by the S.A. and the S.S. a month or so earlier, was one of the losers; his ouster was engineered by his former protegee, General Kurt von Schleicher, who succeeded him as Minister of Defense. After conferring with party leaders and spending "an unusually long time" with Hitler, Hindenburg named a new chancellor–Franz von Papen, a right-winger and former military attaché in Washington. Among the "various bits of contradiction, nonsense, absurdity, and rhetoric" that littered the political landscape, some commentators said that Hindenburg fired Brüning "because he was not severe enough against the Nazis," while others said it was "because he was too severe against them." Harry expected that with Papen as chancellor, the Nazis would get what they wanted, and they did: a revocation of the S.A.-S.S. ban, and new elections for the Reichstag on 31 July. In the weeks following the unbanning, Nazis killed ninety-nine people, most of them in Berlin.[142]

Observing events from a cool distance, Harry listened to Hitler on the radio and attended controversial films. He noted Hitler's plan for a radio address on 14 June, the first time that the Nazis had breached "the democratic defense of the German democracy." He attended a film created by Bertolt Brecht, Hanns Eissler, and others that had been "3 times forbidden by censor." This was *Kuhle Wampe, Or Who Owns the World,* the only Communist film made in Weimar Germany; the title derived from its setting in Kuhle Wampe, a workers' colony. The censors feared that the film's depiction of unemployment and the suicide of an unemployed worker might suggest the inability of the government to care for its citizens and thus provoke disturbances. Not suspecting the film's eventual historical significance–it is now considered a classic of left-wing cinema–Harry thought it would turn audiences off because it was so "boring" and "dull"–surpassed "from the point of view of ennui… only by Richard Strauss's opera 'Ariadne auf Naxos,' 2¼ hours long and much more than twice as long as a Wagner 5-hour affair." Immune to Strauss's lighter touch, Harry missed the aesthetic boat.[143]

In the weeks before the next election, on 31 July, political disturbances multiplied. Returning home one evening from Paul Gottschalk's, Harry

> heard the unmistakable sound of rhythmical nailed boots on pavement, and there came a group of Hitler's S.A. swinging along. A second was following…. They looked young, husky, and determined, but more boy-scout marching style than West Point. There may be 350,000 of them in all, but France need not be particularly alarmed about them. For *Strassenkravalle* [street riots] they are suitable, but in all <u>military</u> aspects they would prove of absolutely no value, having neither the equipment nor training.[144]

Other private militias marched, each with its own uniform. "This uniform business is a great thing in German politics," wrote Abraham Plotkin: "The moment a movement gathers momentum, up pops the uniform." The gray uniform of the Steel Helmet *(Stahlhelm,* a nationalist veterans' organization opposed to the Weimar Republic) resembled that of the Reichswehr; incomprehensibly, Harry's collection of photographs included one of Walter Elberfeld in a Steel Helmet uniform.[145] The colors of the *Reichsbanner Schwartz Rot Gold* (the Black Red Gold Banner of the Reich), which was loosely affiliated with the SPD, indicated its support of the Weimar Republic. The Iron Front (*Eiserne Front*), which was allied with the SPD and also with the *Reichsbanner*, had support from unions; marching "with a zip as effective as that of the Nazis," it held a huge demonstration in Berlin the day before Hitler was named chancellor. The *Rote Frontkämpferbund* (the Red Front-Fighters League, the Communist paramilitary group) was declared illegal by the Papen government because it was anti-government. After Hitler took power, the brown S.A., the black S.S., and (briefly) the gray Steel Helmet remained--this last forced in 1934 to wear "the honorable brown" S.A. uniform, as Victor Klemperer remarked ironically, and dissolved completely in 1935.[146]

The contemporary militias resonated with Harry's reading about the Thirty Years' War, "in which private armies ravaged the land and set Germany two centuries–perhaps three–behind the rest of the western world."[147] He found parallels with the present situation: "Fanaticisms, local, racial, religious, economic class disturbances, barbarisms of assorted types, a vicious particularism engendering differences in whose acid all feeling of community disintegrates, gangsterism raised to a principle"–all this had been "chronic in German history since the 16th century." War became "a profession, with families bred to it...–blood and iron were necessary for practical things." When "slogans of professed humanity" became "coarse and crude..., the *Denker und Dichter* [thinkers and poets]...never protested–or rarely."

The pursuit of scholarship occasionally drew Harry unwittingly to dangerous places. At the *Vorwärts* building, where he hoped to use the bookstore, he found the gates closed and the building guarded by "half a dozen healthy-looking men in khaki, Reichsbannermen." Some hours after he left, there was "an attack on the building by 100-150 Nazis, two men were shot and a third badly hurt." The neighborhood, an SPD stronghold, was like "a superheated steam boiler whose safety valve is being held down" by the government of Papen and Schleicher, "engineers [who] don't arouse my confidence." He was glad he hadn't witnessed the attack and hoped to avoid all disturbances. If the university were closed– "either by the anti-Nazi government in order to prevent rioting or by the Nazis if they take the helm, to clean the faculty of non-Nazi professors"–it wouldn't directly affect him as long as he could "get my *Studienbuch* signed, and...the libraries remain in operation." By then attending only four hours of classes a week, he didn't mind "that there was another *Kravall* [riot] in the university this morning, the first since last fall or early winter."[148] Two weeks later he saw "mobs of students clustered" by the closed gates–yet another *Kravall*. That particular riot alarmed Count Harry Kessler, who wrote in his diary that "the unbridled, organized Nazi terror" had "again claimed seventeen dead and nearly two hundred wounded as its victims."[149] Kessler added: "It is a continuous St Bartholomew's Massacre, day after day, Sunday after Sunday." Less emotional than Harry Kessler, Harry Marks maintained his customary ironic distance. For him, "the most serious factor is not the possible altera- tion of university organization but the fact that the Nazis want to interfere with the opera."[150] He didn't really mean it, though.

In the lead-up to the election, Baron Wilhelm von Gayl replaced Groener as Minister of the Interior. Gayl, who was later to resist the Nazis, was willing to censor newspapers at the government's bidding. The *Vorwärts* and a Cologne paper backed by the Catholic Zentrum (Center) party were both shut down for five days as pun- ishment for their criticisms of the government. The *Vorwärts* had slyly suggested "that there was a connection between the new Nazi uniforms–very expensive–and the shortening of the relief pay- ments," and the Cologne paper had objected to foreign policy to- ward France. Harry reacted cynically: "I can't work up any sympa- thy for anyone concerned.... I don't suppose any SPD or Zentrum members have lost any tears over the almost equally arbitrary 5 day ban of the Berlin Nazi organ *Der Angriff*." Finally, on what became known as "Bloody Sunday," a "pitched battle...in Altona (Ham- burg's Hoboken)," which resulted in eighteen deaths, led Gayl to prohibit all demonstrations.[151]

Nazis and Communists thronged the streets. One Sunday the Kurfürstendamm, a major shopping street, was "swarming with uniformed Nazis. Walking in 3's & 4's, they lounged up and down and across the avenue...saluting acquaintances with the pseudo- Roman gesture of the raised arm." At a Communist demonstration on the following Tuesday, a couple of miles of Communists marched down from the Red north of Berlin and sang the Internationale and other appropriate anthems, shouted couplets in unison against the Nazis and in favor of the KPD [German Communist Party], and raised their fisted hands in the Red salute or gesture of defiance. There were workmen's bands, always red flags and banners with suitable inscriptions, and all ages and both sexes were among the marchers: unemployed looking a little shabby, employed men with white shirts, gray shirts, blue shirts, brown shirts, dirty shirts, hatless or with the nautical caps so much worn by all ages of men; girls in bright dresses, gray-haired women, thin women, fat women, school girls and stenographers, women in white with nurses' caps and bags with contents for all emergencies, and, always, cops. Cops pacing alongside by twos, cops in five-seater open runabouts, cops in the familiar police department riot squad trucks, all in Alarmbereitschaft [emergency readiness], the bands of their helmets under the chin, the side boards of the trucks down to allow instantaneous action.

Such parades reinforced the marchers' "community of feeling" but probably had no effect on the audiences lining the streets. Harry had a certain sympathy with "these hoarse marchers, with their shouts of 'Was haben die Arbeiter? [What do the workers have?] Hunger! Hunger! Hunger! Was wollen die Arbeiter: Arbeit! Arbeit! Arbeit!' [What do the workers want? Work! Work! Work!]."

After a ban on demonstrations, competing parties compensated by littering the street with fly sheets advertising their causes: "People stooped over, men and women, and picked them off the pavement or off the asphalt, and walked along reading them."[152] Harry had a personal experience of anti-Semitism when he and Heinz encountered "two boys handing out fly sheets. I put out my hand for one and the boy turned away and said–Nee–nicht für die Juden [No, not for Jews]."[153] Heinz, unrecognized as Jewish, gave Harry his copy; Nazis, it seemed, were no more adept at recognizing Jews than the admissions officers at Harvard mentioned in Chapter 2. The government, too, practiced political hooliganism. On 20 July,

Albert Grzesinski, an SPD politician, was forced to resign as police president of Berlin by a group of young officers sent by Papen; in a premonition of Nazi methods, they "forced their way in [to police headquarters], hand grenades in their leather belts." Harry considered writing to Artz in Heidelberg: "How do you like living under a dictatorship?"[154]

On the eve of the election, having just left on his travels, Harry strolled the streets of Frankfurt, noting political flags. A neighborhood favoring the SPD and KPD was thick with "red flags with a white sickle and hammer," in one area "completely ablaze and not unfittingly labeled by a sign over the entrance: *Klein Moskau* [Little Moscow].... I thought, lord help a Nazi in this neighborhood, but there were none."[155] The "better off areas" displayed Nazi flags. He saw "a troop of Nazis" and then "a much larger group of the Iron Front." When the election results came in, the Nazis, although the largest party in the Reichstag, did not have a majority, and Hindenburg refused to name Hitler chancellor. The government collapsed. New elections were called for 6 November when, as already noted, both the Communists and the Nazis ganged up against the SPD in the transport strike.

During his travels, Harry followed events in Germany through the *Frankfurter Allgemeine Zeitung*. The "nationalist-militarist internal disposition" of the government, with its suppression of all left-wing thought and "collateral policy of strengthening right-wing opinion and parties," was laying a firm foundation for the Nazis. The government attacked the KPD, whose national headquarters at Karl Liebknecht House "was searched and the *Rote Fahne* [Red Flag, the KPD newspaper] several times banned. Rewards are offered for information about illegal Communist literature–...now they set a price on its head." The one certainty about the upcoming November elections was that the Papen government, which had bitterly criticized Hitler's NSDAP, would face "some 500 or more hostile Reichstag members," for only the DNVP supported Papen's Zentrum. The Nazis lost ground in November, a temporary reprieve. Walking along the Kurfürstendamm a week before Hitler became chancellor, Harry saw "Nazis with 3 *Hakenkreuz* ["crooked cross," swastika] banners marching in the snow, singing about Hitler *unser Führer* [our leader]. Sad demonstration of herdmindedness."[156]

That month, the brief and brilliant academic career of Ernst J. Cohn shuddered to a halt. A year earlier, Cohn had been named "ordinarius [full professor] on the law faculty of the Univ. Breslau...at the extraordinary age of 28" and entered into a torment predictive of later events.[157] His colleagues didn't mind that he was Jewish, but the Nazi students did. In December 1932, the governing body of the university bravely declared that they would not dismiss him–only to do so a week later:

> Why? Because he had answered a newspaper's request, made to a large number of people, to express an opinion whether or not Trotsky ought to be allowed to enter Germany. Cohn answered that he didn't know the details of the matter, but that his principles would be: if Trotsky wanted to come to Germany for his health and as a private gentleman, he saw no reason for prohibiting his entrance. On the other hand, if he came as an agitator–We have enough of such already–Cohn said; Keep him out.

This statement, deliberately misinterpreted as a call for Germany to give Trotsky political asylum, gave the university an excuse to fire him. There followed "a great row and the Prussian *Kultusministerium* [Ministry of Cultural Affairs] intervened." Cohn, having apologized, "was once more returned to the fold," again requiring police protection. Harry concluded: "This is merely one incident out of many to illustrate the penetration of some of the universities by politics of the most vicious order."[158] Two weeks after Harry reported Cohn's troubles, Hitler took over.

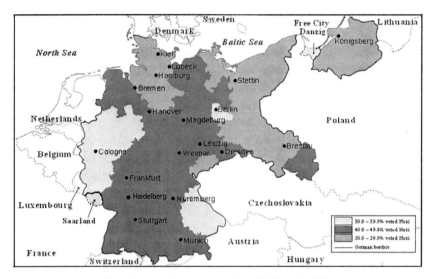

Reichstag election results, 5 March 1933

Deutsche Bank in
Heidelberg on
14 July 1931, when
Harry found it
closed in banking
crisis

Entrance of new
building at Heidelberg
University, August 1931.
The Nazis replaced
Pallas Athena with
the imperial eagle and
replaced the inscription,
Dem lebendigen Geist (To
the Living Spirit), with
Dem deutschen Geist (To
the German Spirit)

S.A. shop at Kantstrasse 173, Charlottenburg, Berlin, June 1933

Shop window in Berlin showing "Heroes of the New Germany--Hitler, Goebbels, Horst Wessel, Göring, Bismarck" (May 1933)

Mommsenstrasse 57, Berlin, photographed 1 December 2005

Grete and Ernst Meyer, 1933

Lisel Meyer, 1 July 1933

Rudy Meyer, 1933

Claire Meyer,
3 July 1933

Paul Meyer, early 1933

Saturday evening at Paul Gottschalk's. From left: Paul Gottschalk, Laura Gottschalk, Flora Mayer (reading newspaper), Betty Elberfeld, Eva Freyhan

Paul Gottschalk in
his Berlin office,
Unter den Linden
3a, April 1933

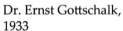
Dr. Ernst Gottschalk,
1933

Laura Gottschalk,
1933

Heinz Gottschalk in Paul Gottschalk's office, April 1933

Lutz Gottschalk, 28 June 1933

Betty Gottschalk Elberfeld,
24 June 1933

Dr. Walter Elberfeld in his "fancy rig," 24 June 1933

Dr. Walter Elberfeld in Steel Helmet uniform, 9 July 1933

Clara Gottschalk Freyhan, 12 June 1933

Dr. Max Freyhan, 1933

Fritz Freyhan, 1 July 1933

Hans Freyhan, 1 July 1933

Martin Hirschbach, 12 June 1933

Rose Hirschbach, 12 June 1933

Ernst Hirschbach, 12 June 1933

HARRY MARKS
STUD. PHIL.

NEW YORK

Harry's card, Arts Faculty, University of Berlin

Reading Room of the Staatsbibliothek, 20 June 1933

4

Germany 1933

Part 1. The New Order Begins

Hitler becomes chancellor

"All through January 1933 Germany fermented," Harry later recalled, "until at the end of the month Hindenburg's cronies had persuaded him to appoint the Bohemian pfc, whose loud voice and startling manners he despised, to the post of Reichskanzler."[1] Anti-Nazis and German patricians may have scorned the Austrian-born Hitler as a mere "Austrian corporal"–equivalent to "private first class" (pfc)–but a "wave of enthusiasm and frenzy swept over Germany" on 30 January when he was named chancellor. It was all "hard to believe," the journalist Bella Fromm wrote in her diary, "if your mind has a leaning toward sanity."[2] Many Germans, agreeing with Harry's prediction that responsibility would make Hitler more moderate, found him laughable. A few days later, attending a performance of Part I of Goethe's *Faust*, Harry was pleased to hear "hearty clapping and chuckles" when a character rejoiced "*Dass ich nicht Kaiser oder Kanzler bin*" (that I'm neither Kaiser nor Chancellor).[3] The chuckles were short-lived. On the eighth anniversary of his *Machtergreifung* (seizure of power), Hitler recalled the Jews' initial "uproarious" laughter; now, he boasted, they were "laughing on the other side of their face."[4] "We believed for a long time that Hitler would not last," said a German Jewish refugee: "But how could we know?"[5] Some people did know, even before the *Machtergreifung*. "To listen to Dr. Freyhan," Harry wrote in 1932, "you'd think the Nazis meant to carry through their pogrom program."[6]

Hitler rose to power through his oratory. Ernst Hanfstaengl, whose antics at Harvard are described in Chapter 6, first heard him in the early 1920s and was enraptured: "He spoke mezzo voice, quietly, soothingly,...words which burned all the more for their softness."[7] Once in power, he took to the air waves. On the evening of 10 February, "all German broadcasting stations were required to transmit the Nazi demonstration in the Sportpalast in Berlin." Harry listened:

> Dr. [Joseph] Goebbels, the editor of the *Angriff*..., did the announcing; it was something like a football announcement–superlatives poured forth in a fluent rattle, we were told that all Germans were being spoken to, including those beyond the boundaries, we heard them sing *Deutschland über Alles*, and the cheers when Hitler "took the word."

Speaking "in a brown chocolaty voice, very emotional, in content perfectly vacuous–but restrained in his inanities," Hitler

> sang, he ranted, he used invective crashing thru to gain effects, he'd go up to a peak notch by notch and explode, and then begin all over again. And all during the entire hour he literally said not a thing. Not a single thing. He counted numbers and called it a program. He blamed some vague beast called "Marxismus" for 14 years of misery, degradation, etc., and promised a land of milk and honey.

Harry's host was among the "millions of people who are captivated by such stuff"; such was the mesmerizing power of Hitler's voice that after a while, "one no longer listened to his words so much as to his voice." Ernst Meyer, although "not typical in as much as he is Jewish," was otherwise representative of "the typical shortsighted *Kleinbürger* [petty bourgeois], uneducated, honest, and dimwitted." Herr Meyer wondered "whether Hitler might not be better than he is painted: only a few changes of personnel in the ministries to give his friends jobs, but as for anything worse– no, unlikely. And if he can do anything to help us, why he should have the chance."[8] In speaking of "us," Herr Meyer meant "us Germans." Before long, Jews were not "Germans."

Harry soon noted indicators of the rising Nazi tide. The right of habeas corpus was effectively eliminated; SPD and KPD leaders were jailed; auxiliary police were mobilized; and "a regular wave of communophobia is being created–the Reichsbahn [railroad] setting armed men to guard bridges & tunnels, the water works being under guard." "Pathological mysticism" spread over Germany, making "for a rejuvenated, purified, guaranteed Aryan Germanic culture."[9] The Prussian Academy of the Arts fell victim to censorship. Two of its prominent members, the writer Heinrich Mann and the artist Käthe Kollwitz, had signed a placard that was posted on kiosks, urging the KPD and SPD to join in "a united proletarian front." Bernhard Rust, the Prussian Minister of Cultural Affairs (*Kultusminister*), told the president of the Academy that it would be shut down unless Mann and Kollwitz were expelled. Called before a special meeting of their peers, Harry reported with irony, "both betrayers of Germany voluntarily resigned rather than cause the whole circus to be closed up."[10]

Other cultural institutions and individuals met similar fates. Principled resistance was not part of German culture; nearly everyone caved or fled. In World War I "there were millions [of Germans] with courage enough to fight & die–but how few–how unbelievably few–with the greater courage not to fight & die." The Free Speech Congress, a mass demonstration attended by 900 people at the Kroll Opera House, included "the anti-anti-Semitic *Altmeister* [old master] of German sociology, Ferdinand Tönnies, who spoke about freedom of teaching [*Lehrfreiheit*]." The Congress was shut down when Rust's SPD predecessor spoke in an "insulting & maliciously contemptuous [way] of the present *Kultusminister*, the valiant school teacher Rust."[11] Fritz Busch, the director of the Dresden Opera and "a pure bred Aryan, was met by a deputation of S.A. & Nazis asking for his resignation" because he had refused to join the NSDAP; at a rehearsal of Verdi's *Rigoletto*, a "bedlam of whistles" made it impossible for him to conduct.[12] The prominent (and Jewish) conductor Bruno Walter was "as good as without an occupation" in Germany; from other quarters, however, "invitations poured down" on Walter, without mitigating his sadness that his birth country rejected him.[13] The renowned Theater am Gendarmenmarkt, which had been without a director for months, "got two Nazis recently." Nazis professed cultural appreciation: "Many

S.A. officers in their best uniforms" attended a performance of *Don Giovanni* at the *Städische Oper* (City Opera), which the Nazis had just "wrecked" by suspending Carl Ebert, its head, as well as two conductors and other staff.[14]

Nazi displays became an everyday matter. One evening at the Meyers', they heard noise and looked out the window to see "a form of mass lunacy": hundreds of Nazis parading four abreast, accompanied by a "heavy police guard, armed with carbines." Police trucks were "flashing their searchlights at the windows of the houses on the streets–looking for anyone interested in peppering the marchers." At the university, Fräulein Brose evinced "rather reactionary" views. She was no Nazi, she said, but "she wasn't so opposed to them as before." She and Harry discussed the "reorganization"–a euphemism for "destruction"–of the Karl-Marx School, a progressive public school that led pupils "towards independence instead of toward the classical Prussian virtue of sheep-like obedience." Fräulein Brose, who had observed democracy while studying in the United States, thought that it was "a fine thing, but not for the Germans." In her view, "free discussion & debate" undermined authority; "the kids should be taught some hard Facts–but which ones, I asked."[15] To Harry, the Karl-Marx School represented the values of his father's P.S. 64.

The closing of liberal schools, the Nazis on the streets collecting money for the upcoming election, the suppression of newspapers– all this, Harry said, was "making an impression on me, the impression of some bad dream where all sorts of foolish things happen without your being able to move a finger. Captive in a daze, you watch the impossible and frightful occur before your eyes." Germany was a *Hexenkessel*, a witches' cauldron. He felt he was witnessing "the end of legalism, the end of order and the birth of chaos," something like "the conquest of Rome by the barbarians." Oswald Spengler's *Decline of the West* needed retitling as "The Decline of Western Culture in Germany." The mood of horror colored everything. Harry admitted a "morbid" fascination with "Pfülf's book on the Jesuits in Germany…a tale of conspiracy, a tale of mysterious organization."[16]

In this "madhouse where the inmates are reckoned by the millions and run around loose," language was ever more perverted.[17]

Magnus von Levetzow, the newly appointed police president of Berlin, denounced "poison plants of Asiatic origin, these murderous political rogues." A person "initiated in the new tongue" would understand a reference to Jewish politicians. It was bitterly amusing "that in ostensibly combating the oriental deficiencies by which Jews defile pure Teutonic culture, the government should gradually assume more and more the traits of an oriental despotism."[18] When Levetzow, in order to promote "traditional Teutonic moralities," issued an order against prostitution, Harry decided to see if he was obeyed. Surveying Friedrichstrasse, a famous haunt of *Nutten* (prostitutes), he found two *Schupos* and two prostitutes. Evidently the prostitutes "hadn't read the newspaper reports of [Levetzow's] indignation. Or maybe they were Nazi *Nutten*?" Two months later, coming home by way of Kantstrasse, another locale favored by prostitutes, he observed "clouds and swarms" of them. Nazi morality took weird twists. All "Germans" were equal under the law, for example, but there was a coda: "Jews are not Germans, and Communists are subhuman (*Unmenschen*), and these must be rooted out."[19] Actually, it was the Jews who were "subhuman"; as *Unmenschen*–literally, inhuman persons, or brutes–the Communists were not human at all.

The Reichstag fire

On 27 February, there occurred one of the signature events of the early Hitler period: a fire at the Reichstag, the parliament building. The next morning, Harry's neighborhood newspaper vendor "derided the government's official attribution of the fire to Communist arsonists. Only the Nazis benefited from the fire, he remarked." The fire gave an excuse to suppress the KPD and suspend constitutional guarantees of free speech and the press, leaving "the Storm Troopers...free to bully, assail, imprison, and kill at will."[20] Was it likely that Marinus van der Lubbe, the simple-minded Dutch man accused of arson, could have brought "immense quantities of inflammables...into the house" without being seen?[21] Was it plausible that the KPD would create its own doom in Germany? From the Stadtbahn, Harry saw "the burnt-out Reichstag...–smoky, sooty, facade projecting, golden dome smoked & without the glass inlays."[22] The fire inspired mordant jokes. In one, Hitler and Moses meet in Heaven, and Hitler asks: "But you can tell me in confidence, Herr Moses. Is it not true that you set the bush on fire yourself?"[23]

In the aftermath of the fire, the authorities pasted orange-and-white paper over SPD and KPD posters on street kiosks and shuttered all the Communist pubs. The police searched Karl Liebknecht Haus, the KPD headquarters, and "turned up hundreds of pounds of ostensibly traitorous & bloody literature.... The whole business smells a little foul, more than a little." Over Berlin there settled a "dull soggy absence of reaction to the most violent changes that a violent government can execute." What was an American to make of all this? Harry thought that "the discrimination here today against Jews doesn't begin to compare with what the Land of the Free exercises towards Negroes."[24] A similar point was made by Sherwood Eddy, an American pacifist evangelist. Speaking in Berlin in 1933, Eddy charged Germany with "acting against the principles of justice.... Don't say it's your affair. It concerns the whole world when we in the United States conduct a lynching.... The world is also concerned when you commit similar injustice."[25] "[T]orrents of applause" flowed from the foreigners in Eddy's audience while the "Nazis, pale with rage, sat immobile, in cold silence." The German habit of fighting political battles with flags continued, but now there was "only a thicket of *Hakenkreuz* [swastika] banners and a waving mass of imperial black-white-red flags of the anti-republicans." Anyone who was "so ill advised as to show" the flag of the Weimar Republic was visited by "troops of Nazis," who trampled the flags and set them on fire, "while howling mobs yelled 'Heil Hitler!'"[26] After the election, a "Berlin flag & banner manufacturer...work[ed] overtime to supply the huge demand" for Nazi flags.[27]

Prominent intellectuals were already "buying one-way tickets out of Berlin," among them Alfred Kerr, the drama critic of the *Tageblatt*, and its editor, Theodor Wolff; Albert Einstein; and the writers Erich Maria Remarque, Emil Ludwig, Heinrich Mann, and Thomas Mann.[28] Grete Meyer wished "she were in Brussels again–and doubtless her wishes are shared by many." At the College of Music, the "left-wing and Jewish teachers" were already "planning to set up a private Conservatory when they finally get bounced"; "reorganization" was expected at the university.[29] All this took place *before* the Reichstag election on 5 March 1933.

Consolidating Nazi control

"This is the morning after the night before," Harry wrote his parents on 6 March. The Nazis won 43.9% of the vote; an alliance with the DNVP, "the party of big business and Junkers," provided an additional eight percent and gave a decisive majority that was solidified, ironically on Bastille Day, 14 July: according to the new mathematics, 43.9%+8% ="100% 'Legal zur Macht'"–legally in power.[30] In the immediate aftermath of the election, Minister of Cultural Affairs Rust proclaimed a holiday, "so that the children could celebrate the Nazi victory"; they marched and sang in the city center "dressed in brown shirts, carrying *Hakenkreuz* flags, and wearing *Hakenkreuz* arm bands."[31] Nazi flags sprouted on official buildings and bedecked the famous equestrian "Quadriga" atop the Brandenburg Gate.

The first "legal" step to consolidate Nazi control took place on 23 March, when the Reichstag passed the Enabling Act suspending the Weimar Constitution and thus abolishing all freedoms of press and person.[32] After twenty-six of the 120 SPD deputies were arrested, the remaining ninety-four voted against the Enabling Act. In their vote, Harry wrote later, the SPD deputies

> proved to the world that Germany was not a monolithic block of barbarians; they took the first step–in public and at risk of their lives–to defy the Evil that was enveloping Germany, a first step toward the heroic anti-Nazi movement... [of Germans who felt a] moral allegiance to–let's call it–Germany and decency.[33]

There was other, sometimes surprising, resistance. A Nazi patient warned his Jewish doctor "to flee before his colleagues came to seize her and throw her into a concentration camp."[34] Several camps were established early in the Nazi period to hold political prisoners: Dachau (near Munich), Oranienburg (including Sachsenhausen, both near Berlin), and Osthofen (in the Rhineland) were founded in March 1933. Before long, they also held Jews.

The SPD deputies and likeminded Germans constituted the "nation of *Dichter und Denker*" (poets and thinkers) revered by Harry and his friends, while the Nazis had "relinquished the *Denken* and content[ed] itself with *Dichtung*." Nazi *Dichtung* was mere hypnotic rants, "poetry" shorn of meaning. With official pronouncements unreliable, Harry now valued hearsay, "the things I happen to hear at the table or in talking with people." There was, for example, the treasurer of a Jewish hospital,

> a harmless, non-political, not excessively Jewish-looking man, [who] was stopped on the street and his briefcase gone through, doubtless with the hope of finding documents proving that the hospital is the scene of "ritual murders," a...refuge for firebugs, a printing plant for illegal propaganda, and a branch of the Internationale. The poor man had... neglected to bring such documents with him, and was allowed to continue on his way.[35]

Repression was omnipresent. SPD supporters were routinely attacked. A doctor who "made the mistake of going last year to operate (or consult) on Stalin...is said to have been beaten up a day ago and may have already lost his job."[36] To the delight of the small businessmen who were a major part of the Nazi base, armed S.A. and S.S. men shut down department and chain stores; department stores "ruined the small businessman," it was claimed, and all of them were supposedly owned by Jews.[37] The Tietz department stores, which were indeed Jewish-owned, were immediately "Aryanized." Other anti-Semitic measures quickly occurred. An invasion of the courts in Breslau by S.A. and S.S. men was puzzling until it became clear that "only Jewish lawyers & judges were threatened."[38] When the courts reopened, all but seventeen of the 364 Jewish lawyers who had practiced there were forbidden entry. In Berlin, where 73.5% of the legal profession was Jewish, nearly all were shut out by a decree limiting Jewish lawyers to the percentage of the total population, which was 3.87%.[39]

Finding out what was happening

Within weeks of the Reichstag election, newspaper editors were required to present themselves twice daily at the Propaganda Office to learn "Nazi newspaper technique."[40] Newspapers that printed something offensive were suspended, so they "all print agency reports and mostly nothing else." Bad news was forbidden: an attack on the apartment of the Berlin correspondent of *Izvestia* went unreported in the German press. Two of the major liberal newspaper publishers, the Ullstein and the Mosse families, were Jewish, spelling doom for their papers. Even before the Reichstag election, one of the Mosse papers, the *8 Uhr Abendblatt*, was suspended "'for an indefinite period'–with no reason assigned." Harry heard an "incredible rumor that the government is going to buy the *Berliner Tageblatt*," another Mosse paper; he supposed that the rumor showed "the extent to which fantasy is nurtured in the dark." But the line between "fantasy" and reality blurred more and more. When the *Tageblatt* failed to note the fiftieth anniversary of Marx's death, Harry thought it had sold its soul.[41] It had not. The historian George Mosse, then a teenager, later constructed an account of the collapse of his family's newspaper.[42] It was on 21 March, the day that Harry condemned the *Tageblatt* as "practically worthless," George Mosse learned, that Wilhelm Ohst, a Nazi commissar, brandished a revolver at Hans Lachmann-Mosse, George's father, forcing him to agree to expropriation. The firm was taken over by a fake "foundation that supposedly aided war veterans." Within two years, circulation of the emasculated *Tageblatt* had fallen by ninety percent.[43] Other papers went under fast. On vacation in Kassel, Harry "saw the broken windows of the now deserted Sozialdemocratic newspaper," which was as ruined "as if it had been struck by lightning, as it has." By May the shelves of the *Staatsbibliothek* newspaper reading room were "pretty empty in some sections–domestic periodicals shut down, foreign ones banned."[44] The *Vossische Zeitung* lasted until April 1934. Countering the loss of credibility of other papers, the *Frankfurter Allgemeine Zeitung* retained its allegiance to truth for a time.

Because editors of Nazi papers had less to fear, they sometimes printed news that the "liberal" press did not dare mention. The *Völkischer Beobachter* (National Observer) noted the "probably frequent" house searches that the foreign press considered too minor to report, or dared not report. The *Beobachter* produced "a flood of vituperation against Jews in general and Einstein, [Lion]

Feuchtwanger, & others, in particular–but nothing about the breaking into Feuchtwanger's home in Grunewald, the theft of the manuscript of his next book, and destruction of other papers."[45] Anyone wanting full information had to consult foreign papers, even before the *Machtergreifung*.[46] On 6 March, the day after the election, Harry bought Dutch, Italian, French, and English papers to cobble together an understanding of the results. Yet foreign papers also fell victim to the Nazis; leading foreign journalists were "followed religiously, and their apartments watched and reported on."[47] "There is always the possibility of expelling troublesome foreigners," the *Angriff* observed. By early August, German-language newspapers from Czechoslovakia and Austria were largely banned, but "every newsstand [carried] Swiss papers–the *Basler Nachrichten* or the *Neue Zürcher Zeitung*"; the circulation of the latter in Berlin was several times that in Zurich itself.[48]

Harry rarely read American papers while he was abroad, although he went occasionally to the *New York Times* reading room, until it closed soon after the Reichstag election. He predicted correctly that when the Nazis discovered that Adolph Ochs, the publisher, was Jewish, they would cite the *Times* as an example of "Jewish world finance."[49] Among American reporters, Harry particularly admired Edgar Ansel Mowrer of the *Chicago Daily News*. Mower's book *Germany Sets the Clock Back* was banned in Germany soon after its publication in 1933, but Harry already had his copy. Ambassador William E. Dodd advised Mowrer to leave Germany by 1 September for his own safety; he was, in effect, expelled.[50] Hoping to meet him, Harry visited Mowrer's office. He was out, but his deputy, an "Urberliner [a Berliner through and through] and a hardboiled leftist," was glad to chat. The deputy expected, "as I do, that incompetency will overthrow the present government" and anticipated that in the meantime the paper would have "to use couriers to get the news out of the country"; he discussed attacks on Americans, a topic Harry omitted when describing his visit in a letter.[51]

Harry didn't wish to disturb his parents, but they were already well informed. Attacks on foreigners were not reported in the German papers, but they were in the American press. On 7 March, Louis and Sophie Marks cabled Harry, begging him to be careful. After

Nazi officers savagely beat the American writer Edward Dahlberg, Harry attempted to relieve his parents' anxiety with wit: now Dahlberg could "write articles for *Scribner's* from his own experience."[52] Another lodger in the Meyers' home, a student from Los Angeles, received a cable from her parents imploring her to return immediately and to "make every effort to save her life. We all had a good laugh," Harry reported, "and I helped her compose a suitable reply, observing that it was safer here than in Los Angeles of the earthquakes." He himself was "in as much danger as in such perilous metropoli as NY or Boston." In fact, there *was* menace in the air. Frau Meyer "seriously suggested that I pack up & send off some of my books lest they be confiscated."[53] Harry's innate recoil from danger protected him during the remaining six months of his stay.

Writing to his parents, he began to couch his views in euphemisms—"very reticent on affairs here"—and in April started numbering his letters so that any interruption in the series would indicate capture by a censor. When one of his letters arrived in New York with a sticker reading "opened for customs inspection," Harry suspected that the censor had removed a Nazi questionnaire that he had enclosed, which was devised to enable undesirable students to be expelled.[54] The questionnaire had arrived, however. Letters *were* opened. Sometimes people asked someone who was traveling abroad to carry a letter, as when Harry's teacher Hajo Holborn asked Paul Gottschalk to take a letter to Paris.[55] Ambassador Dodd's letters, bearing "the stamp and seals of the United States," were opened; he omitted potentially dangerous names from his private diary and knew that his house was bugged.[56]

In these circumstances, anecdotes and rumors flourished. One day an electrician working at the Meyers' apartment told Harry that a man on Uhlandstrasse "was arrested because someone overheard him say he didn't believe the official version of the Reichstag fire. The greatest virtue today is *Mund halten*"—keeping your mouth shut. Official statements required decoding. If the government denied "that the political prisoners, now to be numbered by the thousand, are cruelly treated, mishandled, or abused," that meant "that their lot is a continuous 3rd degree." Harry's visit to the dentist concluded with a half-hour discussion of politics. One of Dr. Stock's patients, a Jewish conductor of an opera company patronized by the Prince of Reuss, "lost his job, despite the Prince of R.'s powerful intervention."[57]

A single, long, intense sentence summed up the seriousness of the situation. Referring to a famous Jewish-owned department store in New York, he asked his parents to

> imagine a crowd of uniformed men standing in front of Macy's, threatening customers who want to enter, forging letters purporting to prove that Macy was supporting the Communist party, closing up the Jewish stores on Broadway, closing Woolworth's, flying their own flags from the City Hall, the Municipal Building, the court houses, and the customs houses, forcing peaceful citizens by threats of violence not to show the American flag, controlling the police so that on inquiring the way from a cop you would be directed to "go back to Jerusalem," where the cops would refuse to [allow] you to enter Macy's, where half the newspapers in New York were forbidden to appear, and theaters showing plays not glorifying warfare would be simply closed, where you would find parades of uniformed men under party insignia–with police participating under the same insignia; with Messrs. Marks and Levy dropped from the Board of Examiners, with the director of the Stock Exchange invited by uniformed forces to resign....[58]

Imagine all this, he said, "and you will have some mild idea of how a nation can be led under flying flags and with striking slogans direct into barbarism." Mistrust dug gulfs between people afraid to share their fears:

> Whisper it. Look over your shoulder to see if anyone heard you. Are you sure the servant in your friend's home isn't a member of the "elevating forces"? Wonder, when you hear auto cut-out explosions at night, if those were shots?

Harry documented the developing disaster through film as well as diary and letters. He photographed a fence on which adherents of the now-suppressed KPD "had painted *Kämpfet gegen das Rote Fahne Verbot*"–Fight against Suppression of the *Red Flag*.[59] The graffito had been "repainted, rerepainted, and so on," and soon would be definitively obliterated despite clandestine efforts by the KPD to repaint it yet again. Most of Harry's documentary effort was expended on current news. He took special note of the victory (at Yankee Stadium in New York) of the American boxer Max Baer over the German heavyweight champion, Max Schmeling. Baer's triumph posed a challenge to Nazi propaganda because he had a German Jewish grandparent. The *Völkischer Beobachter*, celebrating Baer as a German American, did not print a photograph of his boxing trunks, which featured a Star of David. Harry imagined a headline in keeping with the *Beobachter* mind set: "*nicht arysche Abstammung* [not of "Aryan" descent]: Jewboy Assaults German Patriot."[60]

Harry was particularly alert to the Nazi assault on Jewish cultural figures. A few escaped immediate attack. Two Jews performed in Wagner's *Tannhäuser* at the Staatsoper: "Emanuel List, the grand bass," who emigrated to the United States later that year; and the popular conductor Leo Blech, who the *Beobachter* said was "constitutionally unable to understand or appreciate Wagner's nordic music." Because Blech was favored by Göring, who took it upon himself to "decide who is a Jew," he continued (in Harry's words) "misinterpreting the government's favorite composer" until 1938, when he left Germany. Such Nazi inconsistencies were not unusual. Even though the renowned Polish Jewish violinist Bronislaw Huberman "was forbidden to give a recital in Berlin," Wilhelm Furtwängler, the Nazi-leaning Berlin Philharmonic conductor, tried to inveigle him into cooperating. Huberman reportedly "wired his refusal back: 'I refuse to do anything which might suggest that everything was in order in Germany today.'" Most foreign musicians, "Aryan" and Jewish alike, refused to perform in Germany. One exception was Richard Strauss, who though an Austrian was very active in Germany–indeed, "the Nationalist general-utility man," in Harry's phrase.[61] When the "Aryan" violinist Adolf Busch, whose wife was Jewish, was summoned to play, he replied: "My name isn't Strauss." Thomas Mann recorded in his diary that Busch had "left Germany though he is considered to be *the* German violinist. Very gratifying."[62] At the same time, *The Threepenny Opera*, with music by the Jewish Communist Kurt Weill, was still being performed. The "little house was packed," Harry reported, finding "many brilliant touches, with the incomparable Lotte Lenya as Jennie. But above all the music!" The film industry was Aryanized faster than musical culture. Harry attended a new film, *Storm Trooper Brand, a Picture of Life in Our Times* (*S.A. Mann Brand*), which contrasted evil Communists and noble Nazis.[63] In the film, the Nazi salute and shout of "*Sieg heil!*" ("Hail to victory!") were "noble and dignified"; the corresponding Communist gesture and shout of *Sieg Moscou!* ("Victory to Moscow!") were "laughably absurd." The "German greeting," as the sociologist Tilman Allert remarks, was "not only a product of those dark and sinister times but…a contributor to them."[64]

The "gentlemen" take charge

Harry heaped scorn on the "feine Herren," or "fine gentlemen," catalogued their deeds, and became preoccupied by the effects of the *Machtergreifung*.[65] Three crucial laws that were passed on 7 April bore down on several of his friends: the Law for the Restoration of Professional Civil Service; the Law Regarding Admission to the Legal Profession; and the Law Regarding New Election of Assessors, Jurors, and Judges.[66] The first of these disqualified from public employment–which included all universities–anyone with a Jewish parent or grandparent; it was extended on 30 June to cover anyone married to a Jew. The blow to the universities was immediate: the German tradition of *Lehrfreiheit* and *Lernfreiheit* (freedom to teach, freedom to learn) "was killed on 7 April 1933."[67]

Other laws soon followed. A decree issued on 22 April excluded Jewish physicians from the public health insurance plans (*Krankenkassen*). Three days later, the government passed a Law Regarding the Overcrowding of German Public Schools and Schools of Higher Education. Requiring all students to manifest "moral character" and "political reliability," this law was aimed at Jews, Communists, Socialists, and pacifists; it was also intended to limit enrollment of women.[68] A law passed on 14 July was the first of many regulations meant to impoverish German Jewry; it was entitled "Law requiring the confiscation of national wealth in the hands of state enemies." To all these impositions there was no organized opposition. "Each person is searching for a hole to crawl into, a spot all to himself," said the artist Oskar Schlemmer.[69]

The anti-Semitic regulations supposedly exempted civil servants who had been employed before 1 August 1914, as well as *Frontsoldaten*–men who had fought in World War I "at the front for Germany or her allies"–and those "who lost their fathers or sons in the war."[70] These exemptions were meaningless. Victor Klemperer, a *Frontsoldat*, lost his job in 1935 allegedly because of declining enrollment, but he knew the real reason. When Bella Fromm took a book containing the names of 12,000 Jewish soldiers who had fallen in World War I to a Nazi functionary–evidence, one would think, of Jewish *Frontsoldaten* who had given their lives for their country–he explained that these Jews "just died naturally."[71] Jewish lawyers were unemployable, because "no Gentile (or even Jew) would hire a Jewish lawyer to represent him before a Nazi judge or jury."[72] Jewish professionals either lost their positions entirely or found themselves with greatly diminished income. Nazi policy-makers simultaneously advocated emigration as the most convenient means of making Germany *judenrein* (cleansed of Jews) and created currency controls that made emigration more difficult.[73]

As the situation worsened, news reports reaching America could hardly convey "the devastating effects of the cold pogrom," a term describing the "legal" restrictions placed on Jews.[74] By "devastating," Harry added, "I don't mean injurious, I mean ruinous in the deepest sense." He attempted to fill in the gaps in reportage. Noting that "German Mathematics" (a Nazi term) produced questionable economic statistics, he proved by his own "Jewish mathematics" that "the figures have been doctored."[75] A diligent censor who could figure out the verbal cloak lightly thrown over Harry's views might have still been stumped by mysterious references to a friend of Julia Gottschalk. The friend was to bring certain information to Alfred Hirschbach in New York: "She will present a note of identification from me, intentionally illegible (as if I needed to purpose that!) and will explain all. P.G. says it's OK."[76]

Casting caution to the winds, Harry wrote to his parents about anti-Semitism in schools and universities. In the schools, "Gentile kids refuse to sit next to Jewish ones." University students walk "ostentatiously…out of the lectures of a Jewish professor who legally is [still] permitted to teach." At the University of Frankfurt, IDs were reportedly taken away from non-"Aryan" students, Germans and foreigners alike. Nazi prejudices might "find some faint reflection in the American mirror"–doubtless there were American "Jewish school children...whose life is made miserable by their 'Aryan' classmates"–but no one there would bluntly demand his parentage, as happened when Harry registered for his final semester and had to fill out a form that treated foreigners like Germans. In response to a question about religious affiliation, he wrote: "Non-Aryan" and added: "American." Privately he exclaimed: "Praise Allah I'm a free man!"[77] In a prelude to the yellow star, the IDs of the remaining Jewish students bore a yellow stripe.[78]

In Germany, "a kind of Never-Never land where the clock has stopped ticking," the language of Goethe went further down the path to deformity paved by Germans after the Versailles Treaty concluding World War I forbade their country to rearm. "Versailles treaty" meant two "entirely divergent things" in French and in German: in French, it meant "a system of hard-won guarantees for the quiet of Europe"; in German, it meant "a shameful extortion reducing Germany to a subject power." On the anniversary of its signing, the Nazis ordered flags on all government buildings to be flown at half mast–Harry photographed the flag at the university, its swastika waving in the breeze–while "S.A. and S.S. men [paraded] with mourning bands over their usual swastika arm bands." Other meanings changed, too: "The...word freedom...has grown a suffix: 'Freedom–but.' I.e.: there must be freedom of the press, but naturally the SPD press must be completely rooted out."[79]

The "present gentlemen"–a sarcastic euphemism for the Nazi leadership–believed that "the less the people know, the better." Their anti-intellectual campaign promoted a "graphologist-philosopher" named Ludwig Klages, author of a multi-volume treatise entitled "The Mind as Negation of the Soul." Harry accompanied Max Freyhan to the university to hear Klages lecture on the ego for an hour and forty minutes. He observed Klages's "large thin-lipped mobile mouth, gimlet eyes, and...beautiful fluency and cadence of speech," and condemned his speech as a farrago of mystical balderdash. Clichés "unreeled from his mouth like the tracks from an observation platform of a fast train. He...was followed with rapt attention by all the 400 [in the audience]–with one exception," Harry, who "found the last 40 minutes increasingly tedious." Besides Klages, the ranks of approved crackpots included astrologers, "miracle healers, one of whom achieved his cures by the application of a dollop of cottage cheese to the sufferer's forehead, and… all sorts of mediums & quacks."[80]

Harry sought explanations of the current scene. Expressing a common interpretation, Dietrich Gerhard thought "that the sense of inferiority induced by the one-sided peace [following World War I]…was the chief cause" of the Nazi "revolution." Would there be a counter-revolution? Paul Gottschalk pooh-poohed the belief of the now-illegal KPD "that the present crew will in time slide off the scene and then their [the KPD's] day will come." He recalled the mood of the troops in World War I: "We want to eat–we don't want a hero's death." Harry agreed: "[T]he masses…will prefer a full belly and no tanks, military airplanes, or battleships, to armaments and parades and an empty stomach."[81]

In June, Harry summed up the present situation with a witty variant on Lewis Carroll's *Alice in Wonderland*. Transposing the action to the Tiergarten, his scenario featured Hitler's erstwhile ally, the media mogul and DNVP leader Alfred Hugenberg, who two days earlier had been forced to resign as Minister for Economy, Agriculture, and Food:

It's getting dizzier and dizzier, said Alice. She never had expected to see a goat with funny whiskers come hurrying through the Tiergarten. But when the goat came nearer she saw that it carried a suitcase labeled "A. Hugenberg, Berlin." The goat did not run off (and thus avoided being a scape-goat), but the longer Alice looked the more certain she felt the horns were beginning to wobble. One <u>did</u> wobble. Alice felt this was very curious and looked closer. Then she saw that the horns were really ears and the goat seemed to be becoming a donkey. Please, she said politely, are you a goat or a donkey? …. The goat-donkey looked at Alice tearfully, then opened its suitcase and began eating huge quantities of the *Lokal Anzeiger*, *Der Tag*, the *Nachtausgabe*, and reels of Ufa. Lugubriously it half bleated, half heehawed. "My dear Alice," it said, between munches, "if you ever thought I was a goat you were mistaken: I've always been a jackass.[82]

Expecting his parents to recognize Hugenberg's newspapers and film company (Ufa), Harry then interpreted his allegory. He admitted he had been mistaken in predicting a power struggle between the two parties that composed the cabinet, the Nazis and the DNVP. There had been no struggle, "only...an edging out" that ended with Hugenberg's dismissal and the "voluntary" dissolution of the DNVP. The Nazis thus removed the "fine gentlemen" of Hugenberg's class, who had helped them win their first major electoral success in 1930.

Harry's allusion to *Alice in Wonderland* reflects its enormous and widespread popularity, illustrated in Count Harry Kessler's comment on Papen: "The papers publish his photograph...over the caption 'The New Look in Chancellors.' He has the air of an irritable billy goat trying to adopt dignity.... A character from *Alice in Wonderland*."[83] If Papen and Hugenberg were laughable billy goats, what was happening was no comedy. Newspapers reported "a regular wave of suicides–this in the Hitler spring time!"[84] Some "suicides" were actually Nazi murders. Newspapers reported "that the chairman of the Deutschnationale [DNVP], Dr. [Ernst] Oberfohren, killed himself a few days ago." Soon the verb "killed himself" needed correction; rather than being "reflexive,...[it was] more probably passive": Dr. Oberfohren did not *kill himself;* rather, he *was killed*–by the Nazis.[85] An outbreak of Jewish suicides and attempted suicides occurred during the early months of the Nazi period.[86] A foreign paper reported the attempted suicide, "after three months' solitary confinement and questioning," of a distinguished professor in Munich with whom Heinz Gottschalk had studied–August Mayer, the former director of the Alte Pinakothek.[87] The effects of repression were coming closer to home. Reading "that the Berlin libraries are being purged," Harry worried that the Nazis might impede his research.[88] When he went for advice at the American consulate, he learned "that letters were being censored, and that of course my materials might be confiscated."[89] Passed from one authority to the next, he finally met with the director of the Berlin municipal libraries, "Herr Direktor Professor Dr. Fritz–a small, kindly, harried man, who very amiably received me and cleared the matter up. Nothing would happen to his library."

On vacation: exploring opinion in the hinterland

For three weeks in March and April, Harry took the temperature of Germany outside of the capital. He was in Weimar on the morning of 1 April, the day of a nationwide anti-Jewish boycott.[90] This roll-out of Nazi power had variable results. In Weimar, Harry "saw nothing except that the local Hermann Tietz [department store] was closed"; in Erfurt later in the day, however, "the picketing and placatting" were effective, and most of the stores were closed. Later, back in Berlin, he learned that the Kurfürstendamm, the busy shopping street, was considerably affected, and that Unter den Linden in the heart of touristic and diplomatic Berlin, where Paul Gottschalk's office was located, had been spared "because of the impression it would make on foreigners & the foreign diplomatic offices."[91] In contrast to Harry's cool assessment, Count Harry Kessler raged against the boycott–an "abominable" and "criminal piece of lunacy" that "has destroyed everything" that the Weimar Republic had achieved "during the past fourteen years…to restore faith in, and respect for, Germany." To Kessler, the willing submission of the German nation to Nazism was "the most horrible suicide a great nation has ever committed."[92]

On his travels, Harry gained insights into popular thinking by overcoming his shyness to chat with strangers. Able to pass for German, he concealed his personal background; to reveal that he was Jewish would have impeded his wish to understand public opinion. A World War I veteran in Leipzig, shabby but clean, expected the Nazis to "improve Germany's economic status, but [he] didn't tell me how"; the veteran said that Jews who had been living in Leipzig for generations "were practically as clean as Germans, but…East Jews were oily and dirty," the same view espoused by anti-Semites at Harvard. Additional instructive conversations took place at an inn in the picturesque village of Stolberg in the Harz Mountains; it was run by a "pure, guaranteed Aryan" family who believed in "Saint Adolf," through whom "all would be reborn." Harry felt like a spy "in enemy territory, or a detective among crooks, or a crook among detectives." As the family told him "how the Jews had infected the body politic, how they should be driven out of Europe and back to Palestine," he began to feel a "sympathy for the right wing which I lacked before. Everything becomes complicated when you get down close to it, like a drop of water." In Stolberg, too, he gained "a sense of the German minuscule principality" that might come in handy for the history of Germany that he dreamed of writing.[93]

Continuing to document current events, Harry asked an S.A. police officer in Goslar, his next stop, for permission to photograph "the closed socialist newspaper exterior…with a placard in the window." When the officer asked his purpose, he told him: "To show how effective the government is." The officer replied: "Well, why not?" Another instance of government effectiveness was a Jewish exodus: 1,500 Jewish refugees were reportedly in Holland and another 1,500 in Switzerland, where they were at least temporarily safe. Collecting his mail in Hildesheim, he found five "panicky" letters, four from his mother and one from Deborah Hirschbach, all responding to atrocity reports. He immediately sent a cable: "BANISH FOOLISH FEARS NEWSPAPERS DEMENTED NO ILLEGAL TERRORISM AM PERFECTLY SAFE FINE TRIP BIRTHDAY CONGRATULATIONS LOVE HARRY." His mother, who must have been pleased with the birthday wishes, had in the meantime written another alarmed letter, which elicited another cable. To demonstrate his caution, he began sending his letters not to his parents but "to Mr Debanalf at the Broadmoor," the nearby building where Deborah and Alfred Hirschbach lived. The "Debanalf" ruse seemed excessive, and he soon resumed using his parents' address. Several weeks later, for safety's sake, he began to refer to Gustav Mayer as "P.G.'s cousin."[94]

Changes in educational institutions

Harry returned from his holiday just in time for the scheduled start of the semester on 15 April, only to find the date postponed until 1 May "to allow for reorganization"–meaning the "purge, rejuvenation, filtering, ennobling, and thinning of the faculties." Euphemisms proliferated: rather than being fired, professors were "sent on leave." At Göttingen University, the famed mathematics faculty "seems to have been swept clean"; perhaps, Harry speculated, "math may not be needed in the 3rd Reich," where another field,

"German physics," excluded Einstein's theory of relativity.[95] As described below, three professors whom Harry came to know outside of class were affected: Gustav Mayer, Dietrich Gerhard, and Hajo Holborn. Martin Weinbaum, the medievalist who had teased him in his first semester, was another casualty. Student support of "reorganization" appeared in "Twelve Theses Against the Un-German Spirit"–issued on 8 April, published in the *Völkischer Beobachter* on 14 April, and slapped on kiosks all over Germany. They were the work of the major student organization, the German Student Body (*Deutsche Studentenschaft*), which planned the book burnings on 10 May that took place in Berlin on Bebelplatz, directly across from the university, and all over the country. A few of the "Twelve Theses" give the flavor of the whole:

> 4. Our most dangerous enemy is the Jew and those who are his slaves.
> 5. A Jew can only think Jewish. If he writes in German, he is lying....
> 7. We...regard the Jew as alien and...respect the traditions of the Volk [German people]. Therefore, we demand of the censor: Jewish writings are to be published in Hebrew. If they appear in German, they must be identified as translations.[96]

In schools and universities, Jewish students and teachers were disoriented. Lutz Gottschalk's high school, the Grunewald Gymnasium, was "predominantly...non-Aryan, as the official tongue has it, and the question of who can stay is naturally of interest." Lutz was one of the few Jews in his class who remained to graduation, in 1935. Until Nazi textbooks could be produced, teachers had to improvise. History teachers were expected

> to deliver oral explanations of the origins of the great National Revolution. And as the teachers, especially after the spring cleaning, will be uniformly *nationalgesinnt* [nationalist in feeling],...they will execute their duties with zeal.

All children, including Jews, had to sing Nazi songs such as a popular ditty with the lines "When the knife drips with Jewish blood, / Things will be twice as good as before." At the university, where students were "not certain whether they may be admitted or, if they are already in, whether they may stay," Hermann Christern began his first lecture "with a zealous but not very consistent paean on the subject of the national resurrection [revolution] of the past three months." Harry thought that Christern's praise "sounded as if it were made to order, for he depended on his notes," which were unnecessary when he spoke about his subject, the Counter-Revolution.[97] The students gave "no sign of assent or dissent." Harry did not return. Christern later proved to be a devoted Nazi.

In this final semester, Harry's research for his prospective Harvard dissertation commanded serious attention. Paul Gottschalk, Gustav Mayer, Hajo Holborn, and Dietrich Gerhard banded together on his behalf: "They are all going a great deal out of their way to help me–what a grand bunch!" At P.G.'s birthday party, Mayer suggested that he speak to Friedrich Hertneck, an economist and journalist, and Holborn soon made the contact. One Sunday morning Hertneck and Harry talked at length "about the SPD & the unions, materials for its history, and the present situation, its past & future." Hertneck thought that internal conflicts had "ruined" the SPD, "that the SPD agitators who went out and orated on Marx spoke empty words over the heads of the audience, that the SPD… had lost the Marxist tinge" and was "completely bankrupt of ideas. He foresaw only a military dictatorship." He told Harry "confidentially" that the correspondence of August Bebel, a founder of the SPD,

> had been stolen–a few months ago by an employee of the SPD archive who turned KPD–and now lies in the Archives in Moscow. Also confidential was the information that the correspondence of–I think–the older Liebknecht had recently been made over to the Prussian or Reich Archives to avoid destruction.[98]

Atrocity stories

Harry anticipated the "thorough ruin of a large portion of the 600,000 German Jews–and the annihilation of their future."[99] The Nazi slogan was "Juden raus [out]! Out of where?" Harry quoted Hamlet: "Out of the air...Into the grave?" Even before Hitler took power, atrocity stories proliferated, most of them true. In 1932, a friend told William Shirer that "you could hear the yells of Jews being tortured" in an S.A. building. No one was deceived by a law making it illegal "for anyone...to claim...that atrocities were taking place."[100] In fact, the stories served a useful purpose for the Nazis: they terrified the population.

Stories of "something horrible" spread virally, by rumor and in print. When Harry was in Kassel, a German Jew was arrested there "for sending a letter to NY doubting the dementis [denials] of atrocity stories"; he was sentenced to fifteen months in jail. In Paris, *La grande revue* published "a long article listing atrocities." Harry heard from P.G. about a cousin's friend whose son, employed in the Ministry of Finance, had disappeared. A week later, the police notified the mother "that her son had died and would be buried at 4 AM." She told a friend, who reported her to the police, who took the mother in: "After a 3-hour examination she was freed with the warning that the next time she spread such an atrocity story she would land in a concentration camp." Fritz Freyhan's friend in the Nazi Factory Cell Organization (NSBO) told a story to illustrate the Nazi "spirit of justice": "Some S.A. men who had killed some Communists & sewn them up in sacks were straightaway thrown out of the S.A. Wasn't that ruthless?!" Martin Hirschbach knew "2 [Jewish] physicians, front soldiers, who were excluded from Krankenkassen practice." One of the physicians, "a bachelor and [an] energetic veteran, was able by plain talk to recover his rights" as a *Frontsoldat* to practice medicine; the other kept mum because he "didn't dare to imperil himself & family by resolute talk." Frau Meyer overheard "a mother admonish her blond nordic youngster to eat up everything so that he would grow up to be a big SS Mann."[101]

An evening at P.G.'s home, typical of gatherings in Jewish homes, produced a veritable anthology of petty torments.[102] One topic was the "German greeting" or *Gruss*–"Heil Hitler" accompanied by a Roman-style salute–which, made mandatory in July, functioned as a loyalty oath to the chief anti-Semite.[103] Rose Hirschbach, glad to be employed as a teacher, struggled to overcome her "revulsion...in giving the first Hitler *Gruss*–but...now it wasn't so fantastic any more." Eva, the youngest Freyhan and still in school, got into trouble for failing to greet a teacher properly. At Rose's school, a Jewish child "was asked why his father wasn't in prison," and another "was told that the Jews were of inferior stuff"; "the kids are taught that Jesus didn't emerge out of Judaism, and that Heine was merely an imitator."[104] Rose, who "read a lot of Heine at a sitting and Goethe too," admitted "that Heine stood for negation and death, Goethe for becoming." She told another story: a teacher called "an 'Aryan' and [a] 'non-Aryan' child" to the front of the class in order to demonstrate "the inferior qualities" of non-"Aryans," stopping only when "the child broke down."[105] Everyone at P.G.'s "agreed that whether it was true or not, it was certainly possible." The next day, Harry and Fritz Freyhan went "on a snapshooting expedition–meeting marching bands everywhere–Fritz fleeing before the flags to avoid saluting–he heard someone criticized for not raising his hand." In the Nazi version of Sleeping Beauty, the prince greeted the heroine with the German *Gruss*.[106]

One type of semi-atrocity–routine Nazi extortions–affected "Aryans" as well as Jews: *Freiwillige Spende*, mandatory but supposedly "voluntary" (*freiwillige*) contributions to Nazi causes. P.G. knew "a stenographer who received some 80 RM salary a month. She had to pay off some 6 or 7 RM in social taxes and some 9 RM in *freiwillige Spende*–5 RM for NSBO, 1 RM for Hitler *Spende*, etc. so that she receives in the long run some 64-65 RM a month."[107] Victor Klemperer's "shrunken salary" went down still more because of these "'voluntary' deductions." He asked: "Who dares object?"[108]

Part 2. Friends at risk

In April, Heinz Gottschalk traveled to Holland on a train "full of Jews tearing out of the 3rd Reich." These were people with intellectual and financial resources, many of whom had friends and relatives abroad to receive them. At the border, Heinz "was thoroughly searched–coat pockets, between the leaves of his books–...

for *Devisen* [foreign currency], but he had complied with the law." Heinz's Uncle Paul had asked him to carry "the firm's most valuable manuscripts to foreign (Dutch) sanctuary." Harry thought that this was "a precaution of dubious necessity," but it soon proved entirely sensible. On the train Heinz met "an acquaintance, a young economist...bound for England."[109]

Everywhere, Harry wrote, "you hear that so and so has moved to Holland or Paris." One of the Meyers' guests said "that there were 12,000 German Jews in Paris–I wonder."[110] The figure was plausible. In December 1933, the *New York Times* reported that some 60,000 Germans had fled that year, 86% of them Jews; there were 25,000 German refugees in France, all but 3,000 of them in Paris.[111] As an acquaintance of Harry remarked, "recent events make leaving the *Vaterland* much easier than at first imagined"; Lisel Meyer was studying Italian, and Heinz recommended that her parents return to Belgium, where she had been born. Still others thought of Switzerland, Palestine, Egypt, or South Africa: a "new *Völkerwanderung* [mass migration] is in progress, comparable to "the expulsion of the Jews from Spain & England and the lot of the Huguenots after the end of the Edicts of Nantes."[112] In all, somewhere between 236,000 and 350,000 Germans emigrated in 1933-39. In Berlin, some 2,400 university students broke off their studies, nearly a fifth of the total enrollment.[113]

Some of those who fled returned once their panic lessened. Fritz Freyhan's departure had been a "sudden decision–just as in the case of Paul Meyer–the trip with the train load of German Jews, anxious, worried, doubtful that they would be allowed over the boundary, and cussing the country once they were safe in a free land." Fritz and Paul had feared that visas would be denied. On learning that visas were "being liberally distributed," Fritz returned, doubtful whether he could complete his medical studies (somehow he did). Paul Meyer never returned to Germany. Four months later, during Harry's farewell party at P.G.'s, the topic was Palestine: "All the younger people," most of whom a year before paid little heed to their Judaism, were now

talking, planning, dreaming of Palestine, and you hear every week of whole families moving to the Promised Land–

lawyers, physicians, bank employees, school teachers–all of them to begin life anew as farmers, as servants, as farm hands, as anything at all, whether or not it is a profession being quite irrelevant.

Once "indissolubly bound" to Germany, these would-be emigrants were now reading the bi-weekly Zionist newspaper, with its notices of courses in Hebrew and firms that shipped possessions to Palestine. German doctors and lawyers newly arrived in Palestine– so went a current joke–placed newspaper advertisements announcing that they were *"Von der Reise zurück"*–back from a trip.[114] They were part of a much larger exodus: "Practically everybody who in world opinion had stood for…German culture prior to 1933 is now a refugee."[115]

German and Jewish

What did it mean to be German and Jewish, or for that matter American and Jewish? Harry thought that if Jews wanted equal rights, they should "become acclimatized and nationals"; those who "continue feeling themselves superior to, to say nothing of apart from, the Goyim [Gentiles],…had better stop complaining about discrimination." His condemnation ignores the impoverished Yiddish-speaking refugees (*Ostjuden*, or East Jews); having escaped Russian pogroms, they felt superior to no one, were scorned by both Gentile and Jewish Germans, and faced insuperable obstacles to German citizenship. Harry's attitude was related to his disgust for compulsory religious education in schools–a cultural feature that, like the debate about identity, antedated the Nazi takeover. Required religion education drove a "great wedge" between Christians and Jews. "The worst of it all" was that while a child who didn't "look Jewish" could choose to go to Christian classes, the others had no choice. Now Jews of all descriptions had no choice because they weren't "German," as Göring made clear: "The Jew is international and not national."[116]

In Berlin, home to over 160,000 Jews, a special telephone book listed Jewish addresses and occupations.[117] According to German law, every citizen belonged to a religious community (*Gemeinde*), whose members were required to contribute 10% of their state tax to support "religious instruction in the schools, the churches (e.g. rabbis are on state pay), and other institutions like hospitals." Refusal to pay could result in a lawsuit. Formalities such as enrolling in a university required a statement of one's *Gemeinde*, which before 1933 one could change by "go[ing] to court–it's like changing your name at home." In Nazi law, however, people claiming to be "pure Aryans" had to trace their descent to the beginning of the nineteenth century. "Non-Aryan Christians" such as the Hirschbach sons (baptized Lutheran) placed pitiable job-seeking notices in newspapers. A World War I veteran, a lawyer who considered himself Protestant, advertised for work in the *Vossische Zeitung*; he had lost his job, because he was "not of pure Aryan descent."[118]

The phrase "German Jew," the novelist Jakob Wassermann reflected, constituted "a double concept which even to the disinterested lays bare copious misunderstandings, tragedies, conflicts, quarrels and sufferings." In keeping with this unavoidable topic, Gustav Mayer began and ended his memoir with a meditation on his identity.[119] He had grown up in a religiously observant family that participated in civic life yet socialized only with other Jews. As a child in East Prussia, he experienced anti-Semitism, yet he felt no commonality with the *Ostjuden*, who had experienced much more. The *Ostjuden*, in Wassermann's words, were "Jewish Jews," alien and distinct from "German Jews." Their forefathers having lived in Germany for centuries, Mayer and Wassermann were "German Jews," a term that puzzled some German Jews. The question nagged: "Are you in the first instance a German or a Jew?"[120] To the youthful Mayer, this was a false choice. Accepting the tension inherent in his "bifurcated soul," he believed that with time, Jews would be fully accepted members of the German people (*Volk*), free like others to practice their religion. In his youth, this had made sense, because under Bismarck, German Jews had gained full freedom. Yet their consequent greater prosperity inspired a recrudescence of anti-Semitism.

At his bar mitzvah, Mayer had received a customary present: volumes of German literature enshrining Enlightenment values.[121] The classics led him from the confines of observant Judaism to the expansive "world of the German spirit." German poetry, not the ossified religious instruction to which he had been subjected, awakened his thoughts and feelings. Throughout his life he remained bound to the language of Goethe, Schiller, and Lessing, which he loved "as tenderly as a musician loves his precious instrument." So strong was his belief in the enduring values of the German Enlightenment that he was convinced that "the Nazis…would not touch the universities." Harry, on the other hand, knew the minute Hitler became chancellor that Mayer was "in danger of losing his job."[122] He kept it until May.

Mayer never ceased feeling "German." In exile in England, when he included himself in the phrase "we Germans," he would watch to see whether his companion's mouth twisted in a scornful laugh. After the war, he remained lost between worlds: he could neither return to Germany (which had betrayed itself), nor follow his brothers to Palestine (he did not feel Jewish enough).[123] He felt like his "forefather Abraham, who implored God to forgive the cities that, despite the presence of a few just men, were condemned to destruction for their sins." Like Abraham, he "never doubted that among the disgraced German people countless 'just' men and women live and patiently suffer." Through his memoir, he "extended [his] hand to a few of them in a brotherly way." But he could not join them.

The Meyers

Harry witnessed the departure of two age-mates, Paul and Lisel Meyer. Grete and Ernst "exported" Paul to Paris only a week after the civil-service law of 7 April, impelled by a rumor "that passports would require a police OK." At the same time, they heard about a young man, an employee of an SPD official, who had been arrested and spent "3 days in the calaboose [jail] without his parents knowing where he was. Then he was released."[124] It could happen to Paul, who had "spent 8 years study and preparation in order finally to be told that it will do him absolutely no good." Part of a "flood" of German Jews pouring into the Netherlands, he traveled via Rotterdam, where, wrote the *Völkischer Beobachter*, there was an "excellent relief organization," as there was.[125] The refugees were met at the Rotterdam train station, and Paul was received in "the home of a lawyer who entertained him for three days." In Paris, his mother's brother and sister-in-law, Fritz and Gracia Juda, provided an immediate refuge. The French cabinet had just declared that the country's "generous traditions of hospitality...obliged [it] to welcome the German refugees," a sentiment that later cooled. Paul was typical of the German refugees in France, most of whom were young professionals.[126]

Paul's siblings followed his example. Lisel, at an early stage of medical studies, left in July for medical school in Florence, one of the few Jewish students in Berlin who was able to continue her studies abroad. Rudy stayed to complete his final medical exams–at a medical school that now included an Institute for Racial Hygiene–and left for Brazil in November 1934. The youngest Meyer, Claire, a nursing student at the Jewish Hospital, was in no immediate danger, for Nazi nurses would not wish to work in such a hospital.[127] In 1934, she married a German immigrant to Palestine and left. Safely out, the Meyer children could then worry about their parents.

The Hirschbachs

On 30 January, Martin Hirschbach's youngest son, Franz, came home from school and phoned a newspaper to ask in his "squeaky 11-year-old voice" whether a new chancellor had been appointed. "Ja, Hitler" came the answer: "And with that the course of my life changed."[128] Over supper that night, Martin and Rose told their four sons "that the rise of Hitler's National Socialist Party meant that Germany would be divided into 'Aryan' and non-'Aryans'–and that we would be considered part of the latter category, even though we had been baptized Lutheran." Martin was a nonbeliever, and Rose regarded herself as "only nominally Jewish," even though–or maybe because–her father had been a leader of the Jewish community.[129]

To allay Alfred Hirschbach's concerns, Harry visited Martin and Rose as soon as he returned from his travels. In Martin's office, "everything was all right...for the time being." Rose, teaching in a private school, expected to be fired. The oldest son, Ernst, a law student, was in the same position as Paul Meyer, "except that he has studied [only] 3 years, so that Paul has wasted 5 more than he."

Harry cabled: "VISITED HIRSCHBACHS TODAY ALLS WELL MARTIN ANSWERING ALFREDS CARD. IM REMAINING HERE ABSOLUTELY UNMOLESTED...STOP WORRYING." They worried nonetheless, and three days later P.G. cabled to reassure them: "HARRY MOST HAPPELY [sic] USING HIS UNPRECIDED [UNPRECEDENTED] OPPORTUNITY OF STUDYING CONTEM-PORARY HISTORY...AND IS ABSOLUTELY SAVE [SAFE]."[130]

Costing Rose her job, *Gleichschaltung* ("coordination," euphe-mistically translated as "reorganization") came to private schools on 24 May. A "metaphor drawn from the world of electricity," *Gleichschaltung* meant putting "all the switches...onto the same circuit,...so that they could all be activated by throwing a single master switch at the centre"–and the Nazis controlled the switch.[131] All private schools, except for those with 100% Jewish enrollment, were forced to fire "non-Aryan" teachers. Rose's new job in a Jew-ish school, which at first appeared temporary, lasted for some years; she thus became the chief bread-winner. Martin was "considerably worried about the future," which was "not indefinite or distant–it can mean merely 'next week.'" He told Harry "his business turn-over had fallen" precipitously in the past six months: in January he had earned 1000 RM a month; in July, 150 RM. The Hirschbachs were trying to find a job as gardener's assistant for their third son, Peter (they succeeded). They wanted to send Gerhart, the second son, to America soon: "Freddy [Alfred Hirschbach] must be able to do something in his circle of acquaintances." Martin begged Har-ry to impress on Alfred "how desperate the situation was": they would be "crushed" before the Nazis were defeated. They were moving to a cheaper apartment. Ernst would complete his law de-gree, "although it didn't mean anything."[132]

Jewish doctors had been "ruined...[when] a simple stroke of the pen" excluded them from the main insurance scheme, the *Krankenkassen*.[133] At least they had clarity; they knew they were fin-ished. Businessmen like Martin Hirschbach, already affected by the Depression, experienced a more lingering extinction of their prospects. As a result of an order requiring municipal purchasing agents to buy only from "Aryan" firms, "M.H. and great masses of other 'non-Aryans' and outlawed socialists will...be reduced not to penury but to starvation." Losses by Jews in commerce and industry "gnaw[ed] at the vitals of almost the whole Jewish group, since the largest proportion of the Jews in Germany [were] wage-earners or *entrepreneurs* in some form of commercial or industrial enterprise."[134] Boycotts of Jewish businesses were another type of "cold pogrom."[135] Still, if nothing worse happened, the Hirschbachs would survive: Peter at his gardening job; Gerhart possibly retaining his job in a Berlin office; Martin, although suffering financially, "safe for the present under the wing of the Christian mother company"; and Rose, although "carried only from month to month," at the Jewish school. For Ernst, there was nothing. Franz was too young to work.[136]

The Gottschalks

Paul Gottschalk, the other businessman in Harry's social circle, believed that Hitler and his thugs were "finished, on the rocks, through"; nonetheless, prudence made him consider moving his business to the Netherlands, so he was ready when necessity called in 1935.[137] He had kept going during the Depression thanks to his brother, Ernst, whose thriving medical practice enabled him to infuse capital into the business; Ernst also managed the business during Paul's travels. After the *Machtergreifung*, Paul was able to carry on despite Nazi regulations, for his customers paid in dollars.[138]

The experiences of the three physicians in the Gottschalk family were somewhat different from those of the three medical Meyers. The older generation, Ernst and Julia, delayed the inevitable for several years with the support of their patients. In 1933, "swarms of non-Aryan patients" apologized to Ernst "for the general anti-Semitism and [had] to be soothed by him."[139] His supposed exemption as a *Frontsoldat* from the ban on *Krankenkassen* patients was meaningless. When Harry asked him how he was, he replied ironically: "Fine! Have you any *Krankenkassen*?"[140]

As a Communist married to a Jew, the surgeon Walter Elberfeld, Ernst Gottschalk's Gentile son-in-law, was doubly endangered. Walter had had a rocky start in the Gottschalk family. There had been "terrible scenes…when Betty's husband first emerged before the horrified eyes of the powers that be–i.e. Dr. E. G., who…is a sort of (benevolent) despot." The "seriocomic story of family jealousy and selfishness" that unfolded "made life miserable for the entire family for several years." Given Ernst Gottschalk's "gloomy" view that Communism was "the only alternative, and not a consumma- tion devoutly to be wished," it may have been Walter's politics that made him initially anathema.[141] His inter-marriage was not unusu- al, for there were 35,000 mixed marriages at the time, and some 16% of Jewish women were married to Gentiles.[142] By 1933, Betty's fam- ily had accepted Walter; perhaps the birth of their daughter Ursula three years earlier had helped mend fences. He was now "ruined for political reasons" and nearly destitute. Betty, a medical student within five months of completing her internship, was thrown out of the university, even though her father's service as a *Frontsoldat* supposedly protected her; she was now "studying stenography at home."[143]

As they worried about their future, the Elberfelds never ceased promoting their political views. Prudent Harry disguised them with initials: "WE and his brother-in-law E.G." (not otherwise iden- tified) "conspired to talk me over"–that is, to persuade him to be Communist. Although resistant to their efforts, he was willing to help E.G. with a manuscript that he had had "ready for the print- er...when the deluge broke." Two days later, E.G. brought the man- uscript and gave Harry three marks to cover costs; this may have been in his baggage when he left Germany, but nothing more is known of it.[144] Walter "put on a fancy rig" so that Harry could take a photo; he needed to make an impression somewhere. The Elber- felds plotted their escape. Their first choice of refuge was the Unit- ed States, but they were willing to go anywhere. Harry asked his parents to speak to "any Mexicans or Central or South Americans or Canadians" they came across and ask "about the chances for a capable young surgeon in their home countries." He translated and elucidated documents relating to Walter's brief career, attributing his difficulties to his marriage to a "Jewess."[145] In February, Walter landed a job "as surgeon in Berlin-Tempelhof," but it would last only through September. He raged against Betty's family for not doing enough to help him: "Dr G had let a Haitian patient get away without asking him about prospects for Walter,...[and] PG...had not inquired in America." Walter and Betty "now had a hundred marks owed to them and two marks in their pockets." P.G. offered them shelter, but it was "humiliating...to have to beg for pocket money to pay for street car fares." Walter told Harry "he was getting MG [first-aid] training. Very practical, I thought."[146] This desperate situation lasted until the Elberfelds left for the Soviet Union, apparently in 1935.

Harry as confidante and tutor

As pressures mounted, Harry took on new roles among his acquaintances. He listened sympathetically as they spoke of their worries, and he tutored the younger generation in the English language, which they supposed would come in handy when they emigrated. Sometimes he taught English twice daily: "This morning Claire; noon Ulrich [Mayer]." Walter Elberfeld was another pupil. Sympathetic listening, though, was more important than teaching. When Betty and Walter poured out their hearts to him, he asked himself: "Why did they tell me their story?"[147] The answer was plain: his friends valued an intelligent, concerned young man who listened without complaint or comment. Professor Mayer, too, expressed his distress to him, as did his son Ulrich.

After a gathering at P.G.'s, Walter and Betty whispered to him to go toward the Witzleben Stadtbahn station so they could talk privately; they knew the Freyhans would go in another direction. They unburdened themselves at length, Betty of her grief for her mother's cancer, Walter of his "contempt for various hypocrites" in the family who gave "consoling words–no real understanding." They talked about their friends who had left for "Palestine, or France, or concentration camps." Harry felt their intensity: "They both wanted to talk–I listened mostly. It seemed to make them feel better to get it off their chest." Honored by these confidences, he was unsympathetic to garden-variety melancholia. When an American fellow student admitted that "he was a hypochondriacal, narcissistic introvert with an Oedipus complex," Harry "felt sorry for him" but nothing more.[148]

Perhaps the most moving expressions came from Professor Mayer during a "long and cordial" farewell evening at his home.[149] Mayer reminisced about his days as a journalist in Brussels, where he enjoyed "an idyllic existence in that problemless time before the war." He mentioned his "lucky" friends who had been invited to join the New School in New York; he "would have liked to have been plagued with an invitation," but none came. Harry left him "the latest batch of the *Times*, and the new Spengler, and will call for them on Monday when I meet Ulrich." And then they said goodbye:

> We shook hands at the door, he wishing me everything good, and standing in the lighted doorway, saying *lebewohl!* Ulrich walked with me to the garden gate. *Es ist nicht schön,* I said, *Abschied zu nehmen.*

"It's not nice to say goodbye": the emotions were beyond expression.

Ernst Engelberg: a decisive friendship

A bloody suppression of demonstrators on May Day 1928 had shocked Engelberg into becoming a Communist, and he quickly became a youth leader.[150] Prior to Hitler's victory, he belonged to a small group that helped Communists and Jews withstand Nazis. It was dangerous work, and he considered taking refuge in the Soviet Union. Early in 1932, en route to the Soviet Embassy to apply for a visa, he happened upon a friend, Nathan Lurje, who had already emigrated to the USSR. Lurje implored him to call off his plan, and he did. Lurje returned to the Soviet Union and, four years later, met a terrible end: sentenced to death on 24 August 1936 as a "Trotskyite criminal," a charge typical of the Stalinist terror, he was shot the next day. "He sabotaged my emigration to the Soviet Union," Engelberg told his son, "but he saved my life."[151]

Harry came to know Engelberg in May 1933, when both were attending Mayer's seminar: "He is the same age as I–and is completing his dissertation–will read some of it." Before long, fearing a police raid, Engelberg asked Harry to hold his dissertation, since "the Nazis were not likely to raid an American student as a possible subversive. So I took the package from him and kept it in my room with the Meyers...[for] a few months."[152] The friendship took off with a conversation lasting three hours. Engelberg maintained, and Harry agreed, that "the masses were led on by the Sozialismus, the petty bourgeois by the Nationalismus." They were soon proven wrong: the masses found Nazi-style nationalism more appealing than socialism.[153] According to Engelberg, a "small kernel of an organization [would] suffice for the formation of a constantly growing snowball when the 'revolution' should come." He told Harry about "underground illegal organizations" and argued, "very reasonably," for Marxist ideas: "Confound it, I'll have to break my head and work up Marxismus and the rest of it."[154]

Even though Engelberg had temporarily put his political activities on the back burner in order to complete his dissertation, he found time to talk with Harry. One day he told him about a Communist whose S.A. brother invited him

> to speak to a Berliner Stormtrupp. After sending the younger S.A. men home, they asked him what they [the KPD] would do to an S.A. man who had killed a KPD man: stand him up against the wall, was the answer. And to an S.A. Mann who had beaten up a KPD member? See if he proved himself on the side of the workers in the revolution. The evening was spent on such practical questions and at the end they decided to invite the Communist again. The fellow must have nerve.[155]

Harry's other instructor in the ways of the KPD was Walter Elberfeld's brother-in-law, E.G. He explained the organization of the KPD in districts, each of which published a local weekly newspaper. He said that the KPD used "devious ways" to obtain mimeograph paper for party publications, which were "circulated from hand to hand...carried about by people on bikes, motorcycles, or by train." The cost was ten *pfennig* "or if 'affluent,' more."[156]

Nearly another month passed before Harry ran into Engelberg on Unter den Linden. They made a date to meet in the Tiergarten on Sunday, 23 July. For three hours they walked and talked in the park, safe from Nazi spies.[157] Engelberg described arrests of Communists and asked for Harry's views of the United States. They talked "about students in the political labor movement–how the workers had little use for mere talkers–he's been in it for five years now. I told him how I thought I'd try to spread the lesson of the German development over there." When they next talked, after class, someone had gone through the books on the desks in the room dedicated to the History Seminar (i.e., the History Department); Engelberg feared a search of the drawers as well. Generous with research information, he gave Harry "copies of unpublished Engels letters, a book from the SPD Archive, and vital parts of his dissertation." Their conversations took place in an atmosphere of danger: "He is cautious–or worried–on the street keeps constantly looking behind him."[158] Communists were being arrested in large numbers–20,000 in Prussia by the end of March–and intrusions like the search of the History Seminar were common.[159]

When Engelberg failed to show up for an appointment on August 7, Harry "read in the evening papers of 31 arrests and wondered whether he was among them." He was not, yet. By the end of 1933, 2,500 German Communists had been killed and 130,000 arrested–among them Ernst Torgler, head of the Communists in the Reichstag, and Ernst Thälmann, leader of the KPD.[160] Harry's final conversation with Engelberg, decisive for his career, came on 31 August, a week before he left for home: "We talked in a restaurant till an egg [slang for "a guy"] sat down at the same table," his proximity requiring them to switch topics. When the conversation could safely resume, Engelberg told him that both Torgler and Thälmann were "constantly fettered." He advised Harry

> to read the whole of [Marx's] Kapital–and in fact as much of everything as possible–to gather a sufficient basis of judgment. I argued against his enthusiasm of belief [and said] that I wanted to stay critical, didn't want to sell out. He said he had gone through the same stages.[161]

Walter Elberfeld's doctrinaire insistence could not convert him, but Engelberg's gentle persuasion did.

Engelberg was not the sole benevolent influence drawing Harry further leftward from the socialist principles that had inspired his research on the SPD. In early July, Mayer introduced him to Karl Kautsky, "the apostolic repository of the Marxist faith."[162] At seventy-nine, Kautsky was, Mayer said, *"ein ganz famoser Kerl"* (a really famous fellow). Harry rhapsodized that

In two hours I got more ideas from him than in two years from GM. He sat there in his low cheery *Arbeitszimmer* [study] and told me of the perils he was managing to avoid, of the German scene, of the correctness of the M.E. [Marx/ Engels] predictions...and of the *weltgeschichtliche Rolle* [role in world history] of Fascism. We drank tea and I listened, and wished I knew more and had thought more so I could have participated more intelligently.

Harry was then translating Mayer's new book on Engels and read some of it aloud to Kautsky, whose English was excellent. Kautsky "found it good..., and, bless the man, invited me out again. Too bad it is inadvisable to write more here about him" (although Harry had already said too much for a Nazi censor). Kautsky's house was searched not long after, but courteously; "the officer in charge said it had been a pleasure to meet so educated a man." The visit to Kautsky constituted "a decisive step in my leftward march."[163]

Part 3: Historians at risk

In the purge of German academia, the University of Berlin led the pack, firing 32.4% of its faculty in 1933-36, testimony to the large numbers of Jews and liberals on its rolls.[164] The plague was everywhere. "Today's paper," Harry told his parents on 13 April, "contains the first news of thrown-out professors. Mayer's not among them, but if he were, he would be in good company." Harry named three, all Jewish: Emil Lederer, a full professor of economics, who "flew out because he's a socialist"; the legal scholar Ernst Cohn, whose travails are described in Chapter 3; and "Arthur Feiler, economics prof. at Königsberg, author of books on Russia & the U.S., both good, formerly editor (or economics editor) of the *Frankfurter Allgemeiner Zeitung*, but he was too *linksstehend* [left-leaning] for the paper." Exactly a month later, Mayer was dismissed from the university and forced off a national historical commission; in addition to being "non-Aryan," he sympathized with the reform wing of the SPD.[165] Nowhere in Germany was there any "collective resistance"; the afflicted were on their own.[166] The four historians whom Harry came to know–Engelberg, Mayer, Holborn, and Gerhard–were "men of incurable independence of mind,"[167] and broadly *linksste-hend*. Only Engelberg had no familial Jewish connections; at that moment, being a Communist was even more dangerous than being Jewish.

German academia resembled the rest of German society in its attitudes toward foreigners and Jews. University teachers, who usually claimed to be apolitical, in actuality functioned as "mid-wives to Nazism," in Alice Gallin's term. Most of them had already implicitly renounced the Enlightenment conception of education as *Bildung*, the formation of a cultivated human being.[168] Harry, aware of this betrayal by academics, was sheltered from it in two ways. First, his social circle consisted largely of Jews who exemplified Enlightenment values. And second, aside from his talks with Engelberg and the anti-democratic Fräulein Brose, his friendships among his fellow students were shallow, and not only because of his shyness. In his own undergraduate days, Gerhard recalled, it was "quite contrary to the customary conduct of German students" to become friends with one another.[169]

Friedrich Meinecke, the dominant figure among the Berlin historians, was an exception to the rule; he was a leader of the moral minority. In 1926, with Gustav Mayer among those present, he advised an audience of his peers to accept co-responsibility with the government for educating students in democracy.[170] No one listened. Meinecke's general conservatism led some to underestimate him. In 1939, a Jew about to emigrate suggested to one of his friends that Meinecke "must be greatly impressed by the successes of Hitler's foreign policy." The friend responded by quoting Meinecke: "Now there is only this alternative: either we get war–in which case we shall be rid of that gang–but at what price? or there will be no war–and the gang will slowly strangle everything that once used to be German."[171]

Gustav Mayer[172]

By the time Mayer was fired, the government had stopped publishing what Harry ironically called "the honors lists" of dismissed professors; the reason, Mayer said, was "to quiet foreign opinion." The just-completed volume two of his Engels biography was now doubly unpublishable: both author and publisher (Ullstein) were Jewish. Harry's extracurricular contacts with Mayer became more frequent in 1933 for two reasons: beginning in February, Mayer began relying on him for translation services; and later, distraught by the crash of his hopes, he was grateful for a young American's ear. When he needed to write to the English historian G.D.H. Cole, who "doesn't read a word of German," he asked Harry to translate a letter into English. A day later, Harry translated a letter to Harold Laski that began by asking "permission to give a sign of life after a long silence." Puzzled, Harry came up with a common translator's solution: "omitting it altogether." He greatly enjoyed translation; it was possible to make "Hegel quotations more intelligible than in the original."[173]

Before long, Mayer was testing him for a far bigger translation job, his Engels biography. Demonstrating the close-knit nature of the Berlin Jewish intellectual community, Ullstein had asked Paul Gottschalk to store the already-printed copies in his warehouse. Harry picked up a copy from P.G.–"bound, very unbeautiful and solid"–and began translating sample passages. An instructor "competent both in Marxist theory & in English" to whom Mayer gave the sample "pronounced it good. So I translated some more." Mayer had a curious idea that Harry should take a copy to America so it could be translated into Yiddish and a copy given to a public library. Harry asked his father to help find an American publisher:

> The problem is as follows: he has written a life of Engels, a work of fundamental importance not only in the narrow connection with Marx and the history of German socialism but also as an indispensable source for the general history of the European labor movement. The book, which is the only scholarly work on Engels, is in 2 vols., a total of almost 900 pages, printed and partly bound by Ullstein.

Louis Marks had no useful connections. Mayer wrote letters empowering Harry "to act in his name in arranging with NY publishers."[174] None of this activity came to any fruition. The book was published in 1936 in a translation by Gilbert and Helen Highet.

Harry visited Mayer at home two days after his dismissal:

He was pretty crushed, spoke of himself as a ruined man, and entertained the fantastic idea that Rockefeller or Carnegie would found a research institution abroad for the prosecution of studies here impossible. I heard several moving tales, and undertook some correspondence for him–he doesn't leave the house....

A research institute for refugee scholars was not a "fantastic" idea. The Institut des Hautes Études Internationales in Geneva, where Engelberg was based in the later 1930s, received most of its funding from the Rockefeller Foundation. Mayer already knew about the "German University" established at the New School in 1933 (with Rockefeller support) as a haven for refugees.[175]

Mayer seemed to seek the company of foreigners. Another dinner guest was a "brainy young Frenchman named Aaron (or however he may spell it–Aron?)." This was Raymond Aron, four years Harry's senior and well on his way to becoming a famous philosopher and journalist. Some weeks later, an agitated Mayer phoned Harry and asked him to come that evening. Wearing "an orange burlap work jacket" instead of his customary formal suit, he allowed Harry to photograph him in his back yard, looking melancholy. He made an appointment for Harry to review his translation with Karl Korsch, a philosopher of Marxism who had studied in England. Mayer and his wife, Flora, were "working up their English now–on Galsworthy."[176] Harry was touched and sympathetic: "The poor man is having a hard pull and talks about the difficulties of learning a language at his age and of the hardships to be expected in having to settle in a new country." He "seemed to fear" he might have to join the New School "and feared breaking up–he was really disturbed." In a pitiful departure from common sense, he suggested that Harry "call on Ambassador Dodd and tell him to do something."[177]

During that visit, Ulrich Mayer revealed his own response to the crisis. Ulrich, who "hadn't bothered himself about Zionism" until the Nazi takeover, now thought that it was "the sole solution." Repeating an idea voiced by other young German Jews, he said that the younger people should emigrate to Palestine, "leaving the older ones in Germany, supported by international charity"; when the older generation "died out there would be no more Jews in Germany." Having the same goal, the Nazi government encouraged Zionist organizations and repressed assimiliationist youth groups.[178] James G. McDonald, negotiating on behalf of the High Commission for Refugees Coming from Germany, similarly proposed "a ten-year plan for the removal of Jews" from Germany.[179] The next year, Reinhard Heydrich, Hitler's head of Security Services, echoed Ulrich and McDonald, but he went further in considering what to do if the young did not leave. "Street methods" to get rid of Jews should be avoided because they might have "foreign repercussions." Alternative means were preferable: "One does not combat rats with the revolver, but with poison and gas."[180] And so they did.

Hajo Holborn

The other two historians with whom Harry developed a significant connection, Dietrich Gerhard and Hajo Holborn, were a generation younger than Mayer and better able to cope with dislocation because of their command of English. Holborn, a *Wunderkind*, had received his PhD in 1924 at the age of twenty-two. A "rarity" among German scholars for publicly supporting the Weimar Republic, he moved from Heidelberg to Berlin in 1931 to direct a research project on the Weimar Constitution.[181] He held two academic positions in Berlin: as the Carnegie Professor of History and International Relationships at the Graduate School of Politics, and as a *Privatdozent* at the University of Berlin.[182] At the School of Politics, he promoted the teaching of international relations and advocated *Lehrfreiheit* and *Lernfreiheit*.[183] Anyone espousing freedom to teach and learn was doomed. Mayer, who had helped bring Holborn to Berlin, told Harry that Holborn was "writing what promises to be the history of the Weimar constitution," a project still awaiting completion today.[184] In a reminiscence of Holborn after his death, Gerhard recalled an evening in late January 1933, when the Dutch historian Johan Huizinga was a visiting lecturer. Huizinga wanted to know what Gerhard and Holborn thought of Germany's political future. "Deeply depressed" over the likely Nazi success, they had nothing to say.[185] The Holborns and the Mayers, neighbors in the Lankwitz section of Berlin, "experienced together political worries and personal vexations during the incubation period of the Nazi terror."[186] Listening together to the election returns in March 1933, they recognized the destruction of all their hopes.

Harry first encountered Holborn as Huizinga's "large, toothily smiling introducer." In his final semester, he enrolled in Holborn's seminar and found him welcoming out of class: "Talked to Holborn this afternoon. A friendly and helpful person, and our political opinions appear to be in conjunction." He was a "good man to know–and heaven knows not because of his 'influence,' since he hasn't any. I mean ideas." In June, Holborn invited him to his home. Harry had expected a substantial supper but admitted that the Holborns' "light refreshment...won't hurt" (he was chronically overweight). The guests–Holborn's sister, "a stout no longer young woman student, an English PhD, and two former Dozenten" at the School of Politics–discussed politics "on a more microscopic scale than I was used to," so he listened quietly. Already preparing to emigrate, probably to the United States, Holborn shared his private concerns with the young American. When he learned that Paul Gottschalk was going to Paris, he asked Harry to request Paul to carry a letter for him; when Harry called to confirm the arrangement, Holborn "sounded played out on the phone." Already in some danger, he had "to 'conspire' in order to notify the Carnegie Foundation of what has gone on here in respect to his chair," which the Nazis abolished when they took over the School of Politics at the end of May. "It is typical of this new state of affairs," Harry wrote, now referring to his own efforts, "that you have to be a conspirator to find out the whereabouts of the SPD archival stuff."[187]

Talking with Holborn before and after the seminar, Harry heard about the halcyon past: "He told me how it was in the still great days at Heidelberg when there was...a brilliant faculty in the social sciences, when he was a *Privat Dozent* there, at 26 a *Stellvertretender Ordinarius*," substituting for a professor on leave.[188] The "brilliant faculty" was all gone from Heidelberg. "One of the greatest sorrows now disturbing my tranquility," Harry wrote ironically, "is that they have made no phonograph records of Heidelberg professors singing at the end of their faculty meetings the Horst Wessel Lied."[189]

Contact with Holborn became more frequent and more casual. On one occasion, Harry dropped in to chat before the seminar, and "he showed me the obit of a MP who had been beaten to death, as he said he knew from dependable sources." Afterwards, they strolled along Unter den Linden, "and I asked him about the piracy of German capitalists. He thought they did not attain American heights, partly because of the tradition of the state & partly because of legislation." On another occasion, they "Stadtbahned together" after the seminar, and Holborn "told me of the sympathetic treatment he found at the hands of the Carnegie officials in Paris." Eight days later, discussing the "reorganization" of universities, Harry felt Holborn's depression.[190]

During a visit to the Holborns' home,

he played me Mozart and Bach on his phonograph before we turned to talk. He told me of his Heidelberg days, of the university conflicts–the Gumbel case–and about his own plans. England or America?…He said he was *vom Herzen* [in his heart] a historian, had always been interested in politics, particularly *Kulturpolitik*, and would like to help an American university nearer to his heart's ideal. We talked till one, when he gave me a pamphlet to read on the Dehn case, and I took the bus through deserted suburbs home.[191]

Holborn assumed that Harry knew about the controversies swirling around Günther Dehn and Emil J. Gumbel, academics who had both been dismissed in April.[192] Gumbel, a non-practicing Jew and a conscientious objector in World War I, was a mathematician specializing in statistics. After his initial conflict with the authorities, in 1924, "any dispute involving a politically nonconformist professor was termed 'another Gumbel affair.'" Dehn, a Christian theologian, endorsed conscientious objection in 1928 and as a consequence was refused a job at Heidelberg and rejected at the University of Halle. Holborn loaned Harry not just a pamphlet but an "80 page collection of documents on the Dehn case." He copied into his diary Dehn's prediction that "what took place in Heidelberg and Halle is only an example of things to come" should the German state "no longer understand its responsibility to God."[193]

In late August, Harry arrived early at the Holborns' emptying home to find them preparing to leave, their house "in disarray–the shelves empty of books." Their

> small son, one of his two children, came in, a lively young-ster. HH thinks the situation is growing tenser and tenser, expects riots or something of the sort by winter, mentioned the disastrous effects of a large wheat crop. He will prob-ably come to the U.S. by the new year, I gather. I gave him our address.[194]

Holborn mentioned a dozen German professors bound for the New School, which he correctly expected they would "expand and trans-form." He himself landed on his feet (see Chapter 5).

Dietrich Gerhard

Of the four historians, it was Gerhard who had the most lasting ef-fect on Harry's scholarly work. His one published book originated in Gerhard's seminar; and, as mentioned in Chapter 5, he main-tained a connection with him for more than two decades. In Berlin, however, their socializing did not go beyond the expectable. Ger-hard played the host quietly when he invited his seminar for an evening at his home, but at the university he acted as provocateur or interlocutor: "Argued a little with Gerhard after being conten-tious during class." They had a "cordial parting" on the last day of the seminar. Harry gave him "a little bibliography. He still has my Singapore paper; maybe I'll ask him about it if I phone him as he invited me to." They talked at least one more time, on 20 May, about the sources of Germany's inferiority complex. A few days lat-er, Harry again quoted the statement attributed to Sir Edward Gray in 1914 that lamps were "going out all over Europe; we shall not see them lit again in our time."[195] "Our time" now meant Harry's time.

Part 4. Leaving Berlin for Cambridge

When Harry inquired about the voyage home six months in advance, a clerk advised him to "reserve a cabin now because the ships would be full in September"–full of refugees. He waited until May, though. He considered booking on a Jewish steamer line, "the Bernstein Line...by way of reprisal," but settled on the *Veendam*, a Holland America ship, sailing on 8 September from Rotterdam. The Dutch, after all, were "one of the few civilized peoples there are." On the big handsome diagram of the ship he marked his cabin in red: #169, first class, Deck B. He speculated jokingly that P.G., who approved the decision to go Dutch, would write Norddeutscher Lloyd "a stinging letter about the American who refused to return home on a German ship."[196]

With departure looming, Harry "started inquiries (naturally I can't be specific here) to see whether I can use the collection of source materials for my thesis where I worked earlier"–that is, the SPD archives, which he didn't dare name. In another act of preparation, he went on 18 July to "the Alex"–the Berlin police headquarters on Alexanderplatz–to obtain permission to leave, a routine bureaucratic requirement, only to discover that the officials "had returned my papers to the cellar."[197] He made good use of the moment: "I snapshot parts of the neighborhood–the Alex from across Alexanderplatz, 'Horst Wessel Haus'–empty, the Volksbühne am 'HorstWesselplatz'–and inside Bhf. Alex [Alexanderplatz train station]." Horst Wessel Haus, not long before, had been Karl Liebknecht Haus, headquarters of the KPD.

Three activities consumed his final weeks in Berlin: clipping newspapers for a record of current events, paying farewell visits, and "exmatriculating" at the university. Walter Elberfeld, Fritz Freyhan, and another guest of the Meyers named Gertrud helped with the newspapers. He took to "dropping in on P.G. four or five times a week and swapping news–it will be quite a loss not to have him in Cambridge." Ernst Gottschalk "said it will seem strange when I'm no longer around." He grumbled insincerely at the prospect of having his twenty-fourth birthday celebrated at P.G.'s, eventually offering himself up as "P.G.'s victim." "It was *doch* [after all] nice last night with the whole crew there," he admitted, adding typically: "If only they hadn't made me presents."[198]

With so little time for repercussions, he threw self-censorship to the winds in his news bulletins to his parents:

> I won't conceal a recent incident in the north of Berlin. An entire S.A. *Sturm* [Storm Troop] is supposed to have been arrested there. They are said to have marched through the streets in closed formation singing:

> *Lieber Hitler, gib uns Brot.*
> *Sonst sind wir wieder rot.*

In singing "Dear Hitler, give us bread / Or else we'll again be red," the Storm Troops were threatening to return to the other political religion, Communism. Another ditty that Harry reported referred to "the Bavarian concentration camp Dachau, also called Auch da," founded in June 1933 for political prisoners:

> *Lieber Gott, mach mich stumm,*
> *das ich nicht nach Dachau kumm.*

The message was self-censorship: "Dear God, make me mute / So that I don't go to Dachau." By September, Dachau held 3,400 prisoners.[199]

Certain episodes had a particular resonance for Harry. Another American, a young doctor named Daniel Mulvihill, chanced upon an S.A. march that was being reenacted for a film. Onlookers were supposed to give the Hitler salute; refusing, Mulvihill was knocked unconscious. The Berlin S.A. leader, Karl Ernst, was ordered to apologize to Ambassador Dodd, and the German government exempted foreigners from giving the salute. This response was mere window dressing, however; several days later another American was attacked for the same reason.[200]

In his final weeks, Harry busied himself with photographic documentation and exmatriculation. To exmatriculate (and thus retrieve his Harvard documents), he had to answer two items in the racial questionnaire for foreign students. One demanded his "religious affiliation (or former religious affiliation)," worded thus to catch "non-Aryan" Christians. The other asked him to state membership in organizations such as the Reichsbanner, the Human Rights League, the Socialist Student Body, "or any other Marxist organization." Harry had only his "non-Aryan" background to confess. His friends helped with packing, so that his room looked "like the day after the cyclone." The freight charges for his books would be heavier than expected: "I'll land with as many pieces of baggage as a minor film star back from Paris."[201]

Harry's higher emotional temperature during 1933 led him to reflect not only on politics but on possible marriage partners. With very little to go on, he wondered how Margarete Simon, an occasional visitor to the Meyers, would respond if he proposed marriage; he said nothing. His first impression of Gertrud, who perhaps was Margarete's sister, was that she was intelligent and attractive, so he gave her Mowrer to read. After "Gertrud sat here for six hours and clipped newspapers and told me all about herself," he fantasized asking her to marry him; however, "her yearning to 'help build up Palestine' is a brake." Two days later, the glow was off: she "chattered incessantly" and dressed like "a child of fourteen…. We said goodbye and shook hands."[202] This was not the stuff of romance.

Two farewell parties took place at P.G.'s. At the first, on 26 August, there were presents. Ernst Gottschalk gave him "a fine edition of the alien poetaster, as the schools are now describing Heine." P.G. gave him Spengler's *Untergang des Abendlandes* (Decline of the West), which Harry thought "has gotten a false reputation for abstrusity, thanks to the English translation." He reciprocated with books in German about the United States. The second farewell took place on 4 September, the night before his departure. The conversation ran on a dark familiar track. Betty described the financial consequences for two physicians after deductions for *freiwillige Spende*; one of them protested in vain that she couldn't afford deductions, while the other "got only about 1/9 of what was owed her." At 11, Harry said goodbye to the older generation, and "Hans & Fritz & I walked to the Star in the Tiergarten talking about my experiences at the beginning of my stay here in Germany, on how you learn–understand–by relating the new element to the totality of already learnt." Fritz had run into a "normally intelligent" acquaintance who claimed that "he gave gladly, sacrificed gladly," whenever "voluntary" contributions were requested. The Elberfelds later complained that the young people had spent too much time joking: "They took it all very seriously, which I did not."[203]

Harry's train for Holland left just before midnight. He had two competing invitations for dinner that night. Ernst and Laura Gottschalk asked him to stay for supper, but Herr Meyer said firmly: "Under no circumstances," and he returned to Mommsenstrasse 57 for his last hours in Berlin.[204] Frau Meyer had refused his rent for the first week of September: he was their guest. The final parting was emotional:

> It was toward a quarter of eleven when I emerged upon the station platform last night to start the homeward journey. Of the younger generation, Fritz and Hans Freyhan were there and Rudy Meyer and Heinz, and of the older generation: PG and Heinz's mother and father. (I had taken leave of Betty and Walter in the late afternoon).

They were all "wondering to ourselves, without saying anything about it, whether and where we would see each other again."

The next day, ambushed by a different and welcome emotion, he went "singing down the streets of Amsterdam (causing the good burghers some apprehension)." Talking about "German conditions to strangers" gave him "a funny feeling of improbability which is only to be expected after quitting a country where you only discuss such things with trusted intimates, and then only in a low voice." It was strange to be in a country with "no *Hakenkreuzfahnen* [swastika flags], no mustard uniforms, no clacking of heels and Heil Hitler!, no police being rushed about in special fast trucks, no fly sheets, no professionally cheery newspapers, no concealment at all." He signed himself: "Greetings from a free country!"[205]

From Amsterdam Harry proceeded to The Hague, where he went to the office of the eminent publisher Martinus Nijhoff, Paul Gottschalk's friend. P.G. had asked him to buy a copy of a book about the Nazis and leave it with Nijhoff.[206] He would either pick it up or have it sent to him in Paris. Such tricks were necessary to obtain "books which the publishers have 'voluntarily' withdrawn from sale," and which, if found during a search of your house, were "liable to make trouble for you." He chatted with the "tall square-headed and distinguished-looking" Nijhoff (whose firm, years lat-er, was later to publish his monograph on Singapore). That night he read Erich Kästner's novel *Fabian: Die Geschichte eines Moralisten*, "the first full-sized book in German that I've ever read in a day"–a "potboiler," but no matter.[207]

Perhaps the greatest benefit of Harry's two years in Germany was immeasurable: he had become "a 'social' being," the conse-quence of a benign plot concocted at the start of his time in Ber-lin by P.G. and Frau Meyer. Heinz Gottschalk had had the same goal: "The poor feller doesn't know what he is up against," he told his parents. P.G. and Frau Meyer, who did know what they were up against, worked in subtle ways. Harry rejoiced in their success while chatting easily with shipmates during his ten days aboard the *Veendam*. This time, unlike the voyage over, "ten days won't be too long" because "I am not quite the same person" as in 1931. As the ship approached New York, he thought about the people he had socialized with that evening and remembered: "Some two years and three months ago I landed in Hamburg after talking with three persons."[208] On that high note, his diary ends. He was ready for a richer social life, one that was to focus on the Communist Party and include his marriage in 1935. And he was fully prepared for his doctorate.

Harry daydreaming at midnight, the *Voss* at his elbow, 2 June 1933

"Newspaper mountain" in Harry's room, 22 June 1933

Harry at Paul Gottschalk's home, 24 June 1933

Communist graffito on Leibnitzstasse, Charlottenburg, Berlin: *Kämpfet gegen das rote Fahne* (Fight Against Suppression of the Red Flag), 23 April 1933

Three Berlin scenes (top to bottom): Alexanderplatz; Horst Wessel Haus; Volksbühne, on Horst Wessel Platz (18 July 1933)

May Day 1933, Unter den Linden, banner reading *Gemeinnutz geht vor Eigennutz* (The Common Good Takes Precedence Over Self-interest)

May Day parade on Unter den Linden viewed from Pariserplatz, banner reading *Dem deutschen Menschen kann nur ein starkes Deutschland Arbeit geben* (Only a Strong Germany Can Provide Work for the German People), 1 May 1933

Professor Gustav
Mayer in the back
yard of his home at
Lessingstrasse 18 in
the Lankwitz section
of Berlin,
15 May 1933

In diesem Hause wohnte von 1932 bis 1934
KURT SINGER
11. 10. 1885 – 7. 2. 1944
In seiner Wohnung wurde am 15. Juli 1933 der
KULTURBUND·DEUTSCHER JUDEN
gegründet, dessen Leiter er war
1938 floh Kurt Singer nach Holland
Er kam im Lager Theresienstadt um

Memorial plaque for
Kurt Singer, Mom-
msenstrasse 56

University of Berlin
on Versailles Day with
Nazi flag flying at half-
mast to signal rejection
of Versailles Treaty,
28 June 1933

Cards for Harry's final
semester, Staatsbibliothek
and History Seminar

Harry's university card, stamped *un-
gultig* (void) after he exmatriculated

Wilhelm and Therese (Aiple) Engelberg, Ernst and Herta Engelberg, and Ernst and Herta's foster daughter, Marie-Anne-Luis Martinez, in Geneva, 1938

Paul Gottschalk with the author, Amherst, Massachusetts, 1944

5

The Dispersal of the Berlin Friends

Harry's German friends all left the country, and all survived, including those in the Netherlands and France, countries from which many Jews went to the slaughter.[1] Well educated and reasonably well off, the friends did not depend significantly on relief organizations; in addition, some of them had relatives and friends abroad who helped. Living in Berlin conferred an initial advantage, for the presence of diplomats and other highly placed foreigners had some protective value. Eventually, though, Berliners shared the increasing dangers that came with time. Not only did receiving countries place more obstacles, but the German government created financial impediments–on the one hand creating incentives for Jewish emigration, such as more favorable terms for those going to Palestine; and on the other hand inventing financial regulations that penalized Jews attempting to leave. The "Reich Flight Tax," or exit tax, was already 25% in 1935; thereafter it rose ever higher. Jewish emigrants were forced to exchange their marks at punitive rates that reduced their money to practically nil by 1939. These restrictions affected Grete and Ernst Meyer, who by mid-decade had barely enough from a pension and investments to get by; they were miserably "bound to this country where we are not wanted and where they won't permit us to leave with any money!"[2] Jews who were at first better off were in the same boat, unwanted and forcibly impoverished.

When Hitler invaded Poland on 1 September 1939, the Hirschbachs, Gottschalks, Freyhans, Mayers, Gerhards, and Holborns were out of Germany, as were the Meyer children but not their parents. Most of them were out of Europe, but the Gottschalks in the Netherlands and Paul Meyer in France were at risk–and who knew whether the Freyhans in England would be safe? The last letters that Harry received from Engelberg and from Grete Meyer, in 1939, were suffused with fear of impending catastrophe. Grete and Ernst Meyer arrived in Brazil in December 1939, and Engelberg and his girlfriend, Herta, made it to Turkey in 1940. A letter from Ernst Gottschalk, dated 28 October 1945, mingled joy with melancholy in a tale of survival. Nazi brutalities had torn apart the group once gathered around Paul Gottschalk's table, scattering them from Marinsk in Siberia to Porto Alegre in Brazil, but they had all survived those dreadful times.[3]

I begin this chapter with Harry's social circle and conclude with the historians. The older refugees who left later were unable to resume their careers; but the young, including those who left late, did well in their new lives. Some of them achieved fame: Gerhard and Holborn rose to eminence in American academia; Fritz Freyhan prospered as a research psychiatrist in America, and Hans Freyhan was respected in local music circles in England; the youngest Hirschbach, Franz, became a noted professor of German literature (Frank D. Hirschbach in America), and his brother Ernst (Ernest) worked as an administrator of children's agencies; Heinz Gottschalk (in The Hague) and Lutz Gottschalk (in New York) were successful antiquarian book dealers; Lisel Meyer worked as a board-certified pathologist in the United States. The other Meyers created new lives in Brazil, France, and Palestine. Resuming his career in Germany, Engelberg became the dean of East German historians.

While Harry's friends were dispersing around the world, his own life back at Harvard was proceeding in somewhat unexpected ways. His almost light-hearted confidence in his swift attainment of a PhD dissipated with his conversion to Communism early in 1934. Through his political activities in 1934-35, he met and married a colleague in the movement. The ensuing responsibilities of a husband and father served to diminish his political involvement and encourage the tardy completion of his doctorate. By the late 1930s, he was no longer an active Communist; failing to land an academic job, he earned an exiguous living as a high school teacher until after the war, when an influx of veterans opened up academic positions and, thanks to Hitler, anti-Semitism went out of fashion.

Part 1. The tone of the letters

Much of my information regarding Harry's friends comes from letters they wrote to him in 1934-45. The letters vary according to the writers' relationship to Harry–"Herr Marks" to Grete Meyer and for some time to Engelberg, "Harry" to the Gottschalks and Walter Elberfeld. The need to elude the censors sometimes necessitated two tones of voice, a surface ease masking a deeper vein of dis-ease. "You obviously read the newspapers," Grete Meyer wrote, "so you are in the picture and will know when I use the greatest degree of reserve in my communications."[4] Ernst Gottschalk, confident that Harry would read between the lines, regretted that he couldn't "invite you to come back" and claimed to be "satisfied" with his medical practice "in the changed conditions."[5] Since the "changed conditions" encompassed Nazi laws, he was inevitably far from "satisfied." Happy in the Soviet Union, Walter Elberfeld feared no censors, enthusiastically congratulating Harry on his conversion to Communism and taking an aggressively Soviet view of the Nazis.

Harry's other Communist friend, Ernst Engelberg, and his father, Wilhelm, wrote with dignity and, at times, considerable emotion–Wilhelm from Germany, and Ernst from Switzerland. Wilhelm, who seemed unafraid of censors, had the painful task of informing Harry about his son's arrest.[6] Referring ironically to "the free German Third Reich," he lamented the loss of "'freedom of thought' in this land of 'Poets and Thinkers.'" Ernst too wrote with irony, but also with caution: he feared the network of Nazi informers in Switzerland. Recounting his experiences in prison, where he had access to books and newspapers, he expressed an ironic appreciation common among political prisoners–"nowhere in Germany can you develop and learn as much as in a penitentiary." He was bitter: the Swiss "comrade" who offered help was a mere Philistine, and "the Swiss philistine is the most loathsome and narrow-minded philistine in the world." Emotionally exhausted and "completely bewildered," he recognized that he and Herta were "optimists by nature" and "already somewhat hardened" by their experiences with the Gestapo. In his last letter, embarrassed but determined, he asked for help: "For a long time I've restrained myself from asking you if you could procure an affidavit for me. But in my need I'm compelled to overcome this restraint."[7]

Like Engelberg, Frau Meyer made outright appeals in her later letters, but her first letter reflected only depression. Finding two or three of Harry's books left behind by mistake, this once-avid reader wrote that "the most beautiful library does not tempt me–I find that all books pale against the events of the present time." Her husband's mood, like her own, was "not too rosy": "He can't get himself to write." Indeed, Herr Meyer–who like most unemployed men lacked the raison d'être that domestic labor afforded women– never added more than a quick scrawl of thanks to her letters. One of these addenda is unexpectedly emotional. Referring to Harry's assistance in obtaining a visa for Lisel, he wrote:

> Dear Mr. Marks,
> I just want to tell you that I am also very moved by your kindness. I like to think back to the time when we were here together and could not imagine that times like these could possibly happen to us.
> Your Ernst Meyer[8]

Grete, who had been so motherly to Harry, harbored hopes that this quasi-son could help her family. A long letter written on 8 June 1936 conveys a complex mixture of reproof and congratulations. Harry had finally written, after a lapse of two years, during which she had heard about him from Paul Gottschalk. With her characteristic intermingling of reticence and frankness, she was not surprised by "the report of your joining the Party (here my pen resists writing down the taboo word, as if the page could suddenly burst into flames)." Her acerbic humor appeared: "You are sufficiently well informed to know that the 'Red Front is still alive' and that many red hearts still beat inside the brown shirts."[9] Such "deceptive hamburgers," said Secretary of State Walther Funk, were "Nazi brown on the outside, Moscow red on the inside."[10] Grete experienced "meanness and hypocrisy…every hour of the day"; with her friends leaving and her children scattered to four continents, she felt isolated except during visits to Lisel in Italy or Claire in Palestine, when she "just want[ed] to rest and relax."[11] The Meyers' "extreme restlessness and exposure to every form of arbitrariness," their "undignified" life, their reduced financial means–all this tormented her. Her attempts at a stiff upper lip failed, together with her resolve to deceive the censor:

> So now you are in the picture, [and] why should I go on complaining. In any case, this gang is carrying on its diabolical game with so much cleverness and is such a powerful organization that they have engraved their name forever in the annals of German history! Almost all the young people of our acquaintance have left, [and] the old ones vegetate.

Two years later, Frau Meyer's discomfort at asking for help was as evident as her resolve: "In normal times, I certainly would not have bothered you with a visit via a letter–for that I have too many inhibitions."[12] She imagined Harry's thoughts as he read her letter, "smiling ironically and thinking…[that] all the Jews in Europe (I am anticipating–right now it's only in Heil. Europe) remember the acquaintances, friends, and relatives who are overseas." She was punning: "Heil." is an abbreviation for "Heiligen," meaning "Holy"; "heil," meaning "hail," was part of the "German greeting."[13] If Jews in Germany were thinking now of their friends and relatives abroad, soon enough Jews everywhere in Europe would be seeking assistance from outside Europe. "I am not trying to prettify my assault on you," she wrote, for "clever" Harry would "sense where this letter is going…. For ourselves, I would not have brought myself to write a letter, but since it concerns the fate of our daughter Lisel, I put all these thoughts aside and try in any way possible to help her." It was difficult "to write under so much emotional pressure," yet she and her husband felt lucky to be "healthy and emotionally intact and…[to] have good news from the children"; they were better off than "most of our fellow sufferers."[14] At the time of her last letter, on 27 November 1938, she saw no hope for herself and her husband. "Heil Hitler" would soon greet nearly all of Europe, bringing her prediction to horrible fruition.

Part 2. Finding a way out

Grete and Ernst Meyer

Five letters from Grete Meyer written in 1934-38–all but one in a Gothic script so crabbed that Harry had to transcribe her letter before reading it–tell a detailed story of restrictions, threats, and efforts to leave. Her first letter, answering Harry's, ends with "a big compliment on your first-rate German," but her news is gloomy.[15] In March 1934, the family had been given five weeks' notice to leave their Mommsenstrasse apartment because "renovations were planned." But there were no renovations: "the apartment is still free (if you want to rent it!)." The notice to move was no surprise: beginning in April 1933, the Nazis passed numerous regulations promoting the eviction of Jews.[16] The Meyers' new and smaller apartment, in the nearby Schöneberg district, was adequate for their shrunken family. Only Rudy was still living with them, for Frau Juda, Grete's mother, had died recently. Rudy had just completed his medical degree, but he would "never get accreditation." He left for Brazil soon after.[17]

Only in her first letter did Frau Meyer attempt to present a cheerful face. She looked forward to Lisel's visit the next month. She enjoyed sitting on their "small balcony with a view on the Stadtpark and Rathausturm-Schöneberg," where one could "hear one's own voice because the little garden street is so quiet and peaceful." Yet the view lacked "the charm of the balcony on Mommsenstrasse that made you reach for your camera so often. But one consoles oneself!" The Meyers' rich musical life was over; their "piano was sold, the radio is abysmal, and during my mother's illness the apartment did not lend itself to chamber music rehearsals. So I spend hours just sitting here quietly and in silence." Rudy, who had belonged to a physicians' orchestra, now had several part-time jobs–as a violinist in both a new string quartet and the Jewish Cultural League (*Kulturbund*), and as a violin teacher. The Cultural League had been founded (with official permission) by Kurt Singer in response to the exclusion of Jews from "German" cultural institutions. A "major force in Jewish cultural life," it provided "amusement, distraction and edification" for Jews while supporting "their human dignity, after their political, economic and social rights had been taken away from them."[18] Rudy probably had a personal connection with Singer, who was likewise both a physician and a musician–and his neighbor, at Mommsenstrasse 56. A memorial plaque on the building reads:

> In this building from 1932 to 1934 there lived
> KURT SINGER
> 11 Nov. 1885-2 July 1944.
> In his apartment, on 15 July 1933,
> THE CULTURAL LEAGUE OF GERMAN JEWS,
> of which he was the director, was founded.
> In 1938 he fled to Holland.

Moving to Holland did not save Singer from arrest; he was deported and died at the Theresienstadt concentration camp.

In 1934 Ernst Meyer lost his job representing the New York office of the Frankfurt-based Jewish banking firm Lazard Speyer Ellison. The Speyer office in New York, Grete wrote, "had no interest in maintaining their agent or their financial arrangements in Berlin," and the parent firm was liquidated on 1 October 1934.[19] Ernst's forced retirement may have been connected with the dismissal from the Berlin Stock Exchange by 1934 of "[p]ractically all the licensed stockbrokers of Jewish extraction." Three months before the parent firm's liquidation, Hitler had turned on his own. On 30 June 1934, in what became known as the Röhm Putsch or the Night of Long Knives, he ensured the primacy of the German military (the Reichswehr) by murdering and arresting hundreds of S.A. members, including its head, Ernst Röhm. In the weeks after the purge, "an atmosphere of 'mute despair'" prevailed among Berlin Jews.[20] If Nazi Brown Shirts were subject to Nazi terror, what hope was there for Jews?

In 1935, the Meyers went to see Lisel three times. After returning to Berlin from the first visit, they decided to respond to Claire's "urgent invitation" to come to Palestine, stopping to see Lisel en route and again on their return to Europe. It was an opportunity "to get away from Hitler's world." In order to afford another trip, they rented their apartment for five months, from September 1935 to February 1936.[21] Grete recognized the irony of finding relief in Italy, where the fascist government "was the great 'model'" for the Nazis. After "a beautiful trip through Italy (Merano, Florence, Rome, and Naples)," the Meyers "boarded the ship and landed in Haifa on October 10th." In December 1935, en route to Germany from Palestine, they "spent a few more days in Florence at Lisel's," and proceeded to Berlin "to welcome our new daughter-in-law, Rudy's fiancée," who was due to leave for Brazil in May. The Meyers themselves visited Rudy later in 1936.

Grete and Ernst were out of Germany during the first shock of the Nuremberg Laws. Passed in September 1935, these laws gave "legal" grounds for the anti-Semitic principles on which local authorities and mobs had been acting.[22] The Reich Citizenship Law stripped Jews of German citizenship and its rights. The Law for the Protection of German Blood and German Honor forbade Jews to marry "Germans," to have affairs with them, to employ Gentile domestic servants under forty-five years of age, and to display the German flag. Later laws defining "Jew" in minute detail allowed *Mischlinge* ("hybrids") like little Ursula Elberfeld, whose "German blood" came from her father, to be citizens, a move that saved many lives. By then, though, the Elberfelds were living in the Crimea.

At the time of Grete's letter from Florence in June 1936, Berlin was gearing up for the Olympics, which took place in August. The government, wishing to avoid foreign criticism and seeking more time to rearm, reduced its domestic terrorism in 1936-37. Visiting Berlin in May 1937, Victor Klemperer "discovered with pleasure that the temper of Jewry, which had once been so pessimistic, is now hopeful." At that moment, Berlin was still safer for Jews than rural areas and small towns. Meanwhile, preparations for war continued. As early as 1936, Berliners were subject to rationing and air-raid drills, with "Aryans" and "non-Aryans" kept separate in shelters. Schoolchildren studied war *matériel* and were instructed to ask their elders for war stories. After the Olympics were over, the campaign against the Jews resumed. One element involved concentrating Jews in designated apartment buildings. In November 1938, Grete wrote from a new address, some blocks north of their previous Schöneberg neighborhood: c/o Levin, Luitpoldstrasse 20. In this final letter, Grete added a postscript regarding the Levins, a very nice couple–he is an unemployed agent, the 24-year-old daughter is a kindergarten teacher [in a Jewish school], a 15-year-old son can continue as an apprentice locksmith only until Jan. 1st. Do you think it might be worthwhile if the father were to approach the [National Coordinating] Committee [NCC] to ask for help? He has no one in a foreign country to help him.

In the short term, the son's apprenticeship would be terminated by Göring's Decree to Eliminate Jews from German Economic Life, promulgated two weeks before Grete's letter. In the long term, little people like the Levins were almost certainly doomed. [23]

The Meyer children[24]

In the years after they left Germany, the Meyer children managed their lives fairly well–Paul in France, Lisel in Italy and then in America, Rudy in Brazil, and Claire in Palestine. After his precipitate departure for Paris in April 1933, Paul made a living accompanying a well-known *chansonnier*, Jean Lumière. "No doubt it was not exactly Paul's plan to live this kind of a half-life," wrote his mother, "but he is earning so well that perhaps he will eventually be able to begin a new life in a new country." The anticipated "new country" was not France–he thought of going to Brazil–but he remained in France for the rest of his life.[25] Soon after arriving, he enrolled in courses at the Law Faculty that would qualify him "to take an exam in the fall–to little purpose for the time being, since he will surely not get a work permit." When Paul's welcome at his relatives' home wore thin, he found a room with a family and married Lilliane, his hosts' daughter. His next ordeal was imprisonment, shortly after the war began, in a *camp de rassemblement* (internment camp) northeast of Paris; Lilliane, their infant daughter in her arms, won his release.[26] Anticipating worse to come, the family moved to Nice, which was relatively safe for Jews, particularly when it came "under the benevolent eye of the Italian army" in November 1942. But after Italy signed an armistice with the Allies (on 8 September 1943), the Germans took over and instituted a three-month round-up of Jews. Paul and his family fled to the countryside near Grenoble.[27]

After the war, the family returned to Paris, and Paul resumed work as a pianist. He lived in contentment until his death at 75 in 1982.

Lisel moved to Florence in July 1933 to continue her medical studies, supporting herself as a governess in a wealthy Jewish family with whom her parents were acquainted. She had remarkable energy. Besides touring with a women's basketball team, skiing, and hiking, "she gives music lessons to earn money, and she still has time for socializing while her colleagues are stuck behind their books."[28] Passing the qualification examination in 1937, she took a job as a pathologist at a hospital near Naples until forced out in September 1938 by Mussolini's anti-Semitic decree. She then aimed for the United States. Having been born in Brussels, she came under the Belgian quota, which (unlike the German quota) was not oversubscribed. Harry helped her find a sponsor: "It is a tragic situation, and if there is anything I can do I want to do it."[29] In a letter supporting Lisel's affidavit, Harry wrote:

> Dr. Meyer is willing to take any kind of position offered to her here. Her English while not polished is adequate, and from my own knowledge of her, I can say that she is a conscientious, unassuming, hard-working girl, with a likable, and well-balanced, personality. She plays the piano well, and has ability in athletics, holding certificates from the Berlin Institute for Physical Training…in swimming, skiing, and field sports.

Lisel's affidavit came from Raymond Goldschmidt, who along with his brother Lucien appears in Frau Meyer's letters to Harry.[30] Like many other refugees, Lisel received help from the National Council of Jewish Women: $50 on arrival and assistance in finding a summer job as a swimming counselor. Her multiple talents and pleasant disposition made her—Harry wrote, urging his parents to invite her to dinner—"quite a different person from Fritz [Freyhan]," whom Harry had come to dislike.[31] Lisel's youth (she was twenty-seven) was yet another advantage. "I am sorry that I sound so hardhearted," wrote the Executive Director of the NCC in declining to help a doctor of sixty-seven, "but the situation is so terrible that we can only think in terms of helping the younger people who have courage and physical stamina to overcome the obstacles which face them."[32] Lisel was indeed adaptable and realistic: "It is not important to her to be in a major city right away (or at all)," wrote her mother, "or to receive a higher salary than her modest living standards currently require."[33] Lisel already knew the message of an eight-page booklet published by the NCC and addressed to German Jewish immigrants: *New York ist gross–Amerika ist groesser* (New York Is Big–America Is Bigger, 1937). New immigrants, the booklet said, would find work more easily outside New York. Lisel understood. She moved to West Virginia to complete a residency and become board-certified in pathology. Then, having married a Swiss refugee, a sociologist named Kurt Mayer, she worked for a time in New York and then in Cranston, Rhode Island, while Kurt taught at Brown University in nearby Providence. In 1966, they moved to Switzerland, Kurt having been offered the sociology chair at Bern University.[34] The ever-adaptable Lisel, by then an ostensibly retired mother of three, did volunteer work on an electron microscope. Like her sister Claire, she lived to great old age, dying in 2003 at ninety-two.

The third Meyer sibling to leave was Claire, who wrote to her parents from England to announce her engagement "to a friend who had been working for some time as a farmer in Palestine." One of some 30,000 German Jews emigrating to Palestine in 1933-35, she joined her fiancé in February 1934, a girl of twenty eager to find a safe haven and, perhaps, to escape comparison with her gifted siblings.[35] Grete and Ernst resisted the practical incentives encouraging them to join Claire because Palestine evoked emotions all too similar to those they felt in Germany. The Jews there "do appear to be under some threat," Grete wrote, "but who can foresee the future?" They worried "that this property built up with so much work and effort will fall victim to Arab fanaticism."[36] Hence, even though their "thoughts wander[ed] so restlessly from East to West, as is fitting for our wandering people," they felt they could not risk Palestine. Claire and her husband were "so happy there that they cannot understand why we don't…[move] to 'that land.'"[37] The marriage failed, but Claire remained and remade her personal life.

Of the four siblings, Rudy went furthest in a literal sense, for in November 1934, as soon as he finished his medical examinations, he joined the first wave of Brazil-bound refugees. Together with three friends, he went to Porto Alegre, capital of the state of Rio Grande do Sul. They arrived in the nick of time. Some months later, the government restricted immigration to those who could work in agriculture.[38] Rudy and his friends found employment as classical musicians at a radio station in Porto Alegre. His efforts to work as a doctor were complicated because the Nazis had forbidden Jews to do the internship necessary to practice medicine in Germany–or Brazil. The Brazilian government, eager to mitigate the shortage of doctors in rural Rio Grande do Sul, overlooked bureaucratic niceties, and in 1935 Rudy was hired as an assistant to a German doctor in a town in the interior.

Realizing the need for a wife to make life in the boondocks tolerable, Rudy proposed to Gertrud Milch, "a dear companion of his youth."[39] Traute, as she was known, had just received certification as a violin teacher, but with the proviso that she teach only "non-Aryans" in "non-Aryan" institutions. The guileless Rudy told her that she ranked first in his list of female musicians eligible to be his wife. "There were," Traute inferred, "two more girls in question, one of them a good pianist but ugly as the night; so that there could be seen a certain line of preference." Rudy seemed unaware "how funnily he had formulated his bid to marry him"; Traute overlooked his gaucherie and sent a one-word telegram: "Yes."[40]

Rudy's medical career was checkered. For years he worked in rural areas under the name of a Brazilian doctor because regulations imposed in 1937 forbade German doctors from taking the licensing examination. Caught twice for practicing without a license, he was imprisoned for nine months in 1943. On his release, the family–now including his parents–moved from the countryside to Porto Alegre, a more agreeable location for urbanites. He and Traute were involved in the Symphony Orchestra of Porto Alegre from its founding in 1950, both of them as violinists and Traute as assistant music director. The "physician and violinist Rodolfo Meyer" led a bifurcated life.[41] In 1948 he was finally permitted to take the licensing exam but was unable to develop a satisfactory private practice. The marriage collapsed in 1955 when Rudy took a hospital job in a small village of German immigrants, and Traute declined to leave her position in the orchestra to accompany him.

Before long he went to Sao Paulo to work in an orchestra and then, rather surprisingly, returned to Germany in 1957.

Rudy's initial purpose in going to Germany was to apply for reparations; he was eligible because the Nazi regime had deprived him of an income. He consulted a Jewish woman who, having survived the war in Berlin, had established herself as a private restitution counselor. She helped him get reparations, and when a personal relationship developed between the two, the resolutely anti-religious Rudy agreed to be married by a rabbi; he even tolerated her attendance at religious services.[42] Once again he combined his two passions. He was hired as a substitute violinist by the Berlin Philharmonic, and his wife found him a job assessing medical claims from applicants for restitution.[43] His medical job gave him the satisfaction of exacting revenge against the Nazis by approving every claim.

Grete and Ernst in the New World

By the end of 1938, Grete had succeeded in the goal expressed throughout her letters to Harry: her four children were out of Germany. She and Ernst, however, seemed hemmed in on all sides. Their ID cards bore a "J"; their names were now "Ernst-Israel" and "Grete-Sara"; their movements in Berlin were highly restricted; and they had no assets. They were typical of the Jews remaining in Germany in 1939, two-thirds of whom were over forty-five.[44] Foreign countries still willing to receive refugees preferred younger ones.

Toward the end of 1936, Grete and Ernst visited Rudy for the full three months allowed by a tourist visa. Soon after they returned to Germany, Brazilian politics took a turn toward fascism. A secret circular issued on 7 June 1937 banned visas for anyone of "Semitic origins," the only exception being "capitalists, industrialists or intellectuals of special interest."[45] Back in Berlin, the Meyers waited, "month after month, to get a permit to Brazil, without any certainty as to whether and when they might get it."[46] As a settled immigrant, Rudy was entitled to apply for a permit for his parents, but the process was cumbersome and time-consuming.[47] After *Kristallnacht*, the cataclysmic rampage of 9-10 November 1938, would-be emigrants encountered "staggering" difficulties as "a flood of new restrictions and regulations" imposed grossly punitive taxes and forced Jews to sell their possessions at a "discounted" rate that reached 94% by March 1939.[48] A "great dispersal" nonetheless ensued: 115,000 Jews left between *Kristallnacht* and the outbreak of war on 1 September 1939, bringing the total of German Jewish emigration since January 1933 to some 400,000. For a variety of reasons, including pressure from the American government, German emigration to Brazil went from 530 in 1938 to 4,601 in 1939.[49]

In December 1939, Grete and Ernst reached Brazil and joined Rudy's family in the rural town of Vacaria, later moving to Porto Alegre.[50] After Ernst died in 1948, Grete, by then suffering from diabetes, agreed with Lisel's suggestion that she move to the United States for better medical care. Because Lisel's home was crowded with three children, she recommended a residence in New York. Grete's last years, during which she made only one trip to Porto Alegre from New York, were lonely; her knowledge of English could hardly compensate for her distance from family and friends. She died in New York in July 1957–a sad note that may be counterbalanced by the resiliency of her children, who not only remade themselves in other countries but also kept in touch with one another no matter how far flung. In 1937, Lisel went from Florence to help Claire with her second pregnancy, and in later life the sisters (and their children) met from time to time in Israel or Switzerland. Lisel's daughter Eva, a future French teacher, spent time with her Uncle Paul and his family in Paris. Rudy and his second wife vacationed with Lisel's family in Switzerland. The bonds, although sometimes frayed, were not broken.

Paul Gottschalk[51]

As prospects darkened in Berlin, P.G. responded methodically. His first nudge to prepare to leave came in the autumn of 1933: a questionnaire sent by the authorities to all Jewish firms, asking them to state their plans for selling or liquidating. P.G. replied that he would liquidate his business over a period of two years. In 1935, when he learned that his nephew (and junior colleague) Heinz was forbidden to work for him in Berlin, he sent him to The Hague and advised customers to write to him "at the Dutch firm of Heinz

Gottschalk," which was in fact P.G.'s firm. He promised "not to compete with Dutch book sellers," for he knew that they were already in bad financial straits because of the Depression.[52] When the command to liquidate came in 1936, Paul received essential help from two eminent colleagues abroad: "pseudo-agreements" with Bernard Quaritch in London and Martinus Nijhoff in The Hague enabled him to export nearly half a million volumes to the Netherlands.[53] Ernst Gottschalk handled the complicated matter of sending the stock to the Netherlands and liquidating the business. The final liquidation occurred in 1937, again with help from friends in London. Paul's "long and difficult negotiations with the Reichsbank" gave him enough cash to help "some relatives to settle their affairs and emigrate."[54] "Some relatives" may have been his sisters, Julia Gottschalk and Clara Freyhan, and his cousins Gustav, Arthur, and Ernst Mayer. His generosity, which he himself took for granted, was "legendary" among his relatives.[55]

On P.G.'s trips to the United States, he visited Harry whenever he came to Boston. On the occasion of my birth, he sent a telegram from New York that conveyed how greatly he cherished Harry as a quasi-son: "ALL THE WORLDS HAPPINESS TO MY GRAND-DAUGHTER." During his 1938-39 trip, his serenity undisturbed by premonitions of war, he described business as "promising." Asked for his opinion of my not-quite-two-year-old self, he asked with typical dry humor: "What do you expect me to say? That she is a museum piece?" During that visit, I talked with him much more than I did with other newly met grownups, calling him "Grandpa" or "Uncle Paul"; afterwards, there was a reminder in the form of "Uncle Paul's chocolate"–a necessity, Harry explained, "in the peculiar upbringing they give infants in Germany."[56] When he paid my family a visit in 1944, the same idiosyncratic warmth appeared. A snapshot shows the two of us sitting side by side on the front steps of the big old house where my family rented the attic apartment. Uncle Paul, wearing his customary suit and tie, smiles down at me, and I reciprocate with the gap-toothed grin of a child of seven.

P.G. left on his 1939-40 business trip to the United States on schedule, even though war had just broken out. He "thought it was a grand opportunity finally to realize his dream," recalled his nephew Lutz with more than a touch of resentment, for Paul seemed oblivious to the "huge problems" Lutz faced in managing the business in The Hague.[57] When Paul arrived in New York four weeks to the day after Germany invaded Poland, the ship's passenger list gave Fritz Freyhan as his "friend," a nice reversal of their roles in Berlin. He settled in New York, where for some years he had stored his most important books and manuscripts with his broker, Tice and Lynch.[58] Again with crucial help from others, between May 1940 and December 1941 he shipped part of his stock from The Hague to New York. His legal status as an enemy alien in the United States was soon solved through his "excellent connections." Switzerland was the only European country where he could do business during the war, but his admirers among American university librarians eased his financial straits by placing extra orders with him that he could fill out of his stock.[59] All was well with his business, he wrote to his sister Clara in 1942; he was preparing a catalogue of rare books and manuscripts, to remind collectors of his existence. Just the day before, he had bought the manuscript of Beethoven's song "In questa tomba oscura," which he recalled hearing Ernestine Schumann-Heink sing in Berlin.[60]

As early as 1942, P.G. began planning buying trips to Europe after the war. Even if major urban libraries were bombed, private collections in suburban homes would most likely be spared; stock would be there, and the collectors would need money. As soon as the war was over, he obtained a letter from the United States Department of Commerce instructing all American authorities to assist him "because my trip was in 'the essential interest of the United States.'" Having "always used the newest and fastest means of transportation"–he had crossed the Atlantic fifty-nine times by ship before World War II–he traveled from then on exclusively by airplane. He left for Europe in November 1945 and stayed for a year. After meeting his relatives and friends in London, he got down to business. In Germany, he used a passport issued by the American military, which gave him diplomatic privileges. Even though he was not yet an American citizen, the American embassy gave him "energetic help" with European visas. In Holland, he reunited with his brother and nephews; they, like his "huge stock," had "emerged from…hiding."[61] That seeming equivalence–family and stock both "hiding"–suggests why he remained free of family ties that might have interfered with his peripatetic profession. Taking care of his stock, he also helped his relatives.

After the war, P.G. transferred to New York the periodicals in his Dutch warehouse that he had shipped to the Netherlands before the war. Now restricting his wares to Continental scholarly periodicals, one of his constant interests, he no longer published the rare book catalogues that had thrilled librarians and collectors; never again would he deal in such items as "a truly breathtaking [autograph] manuscript" of Beethoven's *Grosse Fuge*, Opus 133.[62] His business never reached his pre-war level; his day was over, and he never repined.

During his regular postwar buying trips to Europe, P.G. interwove business and personal visits. He often visited Karl and Gertrud Mayer Jaspers, by then living in Switzerland. In 1946, Jaspers described the "great joy" that he, his wife, her brother Ernst Mayer, and P.G. felt at being once again "in bodily contact with the intellectual world." About a two-week visit twenty years later, Jaspers wrote:

> It is a great pleasure for Gertrud to revive in her conversations with him ever more memories, reaching back more than half a century, of the various branches of the family, and I share in her pleasure. Paul himself is admirably energetic despite his 85 years, continuing to make business trips all over Europe and to come up all the time with ideas for his secondhand bookstore.[63]

The Jasperses thought Paul's business was doing well, but this was not true. As was the case with other emigré antiquarians, his financial circumstances were exiguous after the war. The decline in his material status is never hinted at in his memoirs, in which he recollects visits with dukes, famous European antiquarians, and leading American university librarians. Yet by the late 1940s, he was reduced to living in a Single Room Occupancy (SRO) hotel near Harry's parents, choosing his dinner every night from the three-item European menu in a dreadful Chinese restaurant. His former stock boy, Arthur Minters, who had himself become an antiquarian dealer, later persuaded him that it would be better to live nearer his office in Greenwich Village, again in an SRO. One night in 1969, he invited my husband and me to celebrate our recent marriage over dinner in his favorite Italian restaurant in Greenwich Village. We met him at his SRO; he came out to greet us, walking serenely past the drug addicts, prostitutes, and other poor souls who were his fellow residents. He was as vivid as ever that autumn night, and his death in February 1970 came as a surprise.

The other Gottschalks

P.G.'s nephews and nieces shared the younger Meyers' facility in accommodating upheavals, but his physician siblings had more difficulties. As noted in Chapter 4, Ernst Gottschalk's supposed exemption as a *Frontsoldat* from Nazi regulations meant nothing; as a woman, Julia had no exemption. With additional decrees imposing further difficulties, it became impossible for Jewish physicians to treat anyone who was not Jewish or to work in non-Jewish hospitals. Berlin, with many Jewish doctors, was a locus of particular repression. Julia Gottschalk was still in Germany when, in 1935, a "Jewish woman doctor, for having attended a wound in the head of someone who had been assaulted, was herself badly beaten and wounded." Julia emigrated via the Netherlands to Britain in 1936 or 1937. Like many refugee doctors of her vintage (she was fifty-five), she did not obtain a license to practice medicine in Britain; she worked in a doctor's practice in Cumbria but apparently spent time in London.[64] Her brother Ernst, kept from emigrating by the lingering death from cancer of his wife, Laura, wrote with touching self-delusion in 1937 that "we hope for improvement [in her health] in the spring." She died in 1938, the year that Jewish physicians were decertified.[65] Without an income and forced to move to a single room, Ernst was sheltered by a patient during *Kristallnacht*. Immediately thereafter, the patient went to see Lutz in Holland and advised him to get his father out before he was deported to a concentration camp. With considerable enterprise, Lutz managed to have Ernst smuggled across the German-Dutch border. He was accompanied by Minna Fens, his housekeeper–"*Arisch!*" (Aryan!), exclaimed a Dutch antiquarian who knew the story.[66] Interned for a time as an illegal immigrant, Ernst was nonetheless able to settle in the Netherlands.

P.G.'s Dutch business was subject to Nazi laws following the invasion in May 1940. Jewish antiquarian booksellers were ordered to close their businesses or hand them over to German-appointed administrators by 1941. German Jews living in the Netherlands–where some 30,000 Germans had emigrated–were ordered to re-emigrate "voluntarily" on 5 December 1941. Lutz, however, continued the business. Anti-Semitic measures in 1942, including a mandatory yellow star, culminated in a round-up; however, instead of reporting to the Westerbork camp, from which Jews were deported to their deaths, all the Gottschalks went into hiding with Dutch families. Heinz, his wife, and their two young daughters survived the war but "suffered terribly," Lutz later said, because they "didn't have the right facilities."[67] Heinz remained in The Hague after the war and re-established his antiquarian business. Ernst and Lutz hid–for exactly 992 days, he remembered–in the home of Charles Gilhuys, chief accountant of the Nijhoff publishing company and an active member of the resistance. In 1946, Lutz moved to New York, married Dorothee, his high school girlfriend, and worked initially for Uncle Paul. Again discouraged by Paul's lack of business sense, Lutz and Dorothee set up an antiquarian firm, Biblion, working out of their home.[68]

Emigrating to the Crimea with their daughter Ursula, Walter and Betty Gottschalk Elberfeld felt that they had entered political paradise. Walter was apparently welcomed for the same reason that brought Rudy Meyer to practice in rural Brazil: a shortage of doctors in the hinterland. They lived "in the country far from any comfort but in a very beautiful area with a good climate," where Ursula was a "happy country child" who "busies herself especially with horses and cattle." Walter rejoiced in the "really remarkable progress" that would shortly make the Soviet Union "the most productive country in the world," putting Hitler's Germany in the shade.[69] He delighted in Harry's new Communist activities, "a significant conclusion" to his years in Germany. He anticipated the politico-military future–"Hitler is driving toward war, and it will end in a crash"–but not the awful fate in store for him and his family.

In 1938, in a cruel reproof of his idealism, Walter was murdered by Stalinist henchmen, Betty exiled to Siberia, and their two children–Ursula and her sister, Renate, born in the Crimea–sent to the Caucasus.[70] "Unfortunately," her father wrote, Betty "remained faithful to her youthful ideals" even after these disasters. After the war, she was reunited with her daughters in Estonia, but she was already "gravely ill from tuberculosis, and died in 1948." After searching for twelve years, P.G. located Ursula and Renate and visited them "every year since 1961 in Leningrad, Kiev, and Moscow"–no mean feat for a man in his eighties, and do-able only through the privations he chose for his daily life. Before his first trip, P.G. hired a tutor to teach him enough Russian to make himself understood. They talked with dictionaries on their laps, Renate apparently without any German and Ursula's deteriorated from lack of use.[71]

Harry wrote to Ernst Gottschalk soon after the war ended, enclosing a letter of recommendation to the American consul, in case his old friend thought of joining his brother in the United States. Dr. Gottschalk did not contemplate further emigration. In a profound understatement, he wrote that "we've all become so much older and so much richer in experiences." He could not disguise his grief over Betty's fate:

> Walter has been taken from her, both their daughters are being brought up in a northern Caucasus home for workers' education, and she lives–as I saw from a postcard–in Marinsk in Siberia between Ob and Tenessie on the Siberian Railroad. It's very doubtful that I'll see her again.... We can't really imagine what your life is like there, and you can imagine even less how modest we have become since we've been deprived of the most essential things, and how thankful we are when one thing or another becomes slowly available here. In any case, everyone here knows with how little a person can manage, when necessary.

The Hirschbachs

Alfred Hirschbach, Harry's uncle, was born in New York and raised in Germany. He worked in New York his entire adult life, employed by the German Jewish investment banking firm Heidelbach, Ickelheimer & Co. at 49 Wall Street. He was, said his nephew Frank, "what every German Jew needed…in those days: a rich American uncle."[72] He brought all the Berlin Hirschbachs to America. Ernst (Ernest within a few years) came first, in 1935, followed within two years by his brother Gerhart (Jerry in America) and his aunt, Hedwig. Ernst, having taken his law degree, had expected to take the second and final juridical examination after his year working for the Berlin municipality. Instead, he was dismissed when new restrictions were imposed on Jewish lawyers. Thanks to his education in a humanistic *Gymnasium*, his English when he emigrated was good enough to read Shakespeare in the original and insufficient to order a cup of coffee. He was twenty-five, young enough to cope with the difficulties of which his Uncle Alfred had warned "in lengthy letters."[73] Arriving with the legal limit of ten marks, he worked at a menial job while improving his English: "I do not know whether I was the only helper on a New York delivery truck with an LL.D. degree in 1936 but even if there was somebody else, that knowledge would not have made things much easier." Modifying his original ambition to become a juvenile court judge, he enrolled at the New York University School of Social Work and embarked on a career with children, eventually directing children's agencies in New Jersey and Montreal. On 18 May 1937, in slightly accented English, he wrote to congratulate my mother on my birth and reflected: "It is only a few years ago that I met Harry for the first time at Paul's house in Berlin, and nobody could imagine at that time that I had to write from Philadelphia to a father…. All good wishes, Your Ernst." When he married an American who asked him to teach her German, he refused: that was his past, and he embraced the New World.

In neither his letters nor his diary does Harry mention the youngest Hirschbach, Franz, who was only eleven in 1933. Franz–who became Frank D. Hirschbach, professor of German at the University of Minnesota–later narrated the successive blows that forced his family out of Germany to America. Enrolled in a non-Jewish high school, he was a minority within a minority; in 1937, fewer than 40% of Jewish children attended non-Jewish schools. Although he "envied the camaraderie and fun" his friends had in the *Hitlerjugend*, Franz had been relatively happy during the 1930s.[74] Until *Kristallnacht*, "a *relatively* 'normal' life was still possible even for young Jews"; then everything changed.[75]

By that time, Franz's father was totally out of work. His mother, as already noted, continued to teach and became the family's sole financial support. Even though the Hirschbachs had thought that the whole thing might blow over, they devised an exit strategy based on Alfred Hirschbach's help. Their plans were already well advanced when, on the morning of 11 November, the day after *Kristallnacht*, Franz was called out of his English class and sent to the principal's office. The principal, in a "not unfriendly tone," told him to get his things, go home, and never return.[76] Franz knew–from the radio, not from the streets of "sheltered" Zehlendorf, where they lived–what had happened the night before. He knew, too, that Alfred Hirschbach had sent affidavits for the four Hirschbachs remaining in Germany (visas followed some months later). A little earlier, when the topic "How do I see my future?" was set for a practice essay for the final exam that he would never take, Franz wrote: "Although in a few months I'll be emigrating to America, I have an unshakable confidence that someday I will again call myself a German."[77] For now, his Lutheran baptism irrelevant, he was not a German; he was a Jew.

Franz's father, Martin Hirschbach, was meanwhile waiting for his brother in New York to complete the onerous tasks necessary for the Hirschbachs to emigrate. Five days after *Kristallnacht*, Harry wrote to his parents: "Any news about Martin? The bestiality of the Nazis is going to prove a very expensive way to divert the attention of the German people from their woes." The United States government had just withdrawn its ambassador from Germany, a futile protest. The Hirschbachs in Germany were rendered destitute by the even more severe currency restrictions put in place immediately after *Kristallnacht*. Alfred must have paid the extortionate exit tax and their transportation costs. They arrived in New York on 3 March, each with a single suitcase and the regulation 10 RM. They were listed on the ship's manifest as Martin (age 65, manager), Rose (age 53, housewife), Peter (age 22, gardener), and Franz (age 17, student). Harry marveled at the "prospect of three-quarters of a dozen Hirschbachs all assembled around one table": Alfred; his wife, Deborah; and the seven Berliners–Martin and Rose, their four sons, and Hedwig. The newest arrivals moved to New Haven, where Martin cleaned mouse cages in a lab and Franz worked in a factory. Not a "housewife" by profession, Rose found a position teaching German at Yale, where she pioneered the native-speaker program.[78]

In 1943, Franz, now Frank, enlisted in the American army and served in Germany: "Among German exiles, almost all of the males of my generation went to war. We knew for what end and especially against what we were fighting."[79] Right after the war, a *Gymnasium* classmate wrote to him from an English prisoner-of-war camp in Egypt, and Frank sent him a CARE package; later on, the classmate having become a German diplomat, they met in Detroit, Belgrade, and Bonn. Sometimes, on his many visits to Germany–he specialized, unusually, in East German literature–Frank would find classmates' names in the phone book or on professional plaques outside their offices, but he never phoned or rang the bell. Despite this reluctance to make contact, he accepted an invitation to the fiftieth reunion of his *Gymnasium* class, who remembered him by his nickname, Fränzchen. As an act more of bravery than of revenge, he wrote an article about his experience, published in a prominent newspaper.[80]

The Freyhans

The Freyhans emigrated in two stages: Fritz to the United States in 1937; and Max, Clara, Eva, Hans, and Hans's wife (Kate) to England early in 1939. The move to England was enabled by an offer to Hans of a teaching post, at a meager ten shillings a week, in a Jewish school in Brighton. The Freyhans' early time in England was difficult. After war broke out, Hans and Max were interned in a camp for enemy aliens on the Isle of Man, where Hans entertained his fellow refuges with piano concerts and lectures on music. Parliamentary debates deplored "the cruelty of internment of refugees at this time," and appeals to release Max and Hans eventually succeeded. The family settled in Bedfordshire, some fifty miles from London, where Hans and Kate taught music in schools; Hans also wrote widely on music, particularly for refugee-related publications. At fifty-eight, Max was too old, and his English at first too shaky, to find paid work. He was nonetheless employed, reading every day at the British Museum and–when his command of English improved–performing as an "immensely charismatic and dramatic lecturer." Both of Hans and Kate's sons, Peter and Michael, became professional musicians. In 1958, they played with the British National Youth Orchestra at the Hochschule für Musik in Berlin, an event that gave their father "a kind of closure on the terrible events of his youth and the Nazis' attempt to destroy him and his family."[81]

Fritz Freyhan's two letters to Harry in 1936 and 1937 indicate both his professional intentions and the nagging quality that annoyed Harry and others who knew him. He told Harry his plans: he intended to complete his exams by the following March, spend three months in intensive study of English, and then "present myself to you in person." He requested information about medical residencies in the United States. Receiving no answer, he wrote again: his previous letter had been "an attempt to revive our somewhat enfeebled relationship," and he "regretted not hearing anything at all from you," not even "through Uncle Paul." If P.G. was not transmitting news, then maybe he too did not care too much for Fritz. True to his plans, he left for the United States in the autumn of 1937, when fewer than a hundred "non-Aryans" were studying in German medical schools.[82]

Harry's persistent remoteness is surprising in view of the long walks and talks that he and Fritz had taken only four years earlier: "a four-hour talk with Fritz Freyhan about politics"; "talked till 12:15 with Fritz & Hans on the hopelessness of the present situation." Other such talks and walks took place. At P.G.'s fifty-third birthday celebration, Harry took photos: "Fritz, who once told me he never let himself be snapped, apparently had forgotten his principles today." In the photo, the handsome Fritz smiles slightly; small wonder that a couple of weeks later, he "seemed enamored of his picture and ordered some more." Harry enlisted his father to meet him on arrival in New York, but his low opinion persisted. Even though Fritz made "a special effort to win the affection of everyone he meets," he had a talent for alienating erstwhile friends.[83] He did well professionally, becoming one of the "pioneering clinical psychopharmacologists in North America," a number of whom had also emigrated from Germany before the war.[84]

Part 3. The Historians

The strains of anti-Semitism that took root in German society in the 1870s-80s, a paradoxical consequence of Jewish emancipation, burgeoned in academia during the 1920s and '30s. Students took the lead, as illustrated in the assault on Ernst Cohn described in Chapter 3, and their teachers followed. Claiming hypocritically to be "above politics," the professoriate was complicit in the ruination of academic life–"personally decent but politically murderous." "The adaptability of a professor is beyond belief," Harry observed: "If you lay him on a red flag he becomes infused with crimson. If you lay him on a Nazi flag he crawls into the hooks of the *Hakenkreuz*."[85] In 1933 alone, 1,200 academics were fired–16% of the entire profession; at the University of Berlin, 33.4% of the faculty lost their jobs in 1933-35, ninety percent of them Jewish. About 60% emigrated; by the end of the decade, more of these scholars had come to the United States than any other country.[86] The University of Berlin lost eleven historians deemed Jewish by the Nazis, as well as Gentiles who (like Hajo Holborn) had Jewish connections or simply could not bear to collaborate with the regime.[87]

In this section, I discuss the emigrations of the four historians with whom Harry had a significant relationship: three teachers–Holborn, Gerhard, and Mayer–who left permanently between 1933 and 1936; and Harry's fellow student, Engelberg, who left in 1934 for Switzwerland, went thence to Turkey, and returned to Germany in 1948.[88] Harry took Mayer's seminar every semester as well as several of his lecture classes, and took every one of Gerhard's courses.[89] Holborn he knew only in his last semester, when the impending departure of both of them fueled a friendship. Their liberal politics impelled Holborn and Gerhard, and indeed nearly all of Meinecke's former students, to leave Germany. Many of them, too, had Jewish connections: Holborn's wife, Annemarie, a scholar like himself, was Jewish; Gerhard's mother, Adele Gerhard, a noted novelist, had a Jewish parent.

Gustav Mayer and his family

It took Mayer three years to arrange his departure. Because he had only twelve years of service, his pension was exiguous. In addition, pensions of Jews were automatically reduced by a quarter and those of the "politically dangerous" by a third; Mayer fell into both categories. In vain, his colleagues petitioned for an increase in his pension to take account of his wife's "delicate health" and his mentally ill son, Peter. Their efforts were ultimately pointless, because his pension was not transferable abroad.[90]

Writing his memoirs at the end of his life, Mayer repeatedly confessed his obtuseness in the face of the Nazi tide rising in the early 1930s.[91] He was not unique: most Jewish historians who wrote post-Holocaust memoirs confessed that they had been so acculturated that they were "baffl[ed by] the upsurge of Nazi antisemitism."[92] During two years of indecision (1934-36), Mayer was appointed to unpaid honorary fellowships at the London School of Economics and was able to cobble together a meager £250 in financial support. Finally, at the end of 1936, Harold Laski secured a three-year commitment for $1,000 annually from a New York institution, and in May 1936 the Mayers sold the Lankwitz house where Harry had visited. English friends helped them move their household possessions to London, but they still had to pay a staggering 65,000 marks in exit tax. Mayer's age and lack of fluent oral English made an academic post impossible, and he had constant problems obtaining long-term support. The Amsterdam-based International Institute for Social History bought his library, and he was a fellow of that organization in London in 1937-40. When his sources of income vanished in 1940, Paul Gottschalk came to the rescue by obtaining a stipend of £300 a year from the Rockefeller Foundation. Rockefeller had no interest in him or his family as individuals, P.G. told his cousin, only in his research. Apparently the stipend continued after the Mayers were forced to leave London for a relatively safer place.

In London, Mayer focused his research on the earlier history of the labor movement in Britain. After the war started, he, his wife, and their son Peter were evacuated to the countryside, where, bereft of research libraries, he occupied himself by writing a memoir. But he could not bear to describe his last lonely years "among foreigners in a foreign country," as he wrote to his wife in 1937. He was torn by private and public tragedies: his son Peter's suicide in 1941 and the Holocaust, which took the lives of family members, although not those closest to him.[93] His other son, Harry's friend Ulrich, struck out on his own. Ulrich was in the middle of his law examination in the autumn of 1933 "when he was dragged out...by a gang of Nazi brownshirts, but he managed to complete his doctorate...before joining his parents in penniless exile in London."[94] In 1936, he acted on his Zionist feelings. Accepting a clerical position in Haifa, he arrived just before the Arab insurrection of 1936-38 that discouraged Grete and Ernst Meyer from emigrating to Palestine. World War II ended his Zionist hopes: he happened to be visiting his family in England when war broke out, stranding him there. Changing intellectual focus, he took a doctorate in anthropology at Oxford and then–now known as Philip Mayer–became a pioneering authority on Xhosa urban life. Thus father and son illustrated the contrasting fates of their generations of exiles, Gustav fading into relative obscurity and Ulrich Philipp recreated as an English social anthropologist.

The tally of the seven Mayer siblings when war broke out was this: one each in England, America, and the Netherlands; two in Palestine; and two in Germany. Gertrud was in the best position because her husband was not only a Gentile but a renowned scholar. Even so Karl Jaspers felt the sting of Nazi repression when, in 1937, a law excluding spouses of Jews from the civil service forced him to retire from the University of Heidelberg. The Jasperses survived the war in Heidelberg, where Gertrud felt in constant danger. Fritz Mayer, dismissed from his post as a doctor, emigrated to Palestine in 1933, where Otto joined him the next year. Another doctor brother, Ernst, delayed his departure until 1938, when he fled to Holland and took refuge in Paul Gottschalk's home; after the German invasion, he and his wife were hidden by a Dutch family. Arthur, who worked for the Warburg bank, escaped to America with P.G.'s help. The most endangered of all, Heinrich and his wife, were sent to Bergen-Belsen, from which they were "freed at the eleventh hour."[95]

Dietrich Gerhard

For temporary refuge in 1933, Gerhard chose Great Britain, where he had spent two Rockefeller-funded years doing research and where he had friends.[96] Walter Adams–General Secretary of the Academic Assistance Council, founded to help German refugee scholars–helped arrange a visiting position in Edinburgh. Arthur Schlesinger, Sr., encouraged him to ask his Harvard colleague William L. Langer about a job, for Gerhard's ultimate goal was America.[97] In his letter to Langer–written in almost perfect English–Gerhard explained that "although not a Jew I am falling under the racial discriminations, owing to the descent of my family" (his Jewish maternal grandparent). Despite having been a *Frontsoldat*, he was "legally excluded from any appointment, at least as the laws are now interpreted, and we shall not be able to carry on financially for a long period." The Rockefeller Foundation was "willing to back me for a limited period of at least one year," paying two-thirds of his salary, as long as he obtained an invitation from a university willing to pay the other third. As for Britain, even "a semi-permanent lectureship" was "very unlikely." His American graduate students, presumably including Harry, thought that he would "fit in especially well there." A letter of recommendation from Howard Gray of Bryn Mawr described him as "a very modest, scholarly & agreeable man.... I should never have suspected Jewish connections...."

Langer's initial reply gave Gerhard the impression that a temporary position was "not quite unlikely."[98] But some two weeks later, Langer wrote that there was "no prospect whatever...for this coming academic year," and there was "little to do beyond waiting and hoping." He hung on through the summer semester of 1935. Finally, in 1936, Harvard offered a temporary position, a toehold from which he proceeded the same year to Washington University in St. Louis, his haven for decades.[99] Gerhard and Harry reunited at Harvard in 1936; the next year, Gerhard wrote a letter of reference for his job file. They maintained contact for at least twenty years. In 1957, Gerhard sent Harry some offprints and invited him to recommend candidates for graduate fellowships at Washington University. Harry's reply ended on a gloomy note: his monograph on Singapore, an outgrowth of his seminar with Gerhard, was languishing with a publisher in London.[100] He had not yet thought of sending it to Nijhoff in The Hague, who published it two years later.

The travails that many refugee academics endured are illustrated in the difficulties experienced by Gerhard's older sister, Melitta, a respected literary scholar who at that time was the only woman teaching German literature in a German university. Fired in October 1933, she admitted that she was a Jew according to Nazi law but asserted that she had always "sharply opposed all Marxist, Jewish, and international outlooks" and boasted of her "unconditional identification with Germanness." A 3x5 card in the files of the Emergency Committee in Aid of Displaced Foreign Scholars, undated but apparently written in late 1933, identifies her as *"Privat Dozent Germanistik"* (lecturer in German language and literature), but she was already *"beurlaubt"* (on leave) from her job.[101] It made no difference that she was *"nicht Jude oder nicht mehr Jude,"* not Jewish or not Jewish anymore. The Department of German at Wellesley College, which was willing to hire her in 1934-35 on a replacement basis, could not find room for her in 1937-38, when she returned to the United States; instead, it hired a German woman who was an out-and-out Nazi.[102]

Hajo Holborn

Holborn, his precocious accomplishments as a historian now irrelevant, lost his position at the Graduate School of Politics at the end of May 1933 and was dismissed from the University of Berlin at the end of the summer session. Facing the disruption of departure, he confided his feelings to Harry, who was only seven years his junior. His American connections–the Carnegie professorship and his American students–inclined him toward the United States. His letters of reference illustrated the coded writing that appears in Harry's letters. Meinecke wrote of "present regulations for civil servants [that] compelled him to seek a position abroad"; Gerhard Anschütz of Heidelberg University explained that "certain obstacles" impeded his academic career.[103]

The Holborns went immediately to England, "trying to conceive of our departure now as a sort of study trip that will one day end [with us] at home again."[104] This dream was short-lived. In 1934, they emigrated to the United States with the aid of the Emergency Committee. Interviews at Harvard led nowhere–he and Langer did not get along–but in May, Yale offered a two-year assistant professorship, with Rockefeller paying half his salary.[105] Holborn was thus well established in America when, in 1937, he wrote a letter of reference for Harry's job file. His tenure at Yale, which lasted until his death in 1969, was interrupted by his wartime work for the Office of Strategic Services (OSS; the wartime predecessor of the CIA), where Langer was his supervisor. Holborn achieved his youthful wish to influence public life not only through the OSS but through his postwar work as an adviser to the State Department on American policy in Germany.[106] After the war, Holborn cooperated with scholars in Germany but refused to teach there. The crowning achievement of his scholarly career was a three-volume *History of Modern Germany* (1959-69). In 1969, he went to Germany as the first recipient of a prize honoring a person who "has linked the world's peoples more closely together in deeper mutual understanding." The night after accepting the award, he died in his sleep.[107] Two years earlier, he had been elected president of the American Historical Association, a fitting capstone to his career.

Ernst Engelberg[108]

Engelberg was the sole fellow student in Berlin whom Harry came to know in any significant way, and they remained in contact through March 1939. In Harry's only surviving letter, he informed Engelberg that he had "gone down the path toward which you pointed me," reaching the blessed destination of the Communist Party, and had thus been "true to my own name"–a joking allusion to Karl Marx.[109] The letter survives in Harry's rough copy, which he kept. A reply came not from Ernst but from his father, Wilhelm, a book dealer in the small Black Forest town of Haslach.[110] Wilhelm had opened Harry's letter (he apologized) and, inferring their friendly relationship, answered because Ernst could not: he was awaiting trial in the remand prison in Moabit, an industrial section of Berlin. He enclosed a slip of paper on which he had written Ernst's address, down to his cell number, in handwriting so beautiful that it could have been an engraved business card. Perhaps, he suggested, Harry would "brighten Ernst's imprisonment with a letter."

Engelberg's story had a prelude. Following the purge that cost his supervisor (Gustav Mayer) his job, two moderate liberals, Hermann Oncken and Fritz Hartung, took on the task of supervision. They did so at some risk to themselves, for Engelberg's was one of only two Marxist dissertations ever presented in Nazi Germany.[111] Oncken's "political biography" of the nineteenth-century German socialist Ferdinand Lassalle made him one of the first German historians concerned with the workers' movement in the nineteenth century, a subject of Mayer's research as well. His opposition to the Nazis, conveyed indirectly in his lectures, became clear to the authorities before long.[112]

When Engelberg's son, Achim, learned of the letters to Harry, which gave fresh biographical information, he happened to be working on a book about refugee German intellectuals. He wrote about the newly discovered letters in a chapter entitled "Sketch of a Thriller."[113] If not exactly a thriller, the revelations contained in Wilhelm's letter disclosed something that Ernst himself had not known: the effect of his arrest on his family. His own letters told the story of his imprisonment, his exile in Switzerland, and his increasingly desperate efforts to find a safe haven from Nazi spies and looming war. The last letter found him still seeking refuge.

Both Wilhelm's letter and Ernst's first letter to Harry gave wrenching details of his arrest and eighteen months in prison. On 22 February 1934, he passed the oral examination that completed his PhD. Four days later, telling his landlady that he was going on his customary after-dinner walk, he went in fact to a secret meeting in a movie house where, still euphoric from his doctoral defense, he failed to recognize the tell-tale sign of an informer.[114] He never returned home. When his landlady inquired at the police station, "they had no information." Three days later came the raid that Engelberg had feared when he asked Harry to hold materials for him. Two criminal investigators searched his room and "took some of his writings, including materials for his doctorate." Wilhelm, whose own father had been in the revolution of 1848, exclaimed: "Slavery of the Soul! What would our fathers and grandfathers–our freedom fighters of 1848–say if they were to visit the Third Reich?"

The police knew that Engelberg was active in left-wing causes but did not connect him with his KPD code name, Alfred.[115] As a dangerous Communist student leader, "Alfred" would have been sentenced to a concentration camp; naturally, Ernst denied all knowledge when the police asked if he knew where "Alfred" was. For six months, he awaited trial in the Moabit jail. For his "parents and sister this [arrest] was a hard blow, a lightning bolt to our hopes" for the brilliant Ernst. In a birthday message to his mother, Engelberg assured her "that she should not be ashamed of him, that he did nothing disgraceful." Jail became bearable when, "after several weeks, he was permitted to have his books brought to his cell." A sympathetic employee of the *Staatsbibliothek*, distressed that such an avid reader was in jail, had arranged for books to be brought to him. "Now I can bear all this and feel lucky," he rejoiced. He asked Wilhelm, who had told him of Harry's letter, to deliver a message: "That Herr H.M. from Cambridge still thinks of me gives me great pleasure; often, walking through the Tiergarten, when we would talk shop, I learned much from him, [and] hopefully he also got a bit from me." Harry got more than "a bit." In the letter that Wilhelm had opened, Harry said that he had "tried my luck occasionally as a public speaker to spread a little enlightenment, and it worked." Wilhelm did not pass on this proof of his son's influence; having a friend who spoke publicly in support of Communism could have made things even worse for Ernst.

In concluding his letter, Wilhelm revealed that he himself had been arrested on 2 August 1933 and imprisoned for three days– "an act of revenge" for his and his family's past political activism. In 1918, like many in the Workers' and Soldiers' Councils formed in the immediate aftermath of the war, he had raised the red flag, signaling the demise of the imperial black/white/red flag.[116] He was editor of a local pro-SPD newspaper; his wife, Therese, together with her father, Franz, kept a pub in Haslach known as a *Revolutionsbeize*–a place where revolutionary political ideas were intensely debated.[117] Many people, he told Harry, had been shocked at the arrest of a man of seventy-one whose family had sacrificed for Germany: not only had his father participated in the revolution of 1848 but his older son, Julius, had fought (and lost a leg) in World War I. Wilhelm still believed "that in a future time we will achieve...the freedom of mankind of every race and faith." He respected but did not share Ernst's politics. In a kind of compensation for Wilhelm's arrest, Haslach later renamed a street after him.

Ernst's upbeat personality made imprisonment bearable. In the weekly letters that he was permitted to write, Wilhelm reported, he assured his family "that in his solitary cell he retains his cheerfulness, although he also has some difficult hours." Finally, on 17 October 1934, he was brought to trial together with nine comrades. Sentenced to a year in prison, he was moved to a penitentiary in Luckau that specialized in Communists–Karl Liebknecht had been held there–but also held common criminals. His first letter to Harry, written five months after his release, described the conditions of imprisonment. While the food was poor and there was no opportunity for exercise, he could "read good books, play chess, and subscribe to a newspaper."[118] His convictions were tested: "I was boxed on the ears, beaten with fists, kicked, choked, and mishandled with a rubber baton and a pipe. A veritable cannonade of insults accompanied the blows." Using "sugar bread and the whip (this was more plentiful)," the Gestapo pretended interest in his "well-being (after they had beaten me black and blue). They gave me to understand that my freedom was there if…yes, if I became an informer." Another prisoner, "unable to handle the mistreatment" and refusing to become an informer, jumped to his death from a third-floor window: "And so in death he found release."

Although Engelberg staved off illness while in prison, when he emerged in September 1935, he experienced a physical collapse and went to Haslach to recover his health. Suffering from fever, an inflamed throat, and heart and kidney problems, he spent ten weeks in bed. Then he went into exile in Switzerland, along with Herta, who had also spent a year in prison. They were determined not "to be defeated by this misery–above all by the Nazis." Still "the threat of expulsion" hung over him, for Switzerland was full of Nazi spies and drove out seventy Communists between 1932 and 1939. Hoping to leave Europe, he began writing to every person and every possible organization he could think of.[119] Wilhelm forwarded Harry's letter of 7 January 1936, which arrived just after Ernst had left for Switzerland. Ernst answered immediately, on 14 January. Asking Harry about the possibility of a job in the United States, he said proudly that his dissertation, "German Social Democracy and Bismarckian Social Policy," was more than "a specialized idea that comes from pure academic thinking," for it derived as well from his practical experience of politics–hardly a recommendation for American employment. He naively wondered if Gustav Mayer could "help me find a publisher. Can you send me his address?" Once again the letters flew across the Atlantic. On 1 February, Ernst replied to Harry's "wonderful letter of Jan. 23," in which Harry evidently wrote about his Communist activities. Ernst felt "very proud of the sudden and complete success of my propaganda efforts towards you. In prison I sometimes thought about what good works you may do." He had had an offer from Emil Oprecht, a Swiss publisher and one-time Communist who supported anti-fascist exiles, but it was contingent upon a guarantee of a certain number of sales; he wondered if American libraries would buy it. Even though he would "need at least half a year to bring [his English] up to speed," he asked whether a job in America would be possible. He overlooked the Depression and his political taint.

Three months later, Herr Engelberg and Herr Marks–the two twenty-seven-year-olds had been writing to each other like middle-aged gentlemen–became Ernst and Harry. "We're so close personally and politically," Ernst began, "that we can speak to each other using the friendly *du* [you]. In Germany we began a brotherly friendship sprinkled with a generous sip of wine."[120] Ernst, a *bon vivant*, went on to give his abstinent friend the benefit of the doubt: "And so I also drink to you in spirit with a full glass of *vin rouge*." But his news was bad. His and Herta's initial reception in Switzerland had fallen far short of expectations. They had been directed to a "comrade" in Zurich–apparently this was Emil Oprecht–who arranged for Ernst to do gardening for half a day and for Herta to do housework, labor that they disdained. To Ernst, Oprecht embodied the contemptuous views that "Swiss philistines have of emigrants." Such anti-Swiss feelings were common among German refugees, whose correspondence is "rich in recrimination against Swiss hostility." Oprecht, however, was hardly hostile; his vigorous and practical support of anti-Nazi emigrant intellectuals was so effective that the Gestapo dispatched a Swiss agent to spy on him and the Germans with whom he was in contact. In any case, Herta and

Ernst were not beholden to him for long. Despite Swiss restrictions on work by foreigners, they found better jobs, Herta as a secretary, and Ernst in the program for refugee scholars at the Institut des Hautes Études Internationales in Geneva. When refugees from the Spanish Civil War arrived in Geneva to work at the International Labor Office, Ernst and Herta, true to their humanitarian convictions, cared for several Spanish children until the families returned to Spain when hostilities ceased.[121]

In 1936, fearing a police raid, Ernst and Herta destroyed their address book as well as Harry's last letter; they had to be careful.[122] Only when Ernst, quite "by chance, found a slip of paper with your address stuck in a book" was he able to resume the correspondence. By then, early in 1939, he was urgently seeking safety: the "very gloomy perspective that I see for Europe compels me to anticipate and prepare for emigration to North America." With the "German emigration quota…very oversubscribed," his "main hope [was] to emigrate to Cuba, and from there to move more easily to the United States," then a common route.[123] This time Harry did not answer quickly; five weeks later Ernst wrote again, on 31 March. The American consulate in Zurich, besieged by an "enormous" crowd of applicants, had absurdly promised him emigration "in 48 months," if he obtained an affidavit of financial support.[124] "Perhaps," Ernst suggested, "some wealthy people among your relatives, acquaintances, or friends would supply this guarantee." Alfred Hirschbach, Harry's only really well-off close relative, was already committed to sponsoring seven Hirschbachs. Not only did Harry lack resources to help but in January 1939 he had resolved to separate himself forever from the Communist Party (see Chapter 6). Ernst had become a danger to his old friend.

Wilhelm and Therese Engelberg were able to visit their son and Herta in Geneva in 1938, apparently the last time Ernst saw his parents. The anguish of the family is not hard to imagine, as the months stretched and war broke out. In the nick of time, in 1940, Max Horkheimer, a prominent philosopher and social scientist, helped Ernst get a position teaching German at the University of Istanbul, where he joined hundreds of German-speaking professors. By happy coincidence, in the very year that a significant number of German scholars lost their jobs, Mustafa Kemal Atatürk, Turkey's great modernizer, instituted a major reorganization of Turkish higher education. In 1933 alone, some fifty German scholars found positions in Turkey; in 1933-35, more displaced German scholars went to Turkey than to the United States. The newly constituted University of Istanbul suddenly became "the best German University in the world"; it was later rivaled by the "German university" at the New School in New York (see Chapter 6).[125]

In Turkey, Engelberg continued with his twin passions: historical research and furthering Marxist ideas. The latter he did under a pseudonym, for the Communist Party was proscribed in Turkey. His personal life improved as well. In Switzerland, marriage would have cost him and Herta their residency permits; that impediment dissolved in Turkey, and the two married. He quickly learned Turkish, and when a daughter was born in 1945, he and Herta named her Renate Sulhiye–Renate "the peace-bringer." Cold-War complexities stymied his efforts to return to Germany after the war to see his father. Wilhelm Engelberg died on 16 June 1947; his son finally made it back early in 1948. Rejected by West German universities because of his politics, he accepted a position at the Karl Marx University in Leipzig.[126] He was among a very small minority of German refugee scholars who returned to Germany.

Throughout his career, Engelberg researched and wrote, no matter how poor the chances of publication, for only one of his writings in the 1930s and '40s was published, an article in a French journal in 1939. In every single year between 1951 and 1990, he published at least one piece and more often multiple works, and he continued publishing in the 1990s, although at a slower pace. His crowning masterwork, a two-volume study of Bismarck totaling 1,680 pages, appeared in Berlin in 1985 and 1990. Together with Waltraut, he worked on his Bismarck for twenty years, putting it though five revisions; the result was "a work of great scholarship that was all but untouched by ideological coloration."[127] Three *Festschriften*–collections of essays by students and colleagues–paid tribute to his sixty-fifth, eightieth, and ninetieth birthdays; and in 2009, a symposium at Humboldt University honored his hundredth. His devotion to his youthful ideals undiminished, he declared in a TV interview on his eightieth birthday that the German Democratic Republic needed to come to terms with its Stalinism, and he publicly regretted the existence of the two Germanies. Six months later the Berlin wall came down.

It seems at first surprising that Harry and Ernst never reconnected. Teaching European history for decades, Harry must have been aware of his friend's accomplishments. When he made his only return trip to Germany, in 1976, he knew that Engelberg had been teaching at Leipzig[128] but not that he had moved in 1960 to Berlin, where he was director of the History Institute, the major locus of historical research in East Germany. Even if he had been in Leipzig, Harry could have written to him there; the letter would have been forwarded, and they could have met in Berlin. But when Ernst's career was flourishing in East Germany, Harry's was in danger of derailment. His political evolution to a strong anti-Communism and his encounter soon after with McCarthyism, experiences recounted in Chapter 7, made impossible a reconnection with any element in his Communist past.

6

Harry and the Communists

Choosing sides

Reading Marx in Mayer's class, Harry had discovered that his own ideas on "historical evolution" were close to "official marxian interpretation." At that point in his own political evolution, though, he regarded both Nazism and Communism as quasi-religions based on an "uncritical mystical acceptance of the bill of fare," with the choice of one or the other depending on temperament. Walter Elberfeld, together with Engelberg the most ardently political of Harry's acquaintances, struck him as "not logical and consistent: he was a Communist." Harry's own temperament was markedly skeptical. He thought that "the certainty afforded by the Nazi faith forms the same sort of refuge as the Catholic Church, being a *Weltanschauung* [world view] which gives positive answers." The same was true of Communism, as he later realized when the scales fell from his eyes.[1]

Until his last months in Berlin, Harry maintained an aloof distance from political passions. When, for example, he heard in 1932 that a Nazi mob had attacked the *Vorwärts* building a few hours after he had been there, he wrote: "Despite all the due interest of the historian in the present troubles, I have no desire to become a participant in them and shall continue to work in more salubrious districts." An American fellow student complained "that whenever he argued against Communist theories I argued for them but that when the Communist side was represented I attacked it." After his conversations with Engelberg, however, he began to choose sides: "Ulrich [Mayer] asked me, in response to my objection to Zionism, what I'd rather do. I answered, slowly, I think I'd rather become a revolutionary than a Zionist." Soon after his return to America, he determined to become a Communist.[2]

Harry's Jewishness may have played a part, however unwitting, in his socialist and then Communist politics, as it did for many German Jewish intellectuals. These Germans "were aware of their Jewishness but thought that through socialism they would arrive at the final point of transcendence beyond Judaism or Germanic roots." The same generalization applied to American Jews, who constituted "at least half if not more" of the academics in the Communist Party of the United States (CPUSA) in the late thirties and early forties. Harry's bourgeois background differentiated him, however, from the majority of young Jewish American Communists, who came from a socialist working-class background. Harry dryly told the House Un-American Activities Committee (HUAC) that he "was not a member of the toiling masses. I was a student."[3]

Why Harry joined

If Harry had not testified before HUAC as a cooperative witness, there would be little information about his Communist passions and activities, for he left few traces. He joined the CPUSA out of an idealistic wish to make a better world–a desire that he himself said amounted to a "religious commitment."[4] This was a universal motivation, but Harry's personal exposure to Nazism placed him in a subset of the converted. A few other academics who became Communists also had first-hand experience of fascism. Among them were Harry's Harvard friend William Parry and his UConn colleague Paul Zilsel, both of whom had witnessed fascism in Vienna: Zilsel as a resident, Parry as a visitor in 1932.[5] Such intellectuals–deeply affected by the suffering of millions during the Depression, fearing that European fascism would engulf the world, and impressed by the supposed success of the Soviet Union in remedying social inequalities–willingly chose membership in a stigmatized group.

At Harry's HUAC hearing, Representative Clyde Doyle, Democrat of California, was puzzled that Harry had been attracted to Communism. All "that fine brain training" must have made him "unusually mature" at twenty-five, Doyle thought, and a mature person would understand the wickedness of Communism.[6] Harry admitted that he was older than the undergraduates who were the majority of his colleagues, "but mature–I wonder in retrospect." Doyle perseverated:

> Mr. Doyle. What was it that got you...to be a youth lead-er in the Communist Party? Why did you do it?
> Mr. Marks. That is–that's the central issue.... It seems to me...we have to recognize–and I say this as a person who is in contact with college students all the time–...the extent to which young people are accessible to ideals.
> Mr. Doyle. What do you mean by "ideals"?

This question, seemingly naive, led Harry to observe that the Communists had taken "the finest ideals of western civilization"–democracy, peace–"and pervert[ed] them to their own ends." In Depression America, "we had poverty in the midst of plenty..., and the students who were not directly, themselves, the victims of the depression tended to have...a sense of guilt, a sense of responsibil-ity." Doyle reiterated his point: Harry was "not a youth...[but] a man." Harry drew a different inference:

> Mr. Marks. All the more reason, I think, for my feeling I must do something to help my fellow man....
> Mr. Doyle. You must then have arrived at the point where you felt you had all the answers.... You concluded that the Communist Party had the answers.... So you were no longer philosophizing.
> Mr. Marks. That is precisely the point. That's what makes it deplorable.

Intellectuals, he said, responded to "a coherent and superficially plausible explanation of everything from causality in philosophy to genetics," and that was what Communism offered. Harry gave an example. The Soviet Union, with its planned economy, claimed to have banished unemployment, whereas Depression America "had between 12 and perhaps 15 million unemployed." The Soviet achievement had "a certain appeal to a person who is not engaged in business life, who has no job, who sees people abstractly as students are apt to see them." The CPUSA assured its followers that because capitalism was "responsible for all crises," its overthrow would enable a paradise of equality to flourish.[7] That the Soviet Union also murdered millions of its own citizens did not, in Harry's brief fervid period, affect his ideals, nor did it occur to him that the murdered millions could not people the ranks of the unemployed. One must keep in mind, too, that most of his political activities took place mainly in 1934-36, before Stalin's horrors were widely known.

Harry's motivations were more specifically rooted in his immersion in Hitler's Germany. While living in Berlin, he had been dismayed by the failure of Americans back home to grasp the dangers of Nazism, and that feeling grew on his return. "[D]istressed at the oversimplified response to Hitler" that reduced Nazism to anti-Semitism, he was "eager to explain to anyone who would listen to me that fascism was an enemy of all democratic rights, and that it was probably [moving] in the direction of war."[8] The appeal of Communism was ultimately "emotional...not purely intellectual." Harry spoke of an "emotional affiliation," a "sense of comradeship" that had moved him when he returned from Europe: "it meant something for me to have friends who were that close." More than once his Berln diary records "a deeper loneliness, a yearning for another home."[9] Other intellectual recruits to the CPUSA also spoke of prior feelings of loneliness. Isadore Amdur, a chemist at MIT, said that before joining he had been a "relatively immature" graduate student who "devoted a great deal of my time to studies and practically nothing to outside activities."[10] The CPUSA gave Amdur a comradeship with people who weren't chemists. To Harry it gave not only comrades but a wife–Sarah Frager, known as Bunny, the best comrade of all.

But the certitudes of Communism did not suit Harry's temperament. As Amdur and other witnesses explained to HUAC, the skepticism characteristic of intellectuals explained why they were attracted to Communism–and why they eventually rejected it. "A scientist, by nature, is a radical person...inclined...to revolt," Amdur said, and the CPUSA was a revolutionary group.[11] But because the CPUSA demanded blind obedience, such people could be only temporary Communists. Asked why he "fell for this phony line," Amdur said lamely that he was not then "as good a scientist as I am now." In his view, mathematicians were "the most radical" of all scientists and therefore the most skeptical, a thesis illustrated by Harry's Harvard friend Herbert Robbins. When he died full of honors in 2001, Robbins was celebrated for "his creativity, perhaps related to the irreverent sense of humour that led to acerbic questioning of dogma, both cultural and scientific."[12] Like Robbins and Amdur, Harry preferred questions to answers. He thought that the most important thing a historian could do is formulate "a fruitful question," for it is easier "to answer a riddle…[than] to devise one."[13]

Harry's endemic skepticism manifested itself during his last talk with Ernst Engelberg. He countered Ernst's "enthusiasm of belief" with his own wish "to stay critical," for he "didn't want to sell out."[14] To sell out what? It could only mean what his colleague Louis L. Gerson called, at his memorial, Harry's devotion to "facts and reconstruction of facts and well tested empirical evidence." But he did sell out. Whatever Rep. Doyle thought, he was not fully formed, and he was vulnerable to the example of Engelberg, who studied as intensely as he engaged in politics. Three weeks before his final meeting with Engelberg, he had a related conversation with Ulrich Mayer. Ulrich remarked that "it would be a great thing…to study exactly how much of democracy is worth rescuing and to study how to organize the revolution. The idea appealed to me at once," Harry wrote in his diary:

[If] I was going to study the lay of the land when I returned, why not study it from the standpoint of the coming revolution? Why not attempt to found a new conception of the American possibility and survey the horizon for openings? And that is the profession for the historian who declines to be a *Stubenhocker*, isn't it? Isn't that the way…to combine study and action? Isn't this what I want?

He thought that it was, yet by nature he was a *Stubenhocker*: a stay-at-home who studied, contemplated, and conveyed his discoveries through teaching and writing. Embracing one element of his quest, he violated his own personality and joined the CPUSA. Four years later, chastened by Stalin's purges as well as by becoming a father, he renounced political activism.

Harry in the NSL and YCL

Harry was supposedly a full-time doctoral student, but this did not necessarily mean taking courses. Without access to his records it is impossible to know what graduate courses, if any, he took at Harvard; he would have received credit for some of his Berlin courses. The major doctoral requirements were comprehensive examinations (known as "generals") and a dissertation.[15] A letter to his parents in the summer of 1932 explained the generals. Of the six required fields, two could be satisfied by upper-level undergraduate courses that he had already taken. He planned to prepare the four remaining fields before he left Berlin:

> 1) economic history of mod. times; 2) Hist of Ger. since 1648; 3) of France since Louis XI; and 4) Italy since the Renaissance. All these will be focused on the 19th century and shouldn't prove at all difficult–merely reading half a dozen books on each and acting bright.

If he took the generals soon after returning, he could accomplish his goal of completing his dissertation and going on the job market in 1935. But there was a catch: his political conversion ruined the timetable. He did not even discuss a dissertation topic with Langer until 1935.[16]

Instead of following the academic route he had mapped in 1932, Harry took a political path. His first step toward the Communist Party–joining the National Student League (NSL) early in 1934–might have been in conscious emulation of Engelberg, who had had his own start in the KPD as a youth leader.[17] The NSL had been founded in 1931 in New York, where student radicals proliferated at both the municipal public colleges and Columbia. The NSL "pretended to be independent of the Communist party," but this was untrue.[18] Still, the NSL stood out among Communist organization in the 1930s, being among "the most competently led" and "more imaginative and less muscle-bound in style than the cliché-ridden hacks who presided over other Communist party enterprises." It was very small potatoes; even at its height in the mid-1930s, it enrolled only a thousand students nationwide. Two other radical organizations also had small memberships–the Student League for Industrial Democracy (SLID) and the Young Communist League (YCL). SLID, founded in 1928 with origins in a socialist group formed in 1905, had more than 3,500 members in 1931. The YCL, founded in the mid-1920s, claimed 3,000 members in 1931.[19] Members of the Harvard branch of the YCL, founded in the fall of 1934, had a central responsibility: "Study, study, study."[20] The NSL leadership belonged to the YCL, characterized as a school "ready to admit those not yet Communists" who were "willing to learn to be Communists." At Harvard, the YCL was "a secret organization," not "for snobbish reasons" like other secret societies but for "practical reasons"–the members did not want to be harassed or worse.[21] When such people graduated to formal membership in the CPUSA, as Harry soon did, they found little difference between the two organizations.

The success of the student groups stemmed not from their minuscule size but from their central emphasis on peace, a concern of many young people from the mid-1920s on. A few students could make a lot of noise. At Harvard, Conant became sufficiently concerned about the NSL that he asked the opinion of A. Chester Hanford, who as Dean of the College had written to Louis Marks in 1927. Conant wanted to know whether the NSL was "a predominantly radical or Communist body," and whom it attracted. Hanford replied that it was mainly concerned with opposing militarism and, although "something of a trouble maker," was not "doing any harm." In characterizing the membership, he used casually sneering anti-Semitic language: "[Eugene] Brown, in spite of his name, I am sure belongs to the chosen race, as his mother's name was Cohen.... [Herbert] Robbins, [Harry] Marks, [Irving L.] Pavlo, [Milton] Weiner, and [Eugene] Bronstein all belong to the particular racial group which in the past has more or less dominated this organization."[22]

When Harry began his Communist activities, 52% of the 26,000 members of the CPUSA were out of work, most of them older than

Harry. Hardly any employed young people belonged; indeed, Harry later suggested, "employment was a prophylactic against Communist membership." Somewhere between 20% and 30% of youth were out of work, among them many college graduates, and that situation helped fuel the student movement. Harry's activities took place under the aegis of the NSL because the YCL was not a registered organization at Harvard; nonetheless, the cover of the *Harvard Communist* says that it was "Published by the Harvard Unit Young Communist League–Communist Party." Although the terms NSL and YCL were mostly interchangeable at Harvard, the YCL complained that all the NSL did was "expound their program at meetings"; the YCL demanded more action.[23]

Harry worked with the NSL as a teacher, speaker, group leader, and minor organizer and recruiter; his only activity outside of the Boston area was attending a national meeting of the NSL in New York. Questioning during Parry's HUAC hearing made it clear–although Parry would not acknowledge the fact–that he had belonged to Harry's NSL group in 1934, when meetings were held in Parry's apartment.[24] Parry's refusal to say whether he knew Harry Marks or Herbert Robbins was my first hint that Robbins had supplied both Parry's and Harry's names to HUAC.[25] "Unfriendly" witnesses typically refused to confirm that they knew particular people, their refusal being taken as confirmation by their interlocutors. Robbins, however, was "friendly." His supposedly secret testimony, now available in any library rich enough to purchase expensive microfiches of "unpublished" testimony, confirms his role:

> Mr. APPELL. Well, let's take…the time when you were in the Young Communist League. Who do you recall as being the chairman…of that particular group?
>
> Mr. ROBBINS: There was a man by the name of Harry Marks–M-a-r-k-s….
>
> Mr. APPELL: Was Harry Marks a businessman in town, or was he a student?
>
> Mr. ROBBINS: No; he was a student….
>
> Mr. APPELL: Can you recall in whose home meetings were held of this group?
>
> Mr. ROBBINS: Well, there was Bill Parry…. He lived in town, a rooming house.[26]

This was the first time the committee heard Harry's name.

In his freshman year, Robbins learned of a coal miners' strike in Kentucky and went down during spring break to see for himself. He had no idea that the newly formed NSL, in its first significant action, had sent a delegation of some eighty students, including two from Harvard, "in the hope of not only providing humanitarian aid to the miners but also of raising the political consciousness of undergraduates."[27] The students did little for the miners, but they accomplished their second goal, "energizing the student movement.[28] Hooked, Robbins joined the NSL and raised money to aid the miners. He attended meetings that he remembered sometimes as NSL, sometimes as YCL.

Robbins's testimony provides a snapshot of NSL/YCL meetings, which customarily focused on a Communist text that the members had been told to read. Robbins would make trouble: "I did not believe in dialectical materialism and...found the philosophy completely absurd....

> Well, finally someone—I'm not sure if it was Harry Marks or not, but it may well have been—said that perhaps the trouble with me was that I should be a member of the Communist Party, that the Young Communist League was just...for the youths, and that maybe I would find a more serious, satisfying purpose if I joined the Communist Party.[29]

Robbins couldn't remember if he had formally joined: "I was never a convinced Communist, and I was repeatedly taken to task by others for not following the party line."

From Robbins's account, the student meetings were more serious than those of the faculty unit of the CPUSA. Harvard and MIT junior faculty members who testified before HUAC described their CPUSA meetings as rather like college bull sessions. When Granville Hicks was at Harvard in 1938-39, "we all felt free...to disagree with party functionaries," and it was wrong to assume that a CPUSA member was a "perfect and willing instrument" of the Party. To Harry, the faculty group seemed "rather rigidly exclusive," lacking contact with its student counterpart.[30] The student and faculty groups were both tiny. Harry estimated that his group numbered twenty or thirty graduate and undergraduate students, at a time when Harvard's total enrollment was 7,300. The faculty group consisted of no more than fifteen junior members–less than 1% of Harvard's 1,878 teachers.[31]

Harry exercised leadership on behalf of the NSL on three occasions in 1934, all of them discussed in detail below: the National Student Strike Against War on 13 April; a demonstration in May against a German Navy ship docked in Boston Harbor; and protests in June against the presence at Harvard of "Hitler's piano player" and liaison with the foreign press, Ernst Hanfstaengl. His more routine work was conducting study groups to introduce young people to "the classics of Marxism, Leninism," with the ultimate goal of recruiting some of them to the CPUSA. In the fall of 1934, he ran weekly groups at both Harvard and MIT. The Harvard course, analyzing "readings from Marx, Lenin, and Stalin," purported to give–in eight sessions–a "scientific consideration" of everything from the class struggle through "democracy as the dictatorship of the bourgeoisie" to "revolution versus reform." The announcement of the MIT course, "Scientific Socialism of Marx and Lenin," said that Harry had "spent several years in Germany as a student, where he gained first-hand understanding of the revolutionary working class movement."[32] He might have gained understanding, but it was not "first-hand." After working some two years with the NSL/YCL at Harvard and MIT, he took on a greater challenge: weekly meetings in neighborhoods in the Boston area with high school students and semi-employed or unemployed youth. Success was doubtful: "The turnover was tremendous…. Frankly, it must have been terribly dull."[33] He later doubted the efficacy of his teaching and public speaking. When he joined the NSL/YCL and CPUSA, he may have felt that initial "sense of elation" described by Granville Hicks–an "intoxicating sense of being in the mainstream of history"–but he later discovered, like Hicks, that "party membership was dull as dishwater."[34]

The peace strikes

The students who struck for peace in 1934 and several years thereafter believed that the "fascist tendencies in our own government" would grow if the United States were to become involved in a war.[35] Anti-militarism appeared logical to those who thought that World War I had failed to bring real peace. Robert Gorham Davis, the first academic witness to testify before HUAC, said that his generation "had been taught that the First World War accomplished nothing despite the 4 years of suffering and slaughter. We were determined that another fruitless war of that kind should not occur."[36]

Along with many other student organizations, the NSL endorsed the "Oxford Pledge," a statement passed by the Oxford Union in 1933. The Oxford students affirmed that in no circumstances would they fight for King and country. Participants in the nationwide strikes in the United States recited an American version: "We will not support the U.S. government in any war it may conduct." Despite (or because of) the presence of the Reserve Officers' Training Corps (ROTC) on college campuses, many American students were pacifists: 33% said in a 1933 poll that they would not fight for the United States unless it was invaded; two years later, 81% said they would not participate in a war fought abroad. The United States had joined in World War I in order "to make the world safe for democracy," declared Joseph Lash, but all the war did was "make it safe for J. P. Morgan." In Lewis Feuer's controversial Freudian interpretation, students were revolting against their parents' generation, which had led the United States into the war. Whatever the psychological cause, they were arguing against militarism precisely when Germany was rearming, thus "disarming [themselves] intellectually and physically before the Nazi advance."[37]

With 25,000 participants, most of them on the East Coast, the anti-war strikes were modestly successful in 1934; they expanded to 175,000 nationwide the following year, when the NSL and SLID were joined by organizations with a wider ideological range.[38] In 1934, the 200 Harvard students who participated, ten times the actual membership of the NSL/SLID, were outnumbered tenfold by spectators. The next year, there were 600 Harvard strikers, but this was a paltry number compared to the 3,500 at Columbia. The strikes marked the end of student apathy.[39]

The 1934 strike consisted of walking out of classes held between 11 a.m. and noon (the hour when the United States entered World

War I). At Harvard, a group of cub reporters on the *Harvard Crimson*, the student paper, organized the "Michael Mullins Chowder and Marching Club," a tasteless burlesque counter-force to the NSL demonstrators. Typifying undergraduate failure to engage intellectually with contemporary politics, the Michael Mullins crowd thought it was funny to dress as Nazis, to goosestep, to yell "Heil Hitler" and give the Nazi salute, and to throw eggs and vegetables at the peace strikers. A socialist student magazine noted that whereas the strike organizers had permission to use the steps of Widener Library, the Mullins group did not, "but the authorities at no time interfered with them."[40] Harvard decided that its "fully mobilized" police did not need reinforcements, because there were "only about twenty" in the NSL and SLID. As the demonstration began,

> the Chowder boys appeared in their regalia, one clad in towels, holding his "Down with Peace" sign, another in black robes with a bomb, a Boy Scout tooting a bugle, and leading cheers for "We Want War," and a Nazi-uniformed gentleman who assisted. They presented a medal to our first speaker, Marks, an N.S.L.'er. Marks pulled the boner of growing obviously sore, and the crowd hooted him and booed as they saw he couldn't take it.[41]

Harry's discomfiture–along with that of all but one of his colleagues–was also recorded in a Boston newspaper: "Irving L. Pavlo, a junior, George C. Edwards, and Henry [sic] J. Marks, graduate students, were forced to retire under a barrage of pennies accompanied by verbal heckling." Being struck by pennies–or, in Harry's memory, a cabbage[42]–while speaking for peace was a price worth paying. Lewis Feuer, representing SLID, endured "all sorts of objects whizz[ing] pretty closely to [his] ears." In the most comprehensive list of vegetable missiles (omitting, however, the cabbage), the *New York Times* reported that the "bombardment…of eggs, oranges, lemons, onions, and grapefruit…continued until the Harvard yard police cut off the source of supply in the kitchen of the Harvard Freshman Union" and confiscated "a large quantity of grapefruit."[43]

The foolish ignorance of the Michael Mullins group and their sympathizers was widespread among undergraduates in many universities. The *Harvard Crimson*, which was generally so conservative that it "might well have been titled the Harvard *WASP*," initially sympathized with the Mullins crowd (who were, after all, its own reporters). It changed course in a retrospective article four weeks later. Now it declared that the strikers had won on the moral battlefield, and that spectators were impressed with the courage and sincerity of the strikers and were revolted by the placards and antics of their opponents. The last speaker for the strikers was warmly applauded when he pointed out that while the other side was using the fascist tactics that had triumphed in Germany, the strikers were here to see that those tactics did not win in America; the strike, he suggested, was a dress rehearsal for what students would do should war come.[44]

Anti-war strikes took place in April in 1935-38, each time with a difference. In 1935, when 3,500 students attended the demonstration at Harvard, the Michael Mullins crowd attempted another disruption, but with less success.[45] In 1936, when half a million reportedly participated nationwide, the Harvard administration supported the strike, and Dean Hanford agreed to speak. In 1937, when the causes discussed broadened to include the Spanish Civil War, Hanford introduced the main speaker.[46] At Harvard and elsewhere, these later events were often presented as "Peace Assemblies" and endorsed by university administrators, who thus preempted the radicals.[47] An isolationist peace strike in April 1938 fizzled because of widespread anxiety of impending war.

The left itself was changing. In 1935, the Comintern established the Popular Front so that Communist organizations could join forces with their socialist brethren; the Communists now favored "collective security" to combat fascist aggression. Repudiation of pacifism and isolationism increased; in 1937, the American Student Union, an amalgam of the NSL and SLID, explicitly endorsed collective security. In the 1936 election, the CPUSA supported Roosevelt, whose poll numbers rose at conservative Harvard to 45%. Even so, when World War II broke out, isolationism prevailed among Harvard students. The Nazi invasion of the Soviet Union in June 1941 finally disabled the pacifist hold-outs; in December of that year, after Pearl Harbor, the American Student Union disbanded.[48]

Harry's activist colleagues

Harry cooperated with six CPUSA or YCL workers, whom he named to HUAC: Mack Libby, the YCL district organizer; Sidney Bloomfield, who taught in the CPUSA school; "a repulsive female named Loretta Starr," who taught for the YCL; David (Dave) Grant, Massachusetts State Secretary of the YCL; John (Johnny) Weber, Secretary of the New England district of the CPUSA; and Nehemiah Sparks, the CPUSA district organizer.[49] Libby and Bloomfield do not appear elsewhere in HUAC indexes; Bloomfield, a dedicated CPUSA worker, published in at least one Communist journal and turns up in Diego Rivera's autobiography. A writer and literary agent named John–never Johnny–Weber is mentioned in testimony regarding Hollywood Communists, but this appears not to be the Boston Johnny.[50] Starr, Grant, and Sparks were known to HUAC in its earliest days, beginning in 1937, when it was called the Dies Committee (after its chair, Martin Dies) and conducted a multi-year "Investigation of Un-American Propaganda Activities in the United States."[51]

It wasn't only YCL or CPUSA personnel who operated openly; the half dozen undergraduate and graduate students whom Harry named also conducted their political lives in public. Their exploits were covered in the *Crimson*, which also printed their letters to the editor. There were four undergraduates: Herbert E. Robbins, '35 (PhD '38); Lawrence S. Levy '39; Allen Kellogg Philbrick (of the class of '35, whom Harvard forced out before graduation); and Daniel Boone Schirmer, '37 (known as Boone to foil easy identification with his famous ancestor). Robbins's activities, which continued during his doctoral studies, have already been noted. Levy helped organize the 1936 anti-war strike at Harvard. As described below, Philbrick had a startling moment of fame before being driven out of Harvard. Schirmer became Harry's good friend. The two graduate students were Saul Friedberg, Harvard Law School '36; and Eugene Bronstein, a first-year graduate student in philosophy in 1934-35. William Parry should be included in this group because he continued to conduct himself as a student after receiving his PhD and becoming an assistant in the Philosophy Department.[52]

Of these friends, Schirmer–"Bunny's 'favorite student'"[53]–

seems to have been the closest to Harry and his wife. "I met Boone a couple of times today," Harry wrote to Bunny three days after my birth, and he "commended [the new father] for not going around crowing and boasting about the baby.... Little does he know what self-restraint it takes"; then he brought Schirmer to the hospital to see the wondrous baby. Schirmer, who belonged not only to the NSL at Harvard but also to several other left-wing organizations, was the only member of Harry's political circle to develop a career in the CPUSA; he was, as Harry testified, "a full-time Communist organizer."[54] In 1952 he went underground; he was caught and, in 1954, spent two weeks in jail after being arrested under the Smith Act. When he appeared before HUAC in 1958, he said that he was a self-employed salesman of a "common household item" that he refused to describe, and was not then a full-time employee of the Communist Party; he declined to give any other information about his life aside from his military service and his year of graduation from Harvard.[55] In the late 1950s, affected by the revelations of Stalin's crimes, he began disengaging from the CPUSA, although not from his ideals. In the 1960s, he undertook doctoral studies at Boston University, writing a dissertation on the Anti-Imperialist League in the Philippines. He devoted the remainder of his long life to the cause of Filipino freedom from oppression, whether foreign or home grown. In 2004, still active although in poor health, he received the Lifetime Achievement Award of the Association of Asian American Studies. His death in 2006 at 91 produced an outpouring of loving tributes from Filipino and other colleagues.[56]

Both of the graduate students whom Harry named, Bronstein and Friedberg, fought in the Spanish Civil War. Friedberg, a member of the Lincoln Brigade, was wounded in two battles; Bronstein, Political Commissar of the second section of the George Washington Brigade, lost his life.[57] Despite initial setbacks caused by his Communist activities, Friedberg went on to a career in law. Bronstein, who had predicted that "I'm going to be killed," died in an aerial bombing on 9 July 1937, age twenty-five. He had left Harvard in 1936 to become a union organizer, changing "his attire, hair style, and speech to be as one of the workers."[58] While in Paris en route to Spain, he wrote a joint letter to Harry and Boone Schirmer in which he expressed mild criticism of Harry's devotion to his dissertation.

He scolded Harry that spending dissertation time with "[August] Bebel, [Karl] Liebknecht, and [Franz] Mehring" had caused him to gain weight; and he warned Boone to "watch out that the *study* of dialectics does not become an end in itself."[59] An obituary in the *Harvard Communist*, which he had helped found, said that his death "made complete the integrity of his life."[60] Another Harvard comrade and fellow soldier, Milton Weiner, witnessed his death:

> I don't mind telling you that I cried when the stretcher bearers confirmed his death. He was killed instantly–I saw him and Dave Walba get hit…. As I told Saul [Friedberg], it seemed almost incredible to me that Gene who was so lively & vital could suddenly cease to exist.

The shock did not affect Weiner's commitment; he knew that "if we lick fascism here, we stop its advance in America." He signed off: "Please give my regards to Bill Parry, Boone & Bunny & the baby…. Comradely, Milton." Earlier, three of his colleagues in Spain–Bronstein, Dave Walba, and "Al G.," the latter most likely Alfred Goldenberg–sent two cards congratulating Harry and Bunny on becoming parents. On the back of an elaborately ornamented card reading "Felicidades," they wrote: "From the Massachusetts delegation in the 19th Battalion, to Carol."[61]

Harry, who kept a clipping headlined "3 Yankees Dead in Madrid Fight," first heard of Bronstein's death over the radio. He recalled his "appalling feeling," a sense of "personal responsibility" because he had "induced him to enter the Communist Party."[62] Harry gave himself too much credit: Bronstein was already a left-wing activist as an undergraduate at the City College, where his participation in a "rowdy" pacifist demonstration led to his suspension.[63] Harry's overestimation of his influence may have reflected discomfort with his own waning commitment.

Politics and love

None of Harry's friendships stemming from his political activities survived into the future–except for one. From a personal standpoint, his most important activist colleague was the young woman he married. A poor Yiddish-speaking immigrant, Bunny was what Jews in Germany called an *Ostjude*, a Jew from despised Eastern Europe. She was born in 1913 in a tiny, apparently nameless place known as Long Village, in a part of Russia that is now Ukraine.[64] Her father, Oscar (Usher) Frager, could barely support his family by small trading; occasionally he would buy a cow, have it ritually slaughtered, and sell the kosher meat among the twenty-five or so Jewish families in the village. His sister, who had emigrated to Boston, recommended that he do the same in order to better his family's economic security. About 1909, he set out, leaving behind his wife, Annie, and three children, two of whom died before he returned. He went far, but not where he meant to go: he boarded the wrong boat and landed in Argentina. Three years later, having saved enough to buy a return ticket, he returned home and, while accumulating funds for another try, begot two more daughters in quick succession. He left for Boston in 1914, when the youngest, Eva, was an infant and Bunny (then Sarah) barely a toddler (her twin had died at birth). No sooner had he arrived in Boston than World War I severed all communication with his family.

Then came the Russian Revolution. The oldest child, Vida, about ten at the time, retained vivid memories of the turmoil. Soldiers were quartered in their little house and later pillaged the village. The residents fled to the woods. By the time they returned, the soldiers had slaughtered the family cow, the sole source of income (Annie sold milk products in the nearest town). Cow's blood drenched the feather beds, which the soldiers had ripped apart. Annie sewed her wedding ring, her only possession of value, into the hem of her skirt and arranged to be escorted across the Polish border in the middle of the night. Carrying their shoes and whatever else they could manage, Annie and her daughters walked to the border through the squelching mud, which pulled at their skin as it dried. They were met not by an escort but by thieves on horseback; they had been betrayed. Bereft and weeping, they walked on until they spied a light in a house, where they were given sanctuary and help to reach their relatives in nearby Rovno. The wedding ring acted as cash.

After some years in Rovno, Annie made contact with Oscar through the International Red Cross. At the beginning of 1921, shortly before Congress passed the first Immigration Law, the family was reunited in Boston. Annie, an illiterate Jew without a word of English, was the kind of person who disgusted A. Lawrence Lowell's Immigration Restriction League (see Chapter 2).[65] She found Oscar changed by his years in America; contrary to his Orthodox upbringing, he now smoked. Nonetheless, Oscar and Annie remained observant, as did their American twins, born a year later in the bitterest winter cold. On 30 April 1923, Oscar–age forty-one, five feet three inches tall, with brown eyes and black hair, a "spot on left eye" his "visible distinguishing mark"–became a citizen; since all of the children were under age, they rode to citizenship on his papers. The children became Americans in spirit as well as law, but Oscar and Annie did not assimilate. Oscar's little shops were unsuccessful until Vida, whose capitalist flair overrode her Communist politics, took over.

The three Russian daughters–Vida, Bunny, and Eva–sloughed off most Jewish practices. Like Harry but for different reasons, Bunny was resolutely irreligious for most of the rest of her life. Judaism and poverty may have been associated in her mind. The Fragers were poor in Russia and, in their early years, were poor in America. All four girls went into the business stream in high school. Bunny kept both of her diplomas. The diploma of the Washington Middle School, from which she graduated in 1929, was an elaborate production almost rivaling the City College diploma of her future father-in-law; a less elaborate but still impressive document showed that she had completed one and a half more than the required 100 credits to graduate from Girls High School. For the three intelligent and curious Russians, with college unimaginable, the Communist Party offered an opportunity to learn through classes and through participation. Describing their early political involvement, Vida recalled an "international hall" in Roxbury, the section of Boston where they lived,

> where all the left-wingers used to meet.... And there were people there recruiting members as fast as they could. When they saw someone was interested, right away they recruited you to the Workers School.... This is where your mother met your father. He was teaching at the Workers School.[66]

This would have been in 1934, not long before the demonstration against the *Karlsruhe* that was to have such an effect on Bunny's life. She was twenty-one, and Harry was twenty-five. Although her level of education was far below his, he was spared "the horror of having a dumb" wife that had once come upon him like "an evil vision."[67]

The demonstrations against the *Karlsruhe*

In the two months following the peace demonstration, Harry took part in two anti-Nazi actions. In May he helped lead protests against the *Karlsruhe*, a German warship docked in Boston Harbor; in June, during Harvard's graduation ceremony, he orchestrated a demonstration against Ernst Franz Sedgwick Hanfstaengl, Hitler's liaison with the foreign press. Because Harry's future wife participated in the *Karlsruhe* protest–and, unlike Harry, was arrested and convicted for her activity–some personal history needs to be recounted. It begins with two of Harry's neighbors in his apartment building in Cambridge: Jerry and Frances Olrich, who both belonged to the CPUSA. An old comrade described Jerry as "a handyman for the party"; an FBI informer, calling him a man with "vast experience and prestige in the party," said that he was "a very able Marxist, a well-indoctrinated, hard-core Marxist, and theoretician." Jerry was subpoenaed by HUAC but refused to testify "before a star chamber proceeding like this." Instead, he whimsically invited the committee to "talk about my political opinions" over supper at his home–even though he would "have a lot to explain to my friends" for inviting Republicans. Because he ruled out discussing his work for the CPUSA, the committee declined his invitation.[68]

Some ten years after his HUAC testimony, Olrich learned that one of his former comrades, Sidney Lipshires, had become Harry's doctoral student after publicly defecting from the CPUSA in 1956.[69] Mentioning his adviser to Olrich, Lipshires was surprised to hear that his friend had known Harry in the 1930s as a neighbor, a comrade, and a man who was "very diffident about relations with women." "All the girls liked your father," Vida recalled; "he was a handsome guy, but he was so shy." Olrich had noticed Bunny's interest in Harry and had encouraged him to make a date with her. Not long before the *Karlsruhe* arrived, Harry took his advice.

Flying the swastika, the *Karlsruhe* was–in the proud words of the German Defense Minister–on a mission to make "friends for the Third Reich" by "conducting propaganda for the German nation and the Fatherland." Some thirty groups protested in Boston against the *Karlsruhe*, among them Jewish organizations and the CPUSA and its affiliates. Official Harvard and other elements of Boston's elite, on the other hand, were glad to entertain the officers and crew, who edified their hosts by "loudly prais[ing] Adolf Hitler and the Nazi government." The German cadets and officers gave an "international touch" to Harvard's annual Military and Naval Science Ball, making it "a colorful and distinguished event."[70]

On May 15, three days before the Military Ball, Allen Kellogg Philbrick, the twenty-year-old Executive Secretary of the Harvard NSL, snuck aboard the *Karlsruhe* at night and was caught while "stuffing anti-Hitler propaganda down a blower" on the ship. The crew turned him over to the Boston police, which took some hours to figure out a reason to hold him. Eventually "he was booked as suspicious person and when questioned gave his name as Ibsen," but he eventually admitted his identity and hired a lawyer.[71] The flyers clogging the blower–written "in good German," said the *Boston Daily Globe*–advised the crew:

> German sailors, don't let Hitler lie to you…. His promises are broken daily. Misery grows. Minister of Commerce Schmidt spoke of a coming inflation only [the] day before yesterday. Is that rebuilding? Salvation lies in Communism. The heroic KPD lives and fights; join and fight, German sailors, for a free Soviet Germany. Long live the KPD.

Omitting any mention of Hitler's anti-Semitism, the flyer declaimed further against Hitler's economic policies. The emphasis on economics, consistent with Harry's interests while in Berlin, hints at the authorship. It was indeed Harry who wrote the exhortation, his German so good that Philbrick later recalled him as a German national; the Boston authorities apparently thought the same, for they made no attempt to identify the author. Doubtful how to charge Philbrick, the police released him, but his ordeal was not over. No sooner was he a free man than he was "kidnapped" by a group calling itself the Anti-NSL League and tied up in a room in a Harvard dormitory, from which he escaped after some hours.[72]

Harry spoke publicly in Philbrick's defense, appearing "much more perturbed" than the nonchalant Philbrick: "As far as we know the government of the United States is not run by Adolph [sic] Hitler and distributing anti-Fascist literature cannot be construed as an infraction of law. The N.S.L. opposes Fascism wherever it develops and we support Mr. Philbrick to the utmost in his courageous attempt to present the truth to the German sailors of the cruiser Karlsruhe."[73] Although Harvard did not formally expel Philbrick, as recommended in a letter to the *Crimson*, it accomplished the same end by rescinding his scholarship, so that he could not return for his senior year.[74] In his HUAC testimony, Harry spoke of him as a "very fine young fellow" who surely would have left the CPUSA; he did in fact leave, later earning a PhD and becoming a professor of geography.[75] In August 1953, the FBI interviewed him in the course of its investigation of Herbert Robbins. Even though all of the names are whited out in the FBI transcript, Harry's identity is transparent. Philbrick, who stated that Robbins had recruited him to the NSL, recalled Harry as an "older student...in his twenties" who "read and spoke German fluently"; he identified Harry and Robbins as "very active in the writing" of the flyer. Although Philbrick had not seen Robbins since 1934, he "felt the subject might be still sympathetic to Communism." Six months earlier, however, Robbins had testified cooperatively before HUAC.

Both Harry and Bunny were involved in a major demonstration against the *Karlsruhe* on 17 May, two days after Philbrick's escapade–Harry as the author of a leaflet, and Bunny as its distributor. For her, the involvement took a serious turn when she was arrested. Some two thousand people assembled at the Charlestown Naval Yard, where the ship was docked, a crowd that included many with pro-German views; the *Boston Post* estimated that fewer than 2% of the students present agreed with the anti-Nazi demonstrators.[76] Something happened–a riot, according to the police and initial newspaper reports; brutal police repression, according to the anti-Nazi demonstrators.[77] In a letter to the *Crimson* on 6 June, William T. Parry described how the police derailed an event that had been planned "to consist of speeches and the adoption of resolutions":

[T]he police brutally attacked the people present, driving them off the lot where they were peaceably gathered, into the streets, where the ensuing congestion provided the mounted police with an excuse for charging their horses into the crowd, riding down innocent and helpless men, women, and children.... Some hundred and fifty patrolmen pushed, kicked, cuffed, clubbed, and arrested all who could not get out of their way quickly enough, as well as those whose arrests had been planned because of their previous political activities. In the police station beatings were administered to many of the twenty-one persons arrested.

Parry's account accorded closely with that given in the *Boston Herald*, which was nonetheless unsympathetic toward the protesters. Shouting "Down with Hitler" and other slogans, the protesters managed to distribute anti-Nazi literature, including the leaflet written by Harry. At Harry's UConn memorial, Sidney Lipshires cited his contribution as an example of his principled stand against fascism; it made so little impression, however, that only one person was charged with "distributing handbills without a permit."[78] Vida and Bunny both demonstrated. Vida, who escaped capture, later recalled "the police...on horseback swinging their clubs." Bunny was among the twenty-one arrested on charges of inciting a riot, disturbing the peace, and blocking the sidewalk; all were sent to the Charles Street Jail and released on $100 bond.[79] Bunny was listed in the newspapers as "Bernice Frazer, 21, of 10 Newbury St."; the age was correct, but the name was a disguise, however thin, in accordance with CPUSA instructions. The *Boston Herald* identified her as "assistant organizer, Young Communist League of America."[80] Not being a student, she was ineligible for Harry's NSL; perhaps she drew a salary from the YCL.

The court was full of supporters of the accused when the trial began on 23 May. Not a single police officer who testified said that there had been a riot, but on 29 May the court handed down twenty guilty verdicts. Fifteen of the twenty, including Bunny, were sentenced to six months in the House of Corrections. International Labor Defense (ILD), the CPUSA legal arm, appealed the verdict, and the defendants were free on $1,000 bail, presumably paid by the ILD.[81] Meanwhile, a Harvard student-faculty committee took sworn statements from witnesses and victims. The committee report, introduced by two distinguished Harvard professors, accused the police themselves of "disorderly conduct"; described two of the officers in charge as "neither competent nor intelligent"; and demanded that the police appoint men "intelligent enough to understand the psychology of the people with whom they are dealing."[82] Such sneering gown-vs.-town condemnation had no effect. On 28 November, eleven defendants, including Bunny, lost on appeal; on December 3, nine of the defendants, Bunny among them, were convicted of inciting to riot.[83] Bunny received the smallest punishment, a $20 fine. The defendants, regarding themselves as "political prisoners" convicted on perjured testimony, insisted on going to jail because paying a fine implied acknowledgment of guilt. Prisoners paid the fine by serving time at the rate of fifty cents a day.

Forty days was a long time in personal terms. The Frager sisters were still living at home, and Vida, as the oldest, was the point person. She did her best to conceal the truth from her parents, who had no idea of their daughters' politics. After stalling for ten days, she ran out of lies to explain her sister's absence and went to the CPUSA office to ask permission to pay her sister's fine so that she could avoid a family crisis. The outraged

> woman sitting at the desk–Alice Ward, sitting at the typewriter there–said to me, "Gee, Vida Frager, if you've got so much money, why don't you give it to the *Daily Worker* instead of paying the fine?" I said, "I didn't come to ask you what to do with my money. I came to ask advice."

Rebuffed, Vida went to the Charles Street Jail and paid the fine, but to no avail. Bunny emerged,

> absolutely fuming! She says, "You have a hell of a lot of nerve to pay my fine. You worked against the rules, and I'm not going out of here with the rest of them here. I'm not going out." And so the guard says to me, "Lady, here's your $20 back. If the prisoner doesn't want to go out, we can't make them go out."

Bunny's intransigence was not surprising; she had initially refused to give the probation officer even the most minimal information.[84] As the days stretched on and their mother's questions became ever more pressing, Vida ran into Harry Castaline, a charming young man who had caught her eye during Party meetings. She thought he was Italian and wouldn't violate her parents' wish for a Jewish son-in-law, "but I had my eye on him just the same." He was not "as militant as some of the old-timers," having just joined the CPUSA. Taking advantage of his inexperience, Vida asked if he would do her a favor. Harry, smitten himself, said: "Sure, anything." Vida had learned that prisoners were forced to leave if their fines had been paid. "'Go into the Charles Street Jail,'" she told Harry, "'and say that you want to pay the fine for Bernice Frazer. Give them the money and run out.' That's exactly what Harry did. He went in and paid the fine, and he ran out." The trick worked.

There were consequences to these encounters for both Harrys. Harry Marks sent Bunny a note in jail, proposing marriage; they married the following March. Three months later, the other Harry–a Russian immigrant, as it turned out–married Vida.[85] More immediately, Vida's violation of Party discipline led to her public expulsion during "a big mass meeting of the whole New England district." She was not permitted to speak in her own defense. Some years later, when the CPUSA learned of her activities on behalf of Russian war relief and the Red Cross, it sent an emissary to persuade her to rejoin the fold. She refused.

Bunny's arrest had repercussions many years later because the State of Connecticut required all applicants for state jobs to report any history of arrests, and UConn was then the sole employer in Storrs. She could have gotten away with a lie, since her real name was never in the court records. But lying was not within her moral power. Throughout her life, whether as a Communist or as a staunch supporter of the Democratic Party, she agreed wholeheartedly with the opinion of a conservative Harvard professor of law, Sam Bass Warner. Suspecting that those who were convicted would consider themselves "martyrs" in the cause of free speech, Warner observed that "the way to prevent Communism is not by unjust sentences that corroborate the radical's conception of the unjustice of present society but by ordering that society so he cannot justly complain."[86]

As a kind of pendant to Bunny's story, her future husband was arrested that summer–for littering. "Hope you aren't in jail!" wrote Harry's friend Herman Walker, apparently aware of his arrest. His offense was distributing CPUSA leaflets calling on Boston longshoremen to strike in sympathy with their West Coast brethren, whose eighty-three-day strike was strongly supported by the CPUSA. He gave an account to HUAC:

> I showed up at the time, received my bundle of leaflets, rather nervously stood in the street leading to the hall where the meeting was to be held. The street was virtually deserted. I may have given out 2 or 3 of these leaflets when a Boston police cruiser with two policemen in it came along and arrested me.[87]

Charged with littering, he went to court and pleaded not guilty; he was convicted and sentenced to pay a $5 fine. "On principle," he appealed; as Bunny's future husband, he could hardly do less. The case went to a jury trial at which one of the policemen testified "that the street was…virtually white in snow with the leaflets." He was found guilty; this time the fine was $10, and he paid it immediately. Outside the building he encountered a political rally that had produced "a good deal of trash, leaflets, and the like…. There were plenty of policemen around, and nobody interfered with the distribution of that litter." He concluded that "there was no justice." If he had not been determined to conceal Bunny's arrest from HUAC, he might have compared his experience of leaflet distribution with hers and observed the failure of the police to make anything of the political origins of his leaflets. They were as "Communist" as hers; he, however, was just an isolated leafleter while she was part of a major demonstration.

The Hanfstaengl affair

A month after the visit of the *Karlsruhe*, Ernst Hanfstaengl, known to his friends as "Putzi," returned to Harvard for his twenty-fifth reunion. His remit at the time was to act as Nazi liaison with foreign correspondents, who "rather like[d] him despite his clownish stupidity."[88] He had already connected Harvard with Hitler by composing a march for his boss's pleasure that was based on the Harvard song "Rah, Rah, Rah." Hoping to avoid adverse publicity, he slipped secretly out of Berlin, but news got out that he would arrive in New York on the *Europa*. As Hanfstaengl was photographed giving the Nazi salute aboard the ship, two thousand demonstrators onshore demanded: "Ship Hitler Back" and, referring to the imprisoned Communist leader, "Free Ernst Thälmann."[89] Reporters dogged his every step, whether he was visiting old friends, attending a Red Sox baseball game, or participating in events at Harvard.

Hanfstaengl, who had "follow[ed] the trail of his master like a faithful hound," boasted that Hitler came "directly from prison to my home" after serving his sentence following the 1923 putsch.[90] Over dinner in Berlin in April 1933, he proposed a "simple" method to take care of the Jews; if one Stormtrooper were attached to each of the 600,000 Jews in Germany, "[in] a single night it could be finished"; his interlocutor understood that "finished" meant "the wholesale slaughter of the Jews." In America he equivocated. After attending a ceremony in Harvard Chapel, he assured reporters that the "position of the Jew in Germany is going to be normal, quite normal, before long. Everything is going to be better."[91] When his next comment proved annoying—"Americans are like children. They are very hard to please, but they are good like children"—he deftly changed course: if Americans were "good like children," they were also like them in "never [being] fooled in the end." With reporters and mostly adoring throngs hanging on his every word, Hanfstaengl swept from social event to social event, glorying in the attention: "A steady, pelting rain did not dampen the spirits of the militantly jovial Dr. Ernst Franz Sedgwick Hanfstaengl who, a glass of his favorite gin ever in his hand, sang, played the piano and gave out interviews every half hour"; he "ecstatically described" his Nazi uniform and, with his "booming voice and stentorian laugh," made the day a success. One day he wore a khaki shirt that reminded a reporter of the Brown Shirts. He contributed an overtly pro-Hitler and anti-Semitic statement to a class book.[92]

The day after Hanfstaengl had assured reporters that the situation of German Jews would soon be "normal," a Harvard graduate, Rabbi Joseph Solomon Shubow, encountered him by chance and challenged him to explain the means by which Germany would solve its Jewish problem: "Did you mean by extermination?" Before he could answer, a Harvard police officer "grabbed Hanfstaengl by the arm and proclaimed the interview at an end." Hanfstaengl, airily saying he was on vacation and would not answer such questions, "proceeded to President Conant's house for tea," an event that slipped Conant's mind when writing his autobiography. Rabbi Shubow's prescient question reflected knowledge of an exterminationist tradition in German anti-Semitism that went back some seventy years and grew in force in the 1930s. A year after Shubow confronted Hanfstaengl, Goebbels said that Jews should be "exterminate[d] like fleas and bedbugs"; the simile must have resonated with Germans all too familiar with fleas and bedbugs. Hanfstaengl's evasion was in keeping with Harvard's efforts to counter the protests. Conant described as "very ridiculous" a related demonstration in Harvard Square.[93]

Then came the Harvard ceremonies. The chief marshal of the alumni contingent invited Hanfstaengl to be his deputy on Class Day, but–after objections considered "extremely childish" by the Crimson–unwillingly rescinded the invitation, sorry to violate "the right of free speech and the toleration of all beliefs." President Conant devoted five airbrushed pages of his autobiography to his version of events.[94] He knew, from angry letters written by alumni, that many strongly objected to the presence on campus of a man known as "a close personal and political friend of Adolf Hitler," but he could not bar an alumnus from a gathering run by alumni. Conant shook Hanfstaengl's hand at a reception; he did not, however, reply to his message of greeting from a German professor whom he had known in 1925 and who, he rightly supposed, was a Nazi.

Class Day ceremonies on 20 June gave evidence of American sympathy with the Nazis. Hanfstaengl marched with the class of '09, giving "a few Nazi salutes" to friends, one of which was photographed.[95] Members of the class of 1924 wore "Bavarian peasant costume, complete with lederhosen, long socks, and dark green hats with feathers, [and]...goose-stepped their way around the stadium, their right hands stretched out in Nazi salutes." Parading just ahead of the 300 members of Hanfstaengl's class, the class of

1919 sang: "We haven't seen Hitler in a H— of a while." Five members of '19 bore a placard reading:

FOR CLASS PRESIDENT,
MAX HANFSTANGEL [sic]
FOR CLASS VICE-PRESIDENT
ADOLPH [sic] KEEZAR.[96]

The names alluded not only to Adolf Hitler but to the late Max Keezar, a Jewish merchant on Harvard Square who saved "many undergraduates from nakedness by his reasonable prices on old clothes." The class of 1919 won first prize for signs, the Hanfstaengl/Keezar sign being "the final and most amusing touch of all."[97] Thus far, five days into his visit in the Boston area, Hanfstaengl had escaped any serious "unpleasantness," much helped by his hosts: Harvard police removed protest posters in Harvard Yard as soon as they appeared.[98]

Biding their time, Harry's group and other anti-Nazi forces saved their demonstration for the next day, when Conant presided over his first commencement. Even though Hanfstaengl prudently absented himself, the protest that Harry helped plan went forward. His task was to plant two well-dressed young demonstrators in the women's section of the class of '09. As Conant was winding up his address, they shouted: "Down with Hitler!...Free Thaelmann!" and "Down with Hanfstaengl!" Then, in a *coup de théâtre*, they flung off their shawls to reveal "anti-Nazi slogans...sewn with red ribbons" on the backs of their dresses; with a touch of humor and misspelling, one slogan read: "Free Hambergers."[99] To make more trouble, the young women (who gave false names to the police) chained themselves to the wooden structure and threw away the keys. Police officers quickly freed them, chains still on their arms; at the police station, they asked for cigarettes and "calmly...puffed away." The protest "was undoubtedly bad manners," Harry later commented, redeemed by an admirable motive.[100] He thought that "the effect was probably the opposite of what was desired," but Conant disagreed: "The protesters...had given vast publicity to Hanfstaengl's relation to Hitler–a relation...that Hanfstaengl never denied."

A similar Hanfstaengl-inspired protest took place when

the commencement ceremonies concluded. A young man who "chained himself to the heavy iron picket fence that surrounds the Harvard yard" was joined by six unchained colleagues wearing T-shirts reading "FREE THAELMANN" and carrying placards that demanded Hanfstaengl's expulsion from the United States. The *Boston Daily Globe* observed that "protesting the confinement of Thaelmann,...now awaiting trial for treason by the Hitler regime, indicated that they were of Communist persuasion."[101] "Agitators" in the crowd shouted slogans and distributed stickers signed by the NSL or the Boston Committee to Aid Victims of German Fascism. This time, the police showed restraint, even when the officer who put his hand over the mouth of one of the chained women was bitten. Conant requested that charges be dropped against the two young women whom Harry had recruited. Later, Governor Joseph B. Ely found it in his heart to pardon the other seven anti-Hanfstaengl demonstrators, who were convicted of "disturbing the peace and of speaking without permits," fined $20 each, and sentenced to six months at hard labor.[102]

The amiable Putzi made further trouble for Harvard by offering an annual "Dr. Hanfstaengl scholarship" of $1,000 to fund a student for a year's study in Germany. He announced his generosity at a Berlin press conference, during which he made out a check to Conant. He had been inspired, he said, by the "American energy, character, and idealism" that he had absorbed as a Harvard cheerleader, an activity that he later claimed had also given him the idea of the Nazi salute and shout of *Sieg Heil*. Conant's response to Hanfstaengl's scholarship offer was affected by regret for his own thoughtless behavior the previous year. He had attended a ceremony during which the German ambassador, Hans Luther, had presented an honorary degree from the University of Berlin to Roscoe Pound, the pro-Nazi Dean of the Harvard Law School. To the German government, Conant's presence had implied approval, even though he had refused to speak or to be photographed with Luther or Pound. Another member of the Law faculty, Felix Frankfurter, had condemned Conant for making Harvard premises available for a "Nazi holiday."[103]

Conant used the inevitable rejection of Hanfstaengl's scholarship as a means of pacifying those who had been shocked by Harvard's friendliness to Nazis: "We are unwilling to accept a gift from one who has been so closely associated with the leadership of a political party which has inflicted damage on the universities of Germany through measures which have struck at principles we believe to be fundamental to universities throughout the world"–the very principles that Hanfstaengl purportedly imbibed at Harvard. The *Crimson*, which had earlier suggested that Harvard award Hanfstaengl an honorary degree as an "honor appropriate to his high position in the government of a friendly country," now agreed that Harvard's refusal of the scholarship "was the only weapon with which Harvard could voice its disapproval of the present German system." The change of heart at the *Crimson* inspired the *Harvard Communist* to observe contemptuously that "the editorial chairman of the *Crimson* last year was awarded a year of obfuscation at the University of Heidelberg, where he is at present."[104]

Refusal of Hanfstaengl's gift was not quite the end of the affair. Matthew T. Mellon–a third-year Harvard graduate student with a Harvard master's and a University of Freiburg doctorate–offered a $1,500 scholarship to give "some deserving student the privilege of study in the New Germany which Dr. Hanfstaengl had in mind." Again the Harvard Corporation refused. Hanfstaengl had Mellon's message to him published in a Nazi paper: "As an American citizen I should like to place my service at your disposal, so that your good intentions will be acknowledged in America." The paper found evidence of Harvard's appreciation of the "New Germany": it had permitted Dean Pound's honorary degree, and it had accepted Hanfstaengl's gift of a bust of the composer Christof Willibald Gluck (although it later rejected a bust of Hitler brought by Hanfstaengl). About the same time, Francis P. Magoun, an openly pro-Nazi Harvard professor of comparative literature, cabled his old friend Hanfstaengl to say that Harvard alumni were "ashamed" of the Corporation's refusal of the scholarship.[105]

A scarcely believable event occurred in 1935, when the Harvard administration allowed the German consul-general, Baron Kurt von Tippelskirch, to lay a wreath with a swastika in Memorial Church, below a tablet commemorating four Harvard graduates killed fighting for Germany in World War I. In the same month, Harvard offered Thomas Mann an honorary degree. The offer carried "undoubted political significance," Mann wrote in his diary, because "this is the university that declined the grant from Hanfstaengl." Einstein, by then in exile, also received an honorary degree, to "tremendous acclamation" from the 6,000 people attending the commencement.[106] Neither degree recipient was then aware of Harvard's anti-Semitism. The next year, Einstein refused to attend the tercentary celebrations because of the invitation to German universities

Harvard and German universities under the Nazis

Harvard's ambivalence regarding the Nazi government was evident when it declined to help Jewish refugee scholars during the 1930s and when it dithered in 1936-37 over official representation at German university celebrations. The decision facing Conant when Harvard was invited to participate in the anniversary celebrations of the ancient universities of Heidelberg (1936) and Göttingen (1937) was whether Harvard should "have any truck with these damaged institutions." Conant's response was affected by his personal experience as a scholar shaped by studies in Germany, until then the model for intellectual excellence. He knew about, but did not agree with, the boycott of the anniversary events by British, French, Dutch, Belgian, Swedish, and Norwegian universities. He knew that Heidelberg had fired forty-four staff for "racial, religious, or political reasons" and had Nazified the curriculum in virtually every field. In Heidelberg's summer course in 1936, for example, "an acknowledged expert" taught "The Intellectual and Historical Basis of the Nazi Movement." German universities taught "German physics," "German mathematics," and "German astronomy."[107]

When the question of Heidelberg arose, Conant proclaimed the need to honor "the ancient ties" uniting all universities, and he sent a representative; privately, he admitted that he feared that if he did not, Heidelberg would boycott Harvard's Tercentenary celebrations the same year–as if Harvard would suffer if Nazis refused to attend. The Harvard delegate, George Birkhoff, thoroughly enjoyed the Heidelberg festivities, at which Goebbels, he reported, "spoke briefly and gracefully and appropriately." In his autobiography Conant made a lame attempt at ex-post-facto exculpation: "Not all the eminent professors had been forced to leave," he wrote, failing to say that all Jews, no matter how eminent, had been forced out. He asked plaintively: "Even if one despised the regime in power, should not one be ready to build a scholarly bridge between two nations?" He might have asked how a bridge could stand on so weak a foundation. When an invitation to the Göttingen festivities came a year later, Conant initially intended to send a delegate, again asserting the need to maintain relationships with German universities "even if we dislike what they are doing." Eventually Harvard decided not to send a delegate, but it never "explicitly declined the invitation." Columbia, in contrast, bowed to an intense campaign and publicly announced it would not send a delegate; soon after it condemned the Japanese, Italian, and German "dictatorships."[108]

Throughout the 1930s, Harvard failed to respond to the crises caused by Nazi control of education in Germany and, later, Austria. Under Conant's stewardship, Harvard was pro-German and anti-Semitic, notwithstanding Conant's private professions of disgust at Nazism. When Harvard celebrated its Tercentenary in 1936–scheduled, despite protests, on Rosh Hashonah–it invited representatives of German universities. Conant's selective memory recalled German scholars in attendance who spoke "to each other cautiously when they spoke at all," and he claimed that the presence of several German refugee scholars showed "what the Nazis had already done to German scholarship." According to a recent history of Harvard, "all but one of the invited German scholars failed to show."[109]

The acid test of academic good faith was created by the burgeoning ranks of dismissed German scholars, a thousand of whom were in exile by the autumn of 1933.[110] Earlier that year, shortly before Conant took over from Lowell, the just-founded Emergency Committee in Aid of German [later Foreign] Displaced Scholars began requesting that American universities make room for refugees. Because of the Depression, the committee arranged for subvention of salaries by donors such as the Rockefeller Foundation and stipulated that the academic positions offered would be temporary. Asked to receive some of them, Lowell declined; his refusal was repeated by Conant and the Harvard Corporation. Dietrich Gerhard's brief stay at Harvard in 1936 was among the rare exceptions to Harvard's intransigence. William L. Langer told Carl Schorske, then his graduate student, that he felt impotent "in the face of urgent letters from German scholars requesting assistance in finding jobs."[111] Langer himself went to considerable lengths to help individual scholars, including providing affidavits of financial support, but he could not shake Harvard's resolve. His sympathies were easy to arouse, for he himself was the son of poor German immigrants, growing up "in South Boston under conditions of penury and asceticism that can only be called Dickensian"; although not Jewish, he was otherwise like the undergraduate commuters at Harvard whom Dean Hanford disparaged.[112] There were very few like Langer teaching at Harvard in those days.

When, after the shock of *Kristallnacht*, Harvard belatedly agreed to accept refugee students, it publicly (if obliquely) asserted that most of them would be Gentiles, even though everyone knew that the vast majority of the refugees were Jewish. There were always excuses. Conant invoked academic principles in refusing assistance to fellow chemists. Many "of the distinguished German chemists were Jews," he explained, and giving jobs to them would affect "the prospects of every young man in that branch of academic life." Junior American chemists, he asserted, could not be shunted aside in favor of mid-career German Jewish chemists; it was beside the point that the Germans might well lose their lives if they remained in Europe. Conant's anti-Semitism, which was typical of chemists in both academia and industry, was evident when, in September 1933, the DuPont Corporation asked his professional opinion of a refugee named Max Bergmann. Even though, as DuPont said, Bergmann "had a great reputation" in Conant's field, organic chemistry, Conant advised against hiring him because he was "very definitely of the Jewish type–very heavy." When it came to non-Jewish German chemists, however, the prospects of junior American chemists were irrelevant. In 1935, Harvard offered a position to a biochemist named Adolf Butenandt, who was definitely *not* "of the Jewish type." Butenandt declined the offer, remained in Germany, and in 1936 took the job of a dismissed Jew and joined the Nazi party. At the end of 1938, after *Kristallnacht*, the Harvard Corporation decided to hire no refugees until there was a national policy on the subject and as late as 1940 maintained that any department that wished to hire a refugee scholar would have "to support him to the end of his working life."[113]

The New School in New York founded a "University in Exile" expressly to accommodate refugees; it received more refugee scholars–over 180–than any other American institution. Ironically, this welcome "served as an alibi for the inaction" of other universities. The University in Exile, sometimes called the "German university," responded forcefully to the Nazi assault on Heidelberg University. Speaking at a convocation in 1937, Thomas Mann suggested that the New School adopt as its own the inscription "To the living spirit" that the Nazis had ripped from the building at Heidelberg that Harry had photographed in 1931. Thus, he said, "the 'living spirit,' mortally threatened in Europe, would have a home in this country."[114] And so it did at the New School, the University of North Carolina, and other institutions–but not at Harvard.

Harry and Bunny in love

Events in the public sphere could not repress developments in the private realm. Released so unwillingly from jail, Bunny never returned to her parents' home. She lived for a while with two women friends and then moved in with Harry, whose apartment was already a crash pad for visiting comrades because he had more resources than many of the faithful. When the checks that he regularly received from his oblivious parents were insufficient to buy food for his guests, his future sister-in-law came to the rescue. Undeterred by her expulsion and already a capitalist in a small way, Vida was willing to help the needy in the CPUSA. Her parents paid her $15 a week to manage their small grocery; with her earnings, she bought a car that she used not only for hauling wholesale groceries but also for theft, bringing supplies to Harry after she closed the store.

In March 1935, Harry brought Bunny to New York to meet his parents. Vida later told the story:

> When he...introduced her–oh boy, she [his mother] had to know her history, her background, where she comes from and all that. And your father says he wants to get married. And your grandmother says, "What do you mean–you want to get married? You're not through with school." He

says, "Mother, I love this girl." And so she didn't say another thing. They got the rabbi to come...to their house, and
marry them.

Harry evidently set aside his anti-religious feelings to win his parents' approval. They were married by Cantor Nathan G. Meltzoff
of Congregation Rodeph Sholom, a Reform synagogue on the Upper West Side of Manhattan; Alfred and Deborah Hirschbach were
the witnesses, but no members of Bunny's family were present. In
marrying her, he unwittingly followed the advice of the financial
magnate Jacob Schiff, who advocated "greater intermarriage between Russian and German Jews."[115] Soon after the marriage, Vida
recounted, Louis and Sophie Marks came to Boston, where the
Fragers invited him for the Passover seder. Unfamiliar with Russian Jewish cuisine, "they didn't eat much," and Louis's knowledge
of Yiddish was insufficient to bridge the social and linguistic gap.
Communist or not, Bunny had married into the bourgeoisie and
had to learn its ways. Eventually she did.

Harry was conscious of their class differences. In a letter to his
parents, he joked, "My wife is a stubborn peasant!" Although it
wasn't entirely a joke, he did admire her intelligence: during a visit
to the obstetrician, "most of the time...they talked about the CIO
and the Supreme Court." Two years earlier, the newly wed Bunny
took a job as a waitress in a summer resort. The NSL and CPUSA
permeate the only surviving letter of the many that Harry wrote
her that summer. He was back in Cambridge after several days in
New York, he told her, where he was "half an hour late in reaching
the Ninth Floor," the headquarters of the CPUSA in New York City.
As a consequence, he "couldn't locate the Fraction at all" and didn't
see "Bill or Sparks."[116] Bill may have been a Soviet agent who operated in New York in 1934-36 under that name. Nehemiah Sparks,
mentioned earlier in this chapter, was the district organizer they
had known in Boston.[117] Harry responded to Bunny's requests for
advice on recruiting fellow waitresses to the NSL and for reading
matter that wasn't "incriminating." Pointing out that "it isn't necessary for someone to be interested in politics to be attracted by the
NSL," he said she need only be ordinarily friendly, and "they will
want to visit you in the fall...[and] we will be able to work together

on them at that time." As he had experienced in talking with Engelberg, "it is hard to like a person without acquiring something of his
mental outlook." He did not answer her request for reading matter that wasn't "incriminating" because, after all, that was the only
material worth reading. He mentioned that he had given material
from the *Daily Worker* to Mona Otway, a Grenadian who had been
his family's housekeeper during his childhood, and had promised
to send her "Race Hatred on Trial."[118] A sympathetic lover, he could
"imagine the type of people that you have to fodder," picturing the
guests as "80 year old frickasee chickens." He longed to see her "in
flowering chiffons, high colored heels, with your face decorated to
resemble a blush. After the revolution...." There are other expressions of love, too.

Why Harry and Bunny left

A variety of reasons, some intellectual and some not, led Harry and
Bunny to separate themselves bit by bit from Communism. Bunny's pregnancy, Harry's incomplete dissertation, and their continued dependency on his parents' largesse combined to make both
of them uneasy. Just as Bunny was preparing to give birth, Harry's
gargantuan dissertation staggered to the end of its two volumes.
The oral examination took place on 25 May; a month later, he received his diploma, in Latin but lacking the grandeur of his father's
City College bachelor's diploma.

In order to complete his degree simultaneously with becoming
a father, Harry had to give up most if not all of his political activity. In his HUAC testimony, and again when interviewed a quarter
century later by Ellen Schrecker, he said that Bunny had opposed
his activism because it interfered with his career.[119] He told HUAC
that he had become a "non-Communist" in the late 1930s; however,
he had at least a nominal connection with the CPUSA as late as
January 1939. It was then that he experienced the final shock that
caused him to cease all activity: his father's discovery that he was
a Communist: "That was the point when the roof caved in, so to
speak."[120] Now that his parents knew, he could recount a visit from
faculty of the Harvard School of Education to observe his practice-
teaching class when he had been only three weeks on the job. The

observers were pleasantly surprised by his poise. "I forgot to tell them," Harry wrote, "that one who has been repeatedly heckled in out-of-door rallies by drunks, opponents, and hell-raisers, is not likely to be fazed by a mere thirty kids."[121]

Harry's gradual disengagement was shared by large numbers of American Communists disturbed by events in the USSR in the late 1930s, in particular the show trials and purges in 1936-37 and the Hitler-Stalin pact on 23 August 1939, just before Germany invaded Poland. As we have seen, the American student movement followed a similar trajectory; once it rejected the Oxford Pledge and the pacifism it represented, few similarities remained "between the student movement of 1934-35 and the one of 1937-38."[122] Nonetheless, as long as the Soviet Union was a wartime ally, Harry could not be an anti-Communist. After the war, he testified, Soviet imperialism accelerated the "gradual process, whereby I shed one delusion after another." Other former CPUSA members described a similar sloughing off of interest and commitment. Isadore Amdur's involvement "just faded out"; Norman Levinson "sort of drifted out" of the Party.[123]

When she talked to me in my teenage years, Bunny credited the Soviet purges with revealing the hollowness of Communist rhetoric; in her recollection, my parents left the CPUSA for ideological reasons. Yet at the time of my birth in May 1937, she was very much in the Party, as attested by a number of letters and telegrams on that occasion. The CPUSA itself sent a telegram addressed to "Mrs Harry Marx"–quite likely a deliberate misspelling–that was headed by Western Union, with inadvertent wit, "Social Message": "CONGRATULATIONS YOUR QUOTA FULFILLED STOP PRODUCTION LOVE AND KISSES=CAMBRIDGE BRANCH." A friend in New York named Belle wrote a jokingly affectionate letter on the letterhead of *Social Work Today*: "Tell me child, can she already quote Marx(ks), Engeles [sic], Lenin and Stalin. She ought to know the history of German Social Democracy by heart. What a bolshevik she will be."[124] Such congratulations were apparently the order of the day. Milton Weiner, in his letter describing Bronstein's death, mentioned he had heard from Saul Friedberg "that you are now the father of a young pioneer. Antifascist greetings to the baby." Bunny had plenty of time for letters, phone calls, and visits, for, as was then normal, she was hospitalized for over two weeks. Three days after she gave birth, Harry sent a sheaf of clippings to instruct and amuse her. The subjects included the bombing of Guernica, Mussolini's good wishes to Franco, Communist attempts to control the CIO, and speeches by John Dewey and Goebbels.

Harry and Bunny were among the earliest of the faithful to fall away. Many American Communists–including Bunny's sister Eva and her husband, Alfred Hirsch–either regarded the purges as an unfortunate deviation from pure Communism or assumed that the Western press exaggerated their horrors. Some of those who suffered could not initially understand what was being done to them. Even while he was being interrogated to the point of torture, one victim regarded the purges as "a temporary aberration," and he continued to believe "that the only way to the socialist transformation of the world was through revolutionary dictatorship of the proletariat."[125] After World War II, Harry cast about for some kind of substitute for the shattered ideals. Like so many other former Communists, he became a firm anti-Communist; unlike many, he did penance for his political sins by cooperating with HUAC. His cooperation demonstrated, at least in his own mind, the secular morality and responsibility that had earlier enabled him to adopt a political religion. A year or two after his HUAC testimony, he performed another act of penance, this time for his display of bad manners in the Prague synagogue. He joined the UConn branch of the Jewish student organization Hillel, the only Jewish organization in Storrs at the time. And he took an active part: he peeled potatoes for Hanukkah latkes, sent his younger daughter to Sunday school, and–most astonishingly–allowed himself to be elected president.

The Knock on the Door:
Harry before HUAC

Those who were caught by the great illusion of our time, and have lived through its moral and intellectual debauch, either give themselves up to a new addiction of the opposite type, or are condemned to pay with a lifelong hangover. (Arthur Koestler)

Koestler's reflections on his Communist past–"the great illusion of our time"–were published in a book with a resonant title: *The God That Failed.*[1] Koestler admitted his inability to "recapture the mood" of his experiences as a Communist in the 1930s: "Irony, anger and shame kept intruding; the passions of that time seem transformed into perversions." Other former Communists played variations on Koestler's themes. For Harry, the dominant emotion was not irony or anger but shame, which he kept tamped down until summoned before the House Un-American Activities Committee (HUAC). Another emotion was an anti-Communism that fell well short of an "addiction of the opposite type"; he became a standard-issue liberal Democrat. And as Chapter 8 suggests, he was indeed "condemned to pay with a lifelong hangover," the decades of a generally happy career shadowed by his few years as a Communist.

Part 1. McCarthyism at UConn

The background

As a Congressional phenomenon, McCarthyism began well before its eponym came on the scene, and it lasted well after his downfall.

Senator Joseph McCarthy's assault on civil liberties began in 1950 with his flamboyant announcement that the State Department was a hive of Communists. Early in 1953, he became chair of the newly created Permanent Investigating Subcommittee of the Senate Government Operations Committee, which he made the launching pad of his fervid anti-Communist crusade. Only a year later, his colleagues in the Senate investigated McCarthy himself for improprieties and, on 2 December, formally censured him. McCarthy thus lent his name to a witch hunt in progress before–and fueled by–the Cold War, yet the main actors were others. HUAC, fed vast quantities of "information" by the FBI, led the pack. Ellen Schrecker suggests that if "observers [had] known in the 1950s what they have learned since the 1970s," when FBI files became available under the Freedom of Information Act, "'McCarthyism' would probably have been called "Hooverism," after J. Edgar Hoover, the *éminence grise* of the FBI.[2]

From the time of its founding in 1938, HUAC busied itself with investigating "Un-American Propaganda Activities in the United States." As Chapter 6 has shown, its early investigations uncovered the pre-war activities of four of the six Communist functionaries whom Harry named in his testimony. Beginning in 1946, it evinced a gargantuan appetite for hearings, producing 93,000 pages of testimony and reports by 1960.[3] It held two types of hearings–public, often conducted to the political advantage of its members; and private (in "executive session"), during which it used promises of confidentiality to inveigle witnesses to give it meat for further investigations. "Private" meant nothing. Harry's testimony was published soon after he testified in executive session; Herbert Robbins's was disclosed decades later. Those who appeared before HUAC were not witnesses in the customary sense of the word; rather, they were defendants in what amounted to criminal trials, although they often did not know who had given "evidence" against them, were not informed of the charges until they entered the hearing room, and lacked such safeguards as an opportunity to cross-examine their accusers.[4] HUAC rules prohibited lawyers for the accused from saying anything effective to the committee.

When it came to investigating Communists, HUAC outshone the two Senate committees engaged in similar activities—

McCarthy's Permanent Investigating Subcommittee, and the Internal Security Subcommittee. HUAC's examination of Alger Hiss in 1948 launched the Red-baiting career of a freshman representative named Richard Nixon. Five years later, under the chairmanship of Harold H. Velde, a former FBI agent, it undertook to examine "Communist Methods of Infiltration (Education)" and became the nemesis of colleges and universities across the nation. Velde's enthusiasm for hunting America's enemies was matched by others. President Harry Truman's Executive Order 9835, issued on 21 March 1947, had opened wide the investigatory gates. Establishing a loyalty-security program for all federal employees, it was widely emulated in both the private and public sectors.[5] The FBI already had a long record of investigating left-wing and liberal activities on American campuses. During the 1930s, aided by college administrators, it produced "information on tens of thousands of Depression America's student activists" and, until unmasked in the early 1970s, managed to keep secret its manifold illegal activities.[6] President Harry S. Truman kept to himself his worry that the FBI might become a kind of "Gestapo."

University administrators had to deal with McCarthyism well before McCarthy. In 1949, the year Harry started teaching at UConn's Storrs campus, the FBI "asked a number of selected colleges to report the names of all textbooks and reference books used in courses in history, government, economics, etc." A UConn administrator duly distributed a request for compliance, but–UConn Provost Albert E. Waugh confided in his journal–"many instructors "object[ed] to giving such information and I had a good deal of time taken up with this matter."[7] With the country in the grip of "a new kind of psychosis, a syndrome compounded of fear, suspicion, and distrust of everybody in public and private life," the investigations into professors were intended less "to expose the few Communists in the colleges and universities" than "to foist thought-control upon the teaching profession." To a contemporary commentator, the investigators were "terrorists" and "Inquisitors"–"political gangsters."[8]

HUAC's investigation of intellectuals began in 1947 with the entertainment industry and continued the next year with inquiries into the State Department (Alger Hiss) and espionage (scientists who had worked on the Manhattan Project). Examination of the supposed Red Menace in universities and colleges commenced at the same time, and a number of states created committees on the HUAC model. In February 1951, the FBI inaugurated its "Responsibilities Program" to identify "Communist or subversive elements" in public employment and pass the information on to state governors and other public officials.[9] It was this program, which ran until March 1955, that led to the investigations at UConn described in the next section. By the time HUAC ran out of "more glamorous targets" and began aiming at academia, many erstwhile liberals agreed with conservatives that Communism posed a danger to the nation.[10] In his journal, UConn's Provost Waugh distinguished between "communism" and "Communism": the latter implied a parrot-like assent to the views of others; the former was a set of beliefs, however "strange and different or even repugnant," to which anyone had a right.[11] Waugh's distinction was far too subtle for nearly all liberals–including, as we will see, Harry.

At its thirty-ninth annual meeting, in March 1953, the American Association of University Professors (AAUP) passed a set of resolutions on academic freedom that gave with one hand and took with the other. Declaring that any teacher who "misuses his classroom...for propaganda practices, or for the advocacy of legally defined subversive action...should be dismissed," it tiptoed gingerly over the protection against self-incrimination afforded by the Fifth Amendment.[12] Yet it also called "for more, not less, freedom to inquire and to express conclusions reached," and it condemned "political tests, standards of conformity, and inquisitorial procedures" as "dangerous enemies of a free society." Such statements had little effect on university leaders.[13] An AAUP resolution endorsed firing untenured faculty only "if reduction of...personnel is unavoidable," leaving the definition of "unavoidable" to administrators on the ground. At UConn, the local AAUP chapter refused the request of an endangered physicist, Paul Zilsel, to bring his case to the attention of the national organization, but it did ask the president and the Board of Trustees to assess "professional competence and personal integrity...on the basis of evidence of actual conduct"–words that fell on deaf ears.[14]

The inquiry at UConn in 1953 did not come out of the blue. Six years earlier, a campus policeman had eagerly assisted an FBI

inquiry into a newly established chapter of American Youth for Democracy, the organization that had replaced the YCL about 1943.
Soon after, UConn administrators forbade a student group from inviting the eminent African American scholar W.E.B. DuBois, whose
Communist sympathies were well known. In September 1947,
UConn President Albert Nels Jorgensen devoted his convocation
address to the threat of Communism. In 1949, HUAC's request for
book lists, mentioned above, cast a "spiderweb of loyalty, anti-sub-
version, and anti-Communism...over Storrs." [15]

These and other intimations of McCarthyism in academia came
to a nationwide climax in 1953. In a statement typical of university
administrators, President Millicent McIntosh of Barnard argued
that any Communist teacher who took "orders from the Kremlin...
[was] not fit to teach because he [was] not free"; she called upon
colleges to "take the responsibility to do their own house cleaning,
[so that] Congress would not feel it has to investigate."[16] Colleges
took that responsibility, but Congress investigated anyhow. Ellen
Schrecker, the leading authority on the Red Scare in academia, estimates that about a hundred academics were fired as a result of
congressional hearings.[17] This figure does not include the hundreds
of others whose careers were interrupted, truncated, or ruined as a
result of local investigations at private and, particularly, public universities–their names unknown outside of their immediate peers,
their fates forgotten.[18]

Accusations at UConn

Four members of the UConn faculty–Paul Zilsel of Physics, Emanuel Margolis of Government, and Harold Lewis and Robert Glass
of the newly formed School of Social Work–were anonymously accused in March 1953 of being, or having been, Communists. Zilsel
had indeed belonged to the CPUSA, but none of the others had.
Lewis's FBI file illustrates the kind of "evidence" used to build a
case against an alleged Communist. The accusation originated in
a memo sent in February 1952 by the New Haven office of the FBI
to the Washington headquarters, recommending that Lewis's associations with "known Communists in Connecticut" be further
investigated. Nothing in the file supports this charge. On 20 March

1952, J. Edgar Hoover gave the go-ahead for an inquiry that also snared Lewis's wife, Celia, in its net. FBI offices in New Haven, New York City, Newark, Pittsburgh, Omaha, and St. Louis provided "evidence," including the misidentification of Lewis with another man of the same name who had allegedly signed a supposedly Communist petition. Lewis himself had signed petitions sponsored by left-wing organizations labeled Communist fronts by the FBI; he had subscribed to *Jewish Life*, which was on the HUAC Guide to Subversive Organizations and Publications; and–like Robert Glass–he had studied at the University of Pittsburgh with Marion Hathway, whose leftist views attracted false charges that she was a Communist.[19] In April 1952, a handwritten note by someone signing himself "Loyal Citizen" insisted that Lewis "was and still is active in the Communist Party." Loyal Citizen got one thing right (or nearly right). He identified Lewis as having changed his name from "Lasikoff" to Lewis. He had indeed changed it from Losikoff in 1943, when he was serving in the army. Toward the end of the war, as Lewis, he was granted security clearance. In October 1952, he was placed on the FBI Security Index, a list of supposedly dangerous subversives to be picked up and put in concentration camps if the government declared a state of emergency.[20]

Lewis's FBI file is a farrago of mostly irrelevant facts, baseless allegations, and outright contradictions. Aside from assertions regarding his activities at the University of Pittsburgh–impossible to verify because of deletions by the FBI censor–most of the supposed information was useless to the FBI. Some of the investigations led to dead ends. The Omaha office could find no "indication he was affiliated with or in sympathy with the Communist Party." "Reliable Confidential Informants" in New York "possessed no information" at all. In one file we learn that an informant in Connecticut claimed that Lewis had belonged to the CPUSA in West Hartford in 1948-49, when he actually lived in Omaha; another informant said he had belonged to the CPUSA in Queens, New York, in 1947, when he lived in Pittsburgh. "All Confidential Informants utilized in this report are of known reliability," wrote the New Haven office. That office asserted he was "in frequent contact with known Communist Party members"–but wrote immediately after: "Confidential informants familiar with...Communist Party activities in the Hartford area, report that the Subject is unknown to them." Despite reports in 1952 that seemed to absolve Lewis, Hoover asked the New Haven office on 28 January 1953 to convey orally the charges against Lewis to Governor John Davis Lodge and to instruct Lodge "that none of the information furnished can be attributed to the FBI."[21] Seven weeks later, having assembled "information" about the other three UConn faculty members, the FBI swung into action.

Shortly before 17 March 1953, four short, undated documents, "blind memoranda" produced by the FBI under its Responsibilities Program, were hand-delivered to Governor Lodge's office.[22] A common means of accusing suspected Communists, such memoranda rendered the viewer "blind" because no one could see where they came from: there was no letterhead, no return address, no signature. Based on "information" gathered through wiretaps, break-ins, and similar illegal methods, the memoranda were designed to encourage the governors, university presidents, and other prominent individuals who received them to cooperate with the FBI in order to avoid publicity.[23] On 17 March, in the presence of an FBI agent, Lodge summoned President Jorgensen, showed him the memoranda, and demanded that he fire the four men. Jorgensen refused on the grounds that he had to preserve university autonomy in matters of personnel. Jorgensen's stand took considerable strength because, he told Provost Waugh, Lodge "was extremely emotional and almost incoherent":

> The Governor raged and stamped, pacing the floor and swinging his arms and shouting. He wanted the President to dismiss them forthwith–no suggestion of a hearing, or the right to defend ones-self, or anything of the kind.... And throughout the whole three and a half hours the entire group sided with him with the exception of [the governor's legal adviser] Charlie House.[24]

Waugh privately thought the memoranda on Glass and Lewis were "the worst form of gossip and informer's cheap talk,...no more worthy of attention than an anonymous letter."[25] Such opinions were inconsequential; in the end, Jorgensen would do Lodge's bidding. All over the United States, university administrations and the FBI cooperated in a "symbiotic relationship."[26]

On 23 March, five days after Lodge received the blind memoranda, the UConn Board of Trustees formulated a policy for dealing with Communists: UConn would not hire or retain any known Communist, and it would fire anyone who failed "to cooperate in instances of alleged or reported subversive associations."[27] The resolution stated that taking the Fifth Amendment would cause "damage to the entire university and to the profession"; a faculty member must "state his position with respect to the Communist Party in the spirit of truth and courage upon the basis of which intellectual freedom is justified and valued." Anyone who refused to cooperate, whether or not proved to be a Communist, would be fired in order to protect "the freedom of all of us."

The Committee of Five

It was at this point that Jorgensen requested the University Senate to appoint a five-member committee to look into the charges and make recommendations to the Board of Trustees; he wanted to maintain institutional control over the firings demanded by Governor Lodge.[28] When Harry was approached to serve on the Committee of Five, Provost Waugh recorded in his journal, he "refused on the ground that he had himself been a Communist and had in the past been investigated in New York. President Jorgensen will come close to apoplexy when I tell him this!"[29] Presumably Harry anticipated that his Communist past might come to light, and he wanted to control the way his employer learned of it. Harry had not, in fact, been investigated in New York; perhaps he had told Waugh about the anonymous phone call that alerted his father that "Harry Marks is a Communist," and Waugh mistakenly thought that the phone call implied an investigation.

In addition to Harry and the four men examined by the committee, one other UConn faculty member had reportedly been a Communist. This was Elmer Luchterhand, a sociologist, who resigned in February 1953. Waugh was relieved: if this case had come "to a showdown," he wrote in his journal, "we would insist on his right to state his own side of the case, and, as I urged again on President Jorgensen yesterday, a man has a right to be a communist if he wants to."[30] President Jorgensen did not agree, but Waugh's gentler and nobler approach was to some extent reflected in the proceedings of the Committee of Five.[31] The committee hoped that those being investigated would speak openly to their peers; however, the two accused members of the School of Social Work refused to cooperate with what they perceived as an illegitimate inquisition. Even so, the committee members were courteous and avoided the antagonistic atmosphere that prevailed when unfriendly witnesses appeared before HUAC.

Unlike the proceedings in a somewhat similar situation at the University of Washington, at UConn the accused attended committee meetings only to testify in their defense; they did not have lawyers.[32] After exhaustive and exhausting meetings from March 30 to June 15, the committee concluded that no charges had been proven against any of the four, and they should all be retained on the faculty. Although Waugh agreed with the Five, Jorgensen did not. He knew it would be easy to get rid of the three untenured men. Waugh advised Margolis, who was in his final semester of a two-year appointment, to let his appointment expire quietly on the contractual date, September 15.[33] Taking Waugh's advice, Margolis entered Yale Law School that fall. Lewis and Glass, just recommended for tenure by Dean Harleigh B. Trecker of the School of Social Work, received terminating appointments giving them a final year at UConn.[34] The problem was Zilsel, who had tenure and was highly respected not only in the UConn Department of Physics but among physicists nationally and internationally. He was the only one of the four accused who had been a Communist, and he had principles.

In Zilsel's case, UConn followed the practice of many institutions, which forced tenured faculty out without explicitly firing them. Zilsel was remarkably above board. He went to Provost Waugh on 13 March to tell him he had just been subpoenaed by HUAC.[35] He freely admitted to Waugh and, later, to the Committee of Five that he had belonged to the CPUSA in 1946-48. He refused to repeat this statement before HUAC, however, because that committee would have demanded that he name names, something for which he had an "extremely strong moral revulsion." During his childhood in Nazi-ruled Austria, he told Waugh, it had been "very strongly impressed on him...that it was absolutely unforgivable to inform on others in political matters." His refusal to testify in Washington cost him his job at UConn. He resigned under overwhelming pressure, the preferred method with which American universities coped with the crisis.

The Committee of Five listed examples of faculty at six other institutions who testified with "candor and frankness," without recourse to the First or Fifth Amendments.[36] Non-tenured faculty at public institutions, which were funded by state legislatures buffeted by political winds, could ensure their jobs only by talking freely about former associates, even though they might not have had contact with them in years. Harry shared Zilsel's distaste but not his moral courage. Many years later, he chaired a subcommittee of the UConn Senate that wrote the university's regulations on dismissal–"among the strongest of their sort in the nation," according to a testimonial honoring his retirement. No doubt he recalled how easy it had been to dismiss his colleagues in the McCarthy era.

Zilsel's testimony

Zilsel's experiences with McCarthyism contrast in several ways with Harry's. First, unlike Harry, he had been outed as a Communist before his politics came to anyone's attention at UConn. He had been denied research clearance when he was a graduate student at Yale and forced to resign a postdoctoral fellowship at Duke because he could not sign the required anti-Communist affidavit.[37] Second, it was the blind memorandum given to Lodge that brought him before the Committee of Five, which had no such prompt to question Harry even though they knew he had been a Communist.[38] Third, Zilsel refused to name names to HUAC, and he suffered the consequences.

Zilsel was the first of the accused to appear before the Committee of Five, on 9 and 10 April, less than two weeks prior to his HUAC testimony.[39] The committee asked him to comment on the three charges contained in the blind memorandum: (1) that while a student at the University of Wisconsin in 1943-45, he had been Chairman of the local chapter of American Youth for Democracy, the same group that had attracted FBI attention at UConn in 1947; (2) that while a Yale doctoral student he belonged to both the CPUSA and the John Reed Club; (3) that he belonged to the CPUSA while a post-doctoral researcher at Duke. Correcting the dates, Zilsel said he had joined the CPUSA at Wisconsin in 1946 and had been expelled in 1948 while at Duke "for violent disagreement with party policy."[40] He had had no contact with the CPUSA or any front organization since then and declared "emphatically" that he would have nothing to do with any such group. He then discussed his "dilemma" with regard to HUAC, with which he wanted to cooperate, but without losing his personal integrity. The committee report summarized:

> If "cooperation" meant that he had to "turn informer to save his own skin," if it meant answering every question under threat of losing his position, and if it meant that he was not permitted in any way to determine for himself what was right and decent, he...could not conscientiously cooperate. He would not sell his soul to save his reputation or his job. He felt that such "cooperation" smacked more of fascism or Communism than of democracy.

Zilsel was glad to cooperate with his colleagues, however. On 12 April, he willingly wrote and signed a statement that he had "not been a member of the Communist Party, formally or in any other way,...since the fall of 1948." Dozens of his colleagues and students in the Department of Physics testified and wrote to the Committee of Five to express their admiration for him as a teacher, researcher, and person of integrity. Harold P. Knauss, the department chair, said that Zilsel's membership in the department had not hindered it from receiving classified government contracts–always a worry with physical scientists–and insisted that his "dismissal...would have a serious effect on the morale of the other members of the Department and would do incalculable damage to the prestige of the University."

Then came the HUAC hearing, on 22 April, attended by two of the Five. In a feat of wishful thinking, they informed their colleagues on their return "that Mr. Zilsel's attitude and behavior... made a decidedly favorable impression upon others, and added rather than detracted from the prestige of the University"–a key consideration for a public institution. On the contrary, however, the

Hartford Times reported on 24 April that Velde considered Zilsel uncooperative. Velde thought optimistically that he might change his mind and name names if UConn denied him permission to teach. UConn cooperated. Velde was wrong.

Zilsel was neither a fully "unfriendly" witness (refusing to say anything) nor a fully "friendly" witness like Harry (answering questions and offering unsolicited observations). His views accorded with those expressed by the prominent playwright Lillian Hellman in her response to a HUAC subpoena on 19 May 1952: "I am most willing to answer all questions about myself…. But…I cannot and will not cut my conscience to fit this year's fashions."[41] This position, known as the "diminished Fifth," ordinarily deprived the witness of the safeguard of the Fifth Amendment because witnesses who agreed to say anything at all were deemed by investigating committees and the courts to have waived all privilege against self-incrimination and were therefore required to answer all questions. To Hellman's surprise, she was simply dismissed, probably because HUAC "didn't want to tangle with" a high-profile witness. Zilsel emulated her stand, in full knowledge of the likely consequences: if he took the Fifth, or the diminished Fifth, Waugh told him, "pressure for his removal…would be very strong."[42]

Asked whether he had ever belonged to the Communist Party, Zilsel answered that he was "not now a member" but would not respond to the question whether he had ever belonged "because to answer it would tend to degrade me…. I am pleading the privilege of the fifth amendment because I do not want to be put into a position where I have to inform on people whom I consider to be perfectly innocent."[43] Zilsel's stand was echoed by other semi-friendly witnesses struggling to speak honestly about their own pasts while not incriminating others. Sigmund Diamond, a young tutor at Harvard who had belonged to the CPUSA in the 1940s, told his employer that if subpoenaed he would not name names; as a consequence, he was not reappointed.[44] That was at Harvard, a private institution lionized by many liberals because it had refused to fire the physicist Wendell Furry even after McCarthy's notorious denunciation of Harvard as "a smelly mess." [45] As a public university, UConn had much less leeway.

Zilsel's ordeal intensified after his HUAC testimony. The next day, Governor Lodge read the newspaper accounts and phoned Jorgensen to demand that he suspend Zilsel immediately–an idea that had already occurred to Jorgensen and Waugh when they heard that Zilsel had refused to answer certain questions.[46] Jorgensen immediately wrote to Zilsel to notify him that he was "suspended... effective immediately and pending receipt of transcripts of your testimony yesterday in Washington and final consideration by the Board of Trustees."[47] When Waugh phoned with the bad news, Zilsel had just returned from the hospital "with his wife and newborn baby daughter." Waugh, suffering from "a miserable throbbing headache, caused...by the mental turmoil over Zilsel's case," felt that he and Jorgensen had been "badgered by the governor's hysteria and unreasonableness into precipitate and unwise action," yet even he "finally became convinced that the suspension was necessary as the lesser of alternative evils."[48] On his own, he would not have suspended Zilsel. The voice of a decent man was drowned out by "the governor's hysteria."

The next day Zilsel came to see Waugh, who explained "the terms of his suspension," which were close to ostracism: "He was not to attend classes. He might use his office on the south campus if he would use reasonable diligence not to come in contact with students. He might get his mail at the main physics office, etc. His pay would continue."[49] The Committee of Five recommended that the suspension be rescinded. Instead, Jorgensen told Zilsel that it would be "helpful" if he resigned. A further incentive came on 1 May, when the agency funding his research wrote to Jorgensen asking "that no expenditures beyond those irrevocably committed be made" from the grant and that all unspent money be returned. The reason: his refusal to name names "raises grave doubts in our minds concerning his objectivity of thought."[50]

Four weeks after Zilsel's testimony, George E. McReynolds, Dean of the Faculty of Arts and Sciences, came forward to report a visit he had received in 1952 regarding Zilsel's views on the Korean War. According to the complainant, Stanley Grean of the Department of Philosophy, Zilsel thought that South Korea had invaded North Korea and that the United States was guilty of "imperialist aggression" (this was the position of Emanuel Margolis). When the admittedly "emotional" Grean repeated his accusation to the Committee of Five, the committee's interpretation was that Zilsel was "an independent thinker rather than a Communist."

Zilsel's maltreatment by Velde and Jorgensen is particularly repellent given his personal history, which he detailed movingly before HUAC. Born into a Jewish family in Vienna–his father, Edgar Zilsel, was a distinguished sociologist of science at the University of Vienna–he left Austria with his family in 1938 and arrived in the United States in 1940, becoming a citizen in 1945.[51] The Zilsels had to leave Austria after the Anschluss "partly because we were Jewish and partly because of my father's political opinions, which were not acceptable to the Nazis." To Zilsel, America was "the country with liberty…the country of Jefferson and Lincoln," but the anti-Communist hysteria made him fear that "what happened over there in Germany could also happen here."[52] Like Harry, he had joined the CPUSA because he thought that the Communists were the strongest force in the fight against fascism in Europe. By the time of his testimony, though, he no longer believed that Communism was a bulwark and was "a very puzzled man," uncertain how best to defend democracy. This honest statement of bewilderment could not have endeared him to Velde and his colleagues, whose defense of "freedom" he implicitly identified as proto-fascist. This was the view of several articles in the *AAUP Bulletin* alleging that government control of universities was "a distinguishing characteristic of every totalitarian society."[53]

Zilsel's remaining nine months at UConn continued with shilly-shallying on all sides. In July, he met to explain his HUAC testimony to the Board of Trustees, which then voted six to five to undo his suspension–a decision then countermanded by their censuring him for refusing to cooperate with HUAC.[54] In November, still under suspension, he wrote to Provost Waugh that it was "courageous" of the Board to maintain his tenure; he said that it had acted "responsibly" and had come as close to "political sanity as could reasonably be expected from a state university."[55] He was looking for a way out; he worried that his students would be tainted by association with him even if he were completely reinstated. In March 1954, having obtained a position in Israel, he resigned.[56] Then, miserable in Israel, he asked to return to UConn and was refused: "It was one thing to protect tenure during the McCarthy era; it was another to welcome back predictable trouble."[57] He did come back to the United States before too long, obtaining a position at Case Western Reserve University, and carried on his career. Looking back at that period some twenty-five years later, Harry wasn't sure whether UConn had behaved as "well to him [Zilsel] as it should have, but I think our record in civil liberties was admirable."[58] What he meant was that he was not harassed. He overlooked everything connected with the Committee of Five.

Emanuel Margolis: a reminder from the past

Harry knew Zilsel only as a colleague and presumably did not know Glass and Lewis at all, since the School of Social Work was not on the main campus in Storrs but in Hartford. He had a personal connection with Margolis, who leaned strongly left but never joined the CPUSA. He had just completed a Harvard PhD dissertation on "Certain Aspects of the Impact of Communism on International Law," and a mutual friend in Cambridge who supposed that Harry had retained his Communist sympathies suggested that Margolis contact him. In spring 1952, Margolis's second semester at UConn, he invited my parents for the evening. It was a disaster. The next morning, my mother told me of their distress at Margolis's assumption that they shared his ardent admiration of the Soviet Union.

Writing his memoirs half a century later, Margolis remembered the evening vividly.[59] A veteran of World War II, in which he was wounded and earned a Purple Heart, he had admired "the heroic role played by the Soviets" in the war and suffered from what he later admitted was "Russophilism (political infantilism might be more accurate) of the most naive kind." Countering his host's romanticism, "Marks had extensive knowledge about the Stalin regime"–he was then teaching Russian history–"and minced no words about it." One example, which Margolis remembered inaccurately, was "the latest instance of Stalin's growing paranoia–the 'Jewish doctors plot'" to poison the Soviet leadership. Harry must have cited other instances of Soviet anti-Semitism, however, since the Doctors Plot, a notorious hoax, was not announced until January 1953.[60] The argument grew hot, Margolis "defending the indefensible" and "Marks and his wife leaving our apartment very angry at us, particularly me, a Jew defending blatant anti-Semitism." Margolis, the son and brother of rabbis, later shed his illusions after Khrushchev's 1956 denunciation of Stalin. The "party line," he wrote, "was a cruel joke played on many socialists, pacifists, idealists, artists and intellectuals."

That evening had repercussions of which Margolis was unaware until I visited him on 8 March 2006. Very soon after Harry and Bunny stormed out of Margolis's home, Harry phoned Curt Beck to say that he had something "very important" to tell him about Margolis, his colleague in the Department of Government. Beck, who had been raised in Prague, was about to take a leave to work on Czech Communism as a State Department intelligence analyst. Harry felt that, given the political hysteria in Washington, Beck should know that Margolis was a Communist.[61] Beck objected that Margolis's critique of the Korean War "did not make him a Communist" and asked for evidence. Harry simply said, "Take my word for it." When Beck told his wife about "this rather unpleasant discussion," they agreed to keep the matter quiet "and to ascribe the episode to the politically charged atmosphere."

Although Harry had no further evidence to corroborate his suspicions, he "reluctantly felt obliged to give...certain information regarding Mr. Margolis' Communist associations" to Dean George McReynolds. In turn, McReynolds informed the Committee of Five (on 19 May) that he had learned of Margolis's views on the Soviet Union from a "man of common sense" who was "competent to recognize the Communist Party line since he is well-grounded in Marxist doctrine." Nine days later, the Committee of Five heard from Harry himself about the evening at the Margolis home. Margolis had already been named by the FBI, so Harry's wrong information did not alter his colleague's fate. As he enacted McCarthyite behavior, he had no idea that a year later the miasma of McCarthyism would spread over him.

Margolis and the Committee of Five

The blind memorandum about Margolis–based, it said, on "reliable sources"–asserted that he had joined the CPUSA in 1947 as an undergraduate at the University of North Carolina (UNC). When he appeared before the Committee of Five on 23 April, Margolis analyzed the origin of this falsehood; his testimony was corroborated by a UConn colleague who had been teaching at North Carolina when Margolis was a student. Both men suggested that those who smeared Margolis at UNC wanted to put the university's president, Frank Graham, "on the spot" for his outspoken opposition to racism and anti-Semitism (he had been a strong supporter of German refugee scholars). When Dean McReynolds asked for evidence of Margolis's CPUSA membership, the FBI did not reply.[62]

Between 15 May and 3 June, ten members of the Department of Government testified about Margolis before the Committee of Five. About half thought that his views were close to those espoused by Communists; the opinions of the others ranged from neutrality to mild expressions of tolerance. The department head said that no students had complained "that Mr. Margolis...upheld a strong Communist position in the classroom."[63] On 28 May, Harry came before the committee. He said that he had been invited to Margolis's home in the mistaken "belief that his own views were similar" to his host's and had been "extremely disturbed" by "the Communist line" expressed by Margolis and his guests. He recalled Margolis's "highly critical" assessment of American foreign policy in the Far East (a reference to the Korean War) but did not mention their argument about Soviet anti-Semitism, which stuck in Margolis's mind for decades.

When, after Harry's remarks, the Five invited Margolis to testify again, he refused, saying that "it was against his scruples to 'defend himself.'" His colleagues Norman Kogan, Louis Gerson, and Curt Beck–whose professional interests intersected with Margolis's–met with the Five on 29 and 30 May. Noting that he was very popular with students, they agreed that he espoused a "Communist line"; Beck, however, insisted that Margolis's ideas did not prove him to be a Communist. To illustrate Margolis's bias, both Kogan and Beck cited his talk in March 1952 before the International Relations Club. His discussion of American policy toward China was, Kogan asserted, a "vitriolic, one-sided attack on the United States." As Margolis had remarked at the outset, "any attitude in this country which is not anti-China is likely to be considered un-American," an observation illustrated by his colleagues' judgment of him.[64] Condemning the State Department for behaving as if "a country numbering 450 million does not exist," he said that "neither recognizing nor reckoning with Communist China" was "complete unrealism" and would, indeed, throw it "into the arms of the Russians." This *Realpolitik*, which his colleagues deprecated as "unscholarly" and "emotional," was adopted eighteen years later by Richard Nixon, who went to China and brought the country around to Margolis's view. Margolis emerged from this ordeal intact. After graduating from Yale Law School, he had a fulfilling career as a lawyer, taught law part-time, and was active in the American Civil Liberties Union.

The risky profession of social work

In the blind memoranda, a "confidential informant of unknown reliability" reported on Glass, while "reliable sources" reported on Harold and Celia Lewis. The memoranda claimed that all three associated with "known Communist Party members" in the Hartford area. On 18 March, the day after learning of the memoranda, Jorgensen and Waugh visited Harleigh Trecker, Dean of the School of Social Work, told him of the charges, and demanded that he suspend both men "immediately and that their salary be placed in escrow."[65] The "flabbergasted" Trecker, doubting that either man was in any way subversive, could only speculate on the origins of these lies. Perhaps they had unwittingly encountered Communists in the course of their social-work practice, which "inevitably brings them in contact with many types of underprivileged persons." Perhaps Lewis had been tainted by association with Marion Hathway at Pittsburgh.

After informing Trecker, Waugh and Jorgensen went on to ambush Glass and Lewis separately, giving each the impression that he was "to see Trecker on some routine matters affecting the school." Instead, the two officials questioned them "regarding their political beliefs and affiliation."[66] They saw Glass first. Jorgensen said: "I merely want to ask you a question or two. First, are you a Communist?" Glass inquired the reason for the question; Jorgensen refused to answer, and they went back and forth again. Glass boldly "reminded us of the importance of protecting staff members against inquisitorial and star-chamber methods." The inquisitors met a less hostile reception in Lewis's office. Waugh's account is worth quoting at length:

> He [Lewis] asked: "To what do I owe the honor of this visit?" The President replied, "I have a couple of questions to ask you. Are you a Communist?" Lewis was obviously surprised to be asked, but replied at once, "No." The President continued, "Have you ever been a Communist?" Lewis replied. "No. I have not. But why do you ask?"

The President explained the charges in the blind memorandum, including the allegation

> that both Lewis and his wife had been active Communists before coming to Hartford and had continued their active affiliation since. Lewis expressed shocked surprise, and we talked briefly about the current hysteria on the matter.... Lewis said...that he knew there was a tendency today to accuse people through "guilt by association", etc. He would welcome any investigation of his past activities and associates. He had nothing to hide.

On the drive back to Storrs, Waugh told Jorgensen that "Glass's reaction might well be perfectly natural for an innocent man," and remarked that had he been in Glass's shoes, "I would myself have been antagonized if someone had bluntly asked me the same question." As for Lewis, though, his apparent candor might have been nothing more than a cover, for "an active Communist...might have no compunction in lying about the situation." Waugh's only certainty was "that we had nothing which any competent, calm, dispassionate body would think of as proof. The President agreed."

When Trecker met with Glass later on same the day, he found him "deeply disturbed" and "despondent"; Lewis, too, was "extremely upset." Rallying to their defense, their colleagues told the Committee of Five that the ambush contravened UConn bylaws and "constitutes a dangerous precedent, as it in effect introduces a loyalty investigation procedure." Both men refused on principle to answer any questions from the committee regarding their politics. The Committee of Five found no evidence of their culpability, but their conclusion had no effect on the Board of Trustees. As Waugh noted bitterly in his journal, the board believed "paid informers of the state police and the FBI" who claimed that Glass and Lewis were "still attending Communist meetings in Hartford." Waugh "pointed out that this was 'police evidence', which the men had never had a chance to rebut."[67]

Ever thoughtful, never heard, Provost Waugh reflected privately on the manner in which the cases of the four accused faculty was decided. From outside the room where the trustees were meeting, he could hear "rather strong argument." He thought that the trustees might have considered more deeply

> how to proceed or whether one should proceed at all. Here are four cases where no one has actually brought a formal definite accusation, and where there is absolutely no evidence which would stand up in any court of law. The Governor has presented very sketchy hearsay evidence and demanded that the President dismiss the staff members without hearing. The President quite properly refused. I rather think it would have been wise not to take any steps at all unless and until someone furnished more evidence or at least offered to appear against them. I think a man has a right to know what charges there are against him and who makes them.

Talking to Jorgensen, Waugh deplored "accusations made in secret without evidence and without opportunity for cross-questioning, etc." But Jorgensen had "for some time been convinced that we would 'have to fire them all.'" The UConn Board of Trustees voted on 27 July 1953 "to give terminating appointments to Glass and Lewis"; during the deliberations, President Jorgensen took a short break, fearing, he said, that he would "blow my top" because Lewis, who had been called to testify, was being recalcitrant. As noted earlier, the trustees' decision allowed the two men one more year at UConn.[68]

Lewis and Glass eventually continued their academic careers, and they kept in close personal touch. Glass, who taught at two other schools of social work, described himself in 1988 as "an old-timer who is still battling for change."[69] Lewis rose to eminence, publishing widely and serving for twenty years as Dean of the Hunter College School of Social Work.[70] There was, however, an interim period when the Lewises suffered continued harassment by the FBI. In 1954-55, when Lewis went to work for a social-services agency in Providence, Rhode Island, both Lewises were pestered by the FBI–at their home and even on the street–with requests for interviews, which they firmly refused. Eventually, the Boston office of the FBI (which covered Rhode Island) recommended that Lewis be dropped from the Security Index. Even so, when he moved to Philadelphia, the Boston office kindly forwarded his file to its counterpart there. Having received a doctorate in social work from the University of Pennsylvania in 1959, the year the FBI finally stopped pursuing him, he continued there as a faculty member until moving to Hunter as Dean in 1970. In 1980, when he was nominated to serve on a committee of the federal Department of Health, Education, and Welfare, a routine background check turned up his FBI record–by then reduced to being a member of a "revolutionary group" (but not since 1948) and "associated with a front organization" (but not since 1952).[71] By 1980, his supposed CPUSA activities didn't matter. Nine years later, he was invited to address the fortieth-anniversary celebration of the UConn School of Social Work.[72] He never mentioned his wrenching experiences there.

Part 2. Harry's testimony

A friendly witness

Reading newspaper articles about Harvard friends subpoenaed to testify, Harry supposed that he was a very small fish in the ex-CPUSA pond and had little cause for concern. The HUAC summons came as a surprise, he told Ellen Schrecker. I vividly remember the knock on the door, about 6 o'clock on a day in late May as Bunny was preparing supper. Harry opened the door, and a man–it was

George E. Cooper, the HUAC investigator–asked him to step out-side. It was presumably then that Cooper handed Harry a copy of Herbert Robbins's secret testimony, given two months earlier, so he knew who had named him.[73] Watching Bunny in the kitchen, I learned the meaning of the expression "to wring one's hands." Board of Trustees policy and Zilsel's example made clear Harry's fate if he did not cooperate fully: he would lose his job. On 2 June, he came to Waugh's office together with Edmund Moore, the kind-ly chair of the History Department. He told Waugh that he had been subpoenaed, and that he had been "for some years a Commu-nist, and intend[ed] to make a full statement to the committee."[74] Waugh, of course, had already learned of Harry's Communist past when he recused himself from serving on the Committee of Five.

On 22 June, exactly two months after Zilsel testified, Harry ap-peared before HUAC. That morning, as Curt Beck passed the Lin-coln Memorial on his way to work in the State Department, he saw two familiar faces waiting to cross the street–Harry and Bunny. Stopping his car, he called out in astonishment: "What are you do-ing here?" Harry began to answer: "I'm testifying this afternoon," but Bunny cut him off, and "he quickly added, please do not tell anybody at Storrs about our encounter."[75] That was how Beck learned, or inferred, that his friend had been a Communist; they never discussed it. Aside from Harry's boss in the History Depart-ment, Edmund Moore, and David Mars of the Department of Gov-ernment, no other colleagues knew. Moore, kind and sympathetic, assured Harry that as long as he testified fully, he would not lose his job, but there would be a penalty: he could never become chair of the department.[76]

Speaking at Harry's memorial in March 1988, I said that his legacy to me was the social idealism that had inspired him to join the Communist Party in the 1930s. I was not sure whether I was dropping a bombshell or a damp squib. It turned out that a few people knew; somehow, word had leaked out, but by then it didn't matter. One of the speakers at his memorial had known for a long time: Harry's former student Sidney Lipshires, who, as mentioned in Chapter 6, had learned from his friend Jerry Olrich.

Harry claimed to HUAC that he had "repressed all of this"–memories of his Communist past–until served with the subpoena.[77]

It would have been more truthful to say that he had tried to repress it. After all, he had been reminded, forcefully, by his encounter with Emanuel Margolis; and just five weeks before the knock on his door, he testified about Margolis before the Committee of Five. In his HUAC testimony, he offered as evidence of his anti-Communist credentials three reviews of books on the Soviet Union that he had published in the *Hartford Courant* in 1949. Reading these books and teaching Russian history surely made him recall the origins of his interest in the Soviet Union. In short, although stimuli to think about his past in the CPUSA had been present at least since 1949, he avoided (or tried to avoid) personal reflection. His self-disgust, not fully evident until the second hour of his testimony, was genuine. Before expressing it, though, he made a false and fawning statement: "Mr. Cooper presented me in the most courteous way possible with a subpena, and I didn't feel distressed. He was reassuring in his manner." Quite to the contrary, as he told Ellen Schrecker twenty-six years later–her notes use quotation marks–the subpoena was an "enormous emotional blow" that made him "terribly distressed." Schrecker was so affected by Harry's recollected emotion that she cited him (as an unnamed "Connecticut professor") to exemplify the pain felt by friendly witnesses. The "revulsion" that he felt toward his Communist self was something that, according to the Schrecker interview, he also felt toward himself as an informer.[78]

Firm anti-Communism was one reason that Harry and other cooperating witnesses testified. Another and probably more powerful motive was fear of losing a job. Trained for no other work, Harry was the sole support of his family; as noted in Chapter 6, Bunny was unemployable in Storrs because she was unable to swear that she had never been arrested. The role of fear in motivating witnesses can hardly be overstated. "Even though you know what takes place in that committee," one cooperating witness said,

> you are so accustomed to respecting government…that your fear is enormous. Intellectually, you understand what's happening, but you can't control the fear. An insidious form of self-guilt sets in. You accept the views of the committee in spite of yourself…. Afterwards, you find yourself guarded and evasive whatever you do, whatever you go.[79]

Some of the witnesses who suffered from this fear were able to fight it off, often at considerable cost. Lawrence Arguimbau, a tenured associate professor at MIT, told HUAC that in the process of deciding what to say, he had "lost 6 pounds and may lose my job and it is a difficult situation." He resolved, like Zilsel, to "give all the information that is pertinent without talking about other people and subjecting them to the same difficulties that I have been subjected to." This was, he said, "what I feel I morally can do."[80] Arguimbau, employed by a private university, did not lose his job. If Harry had taken the same position, Governor Lodge would have had him fired.

Harry used the three weeks between subpoena and testimony "to go prying around in my subconscious," and he concluded his testimony by expressing gratitude "for a very courteous and kind hearing of the story which I am not particularly happy to relate." He even praised HUAC for giving him "the opportunity to discourse informally, intimately," commenting that such a setting "is going to produce testimony which is much less inhibited than testimony given in public."[81] As we will see, however, Harry's testimony was artfully inhibited; he never said a word about Bunny while giving the impression of full disclosure. When Velde left the hearing, thanking Professor Marks "for your very helpful testimony," Harry reciprocated, expressing gratitude toward Velde "for the opportunity to testify in executive session."[82] He could not have known that "executive session" was a tactic meant to soften up witnesses by promising a privacy that HUAC felt no obligation to honor—a way "to gull [a witness] into betrayal and injury of others."[83] Executive session did at least spare him the ordeal of "being interrogated under a battery of bright lights, in the presence of newspapermen, photographers, radio microphones, and television cameras."[84]

Harry testified for nearly three hours before a HUAC subcommittee consisting of Velde and Rep. Clyde Doyle of California. Velde disappeared almost immediately on House business, and Doyle was present only part of the time. Most of the questioning was done by Frank S. Tavenner, a "quiet, unspectacular," and experienced lawyer who served as HUAC counsel from 1949-56 and conducted a large part of the questioning.[85] HUAC did not follow up on the few leads presented in Harry's testimony. From the point of view of its ostensible purpose, this hearing was useless.

At the outset, Harry's friendly demeanor inspired Velde's curiosity, even for irrelevant anecdotes. While giving the standard information regarding his educational background, Harry mentioned assisting "Prof. William H. Burton, for whom I have a stupendous regard," in a summer-session course at Harvard in 1945, when he "had a peculiar experience." While Burton was out for lunch, the phone rang: "Would you tell Professor Burton that the first atomic bomb has been dropped?"[86]

Mr. Velde. Was that the bomb test?
Mr. Marks. No; this was the first one on Hiroshima
Mr. Velde. Oh, the first one.
Mr. Marks. Yes, and I was the first one there who had gotten the news. But this is not a matter of importance to this committee.

This exchange set a tone of casual comment different from the tense exchanges between Zilsel and the committee. Harry's stories disarmed any suspicion that he was withholding anything when he said "I have no idea...I am not sure," an impression supported by his seemingly eager naming of names. But he *was* withholding. Although he discussed the Hanfstaengl episode, he did not tell HUAC about his role in protests against the *Karlsruhe* that took place a month before, which must have been etched in his memory, for it encompassed his proposal of marriage. He wanted to protect Bunny from any exposure. Nor did he mention Jerry Olrich, who had encouraged him to ask Bunny for a date.

During much of the hearing, Harry was a college teacher patiently explaining the chosen topic to willing students. His first expression of emotion came in response to Tavenner's question about CPUSA success in recruiting Harvard students. "[T]his is one thing which causes me a great deal of remorse," he said, becoming somewhat incoherent: "Some of the people whom I had something to do with in bringing into the Communist movement turned out to be irretrievably lost."[87] By "irretrievably lost," he meant that they had remained Communists: "I'm thinking in particular of one person who was a splendid young fellow at the time, a boy of high idealistic temperament and good intellect, who is known now as a

full-time Communist organizer. I am referring to Boone Schirmer—
B-o-o-n-e S-c-h-i-r-m-e-r." He had lost touch with Schirmer but
knew that he had seen him in a scene in *Paisan*, a movie made by
Roberto Rossellini in Italy in 1946. The scene depicted American
soldiers "getting into a boat in a marsh, and I could swear that one
of those soldiers was Boone Schirmer." He was right. Schirmer
served in the U.S. military in Italy in 1944-46, working with Italian
partisans, an activity shown in the film, in which Schirmer was an
extra.[88] Asked for further details, Harry said that his knowledge of
Schirmer's career in the CPUSA came entirely from Herbert Philbrick's notorious book detailing his activities as an FBI informer in
the Boston area.

When Tavenner moved to the supposed central purpose of the
hearing–he wanted names–Harry said he had not been in touch
with those he named for the past fifteen years; they were no longer
his friends.[89] Rather than seeing himself as a betrayer, he felt–as
did all ex-Communists–that he himself had been betrayed by the
CPUSA. Naming names, he sounded spontaneous:

> Wait–there is one, I think–Larry Levy….
> There was one very fine young fellow by the name of
> Alan Philbrick….
> Herbert Robbins I remember….
> There was one student in the law school who was a very
> nice fellow by the name of Saul Friedberg, I think…. There
> was one fellow whose first name I remember–Paul–but I
> can't remember any more.[90]

No wonder he remembered Robbins, who he knew had just named
him. He recalled Eugene Bronstein, too, and his own "appalling
feeling" when he heard of his death in Spain. Tavenner's interest
in the relationship between the YCL and the CPUSA yielded the
names of Party functionaries, all of whom were already known to
HUAC (see Chapter 6). He had nothing new to offer about the Party's largely futile efforts to recruit youth.

In the second half of Harry's testimony, he was intent on explaining the emotional appeal of Communism to Depression-era
students, because of its stated opposition to fascism and war. This

topic gave way to a comparison of Communism and fascism, a feature of his course on Europe since 1918, during which Doyle played the role of the attentive but none-too-bright student.[91] The hearing dragged until Harry brought up "the part which is personally the most difficult to deal with": the way his father had learned about his political activity, through an anonymous phone call to one of his colleagues on the Board of Examiners. The caller, evidently aware of anti-Communist investigations targeting New York City schools, said: "You have Harry Marks' name on your list of teachers in training. Do you know that Harry Marks is a Communist?" The colleague thought the matter over and after a couple of days asked Louis if it was true, and Louis wrote to ask. Harry remembered the exact date on which he received his father's inquiry: January 11, Louis's birthday, "and…it was not a very happy birthday that I could wish him." Anti-Communist investigations in New York City schools made the caller's question all too relevant.[92] Harry replied truthfully that he had been a Communist and untruthfully that he "had dropped out in 1936." He feared that "the effect upon my family" of an honest answer "would have been disastrous," coming just when he himself was hoping to become a New York City teacher. Now his falsehood had come home to roost. Ever since Cooper had served the subpoena, he had been asking himself, "in considerable anguish," what would have happened if he had answered truthfully; at the time, though, either answer "looked to me…like disaster." In any case, his father's letter "was the jolt which effectively severed organizational ties with the Communist Party." When the CPUSA tried to lure him back later in 1939, he resisted, "thanks very largely to the encouragement of my wife." No doubt that was true, and it certainly deflected any potential questions about Bunny's politics.

When Harry said he had become an anti-Communist around 1947 or 1948, Doyle asked why he had not contacted HUAC earlier to "help us in this fight."[93] Harry cited two reasons for his inaction. The first was an earlier doubt that HUAC would be "effective"; this may be an oblique way of saying that he didn't like the adversarial approach, or that he suspected it of witch-hunting. He claimed now to admire HUAC's "professional" approach, a statement that (if sincere) would align him with the view common even among liberals that it was McCarthy's tactics rather than his purpose that were abhorrent.[94] The second reason for stasis was the real one, a feeling that his Communist activity was "a rather revolting thing, which lay 15 years in the past," and he found it "disgusting...to think about it."[95] This language–"revolting...disgusting"–suggests that Harry felt his testimony to be at once an act of self-preservation and a purgation of his repressed past. It was a private moment conducted in what he thought was the sanctuary of a private hearing. Would he have abased himself had the hearing been public?

Resuming his earnest examination, Doyle asked why so many witnesses took the Fifth.[96] One reason, Harry thought, was a "feeling of nausea" that in his own case could be overcome only by "tell[ing] the whole story." Another reason, evident in Zilsel's case, was a sense that there was "something dishonorable" about endangering someone else. He acknowledged that many of his colleagues "will think very poorly of me for talking to you like this." His verb– "will think"–suggests that he feared that the story would get out and was preparing himself to face condemnation; he knew the sympathy that Zilsel had aroused. The third reason why people took the Fifth, fear of self-incrimination, was preposterous given the general assumption that everyone who took the Fifth before HUAC had a Communist past. He gave a strange example to illustrate self-incrimination: suppose he had "had something to do with Gene Bronstein's going to Spain, and had thereby violated some law." Letting that pass, Doyle asked if he thought that the committee was "trying to interfere with academic freedom." He did not. Indeed, he took issue with Einstein, who ten days earlier had said that any intellectual summoned to testify should practice Gandhian resistance and be "prepared for jail and economic ruin"; it was "shameful," Einstein argued, "for a blameless citizen to submit to such an inquisition, which violates the spirit of the Constitution."[97] Harry, however, did not regard himself as blameless. A curious interlude followed on the topic of executive session. Harry was grateful for the promise of secrecy; he felt that if the session had been public, it would have had "very serious effects" on both UConn and his family, particularly his sixteen-year-old daughter. He misjudged in two respects. First, the testimony was published the same year, but no one at UConn read it except for David Mars, an aficionado of congressional publications. And second, the daughter whose innocence he said he wanted to protect would have been grateful for a frank talk.

Although Doyle's curiosity was now exhausted, Tavenner's was not. He had two matters in mind. First, he wanted to know more about Communist indoctrination; and second, he wanted Harry to examine a list of names. Lurking somewhere behind Harry's analysis of indoctrination was his unrevealed friendship with Ernst Engelberg, for he spoke of

> the sense of comradeship; the use of the term "comrade" probably has gone out of style since my day, but I came back from Europe, and it meant something for me to have friends who were that close, so that there is this emotional affiliation which is not to be lost sight of.[98]

Tavenner wanted names, not emotions:

> I hand you a list of persons [in the Boston area] who have been identified as having been members of the Communist Party during the course of our investigation in this field, and I will ask you to examine them and state which of them were known to you to be members of the Communist Party.

Harry did not recognize most of the names and was reticent about those that he did recognize. He said that he knew that Wendell Furry belonged to the American League Against War and Fascism but not that he belonged to the CPUSA. He thought that Louis Harap was close to, but not a member of, the party. He knew that Robbins and Schirmer were member of the YCL, not that they belonged to the Party. The only tidbit he offered was an account of his ineffective distribution of flyers, which resulted in his arrest for littering. It was bathetic.

Harry in "the odious role of an informer"

How is Harry's testimony to be measured today? How was it measured at the time? Half a century makes a difference, whether considering the morality of his cooperation or its effects. My uncle

Alfred H. Hirsch was summoned to testify before a HUAC subcommittee in Milwaukee in 1955. He took the Fifth on nearly every question and scorned Harry for cooperating.[99] A self-employed printer from a wealthy family, he would not have lost his job. Putting aside for the moment both the reasons and the morality of Harry's decision to cooperate, one may ask whether his testimony harmed anyone. Fifteen of the seventeen people whose names are mentioned in his testimony, six of which were fed to him by the committee, had already been publicly connected with the CPUSA or other far-left groups, through either congressional investigations or newspaper reports. These fifteen included one dead man (Eugene Bronstein) and fourteen who were alive.[100] Neither Mack Libby nor Sidney Bloomfield, CPUSA workers, appear in the index to HUAC hearings, and none of the other sources that I consulted mention Libby; Bloomfield, as noted in Chapter 6, was publicly Communist. Scraping the very bottom of the barrel, HUAC had to be selective about whom it subpoenaed.[101] By Uncle Al's moral standards, Harry was an informer, albeit one who had nothing new to contribute–and one who knew that by the time he testified, just about everyone namable had already been named. In fact, few of HUAC's friendly witnesses had any new information.[102] Many Communists and fellow travelers were named in the public record of the 1930s and 1940s. The FBI had been keeping tabs on some Harvard organizations since the early 1930s, always getting "cooperation from the university administration."[103] Much information was available in the *Harvard Crimson*, and President Conant's "respect for the Bureau's work" surely helped.[104]

From 1946–the year he left the CPUSA–to his retirement in 1979, William T. Parry, whose role in Harry's NSL group is discussed in Chapter 6, taught philosophy at the University of Buffalo, then a private institution. Like Zilsel at UConn, he was prompted by a HUAC subpoena to reveal his political past to an internal university committee.[105] He told Buffalo, then a private institution, that he was willing to talk to HUAC about his own membership, in order "to protect the good name of my university"; however, again like Zilsel, he would not "play the odious role of informer."[106] When Velde forced Parry to take the Fifth, the repercussions at Buffalo, while serious, were less severe than they were for Zilsel at UConn.

The difference in consequences reflected the greater dependence of public universities on the public purse and, hence, on politicians' willingness to fund them. Buffalo's policy regarding faculty members called before a legislative committee, established eleven days before Parry testified, required them to "testify freely and frankly"; as at UConn, any Buffalo faculty member presently belonging to the CPUSA would be fired.[107] Three days after Parry's HUAC testimony, the Executive Committee of Buffalo's College of Arts and Sciences resolved to investigate him; as a result, the university revoked his tenure and placed him on annually renewable contracts as an associate professor for a probationary period of at least three years, after which his tenure might be restored.[108] Reinstated in 1961 after eight years, Parry served as department chair during a period of student unrest, demonstrating "a nervous system perfectly adapted to the rigors of that academic climate."[109]

At the other extreme from Parry was Whittaker Chambers, the ex-Communist who unmasked Alger Hiss before HUAC in 1948. Chambers believed that "the ex-Communist informer…uses his special knowledge to destroy others."[110] This was true for him, but the ex-Communists summoned in 1953 had nothing to add to the work of destruction. If Harry's primary reason for testifying was to expose the pestilence of Communism, he accomplished it far more effectively in his history classes than in testimony that no one read. "I probably know more about Communism than I would possibly have known in any academic way," he told Doyle.[111] One could say that ex-Communists were particularly fit to teach. Communists, on the other hand, were thought unfit to teach, a point that Harry made, "as emphatically as I could," during discussions in the UConn chapter of the AAUP. The National Education Association expressed the same view in 1949. The UConn Board of Trustees, the National Education Association, the national AAUP–as well as nearly everyone who opposed McCarthyism–believed that Communists were rigid ideologues committed to spreading their ideology in every possible way. Such a person was, in the words of Norman Thomas, the leader of the Socialist Party of America, "either too foolish or too disloyal to democratic ideals to be allowed to teach in our schools." It took years before calmer heads recognized that most Communist professors separated their CPUSA interests from their teaching and were careful *not* to intrude politics into their classrooms.[112]

Anti-Communism was only half of the explanation for Harry's willingness to testify; self-preservation was the other. Harry's Harvard contemporary Richard Schlatter, speaking at a symposium in 1977, conveyed McCarthyism's "absolutely devastating effect on the academic profession." Before Schlatter appeared before HUAC, three of his Rutgers colleagues who had testified were fired, par for the course in public universities. Like Harry, Schlatter "was married with two children. I had no other training for any kind of work except academic work. I was faced with the possibility of losing my job, and losing my career." Most important, he felt a strong desire "to do something worth doing, something of service to mankind"–to teach. Harry had written in his Berlin diary of his wish to "change things," to be (in Schlatter's words) "of service to mankind"; like Schlatter, he found teaching to be the means to that end. Schlatter figured out how to testify without damning anyone he named. Prior to appearing before HUAC, he contacted all the people he intended to name and got their permission for doing so; he then informed HUAC what he had done, and the committee kept his testimony secret, lest his example inspire others. [113] Harry was not so ingenious.

Motivations for testifying were, like motivations in general, mixed and inconsistent. Praise for cooperation could come from strange sources. A libertarian magazine devoted to "the further discovery and application of the Creator's changeless principles in a changing world"–the kind of balderdash that drove Harry wild– published an article in 1954 praising the contributions to its mission made by Harry and six other "contrite, gracious, humble, wise" cooperating witnesses who spoke to the "gracious and understanding" congressional committees.[114]

Why did HUAC persist?

In winding up Alfred Hirsch's hearing, Doyle remarked that "the records before us, resulting from investigation and records, clearly indicate that we know pretty much about...[the] activities in the Communist Party" of every witness who took the Fifth. What, then, was the purpose of the "surrealistic morality play" performed in the House? When the committee knew in advance that a witness would not cooperate, why did it bother summoning that witness for a tedious public examination? "The main object of virtually every public appearance," writes Walter Goodman, "lay in the appearance itself." Witnesses who cooperated in executive session might be asked to confess in public later but spared the humiliation of naming names publicly. There was, Robert Iversen observes, a strong Christian religious tinge to the language used by congressional committees. Regarding Communism as a pseudo-religious faith, congressional committees wanted the sincerely penitent to achieve "redemption," and the "culmination of the ritual of penance was the 'naming of names.'"[115]

Victor Navasky recasts Iversen's religious metaphor in anthropological terms: the hearings, "fueled by moral indignation," were "degradation ceremonies" meant to stigmatize deviant behavior.[116] These theories apply only partly to Harry. Because his testimony received no publicity, it could not deter others from sinning. While he felt degraded, ashamed, embarrassed—even suicidal, he told Ellen Schrecker—he was also able to dismiss the experience as "water over the dam," and "dirty water at that."[117] He retained the esteem of his peers. In 1954, he was elected to the University Senate, where he served for the remainder of his career. Curt Beck occasionally wondered why Harry, so highly esteemed, was never elected department chair. That was apparently the only price that he paid in public, and not a price that he regretted. As the next chapter suggests, however, he paid a private price.

Sarah (Bunny) Marks, 1935

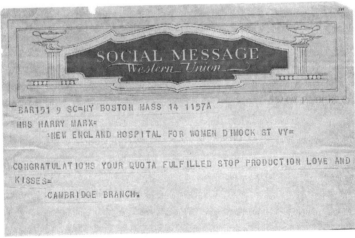

Telegram from Cambridge branch of CPUSA congratulating "Mrs Harry Marx" on the author's birth, dated 14 May 1937

Harry J. Marks, ca. 1960

8

Harry as an Academic

Harry was an academic to his core. Even as new father, he relied on learned authorities. In a letter to his parents four days after my birth, he quoted "'The Care of Your Baby', U.S. Public Health Service, p. 11." The Public Health Service held that babies were to be fed every four hours; if the baby screamed in hunger after three hours, she must not be accommodated for another hour. It was hard to hear "your progeny yowling as if in mortal agony, even if you know it is entirely normal and necessary for her development. There she goes again...." A neighbor had a different attitude. At 5 a.m., Harry and Bunny heard "a coarse male voice" roaring: "Stop that noise!" The U.S. Public Health service also advised that babies be exposed to fresh air four hours a day, in all seasons. Photos show a baby carriage, with me inside, parked outside their apartment building with no attendant visible. Although less concerned about learned opinion, Bunny tended to defer to Harry. Writing to her mother-in-law a week after my birth, she rejoiced "that Carol really looks very much like her Daddy. I did so want to produce something in his likeness."[1] She succeeded in ways she could never have anticipated. Not only did I become an academic but my eventual choice of African Studies as a field owed a good deal to my parents' political ideals, which made the literature of oppression naturally attractive.

Starting a career

In March 1937, Fritz Freyhan wrote from Berlin in a futile attempt to resuscitate a shallow friendship. He demanded an update on

Harry's life: "You used to talk a lot about an eventual academic career. Well??" It was a good question. Five years earlier, Frederick B. Artz had advised Harry go to law school when he returned home, for there would be no academic jobs. Harry had already considered a career in law; after all, "law would be one way to help change things. The secular change effected through education seems...too slow, too negative, too aloof, too indifferent." Once back at Harvard, however, he reconciled his goals: he would work toward "secular change" through Communist organizations while laying the foundation for a career in academia. He had thought further about Artz's warning about the job market during his contemplative vacation in Switzerland in July 1932. He felt "impelled to work" hard because of the "possibility of not getting a job"; he then wrote "probability" above "possibility"and added that "the consequences of getting it by the skin of my teeth would be catastrophic."[2] He did not get it (the PhD) by the skin of his teeth, as shown by the very strong recommendations for academic positions written by his dissertation supervisor, William L. Langer. Nonetheless, he remained without work at the university level until 1946.

Harry's immediate task, once fatherhood loomed, was completing his dissertation. His legwork in Berlin paid off: the pamphlets he had collected were absent in the vast resources of Harvard's Widener Library and unavailable anywhere else in the United States. He passed the oral examination on the dissertation a couple of weeks after my birth. Signing himself A.B. for *"armer Bankier"* (poor banker), Alfred Hirschbach sent a letter celebrating Harry's progress from A.B. to Ph.D. He wrote in elaborate, mock-formal German, a sly way of congratulating his nephew on his mastery of German as well as his doctorate. The first sentence, consisting of seventy-five words arrayed in many clauses, occupied an entire paragraph. Addressing Harry as *"Sehr geehrter* [most honorable] *Herr Doktor,"* he constructed a twelve-line sentence exploiting the wonders of German grammar to the fullest.[3] The grammar was witty–he knew Harry was a connoisseur of the language–but the intention was serious, for Alfred expressed his heartfelt wish that a university would soon take advantage of Harry's brilliance by hiring him. Fulfillment of that wish was deferred for nine long years.

In the meantime, Artz thought that "the best prospect" of a job was with the Federal Writers' Project of the Works Project Administration, which produced guidebooks to localities. Harry began inquiring about a WPA job in May 1937; by September, a position as a writer had come through, and for about a year and a half, he worked at home for $86 a week.[4] In addition to performing a task well suited to a historian, he would have found the Boston office congenial, dominated as it was by left-wing academics from Harvard. One of its directors said that "between one half and one third of the personnel either were members of the Communist Party or were fellow travelers." The Boston office had just been forced to respond to right-wing pressure to revise the first edition (1937) of the guidebook for Massachusetts. The "tiny, cumulative changes" executed under the direction of the supposedly "Communistic" Harvard-connected writers like Harry "pushed dissenting voices to the margins." No one noticed the revisions, which would have done little in the face of investigations by the newly founded House Un-American Activities Committee into alleged Communist influence on Federal Arts Projects.[5]

Harry's WPA earnings were a mere and insufficient stopgap before, as he hoped, he launched his academic career. He put considerable effort into his job search, even inviting William L. Langer's secretary and her husband for tea, unlikely as such a gesture was to influence Harry's dissertation superviser.[6] In March 1937, with the dissertation on the verge of completion, he wrote fifty-two letters of inquiry to colleges around the country and registered with both the Harvard Placement Office and the American College Bureau, in Chicago. His references were evenly divided between his teachers at Harvard (Langer, Artz) and Berlin (Gerhard, Holborn). Langer, already a star, wrote strongly supportive letters. Harry, grateful to receive a copy of Langer's most recent book—this would have been the pathbreaking *Diplomacy of Imperialism 1890-1902*--told his parents: "This feller has written a surprising book, and he isn't 35 years old yet."[7] The longest of Langer's recommendations is also the subtlest. He started by saying that he had known Harry as both an undergraduate and a graduate student; indeed, Harry had taken every one of his courses.[8] Like all writers of recommendation who intend to be taken seriously, he included a mild negative, one that conveyed Harvard's patrician disdain for supposedly Jewish manners–a disdain present even in a scholar who worked hard to help German and Austrian academics fleeing the Nazis. Harry was "not a fellow of great elegance or finesse, but [he] has always impressed me as a man of powerful intellectual endowment and rugged originality," widely read and with a "passion for learning." He dealt with Harry's political passions by saying that he "takes much more than an average interest in the world about him and is profoundly concerned with the great economic and social questions that confront the present age." Clearly aware of Harry's Communism, Langer firmly stated his conviction that his political passions did not contaminate his scholarship. The remainder of the recommendation, devoted to Harry's dissertation, further negated any taint of radical partisanship; it was "an unusually fine piece of work...marked throughout by complete independence of thought and sound scholarly balance." Looking to the future, he had urged Harry to write "a general history of German Socialism," a book certain to be "a splendid piece of work," and one for which he was "unusually well equipped." He ended by comparing him to another recent PhD, "a man of somewhat longer experience, but...rather less promise. Marks's potentialities are very great."

The next recommendation, written on 12 September 1937 with respect to positions at Queens and Hunter colleges in New York, was even stronger. This time Langer wrote to Jewish New Yorkers, to whom, rather than deprecating Harry's rough edges, he praised his "likable personality." Langer declared that as someone "passionately fond of everything connected with his work," Harry would "make an unusual research man and...a competent and inspiring teacher." A generic recommendation for the American College Bureau similarly described him as "a fellow of forceful personality and a great capacity for work, vigorous and clear in his thinking and in exposition." Half a year later, Langer received a request from the Harvard Appointment Office to recommend someone for a position in European History at Sarah Lawrence College. Sarah Lawrence sought someone with a good personality who was married and therefore impervious to the charms of Sarah Lawrence's students, all women and most from well-off families. Langer wrote that besides being "admirably fitted to meet the requirements," Harry possessed "unusual intellectual endowment, firm character and independent judgment." He added that Harry was presently in New York and gave a telephone number. Sarah Lawrence did indeed invite him for an interview; after all, "firm character" reinforced his marital status. Harry thought the college "too rich for my taste"–a pun alluding to the students' families.[9] He didn't get the job.

Harry was not even considered for a position at Hofstra College, a newly founded commuter institution that was initially under the supervision of New York University. Addressing John Musser of the New York University Graduate School, who was handling hiring for the History Department, Langer's recommendation implied his knowledge of Hofstra's anti-Semitic context:

> Marks is a Jew, but [sic] a very fine fellow and far above the average as a scholar. He has travelled widely in Europe and has an admirable language equipment. I think so highly of his work that I am recommending him very strongly for a Guggenheim Fellowship. From the standpoint of Hofstra College I think he would be particularly good, because he is a fellow of a great deal of energy, clear mind and organizing ability.[10]

Evidently suspecting that Hofstra would not hire a Jew, Langer added: "I hope you will feel disposed to consider him, but I should, of course, be happy to make other suggestions if you would like them." Musser's reply noted Hofstra's "peculiar conditions": the college had "a proportion of Jews on the faculty...and several of them are among our outstanding scholars." It was "located in what is almost entirely a gentile community," and there were "very few Jews in the student body." Worse yet, "some phases of the work will be of an executive character," for which a Jew would be ill equipped by virtue of his innate lack of polish. Hence, "I am afraid that we would prefer a gentile."

As mentioned in Chapter 2, the historian Sidney B. Fay had warned the undergraduate Harry that should he become an academic, being Jewish could harm him in the job market. Other historians in training received similar advice. Carl E. Schorske, another of Langer's doctoral students, was "advised that a career in history would be very difficult for a Jew, or even for someone with one Jew-ish parent." Harry suspected prejudice when he was interviewed in September 1938 for a part-time college-level position, at $50 a month, at the Bouve-Boston School of Physical Education. Miss Bouve "said she wanted someone older (maybe not Jewish?) with some experience."[11] The paucity of jobs coupled with the preva-lence of anti-Semitism convinced Harry that teaching high school history was the only immediately possible profession related to his studies and to his pleasure in teaching, which he had discovered while lecturing on Marxism for the CPUSA. In 1938, he enrolled in the Harvard Graduate School of Education for courses that would qualify him for a substitute-teacher's license in New York City. Ap-propriately enough, his first course was with Robert Ulich, a Ger-man authority on the history and philosophy of education.[12] In Oc-tober, he took the New York City teachers examination. His father gave him his results before they were published–the only time he benefited from a personal connection with the Board of Examin-ers. He ranked twenty-fourth (his performance in oral English was mediocre).[13]

In March 1939, aiming at a high-school position, Harry regis-tered with the Harvard Graduate School of Education Placement Office, as well as with a teachers' agency in Chicago; he also can-vassed old friends from his own high school, Fieldston. Langer again wrote a strong letter of recommendation for his file: "I regard him as an unusually gifted young man, widely read and widely interested. He has a most unusually vigorous and original mind, and I consider him admirably endowed for either teaching or re-search work." Months passed. In June, there came an offer of an interview for a position as a teacher-in-training in New Dorp High School in Staten Island. "DEFINITELY GOT JOB THANK CAR-OLS CROSSED FINGERS," he wired Bunny on 11 August. But a two-year-old's crossed fingers could not improve a salary of $4.50 a day; he still needed a parental hand-out. Thus he moved from the brilliant center of the Big Three (Harvard, Yale, Princeton) to "something of a frontier community, but not more than a day's portage from the big city"–by which, like everyone else, he meant Manhattan. It was, he told HUAC, "more like a rural community than a borough of the city." He was there for three and a half years.

In 1941, he moved from his probationary status to that of a full-fledged teacher, redeeming his earlier performance by ranking first in the examination in Social Studies.[14]

Early in 1943, Harry left Staten Island for a job at Amherst High School. He flourished in Amherst, a pleasant small college town in Massachusetts, even though at a salary of $1,800 a year he had to work in the summer–one summer in a lumberyard, another as a teaching assistant in Education at Harvard. He also taught in an army program at the University of Massachusetts, his first college-level job. Meanwhile he enrolled for a Master of Arts in Teaching at Harvard, commuting on weekends, to complete the work he had started in 1938. Three years after he moved to Amherst, students on the GI bill created a sudden expansion of job opportunities, and he was hired at the rank of Instructor to teach at the Hartford branch of the University of Connecticut. In 1947 he was promoted to assistant professor and granted tenure; a man with three Harvard degrees was a catch. In 1949, he was transferred to the main campus in Storrs, where he remained the rest of his life, promoted to associate professor in 1955 and to full professor in 1963. Two years later he was instrumental in founding the New England History Association.[15]

When Harry joined the faculty, UConn was starting its evolution from an agriculturally oriented land-grant institution to a major research university.[16] As a part of that evolution, he needed to publish a book. He returned to the seminar paper on the transfer of power in Singapore from the Dutch to the English that he had written for Dietrich Gerhard at the University of Berlin, a topic that he thought then merited longer treatment. His renewed effort, conducted through trips to Widener Library at Harvard, resulted in a monograph, *The First Contest for Singapore 1819-1824*, published in 1959 by Martinus Nijhoff. It was pleasing to be published by "the oldest and largest Dutch publishing house," run by Paul Gottschalk's friend Nijhoff, whom Harry had met in 1933–"a very fine gentleman and helpful."[17]

Harry as teacher and colleague

Two special events honored Harry for his service to UConn: a teaching award in 1970 and a flurry of honors and tributes when he retired in 1978. Noting that his student evaluations garnered the "highest rating ever recorded by a member of the Department of History," the commendation for the Alumni Association Teaching Award spoke of his "engaging personality...acute sense of responsibility and concern for other people," and his "continuous and enthusiastic sense of humor." A student who did not appreciate the last-mentioned quality once sent an anonymous hate letter that made the recipient smile: "Stop telling jokes. History is serious business." At a "special history colloquium" marking the occasion, the main speaker was Carl E. Schorske, a link with Langer.[18]

The Teaching Award stimulated former students to write to him. "It must have taken them a long time to discover your qualities as a master-teacher," wrote Richard H. Dekmejian, adding: "I could have told them that eleven years ago."[19] Florence Wegman Brisman thanked him for admitting her as an undergraduate to his graduate course in historiography, which "introduced me to an intellectual discipline that only some few of my courses at law school promoted." Harry's letter of recommendation for Miss Wegman showed his admiration of female achievement. Not only was her academic work of "effortlessly high quality," but her activities in the Student Senate showed "courage, stamina, gusto, and unquenchable bounce."[20] In the same year that Miss Wegman applied to law school, Harry published an article about her unknown soul sister, Mary Ann Tucker, a forgotten rural English woman who challenged authority in 1818: "She showed spunk, brains, eloquence, and independence of character on that August morning as she defended her right, at a time when it was no right in English law, to criticize the misconduct of a public official."[21]

A single anecdote sums up his influence as a teacher. One day in 2007, I chanced to meet in a New York art gallery a student from his first year of teaching on the Storrs campus. As a freshman in 1949, she asked a question in his class; the warmth and respect with which he answered persuaded her to major in history. She was in his course in Russian history when Stalin died, in March 1953. He began the class following Stalin's death with a question that made a deep impression on her: "What would have been different if Stalin had died last year?"[22] At the very time that Harry's anti-Communism took center-stage in the investigations described in the previous chapter, his overall approach in the course convinced her that he greatly admired Russia. His personal views were irrelevant to his bedrock insistence that to understand a people, the historian must appreciate (without necessarily approving) their feelings and ideas. He hated Nazism, but made it his business to listen to Nazi sympathizers in 1933, and his admiration for German literature was in no way diminished. If "Russia" meant Dostoevsky, then he did indeed "admire Russia." But if "Russia" meant Stalin, he despised it.

Asking and soliciting questions was the leitmotif of Harry's professional life. Not all students appreciated his pedagogy. A long article in a local paper reporting his retirement observed that some students found his teaching method "unnecessarily difficult" because he pressed them with "apparently irrelevant questions."[23] But most students understood, as was evident in the retirement tributes. "I want to thank you for asking me questions," wrote Hal Keiner, then completing his dissertation. Another, Thomas Osborne, had his own question, one that had "puzzled us through the years: will you really open a delicatessen?" His wit was catching, but his pedagogical genius was not. A student once rushed breathlessly into a colleague's office: "You won't believe it. I just came from a final history class where everyone stood up and clapped!" The colleague reported mournfully that ever since then he had stopped his final lecture five minutes early "to await some such spontaneous demonstration. Silence."

The voluminous material relating to Harry's retirement contains praise that must, of course, be taken with some grains of salt. Besides official resolutions and letters from two UConn presidents, the department compiled a thick notebook containing one hundred letters written by colleagues and former students. One former colleague–Edmund Moore, the department chair at the time of Harry's HUAC testimony–found himself too overcome with emotion to write. Moore scribbled a note to the current chair: "I feel rather too strongly, in the 'matter of Harry,' to translate it into words." Most of the former students who contributed letters had become professional historians, and they credited him with inspiring them to join the profession. A typical letter came from William Sheridan Allen of the University of Buffalo:

It was almost a quarter-century ago that I first attended your lectures in German History, but the moment I think of them I immediately recall my sense of amazement that college lectures, in addition to conveying data, could be literate and witty. Every session yielded a new stock of elegantly contrapuntal analyses plus so many puns (in three languages, yet!) that I was lucky to get half of them down in my notes. But enough was recorded so that even now, after all this time, I find myself echoing some of your ideas in my own lectures.

Most of all, Allen said, he valued Harry's "sense of commitment and integrity; you showed me what was meant by the abstraction 'scholarly ethos.'" Allen had attended two other graduate schools and taught in six colleges: "But you have always remained for me, through all my encounters with other teachers and colleagues, the exemplar of what a university professor ought to be."[24]

A curious preface that Harry wrote in 1951 for an as-yet-unwritten book gives the full flavor of his relationship with students and readers. The "dehumanizing of human relations," he says, has destroyed the former fashion of the author's address to the reader. Nowadays, a book is "supposed to be born parthenogenically in a germ-free environment"; it is "a thing, not the words of one man or one woman speaking to another man or woman." Today the author must not speak authentically "with the hesitant, tentative tones of an often puzzled human being" but must instead take on "the synthetic certainty of a mechanical man." He refused such certainty: "And if this book is read by only one person in the world, then for you I wrote it."[25] This concept of writing history went way back to his youthful fantasies while studying abroad. He aspired to write history that would be "encyclopedic in content"; that would be "thought...through in arrangement and conclusions"; and that "would...be intimate, not as though it were written by a snow man from the third-hand compilations of diplomatic and commercial treaties."[26] This idea of an "intimate" relationship between writer and reader is manifest in a meditation on historical method that he wrote toward the end of his life when he was rejiggering his unpublished book. He admitted that he could be accused of "seizing upon other men's eccentric ideas and exaggerating them"; even such an attack would make him grateful "for two reasons. It would answer the question: Is anybody listening? And it would provoke discussion, correction, and possibly clarification."[27]

There were indeed people listening: his students and colleagues. Again and again the letter-writers exclaim over his extraordinary breadth of knowledge, his kindness (especially to neophytes and newcomers), his genial tolerance, and his puns. The *History Department Newsletter*, announcing his retirement, stated that he had supervised doctoral dissertations "ranging in subject matter from Anglo-German diplomatic history to Scandinavian feminisms." Constantly extending his knowledge, he had taught seventeen different courses; the final new one was on the history of health and disease. His colleagues in the University Senate applauded his eloquence and his ability to steer discussions in fruitful directions. Recalling the "otherwise fetid aura" of faculty and Senate meetings, the Director of the Institute of Material Sciences declared that Harry had "provided the only fresh breath of air." Another Senate colleague, one of several inspired to write verse, wished to convey the

> … warmth of our gratitude
> When Harry would resuscitate,
> Rejuvenate and liberate,
> Illuminate and elevate
> To its proper, lively state
> A dismal, moribund debate.

The testimonial resolution passed by the faculty of the College of Liberal Arts and Sciences emphasized his value to their community. He had served on innumerable committees and in the University Senate; he had taught 6,100 students and been concerned with teaching on the high-school as well as the college level; he had exemplified the highest standards of scholarship. The resolution summed up what the university community treasured: "A penetrating intellect, a sensitive conscience, a sense of humor, combined with personal humility, dedication to duty and broad humanism, these are what Harry J. Marks has meant to us." The writer of the resolution knew nothing about his HUAC testimony, which showed a conscience not only "sensitive" but tortured. It had been a satisfying career notwithstanding the slow start and the traumatic experience of McCarthyism, points not touched on in the testimonial.

Paying the price: Harry's career

Harry paid a price for his past. Although Langer had thought that his dissertation could yield not only several articles but a general-interest book on the history of socialism in Germany, all that came was a single article distilling the interpretive essence of the dissertation.[28] Harry's sole attempt to fulfill his youthful dreams of writing books for the general public failed to find a publisher. For more than fifteen years, beginning around 1957, he labored to realize his vision of a syncretic history spanning many areas of knowledge. His aim was a book devoted to what he called the "pivotal period" (1895-1905) in European history–a synoptic topic suitable to his wide-ranging curiosity and command of European languages. The text and voluminous notes refer to scholarship in English, French, German, Italian, and Dutch. Engagingly written like all his publications, the manuscript shows him as an omnivore of history, for notwithstanding its ostensible focus on only ten years in European history, the book extends back to the Middle Ages and ranges far beyond Europe.

In 1962, Harry prepared a series of lectures based on his progress to date and, at the same time, sent a query letter to Macmillan Publishing. The head of Macmillan's Trade Department replied that "you may have a very noteworthy book."[29] After spending the next decade developing the manuscript further, he sent query letters to twelve more publishers, a few of whom expressed interest. Colin James of Cambridge University Press admired the "clarity with which you present your argument and the easy and readable manner in which you draw on the relevant literature." Elizabeth Sifton at Viking "found it well organized and lucid, an admirable job–in short, eminently worthy of publication." But she could not make an offer, for her colleagues had expressed "a number of reservations…–not so much about your work as about our suitability."[30] Sifton saw the book as intended for the "academic or specialist market," whereas her company aimed at "the general reader." An editor at Norton came to a similar conclusion. While he and his colleagues were "impressed by the breadth of your knowledge" and "your abilities to make brief analyses of causes and trends," they found his writing "too sophisticated for the general reader"; at the same time, the book lacked sufficient detail for use as a textbook. Harry himself summed up the problem with the book in a letter to an editor at Oxford University Press: "The book is not a narrative and is not a textbook."[31] Neither fish nor fowl, the book could not fly. It did, however, greatly enrich his teaching.

While Harry was laboring on the Pivotal Period, a Dutch historian named Jan Romein (1893-1962) articulated a similar hypothesis in a two-volume study published posthumously in 1967. In a three-page overview of Romein's career that concluded his own opening chapter, Harry wrote that Romein "commanded the most inclusive and thoroughly structured view of the Pivotal Period." Describing him as "a refined and subtle and undoctrinaire Marxist," he said that his "monumental work undergirds much of the argument of the present essay, but does not render it superfluous." Why not? The obvious reason was that a book in Dutch had a far more restricted readership than one in English. A less obvious but more important reason (in Harry's opinion) was Romein's neglect of "the issue of periodization as a theoretical problem," a topic to which he himself devoted attention. He expressed his "warmest admiration," and declared that "if the present essay sends any reader to that work, it will be a service to the reader."

With "the present essay" unpublished, the actual service that Harry performed was to write the introduction to the English translation of Romein's book, *The Watershed of Two Eras: Europe in 1900*. One reason that Romein succeeded in publishing while Harry failed was that he had a far better track record, despite being a "maverick" writing in a minor language.[32] Another reason was proximity to sources: as a European, Romein was surrounded by sources. For Harry's research to carry similar heft, he would have had to go to Europe and forage in archives, and this he could not do. In relying solely on published sources, he made a virtue of necessity. There are several explanations for his failure to return to Europe as a historian.[33] He lacked financial support: during his first fifteen years;

UConn had limited research funds and paid low salaries. I was well aware of his salary when I was an undergraduate, for it had to be stated on my annual scholarship applications. When I was hired to teach at Cornell University in 1963 at the amazing salary of $6,500, I earned $500 more than he had made in my last year in college six years earlier. Around 1960, his salary rose and the climate of support improved, but my mother fell ill in 1962 and died a year later. Her death and his younger daughter's serious illnesses soon after were also barriers to a foreign trip, although hardly insuperable.

Lurking behind these impediments to research abroad was the shadow of Harry's past: both his Communist involvement and his inability to land an academic position until 1946. A comparison with the career of his graduate-school colleague Carl E. Schorske may be instructive in analyzing the interplay of anti-Semitism and the Depression as explanations of Harry's slow start. Schorske, we may recall, had received the same warnings as Harry regarding his prospects as a Jew in academia. But Schorske had the good fortune to have his progress toward the doctorate interrupted by military service, and when he completed his degree in 1950, anti-Semitism was out of fashion in academia. Schorske was a Pulitzer-Prize-winning author of five books—one of them his dissertation—and many articles and edited books; he taught at elite universities with substantial research budgets and belonged to the inaugural class of MacArthur Fellows. Harry, a professor at UConn, won no prizes or significant research grants; he published one monograph and a handful of articles. Did his ambition dissipate? Why didn't he try to win a research grant before personal calamity struck? His political past suggests an answer. Perhaps he didn't want to risk refusal of a passport, as had happened to other ex-Communists. He knew, too, of a foreign example: Romein had been expelled from the Dutch Communist Party in 1925, yet his former membership led the State Department to deny him a visa in 1949, making impossible the three-month American lecture tour that had been arranged by the Rockefeller Foundation. Among Americans, a Communist past could jinx reformed sinners, for even cooperative witnesses before HUAC were refused passports. One such witness, the chemist Martin Kamen—who had never been a Communist—was repeatedly denied a passport from 1947 until he successfully sued in 1955. The

Cornell physicist Philip Morrison, an unfriendly witness who was protected by his employer, was invited to conferences abroad but even so thought it wise to delay applying for a passport until 1960.[34] Harry at UConn had greater reason than Morrison at Cornell for lying low. He paid for his past by having a diminished future.

Harry's professional writings

A book centered on a historian must take note of his professional writings. The weightiest of these, literally, was Harry's "exhaustive and scholarly" dissertation on the Social Democratic Party 1890-1903, which Schorske considered "an excellent introduction" to the fraught period after 1903.[35] In the sole published article to emerge from the dissertation, as in the dissertation itself, Harry asked why "the largest political party in the country and the largest socialist party in the world...sank to insignificance and became no more than...a cog to gear the labor movement into the German war machine."[36] He was appalled that in 1914 the SPD had acceded to the government's war policy. His disgust at this betrayal of principles was no doubt affected by his first-hand observation of the SPD's subsequent weakness against Nazism–for, as he later wrote, "the themes which the historian investigates may be very largely determined by present rather than past events."[37] While most of his dissertation is studiously neutral, the Preface is forthright in offering an interpretation inspired by the moment in which he wrote. If the SPD had been the "revolutionary, anti-capitalist Party" that it claimed to be, he argued, it would have shown its mettle on "three decisive occasions": "in July and August, 1914, in the winter of 1918-19, and in the months from July, 1932 through May, 1933," the last of which he witnessed. "On each occasion," however,

> it rejected revolutionary, anti-capitalist action. Had the decision been otherwise, the history of Germany would have been different. Europe would have a different face today. And therefore, of course, the world situation would not be what it is.[38]

In short, Harry's Berlin friends would not have been fleeing Germany. Because the period covered by the dissertation ends in 1914, the topic gave little opportunity to reveal his political sympathies more openly. This dissertation, unlike Emanuel Margolis's, could not be a stumbling block to academic success.

Harry's commitment to intellectual history, nurtured in Berlin, marks him as a European historian in two senses: he was a historian of Europe, and he was intellectually allied with the German émigré historians who fostered the growth of this discipline in America, in particular Holborn and Gerhard. Both men had imbibed the emphasis of their mentor, Friedrich Meinecke, on "the meaning of events rather than their causes," and thus Harry's lifelong interest in the history of ideas had an intellectual-genetic link with one of the fathers of that field.[39] Harry's monograph, *The First Contest for Singapore*, diverges into detailed diplomatic history from his more characteristic concerns with social and intellectual history and for that reason does not typify his historiographical approach. The article about Mary Ann Tucker mentioned earlier, apparently a spin-off from the monograph, represents his fascination with social and intellectual history.[40] Tucker's sole recorded appearance in history took place in a Cornish courtroom one morning in August of 1818, a year before the "contest for Singapore" began. In it, he portrayed an unwitting heroine driven by just the kind of moral imperative that he himself had sought.

Harry's concern with pedagogy, which began when he taught for the CPUSA, went in tandem with the required graduate course on theories of history at UConn, which he continued to teach as a professor emeritus right up to his sudden death at seventy-eight in 1988. He wrote three short pieces addressing pedagogical matters. Two were articles published in the year of his HUAC testimony– one on the American historian Charles Beard's relativism, the other a consideration of the teaching of history in colleges.[41] Seven years later, a former student asked him to write a brief introduction to a handbook for high school history teachers that he was co-editing.[42] Harry also maintained a connection with his early career by teaching in summer programs for high school teachers at Bennington College in Vermont and at the University of Oregon. After he died, UConn recognized his long interest in high-school teaching by establishing a memorial fund in his name to support graduate study by high-school teachers.[43]

Harry began working on the Pivotal Period soon after he completed *The First Contest for Singapore*, publishing his main ideas in a short essay.[44] In the end, though, his culminating published scholarly work was the eighteen-page Introduction to Romein's long book.[45] The Introduction can stand as a summary of his career, for it is resonant with his own biography, even though, with one brief exception, he never says a word about himself. Imbued with a profound concern with the intersection between individuals and history, the Introduction does not–as so many introductions do–rehearse the book's main points. Rather, it probes Romein's life and career to reveal the soil in which his magnum opus grew. Like all of Harry's scholarship, it is written without any care for his own professional reputation. Whether the Introduction had any impact it is hard to know, but the book itself made Romein better known in the anglophone world.

My concern here is for how the Introduction connects with Harry's private history. Some of these links leap out at me in ways inaccessible to anyone else. The person who recommended Harry to the Wesleyan University Press was Rosalie L. Colie, my mentor at Barnard College and a scholar of Dutch cultural history, with whom he had discussed mutual interests. His knowledge of Dutch equipped him to read an essential text: the historian Annie Romein-Verschoor's two-volume memoir of her and her husband's lives. Quoting Colie's article on Johan Huizinga, he had much to say in the Introduction about Huizinga, the best known internationally of twentieth-century Dutch historians. Huizinga had been designated as Romein's dissertation adviser at Leiden University, "but every topic that Huizinga proposed he found too dull, and every topic he proposed Huizinga found too dangerous"–"dangerous" because Romein was a Marxist.[46] Despite his expulsion from the Communist Party in 1925, Romein and his wife "continued to think of themselves as Marxists but hewed to their principles instead of the party line." Harry the ex-Communist appreciated that devotion to *their* principles and the Marxist ideals that he himself had once cherished. He must have been glad that he was spared anything like Romein's twelve-year exclusion from academic positions after his expulsion from the Party. The Romeins sustained themselves through journalism and by writing highly successful popular histories, and then they reentered the profession.[47]

Huizinga connects directly with Harry's biography, for Huizinga lectured at the University of Berlin on two successive nights in 1933. Writing in his diary after the first lecture, Harry admired "the fine manner he had–a healthy humor, too, which is rare in these parts." The next night's lecture was "pretty swell stuff," too:

> The man's an artist as well as a keen mind–and I think I'll try his *Herfsttij der middeleeuwen* [Waning of the Middle Ages]…. Huizinga spoke over[48] Burgundy and its place in European history–its culture and its crucial situation between France & Germany. He made a number of precious observations on history in general, and especially I liked what he said about the place of contingency because I felt the same way about it and had said as much in the last paragraph of Singapore.[49]

Forty-five years later he recurred to this moment in his Introduction. Romein, he wrote, "exhibited that empathy which Huizinga, in a lecture delivered in Berlin three days before Hitler was appointed chancellor (and which I heard), attributed to educated Netherlanders as a consequence of their country's intermediary position in Europe."[50] In Berlin, still thinking about Huizinga's ideas, he endorsed his observation: "While at any given moment, it is impossible to predict what will follow, historians often spend their energy trying to prove that what happened was inevitable."[51]

In Berlin, Harry had "ordered Huizinga's *Leven en denken in Amerika*" (Life and Thought in America) to take back to America itself.[52] In writing about Romein forty-five years later, he took his Berlin experience to America in another sense. Like Harry, Romein was an exponent of "integral history," which aims to understand how social, economic, intellectual, and political elements intertwine. Hidden in Harry's essay about Romein is a private "integral history" of his own that links the ambitious young man who soaked up Huizinga's words in Berlin to the mature historian in the twilight of his career. And it links Romein's experiences as a Communist to his own–a serendipitous closing of the circle.

Timeline of Events in Germany

1918   11 Nov.: Armistice is signed ending World War I. The following year, Weimar Constitution is adopted for postwar Germany.

1919   15 Jan.: In failed revolution, Spartacist (Communist) leaders Karl Liebknecht and Rosa Luxemburg are killed.

   28 June: Versailles Treaty is signed; Article 231 ("war-guilt clause") makes Germany responsible for reparations for "all the loss and damage" experienced by the other powers. Deep and virtually unanimous German resentment follows.

   11 Aug.: New Constitution is signed, formally inaugurating Weimar Republic. It provides for a democratically elected president, a chancellor (appointed by president) with executive authority, and a Reichstag with power to make laws. Article 48, which permits president to suspend temporarily constitutionally guaranteed rights, proves to be its Achilles' heel, paving the way for Nazis to take control in 1933.

1920   24 Feb.: German Workers' Party (soon renamed the NSDAP), led by Hitler, announces Twenty-Five Points, giving main Nazi ideas—abandonment of Versailles Treaty, need for *Lebensraum*, turning department stores over to small tradesmen, denial of citizenship to Jews, exclusion of all non-"Germans" from employment by newspapers, "positive Christianity" that "combats the "Jewish-materialist spirit," nationalization of all businesses, etc. Soon S.S .and S.A. are created, and Nazis adopt swastika (*Hakenkreuz*) and the "Hitler *Gruss*"– outstretched right arm accompanied by shout of "Heil Hitler!"

1923   Economic crisis: inflation reduces most of middle class to poverty.

8/9 Nov.: Beer Hall Putsch in Munich: Hitler, Gen. Erich Ludendorff, and other Nazis attempt to take over Bavarian government as a means to obtain national control. Hitler is arrested, tried for treason, and sentenced to five years; he serves eight and a half months, during which he dictates first volume of *Mein Kampf* (published in 1925).

1924   *Reichsbanner Schwarz-Rot-Gold* (Black-Red-Gold), private militia supporting Weimar Republic, is founded.

1926   Founding of *Nationalsozialistischer Deutscher Studentenbund* (National Socialist German Students' League; NSDStB) is announced in *Völkischer Beobachter*.

1928   20 May: In Reichstag election, SPD wins 153 seats (29.8%) and is the leading party; Nazis win 12 seats (2.6%), and Communists win 54 (10.6%).

1930   23 Feb.: Horst Wessel, thuggish S.A. youth leader, is killed in Berlin brawl; Goebbels blames Communists and makes Horst Wessel Song the Nazi anthem.

29 Mar.: Heinrich Brüning, leader of Zentrum (Center) Party, appointed chancellor.

14 Sept.: In massive voter turnout for Reichstag elections, SPD wins 143 seats; Nazis come second with 107; Communists are third with 77.

13 Oct.: Nazi members attend Reichstag wearing S.A. uniforms and introduce anti-Semitic bills.

1931   20 June: U.S. President Herbert Hoover announces one-year moratorium on international debts, a move welcomed in Germany.

Mid-July: Two banks, Darmstädter und Nationalbank, declares bankruptcy; other banks close.

10 Oct.: Hindenburg offers Hitler position in government; he refuses, on grounds that it is not sufficiently important.

1 Dec.: Ernst Thälmann, Secretary of KPD, proposes forming common front with SPD; SPD refuses on 28 June 1932.

1932   15 Feb.: Unemployment reaches 6,126,000.

25 Feb.: Hitler, born in Austria, becomes German citizen so as to become candidate in Reichstag election; two days later, he announces his candidacy for presidency.

13 Mar.: In first round of presidential elections, Hindenburg wins 49.45% of vote; Hitler, 30.23%; Thälmann, 13.2%.

10 Apr.: In second round, Hindenburg is re-elected president with 52.93%, including some votes from Communists fearing Nazi takeover; Hitler receives 36.68%; Thälmann, 10.2%.

15 Apr.: S.A. and S.S. are banned on orders of Wilhelm Groener, Minister of Interior and Defense. Two months later, on 16 June, Franz von Papen lifts ban.

12 May: Groener forced to resign.

30 May: Brüning and Cabinet resign.

1 June: Hindenburg names Papen as chancellor.

4 June: Reichstag is dissolved. By mid-year NSDStB enrolls 7,600 students.

9 July: Lausanne Treaty signed, freeing Germany from reparation payments.

17 July: Street fight in Hamburg-Altona results in 18 deaths and 100 injured people; two days later, Interior Minister Wilhelm von Gayl bans demonstrations.

31 July: With 84.1% of voters participating, Nazis become largest party in Reichstag, winning 37.4%; SPD wins 21.6%; Communists, 14.3%; Zentrum, 12.5%; DNVP, 5.9%.

2 Aug.: Hitler refuses Papen's offer of vice-chancellorship, holding out for chancellorship.

30 Aug.: Nazis wear S.A. uniforms at first meeting of new Reichstag; Göring is elected its president.

12 Sept.: Reichstag votes no confidence in Papen and is dissolved.

3-7 Nov.: Berlin transit strike, led by KPD with Nazi participation, causes chaos.

6 Nov.: Nazis take 33.1% of votes in Reichstag election; SPD, 20.4%; KPD, 16.9%; Zentrum, 11.9%; DNVP, 8.3%.

19-21 Nov.: Hindenburg discusses with Hitler an offer of chancellorship provided he gains majority in Reichstag and governs with president's approval.

24 Nov.: Hitler refuses the chancellorship unless he has full power.

3 Dec.: Gen. Kurt von Schleicher replaces Papen as chancellor.

1933   30 Jan.: Hitler becomes Chancellor

23 Feb.: Gay rights groups banned.

27 Feb.: Reichstag fire. Dutch Communist, Marinus van der Lubbe, is arrested for arson. Ernst Torgler, leader of KPD deputies in Reichstag, and (in coming days) 4,000 Communists are arrested. At Hitler's instigation, Hindenburg issues decrees removing constitutional protection, using Article 48 of Weimar Constitution as his cover.

28 Feb.: Measures introduced repressing freedom of speech, assembly, press, and other basic rights.

3 Mar.: Thälmann is arrested.

5 Mar.: In Reichstag election, Nazis take 43.9% of votes; SPD, 18.3%; KPD, 12.3%; Zentrum, 11.2%; DNVP, 8%. Hitler's coalition government with DNVP gives him required majority.

8 Mar.: Election of KPD deputies in Reichstag is annulled.

11 Mar.: Display of Weimar flag forbidden.

13 Mar.: Goebbels named propaganda minister.

15 Mar.: KPD banned.

20 Mar.: Himmler announces creation of concentration camp at Dachau, near Munich, to contain political prisoners. Similar camps are soon established near Weimar at Buchenwald and outside Berlin at Oranienburg (Sachsenhausen).

21 Mar.: Reichstag opens; 26 SPD deputies as well as all KPD deputies are excluded.

23 Mar.: Reichstag overwhelmingly passes Enabling Act, which suspends Weimar constitution for four years and gives Hitler dictatorial powers (it is later renewed); SPD deputies vote in opposition, but Zentrum and DNVP support Nazis.

1 Apr.: Nationwide boycott of Jewish businesses and professional offices.

2 Apr.: Decree requires anyone leaving Germany to have official permission.

7 Apr.: Jews are restricted by three laws governing public employees: Law for the Restoration of Professional Civil Service, Law Regarding Admission to the Legal Profession, and Law Regarding New Election of Assessors, Jurors, and Judges.

10 Apr.: Jewish lawyers excluded from German Bar Association.

22 Apr.: Jewish doctors restricted from participating in national health plan (*Krankenkassen*).

25 Apr.: Decree Against the Overcrowding of German School and Universities establishes quotas for Jewish teachers and students.

26 Apr.: Leader of Steel Helmet joins NSDAP, accepting Hitler's leadership. Göring founds Gestapo.

2 May: Labor unions are dissolved by being "coordinated" (*gleichgestaltet*) as German Labor Front; many labor leaders are arrested.

10 May: Students conduct book burnings instigated by Goebbels in Berlin and eighteen other university towns (some a few days later) to protest "unGerman spirit." Socialist parties are outlawed.

Mid-May: *S.A. Mann Brand*, Nazi film depicting events as recent as March, is released.

June: *Jüdischer Kulturbund* (Jewish Cultural League) founded.

1 June: Industrialists create *Adolf-Hitler Spende,* a fund to support NSDAP; "voluntary" contributions are actually mandatory.

5 June: Political parties other than NSDAP are dissolved.

9 June: Arturo Toscanini refuses to participate in Bayreuth Festival to protest Nazi repression of artists.

19 June: SPD governing committee removes Jews from board of directors.

21 June: In "Köpenick Blood Week," S.A. invades working-class district in Berlin, killing 91 residents.

22 June: SPD is banned and its property seized; union funds are confiscated.

26 June: National Party dissolves itself; its leader, Hugenberg, is forced to resign from government.

30 June: Decree for Coordination (*Gleichschaltung*) subjects every aspect of German society to Hitler's ultimate authority; civil-service law of 7 Apr. is extended to apply to Gentile civil servants married to Jews.

5 July: Zentrum "voluntarily" dissolves itself; other non-Nazi parties have already done or will soon do so.

7 July: All SPD deputies banned from Reichstag.

14 July: Law on the Formation of New Parties makes Germany a one-party state. Law for the Prevention of Genetically Diseased Offspring requires surgical sterilization of persons with physical or mental "defects" (affecting mentally ill and handicapped people, blacks, Sinti [Roma], etc.).

31 July: 26,789 political prisoners.

Sept.: 10,000 German refugees in Switzerland.

30 Sept.: Official figure for unemployment is 3,849,000.

4 Oct.: Law Regarding Editors requires journalists to have pure "Aryan" ancestry going back to Jan. 1800.

21 Oct.: Germany announces withdrawal from League of Nations.

12 Nov.: In foregone conclusion, Nazis win 92.1% of vote in Reichstag election.

1 Dec.: Law makes state and party a single identity: *"Partei und Staat sind eins."*

23 Dec.: Van der Lubbe is sentenced to death for Reichstag fire (executed 10 Jan. 1934); case against four accused Communist co-conspirators is dismissed.

1934   18 May: Reich Flight Tax of 25% imposed on transfers of RM 50,000 or more.

23 June: Emigrants are restricted to RM 2,000 in foreign currency, down from 10,000.

30 June: Night of the Long Knives (also known as Blood Purge or Röhm Purge): S.A leader Ernst Röhm and at least a hundred others are murdered by S.S. to remove socialist elements in NSDAP.

25 July: Nazi plot in Vienna succeeds in assassinating Chancellor Engelbert Dollfuss but fails to take over Austrian government; Dollfuss is succeeded by Kurt Schaussnigg.

2 Aug.: Hindenburg dies; Hitler melds offices of president and chancellor; all German troops are required to swear personal loyalty to Hitler, with all civil servants and government ministers soon required to swear likewise.

19 Aug.: Plebiscite endorses Hitler as chancellor and Führer.

25 Aug.: Dorothy Thompson is expelled from Germany by Ernst Hanfstaengl, becoming first American journalist to be formally expelled.

1935   13 Jan.: Residents of Saarland vote overwhelmingly to return the territory to Germany, from which it had been separated in Versailles Treaty.

1 Mar.: Germany occupies Saarland.

16 Mar.: In defiance of Versailles Treaty, law establishes military draft and army of 500,000.

14-15 Sept.: Nuremberg Laws passed, excluding all those not of "German blood" from citizenship, forbidding intermarriage of Jews and Gentiles (as well as extramarital affairs between Jews and Gentiles), and forbidding German women under forty-five from working in Jewish households.

7 Nov.: Steel Helmet, already eviscerated, is formally dissolved.

14 Nov.: Remaining Jews dismissed from public service.

1936-
1937
Because of Olympics in Berlin (1-16 Aug. 1936), these years are relatively quiet. Germany occupies Rhineland (7 Mar. 1936) and sends military assistance to Franco in Spain

1938   11 Mar.: Germany invades Austria, incorporating it within the Reich (Anschluss, or union).

24 Apr.: "Decree on the Registration of Jewish Property" requires Jews and Gentile spouses of Jews to register all domestic and foreign assets.

1 July: Jews who lived in areas including public places (government buildings, theaters, cinemas, concert halls, sports facilities, and the like) must have left by this date; from now on, Jews may not enter such areas.

23 July: "Third Notice Regarding the Identification Card Requirement" mandates all Jews over fifteen to carry photo ID card with fingerprints; cover and inside pages are stamped "J."

17 Aug.: "Second Decree Supplementing the Law Regarding the Change of Family Names and First Names" affects Jews whose given names do not appear on a Nazi list. By 1 Jan. 1939, women must add "Sara" as a middle name, and men must add "Israel." Because list consists of "curious-sounding Yiddish or ghetto" names, most Jews are affected.

30 Sept.: In Munich, Britain and France agree to cede German-speaking parts of Czechoslovakia (Sudentenland) to Germany. Neville Chamberlain predicts that "peace in our time" will result from this agreement, which others see as appeasement.

5 Oct.: Jewish passports are required to be stamped with J.

7 Nov.: In Paris, Herschel Grynszpan, a German-born Polish Jew disturbed because his parents have recently been expelled from Germany, shoots Ernst vom Rath, official at German embassy, who dies on Nov. 9.

9/10 Nov.: In ostensible retaliation for vom Rath's assassination, nationwide pogrom of *Kristallnacht* initiates blizzard of anti-Semitic repression including murders, destruction of property, mass arrests, and enormously punitive financial sanctions.

12 Nov.: German Jewish community is assessed one billion RM to "atone" for vom Rath's assassination. Other penalties include total exclusion of Jews from German economic life and their children from public schools.

3 Dec.: Start of compulsory Aryanization of Jewish businesses.

1939   17 Mar.: Germany invades Czechoslovakia.

30 Apr.: Jews are required to live in *Judenhäuser* (Jewish houses).

23 Aug.: Germany and USSR sign 10-year non-aggression pact dividing Poland between the two countries.

1 Sept.: Germany invades Poland, launching World War II.

1940   9 Apr.: Germany invades Denmark and Norway.

10 May: Germany invades Netherlands and Belgium.

5 June: Germany invades France.

21 June: France surrenders to Germany at Compiègne.

27 Sept.: Germany, Italy, and Japan (Axis) sign military and economic treaty vowing to fight together against US should it enter war.

1941   22 June: Germany invades USSR.

19 Sept.: All Jews in Germany are required to wear yellow badge with Jewish star.

14 Oct.: First deportation orders send Jews to extermination camps further east.

7 Dec.: Japan bombs Pearl Harbor; US enters war.

1942   20 Jan.: Wannsee Conference sets extermination as "Final Solution" of "Jewish problem." Jews still in Germany are "resettled" eastward to extermination camps.

1943   Goebbels declares Berlin *judenrein* (clean of Jews).

1944   6 June: Allies land on beaches in Normandy.

20 July: Assassination plot against Hitler is exposed; some 200 conspirators are executed.

1945   29 Apr.: Hitler writes his will, marries Eva Braun; on 30 Apr., the two commit suicide.

8 May: War in Europe is over.

20 Nov.: Nuremberg war crimes trials start, concluding 1 Oct. 1946.

Notes

Chapter 1

[1] In quoting Harry's diaries and letters, I have silently emended abbreviations and other types of shorthand, along with occasional errors of spelling and punctuation. I have begun the process of donating these letters and diaries as well as all of the letters to Harry from German friends (except those connected with Ernst Engelberg, which are going to Humboldt University) to the Leo Baeck Institute, a renowned center for the study of German Jewry in New York, where they are catalogued as Harry Marks, "The Rise of the Nazis" (ME 1558).

[2] David G. White to William L. Langer, 16 Feb. 1940, papers of William L. Langer, Harvard University Archives, HUG(FP) 19.8, box 2, General Correspondence 1933-41. White, who received his PhD at the University of Berlin in November 1939, was appealing for help in relocating to an American university. Beginning in 1828, the formal name of the university, which was founded in 1810, was *Friedrich-Wilhelms-Universität*; but it was known simply as *Universität zu Berlin* (University of Berlin). In 1949, it was renamed Humboldt University after its founder, Wilhelm von Humboldt.

[3] Munro 2006: 86-87.

[4] On Cohn, see Plotkin 2009: 128 and Chapter 3 of this book. Plotkin arrived in Germany on 22 Nov. 1932 and left on 8 May 1933; on his intention to publish, see the editors' introduction, p. xvi, and Plotkin's reprinted essay, pp. 175-95. The German Diary Archive (www.tagebucharchiv.de) contains unpublished diaries. Unpublished autobiographies by non-Nazis exist in the Houghton Library at Harvard and the Leo Baeck Institute in New York; there are as well many published and unpublished Nazi memoirs (Liebersohn and Schneider 2001; L. Hill 1994: 224-25).

[5] HJM 1980. Even though by 1980 some of his UConn colleagues knew of his political past, Harry preferred not to mention that painful episode.

[6] Klemperer 1998: 6-7, 9 (17 Mar. and 30 Mar. 1933).

[7] Chalmers 1998: viii; xxi-xxii, n5; Klemperer 1998: 134.

[8] Shirer 1941: v. Erik Larson's warmly reviewed book about Dodd and his family, *In the Garden of Beasts: Love, Terror, and an American Family in Hitler's Berlin* (New York: Crown, 2011), appeared just as this book was going to press.

Chapter 2

[1] Margaret Julia Marks, notes on family history. Esther Buck emigrated from Königsberg in East Prussia in 1860.

[2] Family legend held that following Julius's death, Esther traveled to Vienna in search of a husband and found Goldstein, four years her junior. He arrived in New York on 29 Sept. 1888; his obit in the *New York Times* (11 Nov. 1911), my source of biographical information, said that from 1878 until his emigration, he served as "*obercantor* of the *Cultus Gemeinde* in Vienna." A Bessarabian-born and Russian-educated composer of sacred music, he became the cantor of the German-speaking Congregation Shaar Hashomajim and served as President of the Cantors' Association of America. Esther "ran the family dry goods store on the Lower East Side" and was "the breadwinner and general manager" (HJM 1980). At the time of Goldstein's arrival in New York, Congregation Shaar Hashomajim was at 15th Street near 2nd Avenue in *Klein Deutschland*; known today as the Central Synagogue, it merged in 1898 with another German-speaking congregation, which had built an elegant synagogue at Lexington Avenue at 55th Street in 1872 ("Consecration of New Synagogue," *New York Times*, 2 Apr. 1865; Goldstein obit, *New York Times*, 11 Nov. 1911; http://www.centralsynagogue.org/downloads/docs/cs_restoration.pdf (accessed 24 Jan. 2011).

[3] Alfred Hirschbach was the son of David Hirschbach and Pauline Alexander Hirschbach. His German parents married in New York City on 26 Feb. 1871, and Alfred was born ten months later, on 18 Dec. 1871, thus becoming an American citizen; his family then returned to Germany. Alfred married Deborah Levison in 1905. Evidently the Marks family stayed in touch with Alfred's mother's relatives, since Harry refers to "the Alexanders" (HJML, 1, 13, 23 June 1932). I have not attempted to discover whether David Hirschbach was related to Henry Hirschbach, who married Sarah Katz Levison's sister Francisca. I was unaware of Sarah's baby sister Bertha Levison's existence until a recent visit to Mt. Carmel Cemetery in New York, where her grave gives her dates as 1887-1889.

[4] A. H. Levison's death certificate gives the cause as endocarditis. Sarah Katz Levison outlived him by twenty-three years.

[5] My thanks to Waltraut Engelberg for decoding the Gothic script and figuring out the English meaning, and for pointing out that the parents' spelling in German indicates only a basic education.

[6] Harry's self-admonition "to write to Aunt Fanny [Louis Marks's sister] in German, thank her for her check, to Father in German for his birthday" suggests some use of German in by some elements of Louis's family (HJML, 1 Jan. 1933). The anecdote about Cantor Goldstein appears

in Harry's oral history (1980). When Louis suggested that Shakespeare might "match the German writers," Goldstein replied: "*Ach, du hattest Shakespeare im original lesen sollen*" (Ah, you should read Shakespeare in the original). Harry later tucked into his collected Shakespeare the Schlegel-Tieck translation of Macbeth's "Tomorrow, and tomorrow, and tomorrow."

[7] American Embassy to Louis Marks, 19 Aug. 1907. He also visited continuing education classes at the *Friedrichsgymnasium*.

[8] At the time, when some 40% of New York children did not attend high school, only 4% of the Marks brothers' age cohort were enrolled in college (Vesey 1965: 289). Isidore presumably came to a better understanding with his mother when he married her stepdaughter, Irene, on 30 Jan. 1898.

[9] The preceding and succeeding family history is based on public records (census reports, death indexes, passenger lists, and the like, as well as a probate announcement), Harry's oral history (1980), a few notes made by Sophie Levison Marks and her father, and a summary of family history written by Margaret Julia Marks. The least reliable source is the public records, mainly because census-takers often made mistakes.

[10] In May 1908, Louis bought a diamond engagement ring from a relative, Seymour Misrahi; the receipt reads: "S. Misrahi, Importer of Precious and Imitation Stones." Louis's sister, Fanny, crossed the line separating German and Sephardic Jews when she married Joshua Misrahi, a Turkish immigrant.

[11] The phrase "pewless and dueless" was coined by the Free Synagogue's first president, Henry Morgenthau, Sr. (www.swfs.org/About/Heritage, accessed 16 May 2008). In his 1980 interview, Harry recalled Louis's support of the Sacco and Vanzetti defense committee; their execution took place shortly before Harry entered Harvard.

[12] The New York Passenger Lists record Louis as returning from Europe on 1 Sept. 1908 (no doubt with Sophie). Sophie did volunteer work in a hospital later on; in a letter from Berlin, Harry observed ironically that there she wouldn't "be allowed to work in a hospital, being of an inferior variety of mankind"–Jewish (HJML, 25 Jan. 1933).

[13] Harry Marks's first wife, Maud Rubenstein, was the Texas-born daughter of Austrian immigrants; she gave birth to a daughter, Margaret Julia Marks, in 1907 and died in 1911.

[14] Frankfurter 1960: 11.

[15] Rudy 1949: 173-74.

[16] Steinberg 1974: 9, 19.

[17] The high drop-out rate testified less to the students' abilities than to their struggles as immigrants' sons. Only 2,730 of the 30,000 students who entered between 1847 and 1902 graduated (Gorelick 1981: 67). Informa-

tion on Louis's undergraduate achievements is in the handwritten ledger books of the Office of the Registrar and in the somewhat different printed volumes of the *Merit Roll of the College of the City of New York*, both in the City College Archives.

[18] My husband, Marvin Sicherman, recalls that in his time at City College (1947-51), the college song contained the phrase "proud sons of immigrant parents." I have been unable to verify his memory.

[19] "Professor" connoted what would today be called the head of a department.

[20] Qtd. Rudy 1949: 191.

[21] Rudy 1949: 260.

[22] European Jews constituted 30% of the New York City population in 1920 (Steinberg 1974: 8).

[23] In 1918-22, Louis taught "Subject Matter and Methods of Teaching Geography" and "Method and Content in Geography and General Science"; in 1920, he taught a course to prepare candidates for the examination to qualify as an elementary-school principal.

[24] The architectural, educational, and social history of the building is detailed in a report supporting its designation in June 2006 as a historical landmark (Kurshan 2006).

[25] Emerson 1922: xiv-xv, 244, 331-32.

[26] Irwin and Marks 1924: v. P.S. 64 was "probably the only school in New York that had a school psychologist"; Irwin's salary was paid by the Public Education Association, not by the school (HJM 1980).

[27] The experiment began in 1917, when the entering class of six-year-olds was given the Stanford-Binet IQ test, and continued in 1918-20 (Irwin and Marks 1924: 40). Louis's co-written second book also concerned testing (Levine and Marks 1928).

[28] Irwin and Marks 1924: 162, 163.

[29] L. Marks 1921.

[30] Virgil E. Dickson wrote that Irwin and Marks's book deserved the "serious attention of teachers, school administrators, and social workers everywhere" (*Journal of Educational Research*, 13.4 [Apr. 1926]: 301). G. T. Buswell emphasized the book's value in the new and truly "democratic" conception of public education for all children (*Elementary School Journal*, 25.3 [Nov. 1924]: 228-29).

[31] Irwin and Marks 1924: 8.

[32] Harry tells this story in his interview (1980). I have no memory of the episode.

[33] Irwin and Marks 1924: 8-9.

[34] "Dr. Louis Marks, 67, Dies After Illness," *New York Times*, 27 Mar. 1943.

[35] The name "Little Red School House" was retained after Irwin's school moved to P.S. 41 in Greenwich Village. When, in 1932, the Board of Education closed it, the parents banded together to preserve it as a private school with the same name (see http://www.lrei.org/whoweare/wwa_12c.html [accessed 20 July 2006]).

[36] The gavel remains in my possession. The first Schoolmasters' Club was founded at the University of Michigan by the philosopher John Dewey and others. Louis Marks was a disciple of Dewey, whose *School and Society* had an honored place in his living room.

[37] "Dr. Louis Marks, 67, Dies After Illness," *New York Times*, 27 Mar. 1943. Rodeph Shalom, whose rabbi married my parents, had been founded on the Lower East Side in 1842 by "members of a Bikkur Cholim society known for its care of the sick and needy"; in 1930 it moved to the Upper West Side, where Louis and Sophie lived (http://www.rodephsholom.org/aboutus_our_heritage.html, accessed 22 May 2008).

[38] Adler was the son of Rabbi Samuel Adler, who came to New York from Germany in 1857 to serve as rabbi of Temple Emmanu-El, the leading Reform temple in the United States. In 1865, Samuel Adler preached (in German) at the consecration of Congregation Shaar Hashomajim, where Herman Goldstein later served as cantor ("Consecration of New Synagogue," *New York Times*, 2 Apr. 1865).

[39] Gittler 1953. Harry's cousins Margaret Marks and Hannah Marks Bildersee also attended Fieldston.

[40] Karabel 2005: 14.

[41] This achievement is recorded by his mother in the final pages of his baby book. Harry had a different memory: that two other members of his class who went to Harvard, Eddie Grossman and Alex Sarin, "had marvelous records,…far better than mine" (HJM 1980). The three roomed together.

[42] The chaperones on the school trip, about which Harry wrote in his first extant diary, were Augustus Klock–a "remarkable science teacher" at Fieldston who also taught the physicists J. Robert Oppenheimer and his brother, Frank–and Mrs. Klock (Cole 2009: 32). Like Frank Oppenheimer, Harry kept in touch with Klock for decades. When, in 1936, Klock taught "The Teaching of Chemistry in Secondary Schools" at the Harvard summer school, Harry and his wife sent flowers and invited the Klocks for dinner (HJML, 30 June 1936). He kept to his death four photos of Mr. Klock in his lab at Fieldston, where he taught 1910-60.

[43] It must be this relationship to which Harry referred in his diary on 24 December 1931, commenting on certain precious letters that he had brought with him and kept until his return home. In 1927, he remembered, his "rationalistic tendency led [him] to take pulse counts to calculate the

effect of the approach of the writer of these letters." A vertical marginal note in his diary, evidently referring to these letters, reads: "Consigned to the deep, SS. Veendam, Sept. 1933."

[44] Interviewed in 1986, Robert A. Riesman, Harvard '40, remembered that Jewish students tended to socialize in "cliques": "There were the New York Jews who had all gone to the Ethical Culture School [Fieldston] and some had gone to Horace Mann, and they were a group apart" (in N. Rosovsky 1986: 94).

[45] Harvard University, *Announcement of the Courses of Instruction Offered by the Faculty of Arts and Sciences for the Academic Year 1930-31*, 2nd ed. (1930), pp. 110-11 (courses). Harry's 1980 interview is the source for his undergraduate experiences. Harvard's privacy rules forbid access to academic records until eighty years have passed. Because the bulk of my research was conducted in 2005-07, I did not have access to those records.

[46] HJM 1931: 106.

[47] Eliot, qtd. H. Rosovsky 1986: 54; Karabel 2005: 40; N. Rosovsky 1986: 14.

[48] Lowell 1909: lxxxvi; Vesey 1965: 25.

[49] Karabel 2005: 78-86.

[50] Karabel 2005: 47-48, 85, 104. The Emergency Immigration Act of 1921 imposed quotas based on the country of birth, limiting the number to 3% of persons of any given origin recorded in the 1910 census. The Immigration Act of 1924 imposed more drastic quotas–2% of the number of persons living in the country in 1890, which was just before the vast immigration from Eastern Europe and Italy that populated P.S. 64.

[51] Frankfurter 1960: 31. Frankfurter, a City College graduate born in Vienna in 1882, emigrated with his family to the Lower East Side in 1884. He taught at Harvard from 1914 until 1939, when he was named to the United States Supreme Court. The praise of Frankfurter as "clean" and well mannered recalls Joseph Biden's comment during the 2008 presidential campaign that Barack Obama was "the first mainstream African-American who is articulate and bright and clean and a nice-looking guy."

[52] Morison 1936: 147.

[53] The phrase comes from a sermon in 1889 by Rabbi Joseph Silverman of Temple Emmanu-El in New York (qtd. Gorelick 1981: 29).

[54] Keller and Keller 2001: 59-63.

[55] Keller and Keller 2001: 159. See Chapter 6 for more on Hanford's memo to Conant. See also Karabel 2005: 172; Keller and Keller 2001: 38; and Barbara Miller Solomon (Radcliffe '40) in N. Rosovsky 1986: 96.

[56] Keller and Keller 1992: 38.

[57] Cohen 1993: 5-6.

[58] Karabel 2005: 51, 75.

[59] Karabel 2005: 87.

[60] Synnott 1979: 95 (photographs useless); unnamed Columbia alumnus qtd. N. Rosovsky 1986: 12 ("mental alertness tests").

[61] Starr 1986: 76.

[62] N. Rosovsky 1986: 15-16.

[63] Qtd. Steinberg 1974: 21.

[64] N. Rosovsky 1986: 15-17. At the 1922 commencement, Lowell announced the formation of the committee ("Names Men to Study Sifting at Harvard," *New York Times*, 23 June 1922). See Steinberg 1974: 21-30.

[65] "Harvard's Inquiry Starts on 4 Lines," *New York Times*, 24 June 1922.

[66] Keller and Keller 2001: 47.

[67] Starr 1986: 77.

[68] Harry Starr '21, "Plain Talk and High Thinking," *Crimson*, 6 June 1922.

[69] Qtd. Steel 1986: 75. In 1933 Lippmann "described Hitler as 'the authentic voice of a genuinely civilized people' and blamed Jews in Germany for the Nazi attacks on them"; five years later, he recommended shipping "surplus" Jews to Africa (Baker 1984: 349-50).

[70] Karabel 2005: 89, 107-09.

[71] Steinberg 1974: 30; Lewis H. Weinstein in N. Rosovsky 1986: 86.

[72] Synnott 1979: 108.

[73] Qtd. Karabel 2005: 172; see Keller and Keller 2001: 32.

[74] N. Rosovsky 1986: 20, 23; Synnott 1979: 110.

[75] Karabel 2005: 96; Synnott 1979: 98-99.

[76] Qtd. Steinberg 1974: 24.

[77] Karabel 2005: 107-09.

[78] Steinberg 1974: 30.

[79] Karabel 2005: 101.

[80] N. Rosovsky 1986: 23.

[81] Lewis H. Weinstein in N. Rosovsky 1986: 86.

[82] Qtd. N. Rosovsky 1986: 23.

[83] Karabel 2005: 89, 109, 168, 170-78.

[84] Karabel 2005: 97-98; Synnott 1979: 99-101.

[85] Synnott 1979: 114-16.

[86] Karabel 2005: 89, 109, 168, 170-78.

[87] HJML, 5 May 1933. Harry kept his notes on Fay's two-volume *The Origins of the World War* (1928) to the end of his life.

[88] Karabel 2005: 106.

[89] Keller and Keller 2001: 50.

Chapter 3

[1] HJML, 17 June 1931.

[2] HJMD, 19 and 20 June 1931.

[3] HJMD, 20 June 1931 (the day the moratorium was announced); HJM 1981.

[4] Goldschmidt 1992: 22.

[5] Anti-Semitic and radical right-wing ideas, already widespread among German university students, were unleashed when Hitler took power (Bühnen and Schaarschmidt 2005: 144).

[6] HJML, 25 June 1931. Dorn's doctoral dissertation (Dorn 1897) was his "promotion," not the *Habilitation* dissertation that would have qualified him to teach at a university. His 50-page memoir of his two years studying in England was published in Heidelberg (Dorn 1904). According to information gathered by Diana Weber of the Stadtarchiv Heidelberg, he was born 1 Feb. 1874 in Mannheim and died in Heidelberg on 12 Jan. 1960 (email, 25 Oct. 2007). In 1902 he was appointed Professor in the Helmholtz Gymnasium; he also taught German literary history at the Handelsschule in Mannheim. According to Elisabeth Hunerlach of the Heidelberg University archives, he began teaching the summer language course in 1929, and there is no record of his activity there after 1934 (email, 19 Nov. 2007). Dorn's translations from English indicate his humane sympathies: *A Philosophy for a Modern Man* (1947), by Hyman Levy, a member of the British Communist Party until his expulsion in 1958 for criticizing Russian anti-Semitism; and *World War, Its Cause and Cure* by Lionel Curtis (1947), which advocates the British Commonwealth as a model for a government uniting all nations.

[7] HJML, 29 June 1931.

[8] HJMD and HJML, both 27 June 1931.

[9] HJMD, 3 Aug. 1932.

[10] HJM 1980; HJM 1981; HJMD, 26 June 1931; HJML, 29 June 1931.

[11] HJML, 29 June and 2 Dec. 1931.

[12] HJML, 4 July 1931; HJML to Deborah and Alfred Hirschbach, 5 July 1931.

[13] HJM 1981.

[14] HJMD, 15 July 1931. The *Frankfurter Allgemeine Zeitung* was published thrice daily; Harry subscribed (HJML, 29 June 1931).

[15] HJML, 14 and 15 July 1931.

[16] HJML, 15 July 1931 (shop windows). On the building and the postwar restoration of the original inscription and the sculpture, see http://www.dem-lebendigen-geist.de/en/projekt/historie.html (which suggests "creative mind" rather than "living spirit" as the translation; accessed 27

Apr. 2011). The American ambassador to Germany, Jacob Gould Schurman, spearheaded the fund-raising drive for the building.

[17] HJMD, 9 Aug. 1931; Dorn to HJM, 20 Aug. 1931.

[18] HJML, 1 Jan. 1932.

[19] HJMD, 15 July, 31 July, and 3 Aug. 1932.

[20] HJMD, 7 Aug. 1933; Levy 1947.

[21] According to her granddaughter Bettina Basanow, Grete's formal name was Margarita, which she did not use (phone interview, 22 April 2008). The family was of Sephardic origin, as indicated not only by "Margarita" but by her maiden name, Juda, and her brother Fritz's marriage to a woman named Gracia Ascoli (see note 126 to Chapter 5).

[22] HJM 1981.

[23] HJMD, 30 Jan. 1932.

[24] HJMD, 17 and 29 Aug. 1932, 1 Mar. 1933; HJML, 1 Sept. and 26 Sept. 1932.

[25] HJMD, 1 Aug. 1932.

[26] HJML, 5 and 28 Oct. 1931. The Meyers also knew Harry's family, having met his parents on an earlier trip to Europe. On 30 Nov. 1931, he wrote to his parents: "What should I say about the Meyer Family? There are no great changes in them; Frau Juda [Grete Meyer's mother] is feeling poorly, to use New Englandisch."

[27] Harry mentioned the nephew in a letter, 22 May 1932.

[28] Heinz had lived "about 20 minutes away from the [Harvard] Yard" (HJML, 11 May 1933).

[29] HJML, 12 Oct. 1931.

[30] On Stone and Aron, see V. Berghahn 2001: 7. Mayer's mother was a Gottschalk.

[31] HJML, 26 Oct. 1931. According to a family tree constructed by Ernest (Ernst) Hirschbach and emended by his widow, Irene (to whom, my thanks for sending it), Alfred (1871-1951) was the oldest of five siblings: Martin (1873-1969), Walter (1874-1923), Hedwig (1885-1972, a journalist), and Felix (who died as a child). Rose and Martin lived out their old age comfortably in Fort Lauderdale, Florida.

[32] As a young man, according to his son Michael Freyhan (private communication), Max had cast off his family name, Cohen or Cohn, in favor of Freyhan, the name of his birthplace outside Breslau; Hans, who cherished his Jewish heritage, regretted his father's decision.

[33] HJMD, 23 July 1932.

[34] HJML, 20 Jan. and 26 Jan. 1932, and HJMD, 14 Feb. 1932. Harry's perverse enjoyment of his own surliness persisted for some years. The "damned telegrams" congratulating him on his marriage on 2 Mar. 1935 made him realize the advantages of his new state: his wife "put in a miser-

able day" answering the telegrams, and it was "delightful to have someone else do this dirty work" (HJML, 6 Mar. 1935).

[35] On Goldschmidt (later Goldsmith), see Chapter 5.

[36] HJML, 7 Dec. 1931.

[37] GML, 14 May 1934.

[38] Albisetti 1988: 242, 248. Born in 1882, Julia Gottschalk attended the
Royal Elisabeth School for Girls in Berlin from 1895-97 but was otherwise
(and unexceptionally) privately educated through the *Abitur*, the school-
leaving examination and her ticket to medical studies (Freie Universität
Berlin, Institut für Geschichte der Medizin, Dokumentation: Ärztinnen
im Kaiserreich, http://userpage.fu-berlin.de/~elehmus/HTML/rec00280c1.
html, accessed 18 May 2007). Because of insufficient provision for girls'
education, Julia was twenty-six when she passed the *Abitur* and thirty-
four when she completed the final stage of her training in 1916; she began
her private practice in 1919. She makes frequent appearances in a biography of Karl Jaspers, whose wife (born Gertrud Mayer) was her cousin and
"virtually a sister" (Kirkbright 2004: 52). Among the scraps of information
about Julia in this biography are her diagnosis of Max Weber's influenza
as fatal and a suicide letter to her from the young poet Walter Calé, who
was in love with her; Julia "felt she ought to have rescued Calé from his
fate" and sought "eternal penance" (2004: 58, 85, 197).

[39] Freidenreich 2002: 16-17, 81, 87.

[40] Marcus 1934: 244.

[41] Mendes-Flohr 1999: 26.

[42] Tyler 2004: 10.

[43] Mosse 1985: 2.

[44] Qtd. Hilberg 2003, 1: 47.

[45] Gay 1998: 111.

[46] Ludwig Gottschalk, 16 Mar. 1995, interview by USC Shoah Foundation Institute for Visual History and Education, University of Southern
California, accessed at Stanford Univ., tape 1490.

[47] HJMD, 7 Aug. 1933.

[48] Bat mitzvahs for girls did not exist then, and perhaps that lack of
pressure made later observance easier. In America, Lisel Meyer's family
observed Rosh Hashanah and Hanukkah as cultural, but not religious,
holidays. My sources are as follows: for Lisel's family, her daughter Eva
Mayer (interview, 12 May 2008); for Grete and Ernst Meyer's family, Rudy's daughter Bettina Basanow (phone interview, 17 May 2008).

[49] HJML, 15 Dec. 1931.

[50] E. Hirschbach n.d. (a): 2, 15.

[51] HJML, 7 Dec. 1931.

[52] HJML, 11 Oct. 1932.

⁵³ HJM 1981.

⁵⁴ HJML, 9 Aug. 1933. There was one exception to this rule: Lutz Gottschalk, who found his uncle something of a *luftmensch* (16 Mar. 1995, interview by USC Shoah Foundation Institute for Visual History and Education, University of Southern California, accessed at Stanford Univ., tape
1490.).

⁵⁵ E. Hirschbach n.d. (a): 12.

⁵⁶ HJML, 1 June 1931.

⁵⁷ P. Gottschalk 1967: 2.

⁵⁸ On the first of each month, Paul Gottschalk–who lived in the Charlottenburg district at Kuno-Fischer Strasse 13 (*Jüdisches Adressbuch für Gross-
Berlin*, 1929-30)–disbursed the funds that Harry's parents deposited in
P.G.'s New York dollar account (HJML, 7 and 19 Oct. 1931). Alfred Hirschbach took care of money transfers when Harry traveled out of Berlin.

⁵⁹ Paul Gottschalk's memoir appeared in German in 1965/66 in the
Börsenblatt für den deutschen Buchhandel, a professional journal (Kirkbright
2004: 348), and in English in 1967. It is the latter version, now an antiquarian item itself, from which I quote; it was "published at the time of the
dedication of the Research Library, University of Florida," the apparent
publisher (reverse of the title page). According to Arthur H. Minters (telephone interview, 18 July 2007), a librarian at the university asked P.G.
to write down the stories he had recounted so often so that the memoirs
could feature at the dedication; he was assisted in this task by two of his
former helpers–Minters and Robert L. Nikirk (who from 1970 served some
twenty years as librarian of the Grolier Club). I bought my copy from
Minters, who worked for him in 1953-64 first as packer and then with ad-
ministrative responsibilities. Minters persuaded P.G. late in life to move
his office to 84 University Place, where Minters also had an office. Such
was the affectionate concern P.G. inspired.

⁶⁰ P.G. knew a personal example of the fate of Jewish academics. His
cousin Gustav Mayer had worked briefly as an apprentice in his uncle's
antiquarian book business after completing his doctoral dissertation, and
then for years as a journalist before embarking on an academic career
(Mayer 1949: 64). Mayer's status at the University of Berlin was equivocal
even after he had amply proven himself as a scholar (Kater 1991: 90). On
the difficulties of Jews in academia, see Jarausch 2001: 14; Gallin 1986: 46;
Grüttner 2005: 78; Kampe 1993: 85n13, 87-100.

⁶¹ P. Gottschalk 1967: 1-2, 5-6.

⁶² Minters 1979: 138.

⁶³ Minters 1979: 139, 91.

⁶⁴ P. Gottschalk 1967: 12, 42-57.

⁶⁵ Kirkbright 2004: 120.

[66] HJM 1981. The other leading philosopher, he explained in a marginal note, was Martin Heidegger.

[67] P. Gottschalk 1967: 21.

[68] Harry brought Paul "photos of the postcard showing him 18 years ago as a *Schipper*" (HJMD, 22 June 1933).

[69] P. Gottschalk 1967: 20-21.

[70] P. Gottschalk 1967, 24, 34-35.

[71] HJML (in German) to Deborah and Alfred Hirschbach, 5 Oct. 1931.

[72] HJML, 6 Dec. 1931.

[73] HJMD, 7 Sept. 1932.

[74] HJML, 6 Oct. 1932.

[75] HJM 1981.

[76] HJMD, 25 Feb. 1932.

[77] HJM 1981. Sombart became a Nazi (HJM 1980).

[78] Hirsch 1946: 153.

[79] HJML, 11 Nov. 1931. The focus of the History Seminar (department) on medieval and modern history was justified by the existence of related "seminars" devoted to prehistory, ancient history, and Eastern European history (Betker 1997, "Einleitung," p. 1).

[80] HJML, 2 Nov. 1931.

[81] HJML, 25 Nov. 1931.

[82] HJML, 30 Oct. 1931.

[83] HJML, 5 July 1932. On German university ranks, see Grüttner 2005: 76-77.

[84] HJML, 3 Oct. 1931.

[85] HJML, 2 Dec. 1931.

[86] HJML, 25 and 11 Nov. 1931.

[87] HJML, 9 June 1932. Harry was referring to Charles A. Beard and Arthur M. Schlesinger, Sr. He had taken Schlesinger's course on American history 1840-1920 at Harvard (and kept his notes). Oncken had been a visiting professor at the University of Chicago in 1905-06, gaining "as deep an appreciation of American civilizations as possible" (Hirsch 1946: 151); the history of the "Anglo-Saxon world…was to become one of his main interests" (Betker 1997, "Hermann Oncken [1869-1945]," p. 2). Oncken was considered by most to be a masterful teacher, his "brilliant" lectures attracting a large following (Betker, p. 2).

[88] HJML, 2 Dec. and 15 Dec. 1931, 9 Jan. 1932.

[89] HJML, 2 Dec. 1931.

[90] HJMD, 5 May 1932.

[91] HJMD, 3 July 1932.

[92] HJML, 20 Dec. 1931.

[93] HJML, 2 Dec. 1931.

[94] HJMD, 17 Jan. 1933.

[95] HJMD, 15 Feb. 1933.

[96] HJM 1981.

[97] HJMD, 5 May 1933.

[98] HJMD, 3 May 1933. Masur, a student of Meinecke like Holborn and Gerhard, lost his position in 1935 and emigrated the following year to Colombia, one of a number of Latin American countries receiving refugees (Betker 1997, "Gerhard Masur [1901-1975], p. 3).

[99] HJML, 26 Jan. 1932.

[100] HJML, 13 Nov. 1932.

[101] HJML, 30 Nov. and 4 Dec. 1932.

[102] HJMD, 14 and 28 Nov., 7 Dec. 1932.

[103] Traubner 2003: 283.

[104] HJMD, 18 Dec. 1932, 28 Jan. 1933.

[105] HJMD, 12, 13, and 20 Jan. 1933.

[106] HJMD, 11 May, 14 June, 17 July 1933.

[107] *Nazionalsozialistische Deutsche Studentenbund*; see Bühnen and Schaarschmidt 2005: 149.

[108] HJML, 6 June 1933.

[109] HJM 1981; HJML, 11 Nov. 1931.

[110] HJMD, 22 May 1932.

[111] HJML, 22 Aug. 1932.

[112] Klemperer 1998: 51 (16 Jan. 1934).

[113] HJML, 21 June 1932.

[114] HJMD, 2 and 5 Feb. 1933.

[115] HJMD, 11 and 20 Aug. 1932.

[116] HJML, 9 June 1932, 17 July 1933; HJMD, 17 July 1933.

[117] HJMD, 13 June, 3 July, 27 June 1932.

[118] HJMD, 16 Apr. 1932. As he worked on his Harvard dissertation, Harry realized he had collected "a lot of pamphlet material…that you probably can't find elsewhere in this country" (HJML, 10 Nov. 1936).

[119] HJMD, 18, 19, and 21 Mar.; 1 and 5 Apr. 1932.

[120] HJMD, 23 Mar., 7 Apr. 1932.

[121] HJML to Hannah Marks, 28 July 1932.

[122] In actuality, it was a Foreign Office functionary who announced that Germany would target "every building which is marked with three stars in *Baedeker*" (Rothnie 1992: 131).

[123] HJMD, 1 Aug. 1932.

[124] HJMD, 3 Aug. 1932; HJML, 7 Aug. 1932.

[125] Artz listed Harry along with eminent established historians of Europe as readers of the book in manuscript (Artz 1934: xiii; Artz to Langer, 22 Jan. 1934, Langer Papers, Harvard University Archives, Personal Corre-

spondence, Box 1, 1924-36, HUG(FP) 19.9). There are no statistical tables in the book, part of a series edited by Langer. On Artz (born in 1894; Harvard PhD, 1924), see Ropp and Pinkney 1964.

[126] HJMD, 2 Aug. 1932.

[127] HJMD, 25 July 1932; HJML, 5, 7, 20, 24 Aug. 1932

[128] HJMD, 15 and 21 July and 31 Aug. 1932, 19 Aug. 1933; HJML, 5 Sept. 1932.

[129] HJML 8 Sept. 1932; HJMD, 29 Sept. 1932.

[130] HJMD, 20 Oct. 1932 (Bergner); HJML, 18 Oct. 1932 (university) and 26 Oct. 1932 (synagogue). Bergner, who was Jewish, left Germany in 1933 and resumed her career in English, which she had learned out of foresight; for an appreciation of her acting that equals Harry's in enthusiasm, see E. and K. Mann 1939: 41-44. On the rioting at the University of Vienna, see the dispatch dated 20 Oct. 1932 by Gilchrist B. Stockton, the American minister (ambassador) to Austria (http://images.library.wisc.edu/FRUS/EFacs/1932v02/reference/frus.frus1932v02.i0009.pdf).

[131] HJML, 27 Oct. 1932.

[132] HJML, 2 Nov. 1932.

[133] Fromm 1990: 45, 48 (6 and 15 Mar. 1932).

[134] Carsten 1967: 149. In his memoir (1981), Harry did discuss the strike, presumably drawing on both memory and secondary sources: when Papen "failed to crush a Berlin subway workers' strike in which subway workers whether Nazi or Communist joined forces together, the behind-the-scenes maneuvering to replace Papen with an effective government that would avert the danger" made "the conservative and reactionary pillars of society" fear a union of liberal and left-wing forces "that was quite improbable of achievement." The Communists and Nazis united in order to discredit the SPD. On the strike and election, see Large 2000: 249-52.

[135] HJMD, 5 Nov. 1932.

[136] Schupo is a shortened form of Schutzpolizei (literally, protective police), the municipal police.

[137] HJML, 2 Dec. and 4 Oct. 1931; Large 2000: 248 (unemployment figures).

[138] The Voss and the Tageblatt, both Jewish-owned, soon fell foul of the Nazis.

[139] HJML, 17 Dec. 1931 (Pertinax), 7 Oct. 1931 (American magazines); HJMD, 7 Jan. 1933 (Coolidge's death), 5 Feb. 1932 (Framm).

[140] HJML, 1 June 1932.

[141] HJML, 12 May 1933.

[142] HJML, 1 June 1932; Large 2000: 244 (ninety-nine killed).

[143] HJML, 9 and 13 June 1932. Kuhle Wampe is described by a recent critic, Glenn Erickson, as "an unusual mixture of artistry and agit-prop, a fascinating ticket to Berlin in 1932" (review dated 27 June 2009; http://

www.dvdtalk.com/dvdsavant/s2956wamp.html; see also http://www.
dvdtalk.com/dvdsavant/s2919wamp.html, both accessed 20 Feb. 2010).
Kuhle Wampe ("cool [signifying 'empty'] belly") was a former summer
resort on the Müggelsee outside Berlin that had been turned into a tent
camp for the homeless. The film was released in April 1932 and banned
definitively in March 1933. A review in the New York Times (24 Apr. 1933)
leaned toward Harry's assessment ("prosaic," "scarcely lives up to expectations"); in New York, the film was preceded by speeches "denouncing
Hitlerism and the persecution of the Jews."

[144] HJML, 19 June 1932 ("Hitler's SA").

[145] Plotkin 2009: 68. On the back of the photo, Harry wrote "W.E."
and the date (9 July 1933); nothing that Harry recorded of his conversations with Walter can explain his membership in the Steel Helmet. Wulf-
Ekkehard Lucke kindly identifed the uniform as that of the Greater Berlin
branch of the Steel Helmet. My thanks also to Gottfried Niedhart for for-
warding my query to Dr. Lucke.

[146] Klemperer, 27 Jan. 1934; 1998: 52. On the Reichsbanner (founded in
1924 and suppressed in March 1933) and the Red Front-Fighters League
(founded in 1924 and suppressed in 1929), see Diehl 1977: 175-90 and 244-
58; on the Reichsbanner, see also Rohe 1966; on the Iron Front demonstration, see Plotkin 2009: 131. Klemperer noted the "unconcealed hostility between SA and Stahlhelm" (21 Feb. 1934; 1998: 56); the S.A. was suppressed
on 30 June 1934 (the Night of the Long Knives or Röhm Putsch).

[147] HJML, 19 June 1932.

[148] HJML, 30 June 1932. While Harry was in Heidelberg, a Kravall involving Nazi, Jewish, and left-wing students resulted in the closure of the
university and the even-handed expulsion of three right-wing and three
left-wing students (Bühnen and Schaarschmidt 2005: 150-51). Even early
in Harry's Berlin days, it was sufficiently common for the university to be
closed on account of riots that he merely commented: "Wieder Kravall" (a
riot again) and repaired to Aschinger's to discuss "the gloomy situation
over lunch" with a fellow student (HJMD, 4 Feb. 1932). Aschinger's was "a
combination restaurant and bakery chain similar to Child's in America"
(Plotkin 2009: 30; Childs was an American chain founded in New York in
1889 and popular throughout the country in the 1920s-30s).

[149] Kessler 1999: 423 (12 July 1932).

[150] HJML, 28 June 1932 (Vorwärts), 12 July 1932 ("another Kravall"), and
28 June 1932 (opera).

[151] HJML, 30 June 1932 (shutting down papers), 18 July 1932 (prohibition of demonstrations). The two events described in the following paragraph–the swarms of Nazis and the Communist demonstration--took
place on 10 July and 12 July (HJML, 11 July and 14 July 1932).

152 HJML, 18 July 1932; HJMD, 20 July 1932.

153 Josef Gugler, a native German speaker, notes that Harry's German is imperfect; a native speaker would say "nicht für Juden" (personal communication, 9 Apr, 2007). In a similar example, Plotkin's companion, watching a Nazi parade, asked a woman the name of the marchers' song; she replied: "I do not speak to Jews!" (2009: 106).

154 HJML, 18 July 1932 (fly sheets); HJMD, 20 July 1932 (fly sheets), 24 July 1932 ("not for Jews"), 20 July 1932 (writing to Artz); Fromm 1990: 55 (on Grzesinski, 12 Aug. 1932, quoting an eyewitness report of 20 July 1932).

155 HJML, 30 July 1932.

156 HJML, 14 Oct. 1932 ("foundation for the Nazis"); HJMD, 20 Jan. 1933 ("herdmindedness"). For an illustration of the Rote Fahne, see Plotkin 2009.

157 HJML, 18 Jan. 1933; Ascher 2007: 61-65.

158 Leon Trotsky, expelled from the USSR in Feb. 1929, was granted asylum in France in 1933. See Niewyk 1980: 64-66. On Cohn's career, see Lorenz 2004, from which I take some of my facts; Bentwich 1953: 38, 85; and Walton-Jordan 2000: 1, 4. Cohn, who settled in England, later refused to help prosecute war crimes because he considered this task inappropriate for a Jew, who might be biased.

Chapter 4

1 HJM 1981. "Private first class" is the American equivalent of the British term "lance corporal," which translates Hitler's military rank (Gefreiter) in the German army in World War I.

2 Prince Max von Hohenlohe, qtd. E. and K. Mann 1939: 67 ("Austrian corporal"); Carsten 1967: 151-52 ("wave of enthusiasm"); Fromm 1990: 76 (2 Feb. 1933). Hitler became a German citizen on 25 Feb. 1932.

3 HJMD, 30 Jan. (Hitler more moderate), 5 Feb. (Goethe's Faust Part I, line 2096). All references to Harry's diary and letters in this chapter are to 1933, unless otherwise noted.

4 Speech to the Reichstag, 30 Jan. 1939, in Noakes and Pridham 1990, 2:1049.

5 Qtd. M. Berghahn 1984: 70.

6 HJMD, 24 July 1932.

7 Hanfstaengl 1934: 8. Hanfstaengl hid Hitler from arrest following the failed putsch in 1923.

8 HJML, 12 Feb.; cf. Plotkin's muted account of the speech (2009: 155). Goebbels founded the newspaper Der Angriff in 1927. The Nazi hijacking of the German national anthem, popularly known as "Deutschland über

Alles," has led to a common misunderstanding that the song advocated Germany's triumph "über alles" (over all). When August Heinrich Hoffmann von Fallersleben wrote the words in 1841, however, his revolutionary intention was to emphasize a future single nation (*Deutschland*) made up of all (*alles*) the constituent states.

⁹ HJML, 1 Mar. and 19-20 Feb.

¹⁰ HJML, 20 Feb. Rust, a former high school teacher, was appointed *Kultusminister* on 6 Feb.; his portfolio included education. On 1 June 1934, he became Reich Minister of Science, Education and National Culture, a position that gave him full power to reshape German education on Nazi lines. His death by suicide on V-E Day (8 May 1945) was not well enough known to prevent his posthumous indictment by the United Nations War Crimes Commission.

¹¹ HJML, 20 Feb. The *Kongress "Das Freie Wort"* (literally, "free word") was among the last such public anti-Nazi protests; Einstein, Kollwitz, Heinrich Mann, and Thomas Mann were among the participants. Harry's parents could have read about it in the *New York Times* ("Nazis Stop Rally for Free Speech," 20 Feb. 1933). Ferdinand Tönnies (1855-1936) became president of the German Society for Sociology in 1909; in 1933, the Nazis ejected him from both the society and his position at the University of Kiel.

¹² HJML, 8 Mar.; Evans 2003: 392. There is, however, more to the story. According to Kater (2008: 109), Fritz Busch "allowed himself to be sent by the Nazis on a cultural propaganda tour to South America" and later inflated his anti-Nazi credentials; see also Kater 1997: 120-25.

¹³ HJML, 19 Mar.; Kater 1997: 115 ("invitations," sadness). Thomas Mann condemned Richard Strauss and Wilhelm Furtwängler, who replaced Walter, as Nazi "lackeys" (T. Mann 1982: 134 [21 Mar. 1933]).

¹⁴ HJML, 22 Feb. (Gendarmenmarkt); HJMD, 18 Mar. ("best uniforms"), 13 Mar. ("wrecked"). The fired conductors were Paul Breisach and Fritz Stiedry, "the latter one of the finest in the country." Ebert, a "pure Aryan," found refuge first in Turkey and then in the United States (Bentwich 1953: 93).

¹⁵ HJML, 22 Feb. (Karl-Marx School); HJMD, 20 Feb. (Nazi parade), 23 Feb. (Brose).

¹⁶ HJMD, 25 Feb. ("bad dream"), 20 Feb. ("Pfülf's book"). Harry refers to Otto Pfülf's *Die Anfange der deutschen Provinz der neu erstandenen Gesellschaft Jesu: und ihr Wirken in der Schweiz 1805-1847* (Freiburg im Breisgau: Herder, 1922).

¹⁷ HJM, letter (unsent) to Joseph Doob, dated 28 Feb. and pasted in Harry's diary. Doob, who knew German, had already completed his doctorate in mathematics at Harvard (interview with J. Laurie Snell, http://www.dartmouth.edu/~chance/Doob/conversation.html, accessed 9/14/09).

¹⁸ HJML, 28 Feb. ("initiated"; unsent letter to Joe Doob). The German reads: *Giftpflanzen asiastischer Provienz, diese politischen Mordbuben.*

¹⁹ HJML, 1 Mar. ("moralities"), 8 Mar. ("Nazi *Nutten*"), 15 Mar. ("sub-human"); HJMD, 31 May ("clouds and swarms").

²⁰ HJM 1981.

²¹ I quote from Harry's letter to Doob, 28 Feb. Most contemporary non-Nazi commentators agreed with Harry's interpretation; however, recent analyses have concluded that van der Lubbe acted alone (Evans 2003: 328-31).

²² HJMD, 28 Feb.

²³ Klemperer 1998: 50 (13 Jan. 1934).

²⁴ HJML, 28 Feb. (Liebknecht Haus; letter to Doob), 4 Mar. ("dull soggy absence"), 21 Mar. ("Land of the Free").

²⁵ Qtd. Fromm 1990: 123-24 (20 July).

²⁶ HJML, 4 Mar. (anti-republican flags, "troops of Nazis"); Fromm 1990: 82 ("howling mobs"; 10 Mar. 1933).

²⁷ HJML, 15 Mar.

²⁸ HJML, 4 Mar. Kerr, who was forced out of Switzerland because he was denied a work permit, continued reporting in London; he was "the most brilliant dramatic critic in Berlin" and "a determining influence on the development of German drama" (E. and K. Mann 1939: 197; Palmier 2006: 157 re the work permit). Ludwig's full name was Emil Ludwig Cohn; his use of "Emil Ludwig" as a "confusing" pen name offended Nazi officials (Noakes and Pridham 1990, 1: 526-27). Harry "learned privately"– presumably from Paul Gottschalk–about Wolff's departure; he hid briefly in Bavaria, left the country, and settled in Nice, where he was captured and sent to the Orianienburg camp, where he died (Palmier 2006: 91, 94, 197, 449).

²⁹ HJML, 4 Mar.

³⁰ HJM 1981, the source as well of the next quotation.

³¹ HJM 1981 (*"Legal zur Macht"*); HJML, 8 Mar. (children marching).

³² Reichstag rules required the Enabling Act to be passed by a two-thirds vote; this was achieved through persuading the Zentrum to join the Nazis and Nationalists, and then manipulating the process further to achieve a decisive vote of 441 to 94 (Kershaw 1999: 466-68).

³³ HJM 1981, the source also of the following quotation.

³⁴ The physician was probably Julia Gottschalk, who did not leave Germany until 1936 or 1937 (see Chapter 5).

³⁵ HJML, 1 Mar. (*"Dichter und Denker"*), 6 Mar. ("talking with people," treasurer).

³⁶ HJML, 10 Mar. (routinely attacked), 17 Mar. (Stalin).

³⁷ Dawidowicz 1975: 52; Noakes and Pridham 1990, 1: 529.

³⁸ HJML, 12 Mar. The *Frankfurter Allgemeiner Zeitung* reported that "a

strong troop of S.A. men" invaded the Law Courts shouting, "Out with the Jews!" (qtd. Anon, 1936: 36).

[39] Evans 2003: 432 (Breslau courts); Large 2000: 289, 291 (Berlin lawyers).

[40] Fromm 1990: 106 (4 Apr.).

[41] HJML, 15 Apr. ("mostly nothing else"), 1 Mar. (*8 Uhr Abendblatt*), 14 Mar. (rumor), and 19 Mar. (sold its soul).

[42] Mosse 2000: 72.

[43] HJML, 21 Mar. (condemnation of *Tageblatt*); W. Dodd 1941: 258 (circulation).

[44] HJML, 3 Apr. ("as it has"); HJMD, 22 May ("foreign ones banned").

[45] HJML, 22 May. Feuchtwanger, who had spoken publicly about Hitler's poor prose in *Mein Kampf*, was on a lecture tour in America when the break-in occurred; he took the advice of German diplomats in the U.S. not to return to Germany (E. and K. Mann 1939: 37). He incorporated the break-in in his novel *The Oppermanns*.

[46] Fromm 1990: 41-42 (15 Jan. 1932).

[47] M. Dodd 1939: 99-100.

[48] HJML, 1 Mar. (buying foreign papers, *Angriff*), 6 Aug. (Zurich itself).

[49] HJML, 21 Mar. In 1934, Frederick Birchall, the chief European correspondent for the *Times*, said that the Berlin bureau was "the central target of official dislike because of its ownership" (Leff 2005: 51).

[50] W. Dodd 1941: 24, 26. The next month, a British journalist was arrested "on charges of transmitting 'atrocity reports' abroad and espionage" (Norwood 2009: 8). Mowrer, then president of the foreign correspondents association in Berlin, "enraged Propaganda Minister Joseph Goebbels, who said he would expend an army division to capture" him (obit, *Time*, 1977; http://www.time.com/time/magazine/article/0,9171,947282,00.html, accessed 18 Feb. 2008). Dodd, the recently appointed American ambassador, was a University of Chicago historian with a PhD from the University of Leipzig.

[51] HJMD and HJML, 8 Mar. Between 3 Mar. and 10 Oct. 1933, there were twenty-six attacks on Americans, the majority in Berlin; six occurred between 3 and 8 March, all but one before Harry left Germany ("Nazi Attacks on Americans," *New York Times*, 13 Oct. 1933).

[52] HJML, 8 Mar. (cable), 17 Mar. (Dahlberg). See "Another American Attacked," *New York Times* , 15 Mar. 1933. Dahlberg's novel *Those Who Perish* includes scenes in New York in which stormtroopers shout *"Heil Hitler!"* and an anti-war protester is beaten by ushers at a movie house when he screams "Down with war!" (1934: 555, 560).

[53] HJML, 18 Mar. (student from Los Angeles), 10 Mar. (Harry's prudence); HJMD, 16 Mar. (Frau Meyer's suggestion).

[54] HJML, 11 Apr. (censor); HJMD, 26 July (caution), 1 July (letter opened). As a foreigner, Harry was exempt from this questionnaire; how-

ever, as noted later in this chapter, he had to fill out a "racial" questionnaire for foreigners when he "exmatriculated" from the university just before leaving Germany.

⁵⁵ HJML, 28 June ("thinning"); HJMD, 24 and 26 June (Holborn and Gottschalk). In the summer semester of 1933, all students known to have been active Communists were ordered expelled and their names placed on a list to ensure that no other university would admit them (Bühnen and Schaarschmidt 2005: 154).

⁵⁶ W. Dodd 1941: 56, 121-22, 65.

⁵⁷ HJML, 21 Mar. (keeping your mouth shut), 14 Mar. ("3rd degree"), 12 Mar. (Dr. Stock). A Prince of Reuss who managed an opera house in 1918 was perhaps the patron in question (see "Rhineland Moves for a Republic," *New York Times*, 7 Dec. 1918).

⁵⁸ HJML, 12 Mar.

⁵⁹ HJMD, 23 Apr. The *Rote Fahne* reappeared underground; in June 1933, Harry Kessler read in a Vienna paper "that the *Rote Fahne* has once again an illegal distribution of three hundred thousand copies (!?)" (Weitz 1997: 287-88; Kessler 1999: 461 [28 June]).

⁶⁰ HJML, 11 June.

⁶¹ HJML, 26 Apr. (*Tannhäuser*), 19 June (Huberman, Strauss). On Göring and Blech, see Kater 1997: 83, 89-90; see Kater 1997 on Furtwängler's and Strauss's complicated relationship with the Nazi regime (195-211). From exile Huberman wrote an open letter to his erstwhile German musical friends, such as Strauss and Furtwängler: "You should have found the courage to cut adrift from a country which banishes musicians whose standing is equal to your own because their race or their ideas do not suit the regime" (qtd. E. and K. Mann 1939: 216-17).

⁶² HJML, 19 June (Adolf Busch); T. Mann 1982: 174 (4 Oct. 1933). On the anti-Nazi stance of Adolf Busch, younger brother of Fritz, see Kater 1997: 121. Before long, Nazi agents visited Busch in Switzerland, inviting him back to Germany; the "agents retired in disorder" at the prospect of Jewish music played by a Jewish pianist when he agreed, with one condition: that he and his pupil (and future son-in-law) Rudolf Serkin would play Mendelssohn (E. and K. Mann 1939: 260).

⁶³ HJMD, 6 July (*Three Penny Opera*) and 30 July (film). The film was reviewed in the *New York Times* when it opened in New York (28 May 1934).

⁶⁴ Allert 2008: 11.

⁶⁵ HJML, 21 June. The term *"feine Herren"* acquired "a certain pejorative, sarcastic undertone" as it shifted from a literal meaning attached to the nobility to a scornful implication in the mouths of working men (Daniel Becker, email, 20 Mar. 2008).

⁶⁶ Edelheit and Edelheit 1994: 299 ff.; Noakes and Pridham 1990, 1:223-25.

[67] Gallin 1986: 108.

[68] Jarausch 2001: 15; Gallin 1986: 92.

[69] Edelheit and Edelheit 1994: 300 (law); Schlemmer 1972: 312 (letter to Gunda Stötzl, 16 June 1933).

[70] Qtd. Marcus 1934: 8.

[71] Fromm 1990: 133 (20-21 Oct. 1933).

[72] Marcus 1934: 9.

[73] Hilberg 2003, 1: 137-43.

[74] HJML, 6 Aug.

[75] HJML, 11 June. American diplomats came to the same conclusion (McDonald 2007: 80 [14 Aug. 1933]). On Nazified school mathematics texts, see E. Mann 1938: 67-68.

[76] HJML, 16 June.

[77] HJML, 5 May ("gentile kids," university students, IDs, mirror); HJMD, 15 May ("free man").

[78] Marcus 1934: 11.

[79] HJML, 8 May ("Never-Never land," "freedom"), 28 June (flags at half-mast), 26 Sept. 1932 (meaning of treaty)

[80] HJML, 17 Aug. ("the less…the better"), 12 July (Klages); HJM 1981 ("mediums & quacks"). A mystical anti-Semite, Klages fell out with the Nazis by 1936. On his thought, see Rohkramer 1999.

[81] HJMD, 21 May (Gerhard); HJML, 22 May (Gottschalk).

[82] HJML, 28 June. George Grosz's well-known allegorical painting, *Sonnenfinsternis* (*Eclipse of the Sun*, 1926), depicts a blindfolded donkey–symbolizing the people–eating a newspaper; it is now at the Hecksher Museum in Huntingdon, NY (http://www.heckscher.org/pages.php?which_page=collection_george_grosz, accessed 20 Feb. 2010).

[83] Kessler 1999: 419 (11 June 1932). According to Kali Israel, "no one [in the West] was NOT using Alice between the wars" (email, 29 Oct. 2008). She adds that the phrase "Hitler in Wonderland" was common.

[84] HJML, 18 May.

[85] HJML, 18 May ("spring time"), 12 and 15 May (Oberfohren). The Nazis targeted Oberfohren because they thought he suspected that they were behind the Reichstag fire (Evans 2003: 370).

[86] Goeschel 2007: 23-26.

[87] HJML, 19 June. Denounced by some of his own students, Mayer (a Jew) survived the initial horror and emigrated to France in 1933; he was arrested by the Gestapo in 1944 and deported to Auschwitz, where he died (http://www.dictionaryofarthistorians.org/mayera.htm, accessed 2 Dec. 2009).

[88] HJMD, 20 Apr. The report of the purging of libraries anticipated a document entitled "Principles for the Cleansing of Public Libraries," pub-

lished on 16 May 1933, which named many titles that had been consigned to the flames on 10 May 1933; for a list of burned books, see www.library. arizona.edu/exhibits/burnedbooks/documents.htm (accessed 27 Nov. 2009).

[89] HJMD, 21 Apr.

[90] 1 April was chosen because it was the last Saturday before Easter and a major shopping day.

[91] HJML, 15 Apr.

[92] Kessler 1999: 451 (1 Apr. 1933), 454 (5 May 1933).

[93] HJMD, 28 Mar. ("oily and dirty"), 5 Apr. ("principality"); HJML, 8 Apr. (Stolberg family).

[94] HJML, 9 Apr. (photograph, exodus); HJMD, 11 Apr. (cable, "Debanalf"), 3 May ("P.G.'s cousin," a phrase used again in letters on 16 May and 9 Aug.).

[95] HJML, 24 Apr. ("reorganisation"), 27 Apr. ("purge," "German physics"). Philipp Lenard, winner of the Nobel Prize in Physics and author of *German Physics*, expressed his "ecstatic" admiration of Hitler as early as 1924 (Weinreich 1999: 11).

[96] I quote Roland Richter's translation (www.library.arizona.edu/exhibits/burnedbooks/documents.htm). The text can be found in Strothmann 1968: 77-78 and (in a reproduction of the flyer and a translation) in Anon 1936: 172-73. Harry copied considerable portions of the theses into a letter to his parents (26 Apr.). From 1931 on, the German Student Body was dominated by the National Socialist German Students' League (*Nationalsozialistische Deutsche Studentenbund*).

[97] HJML, 3 May (Lutz Gottschalk's high school, history teachers), 26 May (Nazi songs), 5 May (university students); Ludwig Gottschalk, 16 Mar. 1995, interview by USC Shoah Foundation Institute for Visual History and Education, University of Southern California, accessed at Stanford Univ., tape 1490 (Lutz graduating); HJMD, 5 May (Christern). On the Nazi song, see Snyder 1984: 39. On Christern's Nazism, see Betker 2006 ("Herman Christern [1892-1941]," pp. 5-6).

[98] HJMD, 27 June ("grand bunch"), 24 June (contact with Hertneck), 5 July and 16 July (Holborn's intervention; conversation with Hertneck). Hertneck had edited Marx's writings on labor unions, *Karl Marx und die Gewerkschaften* (1928). The "older Liebknecht" was Karl's father, Wilhelm (1826-1900), another founder of the SPD.

[99] HJML, 13 Apr. The census of June 1933 listed 499,862 "Jews by religion." Today historians estimate that somewhat more than 500,000 Jews lived in Germany, along with nearly as many Germans with some Jewish background.

[100] Shirer 1941: 15; Haffner 2002: 127.

[101] HJML, 15 Apr. ("something horrible"), 8-9 Apr. (German Jew arrested); HJMD, 6 Aug. ("article listing atrocities," "son had died," Martin Hirschbach), 11 July (obit of MP), 10 Aug. (Fritz Freyhan's friend), 13 Aug. ("big SS Mann").

[102] Kaplan 1998: 51; HJMD, 26 Aug.

[103] Allert 2008: 30, 89. In some places, Jews were forbidden to give the German greeting, a prohibition later made general as a means of further stigmatization (Allert 2008: 38).

[104] In 1934, Heine's poem *"Die Lorelei"* was still being sung in schools, but ascribed to an "unknown" author (Fromm 1990: 168 [19 June 1934]). Erika Mann estimated that a German child "says 'Heil Hitler!' from 50 to 150 times a day" (1938: 21).

[105] "A favorite anecdote" among Jews concerned a visiting "race hygiene" expert who ironically picked a Jewish child to demonstrate "Aryan" characteristics (Kaplan 1998: 35). For a 1934 photograph of a teacher using a child to demonstrate the "ideal Nordic type of youth," see Guérin 1994.

[106] HJMD, 27 Aug. ("Fritz fleeing"); Allert 2008: 37 (Sleeping Beauty).

[107] HJMD, 28 Aug.

[108] Klemperer 1998: 38 (23 Oct. 1933).

[109] HJML, 17 Apr. The acquaintance on the train was probably Raymond Goldschmidt, who emigrated the next year to the United States. On *Devisen* regulations hampering emigration of German Jews, see McDonald 2007: 511-12, 523, 553-57 (Oct.-Nov. 1934).

[110] HJML, 3 May ("Holland or Paris"); HJMD, 4 May (Meyers' guest).

[111] "60,000 Have Fled from Nazis' Reich," *New York Times*, 6 Dec. 1933. Caron accepts these figures, with minor variants (1999: 2). For the 22,000 in Paris in 1933, see Moore 1986: 21. The German refugee population in France in the 1930s was about 30,000 (Palmier 2006: 184).

[112] HJML, 3 May.

[113] Moore 1986: 17 (emigrants 1933-39); Bühne and Schaarschmidt 2005: 143-44 (breaking off studies).

[114] HJML, 19 Apr. (Fritz's departure), 27 Aug. ("dreaming of Palestine," back from a trip). On 1 Apr., the day of the boycott, Jews were indeed taken off trains at the frontier and required the next day to obtain a permit (Anon. 1936: 41-42). No one could be sure what rules applied.

[115] Dorothy Thompson, qtd. on title page of E. and K. Mann 1939.

[116] HJML, 17 Mar. ("stop complaining"), 21 Mar. (Jews without choice, Göring). Harry was quoting an interview with Göring in *De Telegraaf* (Amsterdam).

[117] Some of the families in Harry's social circle were listed in the *Jüdisches Adressbuch für Gross-Berlin* (1929/30). According to Large, the Berlin Jewish population was 160,564 in 1933 (2000: 289).

[118] HJML, 19 May 1932 (German law), 25 June (lawyer).

[119] Wassermann 1933: 1; Mayer 1949: 6-15, 364-74. Wassermann updated his autobiography, published in German in 1921, with a long final chapter that took into account the *Machtergreifung*. The letters he had "received...from every class of German society" expressed the writers' dismay at anti-Semitism; but these were "empty words," for all had "grown much worse" (1933: 279).

[120] Wassermann 1933: 197; Ludwig Strauss, qtd. Mendes-Flohr 1999: 50, 59-63 (the puzzling question). Dual identity, being German *and* Jewish, was analyzed at length by Franz Rosenzweig (1886-1929), a major figure in the German Jewish Renaissance (Mendes-Flohr 1999: 83-88).

[121] Mendes-Flohr 1988: 27, 34-35.

[122] Mayer 1949: 13-14 (German poetry), 365 ("as tenderly"), 361 ("the universities"); HJML, 1 Feb. ("losing his job").

[123] Mayer 1949: 372.

[124] HJML, 15 Apr. (exporting Paul); HJMD, 24 Feb. ("no good"). For similar stories of sudden arrests, see Klemperer 1998: 9-10 (29 March 1933).

[125] Moore 1986: 36 ("flood"); HJML, 15 Apr. (*Beobachter*). On Rotterdam as "an important centre for re-emigrants" like Paul, see Moore 1986: 197n62.

[126] Qtd. Caron 1999: 16. On the French reception of the German refugees, see Palmier 2006: 184-94; the Netherlands was the most consistently welcoming European country (Palmier 2006:144-45). Google Books makes it possible in an instant to find an announcement in *L'Univers Israélite* for 1907-08 of Fritz Juda's marriage to Gracia Ascoli in Paris on 22 September 1907, as well as a reference in the *American Cloak and Suit Review* of July 1919 to him as an artist who co-created a new fashionable silhouette. Evidently Fritz Ruda worked for a couturier.

[127] HJMD, 3 July (Lisel in Florence); HJML, 15 Apr. (Rudy's exams, Claire at hospital); Bühnen and Schaarschmidt 2005: 157 (few students able to continue); Bernhardt 1989: 69 (Racial Hygiene).

[128] Tyler 2004: 19.

[129] Rose's father was Bernhard Borchard. Rose and her siblings "turned away from their religion," according to Ernest Hirschbach, "in spite of their father's strong involvement in Jewish community affairs–or perhaps because of it" (E. Hirschbach n.d. [a]: 23-24).

[130] HJML, 15 Apr. (visiting Hirschbachs), 16 Apr. (Harry's cable); 19 Apr. (Paul Gottschalk's cable).

[131] HJML, 26 May (Rose's job); Evans 2003: 381 (*Gleichschaltung*). Kaplan (1998) translates *Gleichschaltung* as "nazification."

[132] HJMD, 6 Aug. (new job, MH's business, appeal to Freddy, "desperate" situation, Ernst); HJML, 6 Aug. (worry about future, Peter, Gerhard,

moving); Tyler 2004: 11 (bread-winner). Schools under Jewish auspices in Berlin ranged from two varieties of Orthodox through Zionist to secular (Marcus 1934: 215).

[133] HJML, 6 Aug.

[134] Marcus 1934: 14. The Reich Statistics Office estimated that 48.9% of German Jews were in "Commerce and Trade" (Noakes and Pridham 1990, 1: 522).

[135] Marcus 1934: 16.

[136] HJMD, 17 Apr.

[137] HJML, 17 Apr.

[138] Paul's nephew Lutz later said that notwithstanding Ernst's help, Paul "had great difficulty after 1929," and by 1935 his firm "was a losing business (Ludwig Gottschalk, 16 Mar. 1995, interview by USC Shoah Foundation Institute for Visual History and Education, University of Southern California, accessed at Stanford Univ., tape 1490). Lutz, who had fallen out with Paul after moving to the United States, may have exaggerated the decline in business; there is nothing in Paul Gottschalk's memoir to suggest that it was losing money in 1935. On conducting his business in dollars, see P. Gottschalk 1967: 34.

[139] HJMD, 17 Apr. Sympathetic "Aryan" patients eventually left Jewish doctors (Freidenreich 2002: 171). Many Germans preferred the Jewish doctors for their expertise, and "some also tended to visit them as an act of political disapproval" (Kater 1989: 189).

[140] HJML, 15, 17 Apr.

[141] HJML, 6 June ("despot"); HJMD, 5 June ("seriocomic story"), 24 May ("gloomy"' view).

[142] Evans 2005: 565; Kaplan 1998: 11.

[143] HJML, 9 Aug. (nearly destitute), 17 Apr. (studying stenography).

[144] In his 1980 interview he said: "Some of my Communist friends trusted me with mimeographed leaflets and posters and some underground printed material to take out. I had them with me in my baggage on the train and wondered what was going to happen."

[145] The translated documents are in Harry's papers. The typewriting and typeface resemble his typewritten letters of the 1930s; he did not have a typewriter in Berlin, so he must have done the translations soon after returning to the United States.

[146] HJMD, 19 Aug. (Walter and Betty's humiliating situation), 9 July (MG training). A respondent to my query posted on H-German said that "MG training" meant first-aid training but did not explain what "MG" stands for (Marie-Claude Molnar, 28 Oct. 2009).

[147] HJMD, 20 Aug. ("twice daily"), 5 June ("their story"). German Jewish intellectuals who anticipated a Nazi takeover were already studying English intensively in 1932 (Krohn 1993: 15).

304   Notes

¹⁴⁸ HJMD, 19 Aug. (Walter and Betty), 22 June (fellow student). Laura Gottschalk had been diagnosed with breast cancer in 1932 and was operated on several times (Ludwig Gottschalk, 16 Mar. 1995, interview by USC Shoah Foundation Institute for Visual History and Education, University of Southern California, accessed at Stanford Univ., tape 1490).
¹⁴⁹ HJMD, 24 Aug.
¹⁵⁰ Engelberg 2007: 12; Mertens 2006: 200.
¹⁵¹ Engelberg 2007: 18. Another comrade in the Communist youth movement, Nathan Steinberger, also emigrated to the USSR, where he suffered greatly but survived; he said that Lurje was accused of "Trotskyite" sympathies and that he himself was tainted by his friendship with Lurje (http://www.wsws.org/articles/2005/mar2005/sint-m09.shtml, accessed 23 Nov. 2008). The "Stalin terror" killed some 60% of the German Communists who emigrated to the Soviet Union (Weitz 1997: 280); see also Palmier, who says that 70% were arrested or deported (2006: 171-84, 712n171).
¹⁵² HJMD, 23 July ("same age as I"); HJM 1981 (held the dissertation). Engelberg lived in "Red" Wedding, a working-class district subject to police raids because of the large number of KPD sympathizers (see also Engelberg 2007: 12).
¹⁵³ Weitz 1997: 282.
¹⁵⁴ HJMD, 18 May and 23 July (came to know Engelberg), 21 May (friendship took off, "Marxismus"), 9 July ("small kernel").
¹⁵⁵ HJMD, 30 July. The KPD and the Nazis "regularly invited members of the other party to their meetings" in Berlin (Swett 2004: 208, 210).
¹⁵⁶ HJMD, 9 July.
¹⁵⁷ HJMD, 23 July. Dodd, the American ambassador, and the diplomat James G. McDonald both used the vast Tiergarten as a safe place for private conversations (W. Dodd 1941: 127; McDonald 2007: 44).
¹⁵⁸ HJMD, 26 July.
¹⁵⁹ Evans 2005: 11.
¹⁶⁰ HJMD, 6 Aug.; Fowkes 1984: 171. Torgler, accused of involvement in the Reichstag fire, was released. Thälmann, who spent eleven years in solitary confinement, was shot to death in 1944 on Hitler's orders.
¹⁶¹ HJMD, 31 Aug.
¹⁶² Bonn 1948: 210.
¹⁶³ HJMD, 8 July (visit to Kautsky), 9 Aug. (search of Kautsky's house); 8 Aug. ("leftward march").
¹⁶⁴ Grüttner 2005: 92.
¹⁶⁵ Walther 1989: 221; Niedhart 1993: 407. Feiler and Lederer found refuge at the New School in New York; Cohn, as noted in Chapter 3, settled in England.

[166] Jarausch 2001: 15-16.

[167] The phrase is Lord Beveridge's in his introduction to Bentwich's book on the Academic Assistance Council, which was founded in England in May 1933 to assist academics dismissed because of their religious or ideological background (1953: xiii)

[168] Gallin 1986, *passim*.

[169] Gerhard 1970: 9.

[170] Gallin 1986: 10-11.

[171] Arthur Prinz, "Plunging into Chaos" (1938-39), p. 23, Arthur Prinz Papers, American Jewish Historical Society (Center for Jewish History, New York), Series 2, Box 1. A recent essay suggests that both Oncken and Meinecke caved in the end (Grüttner 2005: 97).

[172] In addition to his memior, my sources for Mayer's biography are Gottfried Niedhart's introduction to Mayer's memoir (1993) and his article about Mayer's English years (1988). I have also used the website of the British Library of Political and Economic Science, http://library-2.lse. ac.uk/archives/handlists/Mayer/m.html, which in turn is based on the Historikergalerie des Instituts für Geschichtswissenschaften, http://www.geschichte.hu-berlin.de/ifg/galerie/texte/gmayer.htm (accessed 14 Jan. 2006).

[173] HJML, 16 May ("foreign opinion"), 6 June (Hegel); HJMD, 1 Feb. (G.D.H. Cole), 2 Feb. (translator's solution)

[174] HJMD, 7 June ("solid"), 12 June ("translated some more") 5 June (Yiddish translation); HJML, 22 Mar. (American publisher), 6 July ("act in his name").

[175] HJMD, 15 May ("doesn't leave the house"), 12 June ("German University"). On Rockefeller funding of the Institut, see Potter 1968: 740.

[176] HJMD, 26 May (Aron), 5 July ("working up their English," Korsch). A German translation of Galsworthy's *Forsyte Saga* was published in 1933 (Chalmers in Klemperer 1998: 471). Perhaps the Mayers were using the method of language-learning that Harry employed in Italy.

[177] HJMD, 9 Aug.

[178] Angress 1988: 18-19.

[179] W. Dodd 1941: 79. The High Commission, which was loosely affiliated with the League of Nations, assisted organizations working to resettle refugees; it was not concerned with Germans still in Germany and hoping to leave.

[180] Hilberg 2003, 1: 34.

[181] HJM 1981 ("rarity"). Meinecke's favorite student, Holborn was the "crown prince" expected to succeed him as king of German historians (Walther 1989: 93). He was a *Privatdozent* at Heidelberg from 1926 to 1931, when he "openly took his stand on the left" in an article on Protestantism and the history of political ideas (Gilbert 1970: 5). On his career in Germany, see Walther 1989: 93-104; Pflanze 1991: 170; and Epstein 1993: 131-33.

[182] Ritter 2006: 24-25.
[183] Korenblat 2006: 406-07.
[184] Mayer 1949: 336-37; HJMD, 26 June. In 1934, Holborn's wife, Annemarie, brought to America the materials that he had collected for the history of the constitution of the Weimar Republic; they remain in the Yale University Archives (Pflanze 1991: 174).
[185] Gerhard 1970: 13-14.
[186] Mayer 1949: 337.
[187] HJMD, 5 May ("introducer"), 30 May ("in conjunction," "good man to know"), 23 June (at Holborn's home), 26 June (confirm the arrangement, "SPD archival stuff"). Holborn's Carnegie chair, a permanent position, was a detriment in Nazi Germany (Pflanze 1991: 170).
[188] HJMD, 27 June. A professor was an *Ordinarius*; a *Stellvertredener* is someone who takes the place of another (my thanks to Peter Th. Walther for this information–email, 11 Sept. 2007).
[189] HJML, 25 June. See Snyder 1984: 97 for the text of the Horst Wessel song, which celebrates the S.A. and the swastika.
[190] HJMD, 27 June (obit of MP), 18 July (officials in Paris), 26 July (depression).
[191] HJMD, 2 Aug.
[192] Friedländer 1997: 345n32.
[193] HJMD, 2 Aug. Gumbel moved to France; Varian Fry helped him to escape in 1940 to the United States, where he worked for the Office of Strategic Services during the war. Dehn sat out the war in obscurity, resuming his academic career in 1946 at the University of Bonn (Lehmann 2003: 85-87). See Brenner 2001: 114-43, 46-65; Isenberg 2001: 106; and, on the significance of the Gumbel case in Germany, Gallin 1986: 71-79.
[194] HJMD, 27 Aug. Frederick Holborn, the "small son," became an academic; he was teaching at Johns Hopkins University at his death in 2005. His sister, Hannah Holborn Gray, became a historian and served as President of the University of Chicago for fifteen years.
[195] HJMD, 27 Jan. (arguing), 24 Feb. ("he invited me"), 21 May (inferiority complex); HJML, 25 May (Gray).
[196] HJML, 18 Mar. (ships full of refugees), 15 May (Bernstein Line); HJML, 6 June (the Dutch), 9 June ("stinging letter").
[197] HJML, 6 June (SPD archives); HJMD, 18 July ("the Alex"). Permission turned out to be unnecessary (HJMD, 1 Sept.).
[198] HJMD, 21 Aug., 26 Aug., and 1 Sept. (helped with newspapers), 18 July (grumbling), 20 July ("made me presents"); HJML, 26 July ("dropping in on P.G."), 13 July (Ernst Gottschalk), 19 July ("P.G.'s victim").
[199] HJML, 23 Aug.; McDonald 2007: 97n3 (number of prisoners). "Auch da," a Swabian greeting, literally means "also there" (Allert 2008: 22). The pun must have been a fleeting joke.

[200] HJML, 23 Aug.; W. Dodd 1941: 26, 47. This may be the episode referred to by McDonald in his diary on 14 Aug., describing the beating of an American who failed to salute the Nazi flag outside the Hotel Adlon (1997: 81). See the *New York Times*: "Nazi Attacks New York Surgeon in Berlin for Failing to Give 'Hitler Salute' at Parade" (18 Aug.); "Nazis Apologize in Mulvihill Case" (23 Aug.); "New Nazi Attack Protested by U.S." (3 Sept.); "Nazi Reported Held in Mulvihill Attack" (17 Oct.; this article also reports another attack on an American). Karl Ernst was among those killed in the Night of the Long Knives, 30 June 1934.

[201] HJMD, 4 Sept. (questionnaire), 28 Aug. ("cyclone"); HJML, 27 Aug. ("minor film star").

[202] HJMD, 9 July and 1, 2, 3, 6 Sept.

[203] HJML, 27 Aug. (presents); HJMD, 5 Sept. (second farewell), 6 Sept. (Elberfelds' complaint).

[204] HJMD, 6 Sept.

[205] HJML, 6 Sept.

[206] HJML, 9 Sept.

[207] HJML, 9 Sept. (visit to Nijhoff; he mailed the letter when the ship stopped at Boulogne, where it presumably was transferred to a faster ship); HJMD, 7 Sept. (reading *Fabian*). The title of the novel translates as "Fabian: The Story of a Moralist."

[208] HJMD, 4 Sept. ("benign plot"), 18 Sept. (ship approaching New York); HJML, 21 Oct. 1931 (Heinz Gottschalk).

Chapter 5

[1] More than half of all Berlin Jews left Germany between 1933 and 1939 (Goeschel 2007: 30). On German Jewish refugees, see Dwork and Van Pelt 2009 and Zucker 2001. The people whom I discuss here all survived, but some of their relatives did not. Some of Gustav Mayer's relatives died, although no one in his immediate family. Most of the family of Laura Perlitz Gottschalk, wife of Ernst Gottschalk, perished (Ludwig Gottschalk, 16 Mar. 1995, interview by USC Shoah Foundation Institute for Visual History and Education, University of Southern California, accessed at Stanford Univ., tape 1490).

[2] Klemperer 1998: 127 (30 June 1935; Flight Tax); Friedländer 1997: 62 (punitive rates); GML, 8 June 1936 (Meyers). Hitler used the Reich Flight Tax–introduced in 1931 to prevent wealthy Germans from taking their capital out of the country–to strip emigrating Jews of their money.

[3] The information that I summarize in this paragraph comes from Ernst Gottschalk's letter and other sources, indicated later.

[4] GML, 14 May 1934.

[5] Ernst Gottschalk to HJM, 22 Apr. 1937.

[6] Wilhelm Engelberg to HJM, 20 July 1934.

[7] EEL, 14 Jan. 1936 (prison experiences); 21 May 1936 ("Swiss philistine"); 31 Mar. 1939 (last letter).

[8] GML, 14 May 1934 (moods); Ernst Meyer, addendum to GML, 27 Nov. 1938. On moods, see Kaplan 1998: 51-52 and Lasker-Wallfisch 2000: 22.

[9] Even in 1944, there were German Communists brave enough to write the slogan "the Red Front is still alive"; it appeared "in thick red block letters on the remains of many walls" in Frankfurt (Hahn 1974: 321).

[10] Qtd. Bella Fromm 1990: 204 (28 July 1935).

[11] GML, 8 June 1936.

[12] GML, 16 Sept. 1938.

[13] My thanks to Lily Munford, the translator, for explaining Grete's pun. Tilman Allert suggests that "Heil Europa" also alludes to the Holy Roman Empire of the German Nation, long in decline until its demise in 1806 (email, 1 Nov. 2009). For a detailed analysis of Heil, see Allert 2008: 39-42.

[14] GML, 13 Nov. 1938.

[15] GML, 14 May 1934.

[16] Hilberg 2003, 1: 170.

[17] As early as June 1932, only Aryans could sit in the front row at clinical demonstrations at the University of Berlin (Mowrer 1939: 233). Because anti-Semitic restrictions on medical students were less stringent in Berlin than elsewhere, Rudy Meyer and Fritz Freyhan were able to complete their degrees. See Marianne Silber, qtd. Laub 2001: 19.

[18] HJML, 30 Nov. 1931 (Rudy in orchestra); M. Berghahn 1984: 52 (major force). Singer had been deputy director of the City Opera (Städische Oper). At its founding in Berlin, the Cultural League received about 2,000 applications for 200 positions from musicians and other artists, and counted 20,000 members in 1934; Kulturbünde were founded in other cities, all of them forced to unite in 1935 under the name Jewish Cultural League (Kater 1997: 97). The League, which was dissolved in 1941, strenuously defied Nazi attempts to ghettoize Jewish creative expression (Mosse 1985: 78-81). Klemperer, however, thought that its leaders "should be hanged," because any cooperation with the government was disgraceful (1998: 189 [9 Sept. 1936]). See also Hilberg 2003, 1: 88-89.

[19] GML, 8 June 1936. The New York office remained open until its chief, James Speyer, retired in 1938 ("International Bankers," Time, 13 June 1938). Ernst Meyer of Mommsenstrasse 57 is identified as a businessman in the Jüdisches Adressbuch für Gross-Berlin (1929-30). On his employer, see "Speyer Banking Firm in Reich to Liquidate," New York Times, 17 July 1934; and "Beit von Speyer, Banker, 72, Dead," New York Times, 9 March 1933. I am

grateful to the reference staff of the New York Public Library for unearthing these articles and for finding advertisements for Speyer & Co. (24/26 Pine Street, New York) in the *Times* in 1930 and 1934.

[20] Marcus 1934: 15 (dismissal of Jewish brokers); Klemperer 1998: 78 (29 July 1934, "mute despair").

[21] GML, 8 June 1936. Grete's chronology is not entirely clear, since she says that they returned to Berlin in December 1935, before their renters would have left.

[22] Noakes and Pridham 1990, 1: 530-41.

[23] Noakes and Pridham 1990, 1: 547 (reduced domestic terrorism); Klemperer 1998: 221 (22 May 1937); Fromm 1990: 217 (20 Feb. 1936, shelters); E. Mann 1938: 59 (war stories); Hilberg 2003, 1: 170, 185 (apartment buildings); GML, 27 Nov. 1938; Edelheit and Edelheit 1994: 306 (Decree). The National Coordinating Committee for Aid to Refugees and Emigrants Coming from Germany operated from 1934 to 1939, when its name changed to National Refugee Service. It was established by the Joint Distribution Committee, a Jewish organization, at the suggestion of the U.S. Department of State, to coordinate the efforts of private agencies. Its work load became enormous. Referring to the immediate fall-out of *Kristallnacht*, the Executive Director wrote: "We have had at least 1500 callers each day this past week; a thousand letters a day come in; there are many hysterical people in the office–the atmosphere is tense and feverish" (Cecilia Razovsky to Andrew Fried, 21 Nov. 1938; Razovsky Papers, American Jewish Historical Society [Center for Jewish History, New York], P-290, Box 3, Correspondence, NCC, Nov. 10-30, 1933).

[24] In addition to Grete's letters, there are other sources of information about the Meyers. Ernst Gottschalk's letter of 28 Oct. 1945 contains news relayed through Heinz Gottschalk. Rudy's widow, Gertrud Milch Meyer (in Porto Alegre, Brazil), as well as his daughter Bettina (in Denver, Colorado) and his niece Eva Mayer (in Stamford, Connecticut) provided a wealth of detail. Grete's letters to Harry exist in two archives–the Leo Baeck Institute in New York, which has the originals (Harry Marks Papers, ME 1558); and the Instituto Cultural Judaico Marc Chagall in Porto Alegre, which has scanned copies. Each archive also has a copy of Gertrud Meyer's brief memoir, written in English (G. Meyer 1995). Eva Mayer obtained additional information from Paul Meyer's daughter, Edith.

[25] GML, 14 May 1934 ("new country"), 16 Sept. 1938 (Brazil).

[26] I owe most of my information about Paul and his family to Eva Mayer, his sister Lisel's daughter. Paul was in the camp at St.-Juste-en-Chaussée, which was established immediately after the outbreak of war to hold German and Austrian nationals. On the history of the *camps de rassemblement*, see Michel Annet, "French Internment Camps in 1939-1944: A Philatelic

and Historical Study" (15 Sept. 2006 ["Chronology" updated on 2 Mar. 2008], http://www.apra.asso.fr/Camps/Fr/, accessed 24 July 2008). Additional information came in an email from Michel Annet (31 Aug. 2008) identifying the specific camp where Paul was held; St. Juste-en-Chaussée is documented as existing between Nov. 1939 and Mar. 1940.

[27] Marrus and Paxton 1981: 319 ("Italian army"); Zuccotti 1993: 181-87 (round-up of Jews).

[28] GML, 8 June 1936.

[29] HJML, 27 Oct. 1938. According to a letter from Harry to the National Coordinating Committee supporting Lisel's application for an affidavit–undated but evidently written in late Oct. or early Nov. 1938–the Meyers moved from Brussels to Berlin when World War I broke out; only Claire, their youngest child, was born in Berlin (in 1914). This letter is the source of some of my other information about Lisel.

[30] Raymond, later a leading economist, moved to New York in 1934 and changed his name to Goldsmith (Glen Fowler, "Raymond Goldsmith, Noted Economist, Dies at 83," New York Times, 15 July 1988). Lucien moved to Paris after the Machtergreifung and then (in 1937) to New York, where he became a prominent rare-book dealer (Dickinson 1998: 75-76; "Lucien Goldschmidt, Rare-Book Dealer, 80," New York Times, 18 Dec. 1992). The Goldschmidt brothers were born in Brussels, which presumably facilitated their emigration. Raymond (b. 1904) received his doctorate from the University of Berlin in 1927. Lucien (b. 1912) was educated in Berlin at the Collège Royal Français; he served in the U.S. military in World War II. Lucien had been in touch with Harry soon after arriving in New York. Frau Meyer expected Lucien to meet Lisel when her ship docked in New York on 11 December 1938 (GML, 16 Sept. 1938, 27 Nov. 38; HJML, 9 Dec. 1938); Raymond Goldsmith, however, was listed on the ship's manifest as the "friend" who would meet her. Under the category "Ethnicity/Race/Nationality," the manifest reads confusingly: "Italian; Hebrew (*Italian*)," although it correctly indicates Belgium as her country of birth. The United States was the destination of the majority of German refugee doctors (Kater 1989: 218, 209-10).

[31] HJML, 9 Dec. 1938. When I mentioned Harry's dislike of Fritz Freyhan to Dorothee Gottschalk, Lutz's widow, she answered: "He wasn't the only one to find Fritz annoying." Harry advised his parents: "Don't take a bum line on refugees because Fritz & Irene [Fritz's wife] turned out to be sour apples" (HJML, 14 Dec. 1938).

[32] Cecilia Razovsky to Elizabeth Dutcher, 9 Nov. 1938, Razovsky Papers, American Jewish Historical Society (Center for Jewish History, New York), P-290, Box 3, Correspondence, NCC, Nov. 1-9, 1938.

[33] GML, 16 Sept. 1938.

[34] Lisel's name (now with the American spelling, Elizabeth) appears regularly in the *American Medical Directory* through 1967.

[35] GML, 14 May 1934 (Claire's engagement); Moore 1986: 48 (Jews emigrating to Palestine). Most of my information about Claire comes from her niece Eva Mayer, augmented by a letter to Harry from Ernst Gottschalk, 22 April 1937.

[36] GML, 8 June 1936. Grete is presumably referring to unrest earlier that year. Arabs continued to protest Jewish immigration until the British authorities put their feet down in 1939, permitting additional emigration (Kater 1989: 214). Jewish emigrants could transfer assets from Germany to Palestine, and in all some 52,000 German Jews emigrated there in 1933-39 (Friedländer 1997: 62-63; Evans 2005: 555).

[37] GML, 16 Sept. 1938.

[38] Mühlen 1993: 11-13. Further limitations on immigration followed.

[39] GML, 8 June 1936.

[40] G. Meyer 1995.

[41] Espindola 2001: 110.

[42] Rudy and his second wife were not married in a civil ceremony, because that would have cost her her pension. Traute also received a German government pension.

[43] To practice as a doctor, Rudy would have had to do an internship in Germany—an impossible task for an experienced physician of forty-eight. He was disqualified from permanent employment in the Philharmonic because he was beyond the age limit of forty-five. Suffering from the delayed effects of a skiing accident when he was seventeen, he died in Jan. 1979, some months before his seventieth birthday.

[44] See Hilberg 2003, 1: 143-44; Chalmers, Preface to Klemperer 1998: xv. A Nazi decree of 29 March 1938 deprived Jewish relief organizations of tax exemptions; on 19 November 1938, another decree excluded Jews from public relief (Hilberg 2003, 1: 144). The requirement that men add "Israel" and women add "Sara" to their names came in a decree of 17 Aug. 1938 that also mandated a *J* on Jewish passports (Edelheit and Edelheit 1994: 305).

[45] Lesser 1995: 1 and Berdichevski 2001: 46.

[46] Lucien Goldschmidt to HJM, 14 Oct. 1938.

[47] On the process, see Berdichevski 2001: 47-50. Some immigrants obtained visas by paying a generous bribe (Laqueur 2001: 215; Mühlen 1993: 13).

[48] Arthur Prinz, "Plunging into Chaos" (1938-39), pp. 5-6, Arthur Prinz Papers, American Jewish Historical Society (Center for Jewish History, New York), Series 2, Box 1. Prinz was a top official of the Association in Aid of Jews in Germany.

[49] Evans 2005: 599 (total emigration); Lesser 1995: 52 (emigration to Brazil). Some 10,000 Brazilian visas were issued to Jews in 1939-42 (Lesser 1995: 120-35).

⁵⁰ My main sources for the post-Berlin history of the Meyer family are interviews with Gertrud Milch Meyer (telephone, 12 May 2008, when she was approaching her ninety-seventh birthday), with Gertrud and Rudy's daughter Bettina Basanow (telephone, 17 May 2008), and with Lisel's daughter, Eva Mayer (12 May 2008).

⁵¹ In addition to the cited sources, I owe information regarding the Gottschalk family to Ludwig Gottschalk, 16 Mar. 1995, interview by USC Shoah Foundation Institute for Visual History and Education, University of Southern California, accessed at Stanford Univ., tape 1490; to Dorothee Gottschalk in several telephone interviews; and to Dr. Claudia Schoppmann of the Gedenkstätte Deutscher Widerstand (in an email, 9 Dec. 2005, drawing on German archives). For photographs of a young Paul Gottschalk and of Julia Gottschalk with her cousin Gertrud Mayer Jaspers, see Kirkbright 2004, photos 26, 27.

⁵² P. Gottschalk 1967: 35-36; Moore 1986: 29-31; Buijnsters 2006: 255-57.

⁵³ Other German Jewish booksellers used similar "fictitious sales or on-approval shipments" and then "nullified [them] as soon as the bookseller followed in person" (Rosenthal 1987: 10). Information on Ernst Gottschalk's role in the business comes from Lutz Gottschalk's Shoah Foundation interview (see note 51).

⁵⁴ P. Gottschalk 1967: 36.

⁵⁵ Kirkbright 2004: 143-44 and Niedhart 1988: 104 (assisting his relatives); Michael Freyhan, email, 28 Nov. 2007 (generosity). Ernst Gottschalk, who had been comfortably off, presumably fell victim to the punitive regulations. Heinz and Lutz Gottschalk left Germany to work for P.G. in the Netherlands early enough not to need financial help. P.G. continued to help his relatives during the war. Writing to Clara on 20 Feb. 1942, he mentioned a birthday gift and a substantial sum that he had sent for her dental care, insisting that regardless of cost she go only to a highly recommended dentist. Eight years later, he wrote affectionately to say how glad he was that they had never had any real differences and that now as they grew old, they felt closer than ever; wishing her a good recovery from an operation, he wanted to pay for nursing care and such extras as "a bottle of good Bordeaux" and fresh fruit–still precious items in postwar England (26 June 1950). Copies of letters were kindly provided by Michael Freyhan.

⁵⁶ HJML, 9 Feb. 1939 ("promising"); 15 Feb. 1939 ("museum piece"); 13 Feb. 1939 ("Uncle Paul"); 21 Feb. 1939 (chocolate).

⁵⁷ Ludwig Gottschalk, Shoah Foundation interview (see note 51). The conflicted relationship between P.G. and his nephew (and, later, between P.G. and Lutz's wife, Dorothee) is the only intra-familial tension that I have observed aside from temporary stress described in Chapter 4 between Betty Elberfeld's parents and Walter Elberfeld.

⁵⁸ Arthur H. Minters, telephone interview, 19 July 2007. Lutz Gottschalk's girlfriend (and, later, his wife), Dorothee Korach, came to work in Paul's New York office when she emigrated just before the war.

⁵⁹ P. Gottschalk 1967: 36 (shipping to New York), 33 (extra orders).

⁶⁰ Paul Gottschalk to Clara (Lotte) Freyhan, 20 Feb. 1942. In his memoir, P.G. mentions buying the Beethoven manuscript from the widow of the musicologist Max Friedlaender (1967: 43).

⁶¹ P. Gottschalk 1967: 36-39 (postwar trip) and 1 (traveling by plane). P.G. was prevented from buying in Germany because of interference by the State Department on behalf of a commission acquiring items for the Library of Congress.

⁶² P. Gottschalk 1967: 40, 43, 52.

⁶³ Arendt/Jaspers 1992: 56 (18 Sept. 1946) and 662 (16 Nov. 1966; if P.G. was planning a "secondhand bookstore," it never materialized). In 1950, Jaspers wrote to Arendt that he and his wife hoped that P.G. would join them during a vacation in St. Moritz (Arendt/Jaspers 1992: 152; 29 June). Other references by Jaspers include mentions of visits from P.G. in 1950 and 1956 (159 [25 Dec.1950], 293 [1 Aug. 1956]) and P.G.'s report of a speech by a German general that he had read in an Italian newspaper (631; 9 Mar. 1966). In 1968, Gertrud Jaspers asked Arendt to tell P.G. that Jaspers's health was improving (678; 4 Apr.).

⁶⁴ Kater 1989: 187-88 (repression of Jewish physicians); Anon. 1936: 67 ("Jewish woman doctor"). I have pieced together information about Julia Gottschalk from Kirkbright 2004: 328n8 and an online resource of the Free University: Freie Universität Berlin, Institut für Geschichte der Medizin, Dokumentation: Ärztinnen im Kaiserreich, http://userpage.fu-berlin.de/~elehmus/HTML/rec00278c1.html. The online source lists her date of emigration as 1936 but says that her name appears in 1937 in a listing of Jewish doctors in Berlin. She gave professional help in London to her old friends Gustav and Flora Mayer (Gottfried Niedhart, email, 29 Nov. 2008). On British non-acceptance of German doctors, see M. Berghahn 1984: 83; and Dwork and Van Pelt 2009: 269-70.

⁶⁵ Ernst Gottschalk to HJM, 22 Apr. 1937; Kater 1989: 192-98 (decertification).

⁶⁶ G. J. de Kievit to Piet J. Buijnsters, 31 Dec. 1996. My thanks to Dr. Buijnsters for a copy of this letter, which includes a few other unpublished details about the Gottschalks. Presumably Minna Fens was over forty-five and hence legally allowed to work for a Jew; she may have left in anticipation of the treatment given the Klemperers' housekeeper, who met the age limit but was nonetheless told to quit her job lest her children's careers suffer (Klemperer 1998: 258 [23 May 1938]). According to Lutz's interview with the Shoah Foundation, which is the source for other information in

this paragraph, she returned to Germany after the war (see note 51). Because she did not need to go into hiding, she remained in the Gottschalk home in Driebergen. The occupation authorities had forced the family to move inland to Driebergen, and until going into hiding Lutz commuted daily to The Hague to conduct business.

⁶⁷ Palmier 2006: 145 (30,000 refugees); Buijnsters 2006: 265, 267, 289 (regulations governing German Jews in Netherlands); Ludwig Gottschalk, Shoah Foundation interview (see note 51).

⁶⁸ Buijnsters 2006: 288. In his Shoah Foundation interview (see note 51), Lutz spoke movingly of the selfless insistence of the Gilhuys family that he and his father stay with them, no matter the risk, rather than reporting for deportation. Gilhuys asked them to remove their Jewish star; Lutz kept his and displayed it for the camera at the end of the interview. Earlier, Gilhuys had managed to shield the Gottschalk firm from German scrutiny. Biblion apparently dealt in art as well, selling an ancient Greek vase to the Walters Art Museum (http://art.thewalters.org/viewwoa.aspx?id=13207; accessed 22 Dec. 2009).

⁶⁹ Walter Elberfeld to HJM, 25 Mar. 1936. Walter's trajectory from happy arrival to death by murder was typical of German refugees in the Soviet Union (Palmier 2006: 172-73); see also Chapter 4, note 151.

⁷⁰ Ernst Gottschalk to HJM, 25 Oct. 1945; Lutz Gottschalk, Shoah Foundation interview (the source as well for Betty's reunion with her daughters and her death; see note 51).

⁷¹ P. Gottschalk 1967: 8. Dorothee Gottschalk remained in contact by phone for decades with Ursula, who married a man condemned to a penal colony near Siberia.

⁷² Tyler 2004: 11. On the immigrants who founded Heidelbach, Ickelheimer, see Supple 1957: 147, 164, and 166; and "Heidelbach, Ickelheimer & Co.," New York Times, 1 Jan. 1886. Ickelheimer was from Frankfurt, where Alfred Hirschbach "spent some years of his youth" (HJM to Hannah Marks, 28 July 1932). Alfred Hirschbach died in 1951, his widow outliving him by a dozen years; her ill health depleted nearly to nil her inheritance, which had already been (according to my cousin Robert Bildersee) considerably reduced by her profligate spending. Ernest Hirschbach's widow, Irene, is my main source of information regarding her husband and his family, in a telephone interview (13 Jan. 2008) and in unpublished materials that she shared. Hedwig Hirschbach is on the list of passengers of the Berengaria, arriving 28 Dec. 1937; her age is given as 52, her "nationality" as Dutch although her "nativity" was German. I do not have a precise date of arrival for Gerhart.

⁷³ E. Hirschbach n.d. (a): 7.

⁷⁴ On Jewish children's school enrollment, see Angress 1988: 12-13 and

Kaplan 1998: 98. On Frank Hirschbach's life, see Tyler 2004 and "In Memoriam: Frank D. Hirschbach," *GSD Magazine* 2 (Winter-Spring 2006): 19. He earned his PhD at Yale after the war. For another example of the common Jewish envy of children in Nazi youth organizations, see Lasker-Wallfisch 2000: 18.

[75] Angress 1988: xii.

[76] Tyler 2004: 11 (financial support); F. Hirschbach 1989 ("never return"). Four days after Franz was dismissed, all Jewish children remaining in state schools were expelled (Angress 1988: 9).

[77] F. Hirschbach 1989.

[78] HJML, 15 Nov. 1938 ("their woes"); Tyler 2004: 11 (Hirschbachs' arrival); 8 Mar. 1939 ("around one table"). The hiring of Rose Hirschbach and, earlier, Hajo Holborn belies the "indifference" to the plight of refugee intellectuals that Norwood ascribes to Yale (2009: 33).

[79] Tyler 2004: 12.

[80] F. Hirschbach 1989.

[81] According to Michael Freyhan (email, 11 Nov. 2008), Hans came in Jan. 1939; Kate came with their infant son, Peter, in March, possibly accompanied by Clara. Max and Eva came together, presumably at about that time, their expenses most likely paid by Paul Gottschalk. Most of my information about the Freyhans after 1933 comes from Michael Freyhan–in his published essay on his father (2003) and numerous emails Nov. 2007-Nov. 2008–and from Margot Pottlitzer's 1974 interview with Kate Freyhan, available in the Leo Baeck Institute in New York (LBI Archives, ME 242; available online). When Clara died in 1974, age 95, she left suitcases full of family letters.

[82] Kater 1989: 171 (German medical schools); Fritz Freyhan to HJM, 25 May 1936 ("in person"), 2 Mar. 1937 ("Uncle Paul"). On dislike of Fritz, see note 31.

[83] HJMD, 14 Mar. 1933 ("about politics"), 18 Apr. 1933 ("present situation"), 24 June 1933 ("forgotten his principles"), 1 July ("ordered some more"); HJML, 1 Dec. 1938 (alienating friends). Fritz had written an "insulting letter" to Harry's parents; he then wrote to apologize, possibly advised to do so by Deborah Hirschbach (HJML, 6 Dec. 1938).

[84] Healy 1998: 193. In addition to the achievements listed in Fritz's obit in the *New York Times* (12 Dec. 1982), he served as President of the American Psychopathological Association in 1969-70.

[85] Gallin 1986: 21 (above politics); Jarausch 2001: 23 ("murderous"); HJML, 2 Aug. 1933.

[86] On academic firings, see Krohn 1993: 11-13 and Jarausch 2001: 17; on emigration, see Krohn 1993: 15. For citations of the voluminous literature on this emigration, see the text and notes in Barkin 1991: 150-51.

[87] See Jarausch 2001: 20. Cf. Mommsen 1991: 63-64; Iggers 2005: 10.

[88] Martin Weinbaum, who taught the medieval seminar that Harry took in his first semester, was forced out in 1933 as was (in 1935) the "Aryan" Gerhard Masur, whose seminar Harry took in his final semester. On Weinbaum, see Epstein 1993: 330. On Masur, see Mommsen 1991: 52, 54-55; Kater 1991: 85-86; and Epstein 1993: 210. Since Harry had no relationship outside the classroom with Weinbaum or Masur, I do not discuss them.

[89] HJM 1981.

[90] Walther 1989: 221 (twelve years); Bonn 1948: 347 (reduction of pensions); Walther 1989: 222 (petition); Niedhart 1988: 99 (not transferable). Betker lists the signatories of his colleagues' petitions (2006, "Gustav Mayer [1871-1948]," p. 3).

[91] I draw most of the information regarding Mayer's exile from Niedhart 1988. The International Institute for Social History was established in Amsterdam in 1935 as a repository "for the papers, books, and other materials of the organizations and individuals persecuted by Hitler" (Kunoff 1975: 147).

[92] Popkin 2003: 3 (pagination refers to a printout of the text of Popkin's article, accessed through JSTOR).

[93] Niedhart 1988: 102 (letter to wife). Mayer dedicated his memoir to Peter. He wrote it between 1943-45 in the small town of Malvern Hills in Worcestershire, where his ashes were buried next to Peter's on 16 March 1948, the seventh anniversary of the young man's death (Niedhart 1993: 412-13).

[94] McAllister 1995.

[95] Kirkbright 2004: 165-67 and 178 (Jasperses in Heidelberg); 143-45, 317n13, and 318n28 (Fritz and Otto Mayer in Palestine); 144 (Ernst Mayer in Holland); 143 (Arthur Mayer in America); 317n20 (Heinrich and wife).

[96] Walther 1989: 327-30; Ritter 2006: 29.

[97] Gerhard to Langer, 29 Mar. 1934, papers of William L. Langer, Harvard Univ. Archives, HUG(FP) 19.8, box 1, Correspondence 1934-35. The other letters to which I refer are in the same folder: Howard Gray to Langer, 7 Apr. 1934; Gerhard to Langer, 11 May 1934; and Langer to Gerhard, 26 May 1934. Professors and clergy who had been working in their professions for at least two years prior to immigration were eligible for non-quota visas if they had job offers from American institutions. Rockefeller regularly supplemented funding for refugee scholars obtained by the Emergency Committee in Aid of Displaced Foreign Scholars, founded in May 1933; by the end of the war it had spent $1,410,778 helping 303 scholars (Duggan and Drury 1948: 78). The committee files are in the New York Public Library (MssCol 922).

[98] Gerhard to Langer, 11 May 1934 (see previous note).

[99] Betker 2006 ("Dietrich Gerhard [1896-1985]," p. 3); Ritter 2006: 30; Epstein 1993: 83-84.

[100] HJML, 28 Sept. 1938 (alludes to Gerhard's recommendation that he take a course with Robert Ulich); HJM to Dietrich Gerhard, 11 Mar. 1957, Washington University Archives, Gerhard Papers, Series 02, Box 02 (my thanks to Miranda Rectenwald for sending a copy). The next year Harry sent Gerhard a copy of his article setting out the hypothesis of the Pivotal Period (HJM 1958; copy in Gerhard Papers, Series 04, Box 09); on the Pivotal Period, see Chapter 8.

[101] M. Gerhard, qtd. Freidenreich 2002: 161 ("Germanness"); Emergency Committee in Aid of Displaced Foreign Scholars, New York Public Library, Box 11, Melitta Gerhard folders (3x5 card). These records, which include an autobiographical outline, contain extensive evidence of her troubles. The secretary of the Emergency Committee wrote in 1938 that although she was "technically non-Aryan," she "belong[ed] to the Protestant faith" and was qualified to teach Protestant theology. She helped her mother emigrate as well. Adele Gerhard returned in 1955 to Cologne, the city of her birth, where she died the following year. In 1980, Melitta donated Adele's papers to the German and Jewish Intellectual Émigré Collection at the University of Albany (http://library.albany.edu/speccoll/findaids/ger039.htm; accessed 4 Mar. 2008).

[102] Norwood 2009: 105. Melitta Gerhard supported her mother as well as herself in a series of short-term jobs, although they sometimes had to take refuge with Dietrich in St. Louis. Harders (2005: 198) contends that she failed to land a decent job because elite American universities were reluctant to hire women, this may explain why, aside from Wellesley, she did not apply to any elite institutions. She was let go by a small sectarian college because enrollment in the German Department plummeted when the war broke out, and the department had to be closed.

[103] Walther 1989: 200-02 (dismissal); Fermi 1971: 348 (American connections). The letters of reference are in the records of the Emergency Committee for Displaced Foreign Scholars, Box 15, Hajo Holborn folder 1; both testimonials were translated into English for use in America—Meinecke, 29 Jan. 1934; Anschütz, 14 June 1933 (referring to his job at the Graduate School of Politics).

[104] Holborn to Gerhard, qtd. Ritter 2006: 25. Holborn's and Gerhard's common experiences cemented a bond; following his younger colleague's death in 1969, Gerhard wrote "Reminiscences" of Holborn (1970).

[105] Ritter 2006: 25 (Emergency Committee); Pflanze 1991: 173 (Yale position). Princeton and Yale fought a bidding war for Holborn, according to the records of the Emergency Committee (box 15, Holborn folder 1). He was appointed to a chair at Yale in 1938 and promoted to full professor in

1940, the year he became an American citizen (Emergency Committee, Box 15, Holborn folder 2).

[106] Pflanze 1991: 177; Coser 1984: 284-85. Annemarie Holborn, her husband's scholarly collaborator throughout his life, was also among the refugees who contributed their expertise to intelligence analysis (Katz 1991: 136-39; Walther 1989: 96).

[107] Ritter 2006: 26-27 (refused to teach); Pflanze 1991: 178 (death).

[108] This section draws principally on the letters to Harry from Wilhelm and Ernst Engelberg; additional essential information comes from Ernst's son, Achim, and his second wife, Waltraut, as well as from his biographer, Mario Kessler. When I visited Engelberg toward the end of 2005, I found him too frail in body and mind to recall that distant friendship, but still able to show the warmth and commitment that had drawn Harry to him and his ideas. I intend to donate the Engelberg letters in my possession to the archive of his papers that Achim and Waltraut Engelberg are establishing at Humboldt University following his death on 18 Dec. 2010. There are five extant letters to Harry, three written in 1936 and two in 1939.

[109] HJM to Ernst Engelberg, 13 May 1934.

[110] Wilhelm Engelberg to HJM, 20 July 1934.

[111] Niedhart–currently writing Mayer's biography–singles out the problem of Engelberg's dissertation to illustrate the serious consequences of Mayer's dismissal (1988: 98). Oncken, who was both a backer of the Weimar Republic and an ultra-nationalist, was close to Mayer (Iggers 1968: 236-37; Niedhart 1988: 98).

[112] Gallin 1986: 101-01; Hirsch 1946: 157; Betker 2006 ("Hermann Oncken [1869-1945]," p. 2). Late in 1934, Oncken agreed to supervise a doctoral dissertation by an American student, David G. White, but then "Professor Oncken was retired very soon afterwards–for political reasons" (White to William L. Langer, 16 Feb. 1940, papers of William L. Langer, Harvard University Archives, HUG(FP) 19.8, box 2, General Correspondence 1933-41; the same file contains a recommendation for White from Oncken, who signed himself with his university title [Oncken to Langer, 18 Apr. 1939]). Oncken's first "retirement" was rescinded because of student protests, but the reprieve did not last long (W. Dodd 1941: 219-20, 250). His offense was insisting on autonomy of expression. Dodd's description (pp. 193-94) of a dinner party at Oncken's home revealed an intellectual community capable of ridiculing Nazi ideas while eluding possible censure.

[113] Engelberg 2007: 9-20.

[114] Engelberg 2007: 14.

[115] Achim Engelberg (2007: 16) quotes his father's notes about his code name (*Deckname*) and his good fortune in being arrested as himself. While archivists have decoded upper-level KPD *Decknamen*, they have not done so for those like Ernst at lower levels (Swett 2004: 219n85).

[116] Carsten 1967: 85.

[117] Müller-Enbergs 2006: 222-23 (editor). *Beize* is a regional term for pub (thanks to Achim Engelberg for this information, email 25 Apr. 2007).

[118] Engelberg 2007: 16 (common criminals); EEL, 14 Jan. 1936.

[119] Palmier 2006: 156-57 (dangers to exiles); Engelberg 2007: 9 (hoping to leave); Palmier 2006: 156 (expulsion of Communists).

[120] EEL, 21 May 1936.

[121] Palmier 2006: 155 ("rich in recrimination"); Bentwich 1953: 17 (Institut); Renate Engelberg Rauer, email, 16 June 2011 (Spanish children). On Oprecht, see E. and K. Mann 1939: 201 and Palmier 2006: 156-58, 380; on the Swiss who spied on Oprecht, see Hall 2009: 260. The friends who helped Ernst obtain a two-year fellowship at the Institut were Else Eisner, the widow of Kurt Eisner (a revolutionary murdered in 1919), and Ernst's fellow exile Hans Mayer, a literary scholar who years later was his colleague at Leipzig (Engelberg 2007: 16).

[122] The 120 German refugees categorized as "political" by Swiss authorities were subjected to "police surveillance,…forbidden to practice any kind of activity,…always under threat of expulsion," and permitted to remain for only three months (Palmier 2006: 154-56). According to Achim Engelberg, previous publications refer to Ernst as a political refugee, but he cannot confirm that that was Ernst's official designation (email, 2 Feb. 2010). Given Palmier's definition, if Ernst had been officially classified as "political," he could not have continued to live in Switzerland.

[123] EEL, 22 Feb. 1939. No other countries imposed as severe restrictions on refugees as Switzerland, where Communists and Jews suffered the most (Palmier 2006: 155). The 1924 United States immigration law set the German quota at 26,000 per year, but during the 1930s only a fifth of those hoping to emigrate to the U.S. were accepted, aside from those like Holborn and Gerhard admitted as non-quota immigrants (Walther 1989: 247; Zucker 2001: 112-21). In September 1933, the German quota was "far from filled" according to a State Department official (Pierrepont Moffat, qtd. by the editors in McDonald 2007: 101); the Berlin consulate was issuing 250-300 visas monthly, and the consulates in Stuttgart and Hamburg issued more (McDonald 2007: 187). Until 1938, the German quota was never filled (Moore 1986: 44).

[124] The American consul in Zurich, who was "notorious" for his hostility to refugees, refused to grant visas even to those with affidavits (Zucker 2001: 149-50); he also rejected out of hand nearly all the affidavits of Austrian Jews who had found temporary refuge in Switzerland (Dwork and Van Pelt 2009: 145-46). American consulates in Germany were later similarly beset by would-be immigrants; in 1938, the Stuttgart consulate received 110,000 applications for the 850 visas issued monthly (Deutschkron 1989: 49).

¹²⁵ Mertens 2006: 200 (teaching German); Reisman 2006: 24; Krohn 1993: 15-16 (first phase; see Reisman 2006: 9); Bentwich 1953: 54 ("best German University"). Walther (1989: 192n15)–who gives Engelberg as an example–directs readers seeking an overview of German scholarly emigration to Turkey to Horst Widmann, *Exil und Bildungshilfe: Die deutschsprachige akademische Emigration in die Türkei nach 1933* (Berlin: Lang, 1973). Since hardly any of the German scholars knew Turkish, they depended on "interpreters who translated their lectures sentence by sentence" (Palmier 2006: 222). Teaching German, Ernst may not have been in this position.

¹²⁶ Engelberg 2007: 30 (Engelberg's return). For the details of Engelberg's illustrious career see Mertens 2006: 200-01 and Müller-Enbergs 2006: 222-23.

¹²⁷ Craig 1999: 63.

¹²⁸ HJM 1981.

Chapter 6

¹ HJMD, 31 May 1933 ("marxian interpretation"), 12 Mar. 1933 (Elberfeld), 24 Mar. 1933 ("Nazi faith"); HJML, 12 Mar. 1933 (accident or temperament).

² HJML, 28 June 1932 (*Vorwärts* building); HJMD, 28 July 1933 (fellow student), 11 Aug. 1933 ("Zionist").

³ Mosse 1985: 55 ("Germanic roots"); Schrecker 1986: 3 (academics in CPUSA); HUAC 1853f: 1857 ("student").

⁴ Ellen Schrecker, interview notes, 3 July 1979.

⁵ Schrecker 1986: 33 (Parry); HUAC 1953c: 1045 (Zilsel's testimony). Both Parry and Zilsel are discussed in Chapter 7.

⁶ HUAC 1953f: 1857-59.

⁷ Manifesto issued on behalf of Communist candidates in the 1932 election, qtd. Hicks 1954: 35.

⁸ HUAC 1953f: 1846. In 1933, Paul Gottschalk also used personal experience to convince unbelieving friends in the United States "that a civilized people could sink to such a level" (1967: 34).

⁹ HUAC 1953f: 1868 ("friends...that close"); HJMD, 4 Feb. 1932 ("another home").

¹⁰ HUAC 1953c: 1047.

¹¹ HUAC 1953c: 1054.

¹² International Statistical Institute, *Newsletter*, 25.3 (2001), http://isi.cbs.nl/NLet/memoriam01-3.htm (accessed 15 March 2006).

¹³ HJM 1966: 20; cf. an earlier article about pedagogy, in which Harry argued that "without the significant question, facts are useless" (HJM 1953b: 21).

[14] HJMD, 31 Aug. 1933.

[15] Information from *Official Register of Harvard University: The Graduate School of Arts and Sciences Containing an Announcement for 1934-35* (vol. 31, no. 31): 40-41. Information on requirements of the Department of History comes from *Official Register of Harvard University: Division of History, Government, and Economics Containing an Announcement for 1934-35* (vol. 31, no. 33): 77-84. Information on academic credit for his Berlin courses comes from his 1980 interview.

[16] HJML, 22 Aug. 1932 (plans for generals); HJM 1980 (discussion with Langer).

[17] Harry told HUAC that he "entered the Communist movement in 1934" (HUAC 1953: 1853).

[18] Cohen 1993: 25; Klehr 1984: 309-10 (pretended independence). In its inaugural issue, the *Harvard Communist*, which the masthead says was published by the YCL of Harvard, labored to distinguish between frankly Communist organizations and the NSL. It described the function of the NSL at Harvard as "forward[ing] the interests of the student body, considering students as those who are primarily interested in education. Communists at Harvard will aid in this fight, in whatever way possible, at the same time that they present the full program of the Communist Party and the Young Communist League" (1.1 [16 Jan. 1935]: 4-5).

[19] Draper 1967: 166 (difference in quality); Klehr and Haynes 1992: 74-75 (small potatoes); Brax 1981: 20 (SLID membership); Klehr 1984: 307 (YCL membership). There were about a million college students at the time.

[20] "The YCL at Harvard," *Harvard Communist*, 3.2 (April 1937): 11-13. YCL members did not have to belong to the CPUSA. Estimates of nationwide membership in the YCL vary from source to source. According to a report prepared in 1935-36 for the American Association of University Professors, when the NSL and SLID joined to form the American Student Union (ASU) in December 1935, each enrolled about 3,000 students; in 1937, the total ASU enrollment was 20,000 (Committee Y 1937: 316-17).

[21] Klehr 1984: 308 (YCL as a school); *Harvard Communist*, 3.2 (April 1937): 13 (YCL secret).

[22] Keller and Keller 2001: 159. The names all occur in the *Crimson* (all but Pavlo in connection with NSL activities). This mention of Harry's name in connection with his Harvard politics is one of two that I have found in published books; the other is in Lipset and Riesman (1975: 158): Robbins "helped to form a chapter of the NSL of which Harry Marks (now Professor of History at the University of Connecticut) became president."

[23] Klehr and Haynes 1992: 73-74, 305 (CPUSA statistics); HUAC 1953f: 1856 (Harry's view); Draper 1967: 155-56 (out of work youth); *Harvard Communist* 1.2 (Feb. 1935; YCL complaint).

24 HUAC 1953f: 1871 (Harry's work with NSL); HUAC 1953e: 1520-22 (Parry's testimony).

25 Named in February 1933 by Robert Gorham Davis (HUAC 1953a), Robbins testified the next month (see next note). His FBI file shows that the agency knew about his past Communist membership when, as an officer in the Naval Reserve, he taught mathematics at the U.S. Naval Academy (1942-46). In 1952, the FBI made futile attempts to demonstrate that he had attended Communist meetings in the period between Harvard and his Navy service. His father-in-law, Judge Edward J. Dimock, presided over the second Smith Act trial of CPUSA members; because the CPUSA considered him fair, both Dimock and (by association) Robbins were labeled pro-Communist, as noted numerous times in Robbins's FBI file. After Robbins testified, further FBI investigations drew the Bureau's attention to Robbins's old comrade in arms, Allen Philbrick, as appears below. An agent's report, dated 16 Dec. 1953, in Robbins's FBI file quotes Harry's HUAC testimony. It appears that Lipset, who gives no source for the following statement, had read Robbins's testimony: "Robbins...helped to form a chapter of the NSL, of which Harry Marks...became president" (Lipset and Riesman 1975: 158).

26 Herbert E. Robbins, testimony in executive session, HUAC, 25 March 1953, unpublished U.S. House of Representatives Committee Hearings, microfiche 1412, CIS-NO 83 HUna-T.13, pp. 326-27.

27 Cohen 1993: 44-45. Cohen counted two Harvard students among the delegates, though it isn't clear whether this included Robbins (1993: 356n20). According to Alan Lomax's mimeographed letter addressed to Harvard students on 30 Apr. 1932, the NSL chapter was then being organized (Harvard University Archives, National Student League folder, HUD 3598).

28 Brax 1981: 22.

29 Robbins testimony, pp. 328-29 (see note 26).

30 Hicks 1954: 46-47; HUAC 1953f: 1868 (Harry's description).

31 Ellen Schrecker, interview notes, 3 July 1979 (Harry's estimate); Eagan 1981: 81 (Harvard's enrollment); Hicks 1954: 63-64 (faculty group).

32 HUAC 1953f: 1847 (study groups on classics); "N.S.L. Organizes Group for Study of Marxism," Harvard Crimson, 17 Oct. 1934 (Harvard course); MIT course, announced in MIT newsletter, The Tech, in Calendar for 4 Dec. 1934 (http://64.233.179.104/search?q=cache:qgkfC54vj28J:www-tech.mit.edu/archives/VOL_054/TECH_V054_S0251_P004.pdf, accessed 2/23/06).

33 HUAC 1953f: 1850, 1856-57.

34 Hicks 1954: 43.

35 Wechsler 1973: 175; Cohen 1993: 96.

[36] HUAC 1953a: 5.

[37] Cohen 1993: 73 (American version); Wechsler 1973: 174 (1933 poll); Cohen 1993: 95 (1935 poll); Lash, qtd. Cohen 1993: 73; Feuer 1969: 363. Feuer's later trajectory led him even further from Marxism than Harry; he became a neoconservative and liked to say: "For Hegel I would not give a bagel!" (Wolfgang Saxon, "Lewis Feuer, 89, Scholar in Sociology and Government," *New York Times*, 30 Nov. 2002).

[38] Wechsler 1973: 171-72, 174; Cohen 1993: 91-95; Lipset and Riesman 1975: 158.

[39] Lipset and Riesman 1975: 159 (Harvard, 1934); Wechsler 1973: 179-80 (Columbia,1935); Eagan 1981: 117 (Harvard, 1935); Cohen 1993: 92 (end of apathy).

[40] *Crimson*, 11 May 1934 (Michael Mullins crowd); "Students Strike Against War," *Student Outlook*, 2. 5 (May 1934): 12-13 (socialist magazine).

[41] "Students Strike Against War," *Student Outlook* 2.5 (May 1934): 12-13. According to the *New York Times*, the first speaker was Allen Philbrick, "Harvard junior and executive secretary of the National Student League" ("Harvard Pacifists Routed by Barrage," 14 Apr. 1934). The student reporter who said that Harry spoke first may have been more accurate; the *Outlook* account also differs from that in the *Times* by calling George Clifton Edwards of SLID "the success of the day" and reporting that he spoke in a "pleadingly rational voice" and "met the hecklers with banter and repartee." Of the two others mentioned in the next sentence, Pavlo, who died in Cambridge in 2009, became an ophthalmologist; and Edwards, who died in 1992, became a judge on the Michigan Supreme Court.

[42] Ellen Schrecker, interview notes, 3 July 1979. In Harry's 1980 interview, he was vague about his role and never mentioned that he was president of the Harvard chapter of the NSL.

[43] *New York Times*, "Harvard Pacifists Routed by Barrage," 14 Apr. 1934 (vegetables); "Fighting Marks Harvard Anti-War Demonstration," *Boston Traveler*, 13 April 1934 (grapefruit, cited from clipping in Harvard University Archives, National Student League folder, HUD 3598). Feuer, as noted in Chapter 2, knew Harry, no doubt through their common political activities.

[44] Eagan 1981: 84 ("Harvard *WASP*"); *Crimson*, 11 May 1934.

[45] *Student Outlook*, 3.5 (May 1935): 4 (3,500 students; FDR's son John, an undergraduate, reportedly raised his hand in a mock Nazi salute); Lipset and Riesman 1975: 161 (less success).

[46] *Crimson*, 27 Mar. 1936 (1936 strike; an Associated Press poll suggested that 190,100 was a more likely figure [AAUP 1937: 319]); *Crimson*, 22 Apr. 1937 (1937 strike).

[47] Draper 1967: 178; Brax 1992: 81-82 (later events); Cohen 1993: 180-83 (1938 strike).

[48] Cohen 1993: 173 (endorsement of collective security); Lipset and Riesman 1975: 162, 171-72 (1936 election), 174 (isolationism); Feuer 1969: 373 (ASU). The Comintern was the association of worldwide Communist parties; it was run from Moscow.

[49] 1953f: 1847-48, 1853-54.

[50] Testimony of Martin Berkeley, a screenwriter, on 18 Sept. 1951 (HUAC, "Communist Infiltration of Hollywood Motion-Picture Industry–Part 4" [Washington: Government Printing Office, 1951], p. 1587).

[51] In 1938, Starr worked on a variety of YCL projects–writing an article on problems of youth relief, working with Polish youth, and participating on a recruitment drive (HUAC 1938-44: 5559-60, 5680, 5682, 5689); after that, she disappears from the HUAC index. In Boston in 1937-38, Grant was a leader in both the YCL and the CPUSA (HUAC 1938-44: 313, 588, 748, 771). Sparks, who spent two years in the Soviet Union (1931-33), had an extensive CPUSA career ranging from Boston to Los Angeles, where he worked for many years. Born Nehemiah Ish-Kishor, he used the names Ned, Nemmy, and Nehemiah; while in the USSR he used a pseudonym, Harry Kweit (or Kwite). Information on Sparks's names appears in the two indexes to HUAC hearings (one for 1938-54, the other for 1955-68). He is frequently mentioned in the early HUAC hearings in 1938-39 (see pp. 218, 249-50, 252, 315, 4592, 6149, 6545, 6622-25, 6736). For later references to his work with the Los Angeles County Communist Party, see (for example) HUAC, *Hearings*, Eighty-fourth Congress, second session, Communist Political Subversion, Part 1, 5 Dec. 1956 (Washington; Government Printing Office, 1957): 6647; and HUAC, "'United Front' Technique of the Southern California District of the Communist Party" (Washington: U.S. Government Printing Office, 1962): 57-58. On his wife, Alice Ward, see below, note 83.

[52] *Crimson*, 27 Mar. 1936 (Levy). Parry belonged to Harry's NSL group (1933-34), the Young Communist League (1934-35), and the CPUSA (until 1942). Like Harry, he supported himself through the Federal Writers' Project, losing his job in 1940 because of his membership in the CPUSA. One of the founders of the Marxist journal *Science and Society*, he served as its first managing editor in 1936-37. Information on Parry comes from Hare 1999; from the Biographical Note in the William T. Parry Papers, University of Buffalo Archives, 22/5F/67; and from his FBI file. See Chapter 7 for Parry's experience with McCarthyism.

[53] HJML, 14 May 1937.

[54] HUAC 1953f: 1849. For Schirmer's activities, see, for example, *Crimson*, 12 Mar. 1934, 2 May 1934, 22 Apr. 1955.

[55] HUAC 1958b: 2258, 2264.

[56] My sources for Schirmer's biography are the nominating statement

for this award (http://maillists.uci.edu/mailman/public/pasacaucus/2003-October/000002.html) and several of the tributes published after his death: http://www.philippinerevolution.org (Communist Party of the Philippines); http://qc.indymedia.org/news/2006/05/7098.php (International League of Peoples' Struggle, statement by Jose Maria Sison); and Walden Bello, "Schirmer, 91: Marcos Critic, Filipinos' Friend," *Philippine Daily Inquirer*, 4 May 2006: A1 (http://news.inq7.net/thegoodnews/index.php?index=1&story_id=74624)–all accessed on 26 May 2006.

[57] Rolfe 1974: 304. Technically battalions, the Lincoln and Washington brigades were usually grouped together under the name Lincoln Brigade. According to Friedberg's obituary in *The Volunteer: Journal of the Abraham Lincoln Brigade* (23.3 [2000]: 20), it was being "beaten and arrested" in the *Karlsruhe* protest (described later in this chapter) that got him "hooked on political action," and he joined the YCL. On the rest of his career, see his Harvard Law School obit (http://www.law.harvard.edu/alumni/bulletin/2001/spring/memoriam_main.html, accessed 8 Aug. 2007).

[58] Rolfe 1974: 101-02 (Bronstein's death); Feuer 1969: 367 (union organizer). Feuer gives 1935 as the year Bronstein left Harvard, but an anonymous colleague wrote that he studied at Harvard for two years ("Eugene Bronstein," *Harvard Communist* 4.1 [1937]: 4). The archive of the Abraham Lincoln Brigade records his occupation as "rubber worker" (http://www.alba-valb.org/volunteers/eugene-david-bronstein, accessed 27 July 2011).

[59] Although the letter is undated, internal evidence shows that Bronstein wrote it in June 1937. He expressed regret that he hadn't seen Friedberg. A letter from Bronstein written from Spain shows him in full command of Communist jargon (qtd. "Eugene Bronstein," *Harvard Communist* 4.1 [1937: 4]). Besides Friedberg and Bronstein, three other members of the Harvard YCL fought in Spain–Milton Weiner, Griffin Washburn, and Joseph Siegel ("Harvard in Spain," *Harvard Communist* 4.1 [Nov. 1937]: 5).

[60] "Eugene Bronstein: A Tribute," *Harvard Communist* 4.1 (Nov. 1937): 4.

[61] Weiner to HJM, 12 Oct. 1937. The earlier card is undated. Dave Walba (Moses David Walba) is identified in the archive of the Abraham Lincoln Brigade as a member of the YCL from Boston; he was killed in the same bombardment at Brunete in July 1937 as Bronstein (http://www.alba-valb.org/volunteers/moses-david-walba, accessed 27 July 2011). Alfred Joseph Goldenberg of Boston, who is probably "Al G.," was also in the Abraham Lincoln Brigade; listed in Harry's clipping as wounded in the battle that killed Bronstein and Walba, he died on 13 October 1937 at Fuentes de Ebro (http://www.alba-valb.org/volunteers/alfred-joseph-goldenberg, accessed 27 July 2011).

[62] HUAC 1953f: 1851.

[63] "City College Ousts Six More for Row," *New York Times*, 6 June 1933.

Bronstein graduated from City on 20 June 1934 (*New York Times*, 20 June 1934). Lewis Feuer, who probably knew Bronstein at Harvard, decried his fanatical obedience to a "political-mystical philosophy" in a way that entailed "self-destruction of himself as an intellectual" (1969: 366, 367).

[64] The village was near the town of Olevsk; Oscar Frager's World War II draft registration card gives his place of birth as "O Levse, Russia." Despite advanced Alzheimer's disease, Vida Castaline was able to translate into English the Ukrainian name of the village. Earlier oral interviews with Vida are the basis of much of my information regarding the Frager family, including Bunny's political activities.

[65] At this time, about 25% of Eastern European Jewish immigrants were illiterate (Ehrenfried 1963: 510); most of the illiterates, presumably, were women.

[66] The CPUSA began Workers Schools in 1923. Asked in his testimony for the name of the school, Harry said that it had no name (HUAC 1953f: 1853).

[67] HJML, 24 Apr. 1933.

[68] Sidney Lipshires, telephone interview, 21 January 2006 ("handyman"); HUAC 1958a: 2110 (FBI informer); HUAC 1958c: 2377-80 (Olrich's testimony). The notorious FBI informant Herbert Philbrick testified that he had worked with Frances Olrich (when she was known as Frances Smith) on a CPUSA training manual (HUAC, "Exposé of Communist Activities in the State of Massachusetts," 23 July 1951 [Washington: U.S. Government Printing Office, 1951]: 1281).

[69] Sidney Lipshires (telephone interviews, 21 January 2006 and 18 March 2006). Lipshires was a defendant in one of the last Smith Act trials, shortly before the Smith Act–which made it an offense to advocate the violent overthrow of the American government–was declared unconstitutional; he left the CPUSA after his indictment was lifted, having been disillusioned by the Soviet invasion of Hungary and Khrushchev's denunciation of Stalin. Illustrating the small world of the CPUSA, Lipshires took over its Springfield (Massachusetts) office from Peggy Schirmer, who in turn had taken it over from her husband when he left for military service in 1944 (testimony of Jack Davis in HUAC, Investigation of Communist Activities in the Albany, N.Y. Area–Part 5, 8 Apr. 1954 [Washington: Government Printing Office, 1954]: 4417). According to the informer Armando Penha, Lipshires had served as Western Massachusetts district organizer of the CPUSA, working with Schirmer in the early and mid-1950s (HUAC 1958a: 2111-16).

[70] Defense Minister, qtd. in "Germany Welcomes Warship on Return," *New York Times*, 19 June 1934, p. 7; Norwood 2009: 42 (official Harvard); "Military and Naval Ball To Take Place This Evening: Colorful Event To Be

Attended By German Cadets and Officers," *Harvard Crimson*, 18 May 1934. The ball illustrated the acceptance of militarism on American campuses that was being challenged by the peace strikes.

[71] *Harvard Crimson*, 16 May 1934. Other newspapers said he gave his name as Charles I. Allen. See *New York Times*, "Harvard 'Red' Seized on German Cruiser," 16 May 1934, p. 3; *Boston Daily Globe*, "Seize Harvard 'Red' on German Cruiser," morning edition, 16 May 1934: 32. The *Times* added that a "search of his rooms at Adams House revealed a considerable amount of Marxian literature."

[72] *Harvard Crimson*, 18 May 1934. Jerry Olrich told Sidney Lipshires that Harry had written the German text of the flyer (Lipshires, telephone interview, 22 June 2006). Philbrick's interview with the FBI about Robbins, in the latter's FBI file, confirms the information (interview in Indianapolis, 10 Aug. 1953).

[73] Raymond Dennet, "International Difficulties," *Harvard Journal*, 16 May 1934 (clipping in Harvard University Archives, National Student League folder, HUD 3598). The article, which quotes an English translation of Harry's flyer, reports that "Albert A. Mallinger, Harvard student speaking for the anti-war faction, was alone permitted to get through his speech."

[74] *Harvard Crimson*, 17 May 1934 (letter from Nixon de Tarnowsky '35); *Harvard Crimson*, 2 Oct. 1934. Philbrick told the FBI that he had dropped out in 1934 because of the publicity given the incident.

[75] HUAC 1953f: 1850. After a long career at the University of Western Ontario, Philbrick died in 2007.

[76] Norwood 2009: 44.

[77] "Karlsruhe Protest Parade Ends in Riot," *Boston Evening Globe*, morning edition, pp. 1, 8.

[78] "Police Defend Selves as They Prosecute Reds," *Boston Herald*, 24 May 1934: 1.

[79] "German Envoy to Be Guarded by Police Here," *Boston Herald*, 18 May 1934: 1. The Charles Street Jail–a national, state, and city landmark built in 1851–was converted in 2007 to a luxury hotel (Joyce Wadler, "Luxury Living Where Once the Residents Were Felons," *New York Times*, 30 Aug. 2007: F3).

[80] "21 Arrests, Many Casualties as Reds and Police Fight Hot Battle in Charlestown," *Boston Herald*, 18 May 1934: 1, 16.

[81] "20 Found Guilty on Riot Charge," *Boston Daily Globe*, morning edition, 30 May 1934: 6; "20 Held Guilty in Anti-Nazi Riot," *Boston Herald*, 30 May 1934: 6. Eugene Bronstein was among those arrested. "Belle Lewis," perhaps using a false surname, got seven months; she was described in the *Herald* as "leader of Young Communist League." She was presumably the

"Belle" who wrote to Bunny three years later from New York, as recounted later in this chapter, and may have been Belle Keller, to whom Schirmer gave money for the Kentucky miners, who was "connected with…the Workers' International Relief in Boston" (Robbins 1953: 325).

[82] Harry's friend Herman Walker was a member of the committee. Its report, issued on 4 June 1934, is summarized on that date in the *Boston Herald* ("Harvard Group Hits Hultman in Riot Report," pp. 1, 12); the *Boston Globe*, morning edition ("Harvard Groups Denounce Police," pp. 1, 2); and the *Harvard Crimson* ("Students Describe Slugging by Boston Police During Riot in 16-Page Report"). Herman Walker also gave a sworn statement as a witness, as did two other of Harry's friends, Saul Friedberg and William T. Parry. The *Harvard Crimson* conditioned its support of the committee report on a commitment to exclude Jews from membership (Lipset and Riesman 1975: 159).

[83] "11 Guilty in Karlsruhe Case," *Boston Daily Globe*, morning edition, 29 Nov. 1934: 32; "Nine Go to Jail on 'Principle,'" *Boston Evening Globe*, morning edition, 3 Dec. 1934: 3. Alice Ward, whom Vida mentions in the quotation in the following paragraph, was the wife of Nehemiah (Nemmy) Sparks (see note 51). Herself active in the CPUSA, she was mentioned in HUAC, *Investigation of Communist Activities in the Los Angeles, Calif., Area, Part 4*, 1-2 July 1955 (pp. 1795, 1814, 1820, and 1856).

[84] "Nine Go to Jail on 'Principle,'" *Boston Evening Globe*, morning edition, 3 Dec. 1934: 3.

[85] Harry Marks married on 2 March 1935, Harry Castaline on 30 June.

[86] Richard O. Boyer, "Severe Judges Seen as Aiding Cause of Reds," *Boston Herald*, 1 Dec. 1934: 1, 3.

[87] HUAC 1953f: 1870. The strike began on 9 May; on 21 July, the strikers agreed to go to arbitration, returning to work the next week. The date of Walker's letter, 28 Oct. 1934, suggests that he had not been in touch for some time.

[88] Shirer 1941: 17.

[89] Conradi 2004: 150-51.

[90] Fromm 1990: 92 ("faithful hound"); Hanfstaengl 1934: 9 (putsch).

[91] McDonald 2007: 28, 69 ("simple" method); "Hanfstaengl in Hub Under Strong Guard," *Boston Daily Globe*, morning edition, 18 June 1934: 1, 6 ("slaughter," "better").

[92] Richard O. Boyer, "Hanfstaengl Life of Party," *Boston Herald*, 20 June 1934: 1 ("stentorian laugh"); Geoffrey Parsons, Jr., "'Hanfy' Has Time of Life with '09," *Boston Daily Globe*, morning edition, 20 June 1934: 23 (khaki shirt); "Hanfstaengl Hits Lusitania 'Myth,'" *New York Times*, 20 June 1934 (class book).

[93] Geoffrey Parsons, Jr., "Hanfstaengl Enjoys Social Round in Hub,"

Boston Daily Globe, morning ed., 19 June 1934: 4, and Norwood 2009: 52–53 (Shubow); Goldhagen 1996: 71 (exterminationist tradition); Klemperer 1998: 128 (quoting Goebbels). Raul Hilberg contends that until 1941, Nazi policy toward the Jews was "expulsion and exclusion," not "extermination" and that as late as 1938 the Final Solution could not have been forecast (2003, 1: 4, 50). Hitler, however, told James G. McDonald on 8 Apr. 1933: "I will do the thing that the rest of the world would like to do. It doesn't know how to get rid of the Jews. I will show them" (2007: 48–McDonald qtd. by Rabbi Stephen S. Wise). On reports that year of Nazi plans to "eliminate" Jews from Germany, causing their "physical extinction," see Norwood 2009: 9. Two years later Hanfstaengl told Varian Fry that radical Nazis "intended to 'solve' the 'Jewish problem' by the physical extermination of the Jews": "Extermination was, I am almost certain, the exact word he used" (qtd. Isenberg 2001: 62).

[94] Conradi 2004: 144-46 ("all beliefs"); Conant 1970: 140-45 (his version).

[95] "Harvard's Alumni Spoof New Deal," *New York Times*, 21 June 1934.

[96] Conradi 2004: 155; "Harvard's Alumni Spoof New Deal," *New York Times*, 21 June 1934. The *Boston Daily Globe* reported the song ("Harvard '19 Banner Alludes to 'Hanfy,'" 21 June 1934: 1).

[97] "Signs and Costumes Amuse at Stadium," *Boston Daily Globe*, 21 June 1934, morning ed.: 25 (sign); "Harvard '19 Banner Alludes to Hanfy," *Boston Daily Globe*, 21 June 1934, morning ed.: 1 (Keezar).

[98] "There was no unpleasantness at Harvard at all yesterday," according to Geoffrey Parsons, Jr., "Hanfstaengl Enjoys Social Round in Hub," *Boston Daily Globe*, 19 June 1934: 1.

[99] Conradi 2004: 156; "Girls in Anti-Nazi Move at Harvard," *Boston Globe*, 22 June 1934, morning edition: 1, 8; "Two Anti-Nazis Freed Upon Conant's Request," *Harvard Crimson*, 18 Oct. 1934. The young women were identified as Sarah Barr and Jean Lentier. According to the *Globe*, any Harvard senior or alumnus could obtain visitors' tickets.

[100] HUAC 1953f: 1849.

[101] "Girls in Anti-Nazi Move at Harvard," 22 June 1934, morning edition: 1, 8.

[102] *Harvard Crimson*, 24 Oct. 1934 (Conant's request) and 30 Nov. 1934 (conviction).

[103] Tuttle 1979: 55 (Berlin press conference); Norwood 2009: 48 (*Sieg Heil*); Baker 1984: 346-47 (Pound, Frankfurter). During a tour of Germany in summer 1934, Pound "several times...congratulated Hitler for bringing domestic tranquility to the country" (Tuttle 1979: 58).

[104] *Harvard Crimson*, 13 June 1933 (honorary degree) and 23 Nov. 1933 (refusal of scholarship); *Harvard Communist*, 2.2 (Apr. 1936): 4. Conant's letter of refusal was quoted in support of the British academic boycott of

the Heidelberg University celebrations, to which (as noted below) Harvard sent a delegate (Burlingham et al. 1936: 30).

[105] "Translation of 'Deutsche Allgemeine Zeitung' Story Gives Cables Sent by Mellon and Magoun," *Harvard Crimson*, 23 Nov. 1934 (decision to reject); "Harvard Renews Rebuff to Nazis," *New York Times*, 23 Nov. 1934; "Professors Regret Hanfstaengl Snub," *New York Times*, 1 Dec. 1934 (reporting on article in *Deutsche Allgemeine Zeitung* and also Magoun's cable, referred to immediately below; E. and K. Mann 1939: 120 (bust of Hitler). The *Deutsche Allgemeine Zeitung* was a right-wing paper published in 1861-1945. A bilingual Russian/German newspaper of the same name began publishing in Kazahkstan in 1966 (http://deutsche-allgemeine-zeitung.de/de/content/blogcategory/41/77/).

[106] Norwood 2009: 58 (wreath with swastika); Mann's diary, 16 Mar. 1935 ("grant from Hanfstaengl") and 21 June 1935 (Harvard commencement)-T. Mann 1982: 236, 242.

[107] Keller and Keller 2001: 156 and Tuttle 1979: 61 (boycott); Norwood 2009: 61-63 (Nazification at Heidelberg); A. Hill et al. 1936: 56, 58 (summer 1936 courses at Heidelberg, "German physics"). Kirsopp Lake, Winn Professor of Ecclesiastical History at Harvard, and Reginald Aldworth Daly, a Harvard professor of geology, received honorary doctorates at the Heidelberg celebration ("Blaney Omits Nazi Salute," *New York Times*, 30 June 1936; Norwood 2009: 67). After Conant became American ambassador to Germany in 1953, he wrote articles for the State Department reflecting on his own dilemma (Tuttle 1979: 51, 67n5); he also exerted his influence to afford convicted Nazis early release from prison (Norwood 2009: 243-50). In 1935, Heidelberg renamed its Physics Institute after Philipp Lenard, who invented "German physics"; in the concluding address at the renaming ceremony, Lenard endorsed the preceding anti-Semitic speeches, exhorting "all to continue energetically the fight against the Jewish spirit" exemplified by Einstein (Burlingham et al. 1936: 47-49, 51; Norwood 2009: 62-63). On Heidelberg's nazification and denazification, see Remy 2002.

[108] Hershberg 1993: 96 (Conant in public and private); Keller and Keller 2001: 157 (Birkhoff reporting Goebbels); Conant 1970: 146; Keller and Keller 2001: 157 (quoting Conant re Göttingen); Tuttle 1979: 66 (never "explicitly declined"); Norwood 2009: 101 (Columbia). Einstein refused to attend Harvard's tercentenary celebration in 1936 because German universities were invited (Tuttle 1979: 64).

[109] Norwood 2009: 37 (invited representatives); Conant 1970: 151 (selective memory); Keller and Keller 2001: 157 (failed to show).

[110] "By 1935," according to Keller and Keller (2001: 155), "1,684 faculty members had been dismissed from German universities, including 5 Nobel Prize winners. Harvard eventually appointed some of them, but

only after they had been vetted by a stay at another American university. And many of Harvard's émigré scholars…were not Jewish." According to Scheffler (2004: 34), Robert Ulich, who was not Jewish and not fired, resigned his post to protest firings at Dresden Technical University in 1933 and was invited by Conant to join the Harvard faculty (see Chapter 8). Dietrich Gerhard's very brief appointment at Harvard enabled him to get a visa and emigrate (see Chapter 5).

[111] Fermi 1971: 77 (subvention of salaries); Tuttle 1979: 52-53 (Lowell and Conant declined); Schorske 1991: 141 (Langer's wish to help refugees); Schorske 1978: 1151 (Langer's childhood).

[112] Langer papers, Harvard Univ. Archives, Correspondence 193[3]-35, HUG(FP) 19.8, box 1, folder Correspondence 1934-35; General Correspondence 1933-41, European Refugees, HUG(FP) 19.8, box 2, folder European Refugees 1939-40.

[113] Norwood 2009: 234 and Keller and Keller 2001: 153-58 (gentiles); Diamond 1992: 115 (Conant on German Jewish chemists); N. Rosovsky 1986: 31 (Conant's anti-Semitism); Norwood 2009: 39 (Bergmann); Lohff and Conrads 2007: 123-24 (Butenandt); Keller and Keller 2001: 158 (as late as 1940). Shortly after he turned down Bergmann, Conant was willing to assist another German chemist, described as having "no Jewish blood," who had been dismissed because of his support for a Jewish colleague (Norwood 2009: 39).

[114] Krohn 1993: 76 ("alibi"); Mann, qtd. http://www.newschool.edu/gf/about/history.htm (accessed 17 March 2006).

[115] Bell 1986: 4.

[116] HJML, 3 Jan. 1937 ("peasant"), 8 Mar. 1937 (intelligence), 15 July 1935 (letter to Bunny). The CIO (Congress of Industrial Organizations) was a trade-union federation. With respect to "the Fraction," Harry explained that YCL members who joined another group that they hoped to influence would privately caucus as a "fraction" before a meeting so that they could agree on the best way to achieve their purpose; they might also caucus afterwards for a post-mortem (HUAC 1953f: 1848).

[117] Weinstein 1978: 127-30 ("Bill"). In Harry's letter to Bunny on 15 July 1935, he also mentioned meeting "Rader…a nice fresh engaging youth," in New York. This youth was not the left-leaning, non-Communist Melvin Rader, a target of McCarthyite witch hunts at the University of Washington, whose first visit to New York was in 1945 (Rader 1969: 77). The persecution of Melvin Rader is recounted by a number of authors (for example Caute 1978: 410). The informant who claimed Rader had been in a CPUSA school in 1938 (and who was later convicted of perjury) insisted that the Rader he was confronting was the very same person he had taught in the CPUSA school. Is it possible that he had confused him with the Rader whom Harry met?

[118] *Race Hatred on Trial,* a 47-page booklet published by the CPUSA in 1931, provided the abridged proceedings of the CPUSA "trial," held before 1,500 white and African American workers, of August Yokinen, a Finnish immigrant and CPUSA member, who had failed to intervene when three African Americans were excluded from the Finnish Club in Harlem (see Jacobson 1998: 252-55). The CPUSA used the trial to demonstrate its anti-racist credentials; since it was widely publicized, Mona Otway would presumably already have known about it.

[119] Schrecker, interview notes, 3 July 1979. Schrecker cites him as "typical" in leaving the CPUSA for "personal, rather than ideological reasons" (1986: 57). Lewis Feuer was clearly referring to Harry when he cited the emotion expressed by the "leading member of the National Student League at Harvard in 1933" (in fact, 1934) (1969: 359); Feuer incorrectly says that Harry's testimony excludes any mention of "the economic impact of the terrible depression years."

[120] HUAC 1953f: 1865. On his father's discovery, see Chapter 8.

[121] HJML, 8 Mar. 1939.

[122] Brax 1991: 8.

[123] HUAC 1953f: 1862-63 (Harry); HUAC 1953c: 1054 (Amdur); HUAC 1953d: 1074, 1981 (Levinson).

[124] Possibly this was Belle Keller, to whom, as mentioned above (note 81), Herbert Robbins turned over money he collected for miners in Kentucky.

[125] Weissberg 1951: 59. Weissberg's memoir of his three years of interrogation, imprisonment, and torture in the Soviet Union was discussed by members of the UConn Department of Government and International Relations, as noted in the report of the Committee of Five (see Chapter 7). On 29 May 1953, Louis Gerson told the committee that he had borrowed Weissberg's book from Emanuel Margolis and found it "a well-written account"; Margolis told Gerson, the latter said, that it was "trash" and "utter nonsense," even though he had not read it (today, Margolis has no memory at all of the book).

Chapter 7

[1] Koestler (1949) in Crossman 1963: 54-55.

[2] Schrecker 1998: 203, 203-39.

[3] O'Reilly 1983: 99.

[4] Silin 1953: 593.

[5] Schrecker 1994: 151-54. During the period with which we are concerned, the Internal Security Subcommittee was chaired by Patrick McCarran (1951-52) and William Jenner (1953-54). McCarran sponsored the act

that established the Subversive Activities Control Board and the requirement that Communist organizations register with the government. The
Senate overrode Truman's veto of the act.

[6] Cohen 1993: 99; O'Reilly 1983: 217-29.

[7] AEW, 13 June 1949, Series V, Box 16, folder 22 May-18 July 1949. In
1938, UConn President Albert N. Jorgensen received a letter advising him
to "look into the Reds around the college and release [i.e., fire] a few" (qtd.
Stave 2006: 73).

[8] Silin 1953: 584, 596 ("thought-control"); A. Meyer 1953:558, 560-62
("political gangsters").

[9] O'Reilly 1983: 207.

[10] Schrecker 1994: 83; O'Reilly 1983: 169-71.

[11] AEW, 31 Mar. 1953, pp. 118-19; DRC, Series V, box 16, folder 21 Mar.-
22 Apr. 1953. In keeping with Waugh's distinction, throughout this book
I have silently altered "communism/ist" to "Communism/ist" when the
Communist Party is meant.

[12] AAUP 1953: 92, 96. Other references to this statement in this paragraph are to pp. 94-95 and p. 97.

[13] A. Meyer 1953: 568-69.

[14] Resolution passed by UConn chapter of AAUP on 20 May 1953, attached to Philip E. Taylor to Jorgensen and Trustees, 5 June 1953 (DRC,
Jorgensen papers, Series II, box 35, "Communism"). Taylor, president of
the UConn chapter, told Waugh of Zilsel's request the day after UConn
suspended him (AEW, 24 Apr. 1953, p. 164, box 16, folder 23 Apr.-21 May
1953).

[15] This paragraph draws mainly on Stave 2006: 73-75. In the 1940s,
UConn officials gave the FBI information about members of the American
Student Union chapter who were "inclined toward Communism"–appar-
ently a reference to American Youth for Democracy (Cohen 1993: 326).

[16] "Educator Assails 'Fear of Russia,'" *New York Times*, 20 Mar. 1953, p.
28. When I entered Barnard the following year, I was unaware of McIntosh's statement. Nor did I know that in 1935, her predecessor, Virginia
Gildersleeve, had applauded Hitler's policies with regard to women and
Jews; according to Norwood, she worked to reduce Jewish enrollment at
Barnard (Norwood 2009: 104-05). It is difficult to generalize about an individual's opinions: the next year Dean Gildersleeve signed a statement by
leading American educators condemning the new Nazi policy of excluding Jewish children from public schools ("Educators Decry Nazis' School
Ban," *New York Times*, 20 Apr. 1936).

[17] Schrecker 1994: 84.

[18] Caute 1978: 406.

[19] Lewis's subscription to *Jewish Life* is indicated in an FBI memo in

Lewis's file, 22 May 1952. He was listed on a petition supporting the Stockholm Peace Plan (against atomic warfare; FBI file, NH 100-14162, apparently June 1952). In 1950, Lewis was a cosigner of a letter to a Pittsburgh paper "attacking the Mundt-Nixon bill that proposed restrictions on the rights of political leftists" (Reisch and Andrews 2001: 105). The University of Pittsburgh resisted public demands in 1950 to fire Hathway; she resigned in 1951, however, taking a position at Bryn Mawr (Reisch and Andrews 2001: 101-08, 121). For an overview of Lewis's life, see Reisch's "Editor's Introduction" in H. Lewis 2003: xi-xiii.

[20] Lewis, FBI file, memo from Director, FBI, to New Haven office, 16 Oct. 1952.

[21] Information gathered from Lewis's FBI file: Omaha office (9 June 1952); NH 100-14162 (apparently June 1952, giving a summary replete with contradictions); and New Haven office (15 Feb. 1952 and 16 June 1953).

[22] My main source here is "Report to the Board of Trustees of the University of Connecticut by the Committee of Five Investigating Charges of Communism Against Four Members of the Faculty," as well as the minutes of the meetings of the Committee of Five–all in the Thomas R. Dodd Archives at the University of Connecticut. According to a Chronology prepared in connection with the report, Jorgensen notified the Chairman of the Board of Trustees and Gov. Lodge of Zilsel's subpoena as soon as he learned of it, on 13 Mar. (DRC, Jorgensen papers, Series II, Box 35, "Communism").

[23] Schrecker 1998: 224, 212.

[24] AEW, journal, 18 Mar. 1953, DRC, Series V, box 18, folder 10 Feb.-20 Mar. 1953, p. 97.

[25] AEW, journal, 18 Mar. 1953, DRC, Series V, box 18, folder 10 Feb.-20 Mar. 1953.

[26] Diamond 1982: 365, 367.

[27] The policy is quoted at length by L. Lewis (1988: 241-42); his discussion of the Zilsel case (242-45) naively depicts Jorgensen as "an honest broker, not a partisan," concerned only with "the facts."

[28] The UConn bylaws provided for a committee of five to hold a hearing for any faculty member being considered for dismissal before the expiration of his contract; the person in question had the right to appear in his own defense.

[29] AEW, journal, 30 Mar. 1953, Series V, box 16, folder 21 Mar.-22 Apr. 1953.

[30] AEW, journal, 14 Feb. 1953, Series V, box 16, folder 10 Feb.-20 Mar. 1953. On 24 Apr. 1953, the FBI Special Agent in Charge in New Haven listed six persons at UConn as possible subversives (Diamond 1992: 204; he

does not provide names)–presumably the four people in the blind memorandum plus Luchterhand and Harry. For an overview of Luchterhand's life and career–with no mention of Communism–see the biographical sketch in his papers at Brooklyn College: http://library.brooklyn.cuny.edu/archives/findaid/luchterhand/bioluchterhand.html (accessed 5 Nov. 2009).

[31] Curt Beck, who taught in the UConn Department of Government his entire career, describes Waugh as "a principled and effective defender of academic freedom" (pers. comm., 8 July 2006).

[32] On Washington, see Rader 1969: 112, 114.

[33] AEW, journal, 27 Aug. 1953, Series V, Box 17, folder 12 July-1 Sept. 1953. Margolis worried that the Board of Trustees would inflict some kind of censure on him, but it did not.

[34] It is not clear whether Lewis and Glass took advantage of the opportunity to teach in 1953-54 (Bruce Stave, email, 3 Dec. 2009). Lewis's FBI file has no information on him in 1953-54 aside from two memos: one, dated 11 Aug. 1954 from the New Haven office saying that he was now living in Providence, Rhode Island, which fell within the bailiwick of the Boston office; and another, from the Boston office on 28 Oct. 1954, saying that he had recently moved to the area. It is therefore possible that he continued at UConn for another year.

[35] I am drawing on two sources: Waugh's journal, 13 Mar. 1953, Series V, box 16, folder 10 Feb.-20 Mar. 1953; and the Chronology drawn up by the Committee of Five (DRC, Jorgensen papers, Series II, box 35, "Communism").

[36] Two of the six universities were public (Rutgers and Ohio State), while the other four were private (Harvard, New York University, Dartmouth, and Yale) ("Chronology," pp. 6-7, DRC, Jorgensen papers, Series II, box 35, "Communism").

[37] Gavroglu 1995: 240-41. On the cooperation of Yale administrators, faculty, and alumni with the FBI, see Diamond 1992: 204-41.

[38] Harry did appear before the Five, but not with respect to his own past; as seen below, he supported accusations against Margolis.

[39] Committee of Five report, pp. 2-9; this report reproduces Zilsel's HUAC testimony, which I use here to fill in details. Zilsel expected to testify before HUAC on April 16, but the date was moved forward by six days.

[40] See Gavroglu 1955: 241.

[41] Hellman 1976: 92-93.

[42] AEW, journal, 13 May 1953, Series V, box 16, folder 10 Feb.-20 Mar. 1953.

[43] HUAC 1953c: 1036-37.

[44] Diamond 1977: 14-15.

[45] Schrecker 1986: 203. Furry was cited for contempt for refusing to name names before congressional committees; the only sanction that Harvard imposed was placing "a finding of grave misconduct on the books for three years," with the threat of firing if he committed any further misdeeds (Keller and Keller 2001: 202-03). Furry's promotion to full professor was also delayed, a minor penalty in McCarthyite times.

[46] AEW, journal, 22 Apr. 1953, Series V, box 16, folder 21 Mar.-22 Apr. 1953.

[47] Qtd. L. Lewis 1988: 245.

[48] AEW, journal, 23 Apr. 1953, Series V, box 16, folder 23 Apr.-21 May 1953.

[49] AEW, journal, 23 Apr. 1953, Series V, box 16, folder 23 Apr.-21 May 1953.

[50] Charles H. Schauer, Director of the Grants Division of the Research Corporation, to Jorgensen, 1 May 1953; Clark L. Bailey to Schauer, 4 May 1953; Zilsel to Schauer, 4 May 1953 (DRC, Jorgensen papers, Series II, box 35, "Communism)"

[51] Edgar Zilsel was assisted by the Emergency Committee in Aid of Foreign Scholars (Duggan and Drury 1948: 208). Interviews with Paul Zilsel include poignant details: his father's suicide in 1944 and his mother's residence in a mental hospital nearly the entire period of her stay in America (she returned to Austria in 1948 and remained there until her death; Gavroglu 1995: 264n167).

[52] HUAC 1953c: 1044-45.

[53] See Barth 1953: 12 and Silin 1953: 585.

[54] L. Lewis 1988: 246; "Dr. Zilsel Reinstated [and] Is Censured by U of C," Hartford Courant, 29 July 1953: 33; "Defiant Teacher Back on Faculty," New York Times, 29 July 1953; AEW, journal, 28-29 July 1953, Series V, Box 17, folder 12 July-1 Sept. 1953.

[55] Qtd. L. Lewis 1988: 247.

[56] AEW, journal, 19 Oct. 1953, Series V, Box 17, folder 19 Oct.-30 Nov. 1953.

[57] Stave 2006: 81.

[58] HJM 1980. In this interview, he never mentioned his intervention in the case of Emanuel Margolis.

[59] Both Margolis in his memoir and Harry in testimony before the Committee of Five gave the year of their argument as 1952, Harry placing it in March (Committee of Five report, 28 May 1953). I am grateful to Margolis for an illuminating talk on 8 March 2006 and for generously sharing the pages of his memoir concerning the evening with Harry and Bunny. This paragraph is based on his recollections. Also present at Margolis's

home were Clifford McAvoy and his wife; Harry told the Five that McAvoy "was visiting various college campuses for the purpose of dissuading physical scientists from engaging in research connected with national defense" (report, p. 61). McAvoy, a former union organizer, had been cited thirty-seven times in HUAC testimony by 1946 (Carr 1952: 237-38).

[60] In Jan. 1953, Stalin claimed that Jewish doctors were plotting to poison members of the Soviet leadership (the accused went to the gulag or death); after Stalin's death on 5 Mar. 1953, his successors admitted the plot was a hoax. There were plenty of earlier instances of Soviet anti-Semitism that Harry could have cited.

[61] Curt Beck, priv. comm. (Jan. 2006) and unpublished memoir. Ironically, in his second (and last) year at UConn, 1952-53, Margolis was replacing Beck. Stanley Grean, Zilsel's accuser, told the Committee of Five (4 June 1953) "that he has never met Mr. Margolis and had received the information about his Communist tendencies from Messrs. Marks and Beck."

[62] Committee of Five minutes, 19 May 1953.

[63] Committee of Five minutes, 19 May 1953; other testimony on 15, 28, 29 and 30 May and 3 June 1953. Some months later, G. Lowell Field, chair of the Department of Government, told Provost Waugh that he had no way of knowing whether Margolis was a Communist and–incredibly–that the report of the Committee of Five was "never brought to my attention" (8 Oct. 1953; qtd. L. Lewis 1988: 40).

[64] "IRC Hears Margolis on U.S.-China Policy," *Connecticut Campus*, 3 Mar. 1952: 1, 3; Committee of Five report, 29 May 1953 (meeting with two members) and 30 May 1953 (meeting with Beck).

[65] AEW, journal, 18 Mar. 1953, Series V, box 18, folder 10 Feb.-20 Mar. 1953. Both Glass and Lewis taught group work, an element of their profession that suffered damaging attacks at the time (Reisch and Andrews 2001: 120-26).

[66] "Statement of the Faculty of the School of Social Work" submitted to the Committee of Five; AEW, journal, 18 Mar. 1953, Series V, box 18, folder 10 Feb.-20 Mar. 1953.

[67] AEW, journal, 29 July 1953, Series V, box 17, folder 12 July-1 Sept. 1953.

[68] AEW, journal, 14 July 1953 (on Waugh's wish for deeper consideration), 21 July 1953 (on Jorgensen's reaction and "have to fire them all"), and 27 July 1953 (on "accusations made in secret" and the final decision); all in Series V, box 17, folder 12 July-1 Sept. 1953.

[69] Reisch and Andrews 1999: 100; Robert Glass, letter, *Social Work* 33.3 (1988): 288. I have been unable to find more than two other brief contributions by Glass to social-work literature ("The Current Dilemma in So-

cial Group Work Methodology," *Journal of Jewish Communal Service*, 44.4 [1965]: 310-15; "Comment," *Jewish Social Work Forums* 4.2 [1967]: 18-19). He taught at the University of Nebraska and at Fordham University (obituary, *Hampton Chronicle-News* 14 July 1994, p. 15). Glass, Lewis, and their families and colleagues were hounded "well into the 1960s" by the FBI (Reisch and Andrews 2001: 121).

[70] At Hunter, where Lewis was Dean in 1970-90, he "played a central role in making it a leader in its field among public universities" (Wolfgang Saxon, "Harold Lewis, Social Work Dean at Hunter College, Is Dead at 83," *New York Times*, 22 July 2003; see also http://www.naswfoundation. org/pioneers/l/lewis_h.htm, accessed 11 Nov. 2009). One of Lewis's relatives recalled the close friendship with Glass (pers. comm.). Since Glass and Lewis both worked in Omaha, in 1948-50, the friendship probably originated there (Lewis remained in Omaha until 1951, when he started teaching at UConn). Trecker said that Glass had taught at the University of Nebraska School of Social Work in 1948-50 and at UConn since 1950 (report of the Committee of Five, p. 40).

[71] Documents in Lewis's FBI file. The Boston FBI office recommended on 17 Mar. 1955 that he be removed from the Security Index. Lewis's FBI file does not show the investigation continuing into the 1960s about which Lewis spoke in a 1995 interview (Reisch and Andrews 2001: 163).

[72] H. Lewis 2003: 208-18.

[73] Schrecker interview notes, 3 July 1979. Cooper served the subpoena "in the neighborhood of 3 weeks" prior to Harry's testimony (HUAC 1953f, 1863; on Robbins's testimony, see p. 1869).

[74] AEW, journal, 2 June 1953, Box 17, folder 23 May-11 July 1953. On 7 July, Harry again visited Waugh, this time to say that he had "answered all the questions which were asked of him" (AEW, journal, Box 17, folder 23 May-11 July 1953).

[75] I am quoting from Beck's memoir-in-progress, which he kindly shared.

[76] My mother, my source of information regarding Moore's promise, told me at the time that a member of the Department of Government had informed Harry that he had read the hearing transcript; thus Harry learned that "executive session" meant nothing at all. Curt Beck identified his colleague as David Mars, and Mars has confirmed that he was then closely following HUAC publications (email, 13 July 2011).

[77] HUAC 1953f: 1863.

[78] HUAC 1953f: 1853 ("reassuring"); Schrecker, interview notes, 3 July 1979 ("terribly distressed"); Schrecker 1994: 60 (friendly witnesses); HUAC 1953f: 1863 ("revulsion").

[79] Donner 1961: 69.

[80] Lawrence Arguimbau, HUAC 1954: 4014.

[81] HUAC 1953f: 1863, 1873.

[82] HUAC 1953f: 1850-51.

[83] Donner 1961: 111.

[84] Silin 1953: 594.

[85] Carr 1952: 267.

[86] HUAC 1953f: 1845.

[87] HUAC 1953f: 1849.

[88] Schirmer, listed in the film credits as "Dan," recalled that during the McCarthy period, censors excised a scene in which his character tells another American soldier, who is reluctant to aid the partisans because some of them are Communists, that they must work together with Communists and socialists to defeat fascism (Emmanuel 2006).

[89] HUAC 1953f: 1850-51.

[90] Lawrence S. Levy graduated from Harvard in 1939. I have no further information on him.

[91] HUAC 1953f: 1860-61.

[92] HUAC 1953f: 1864-65 (Harry's testimony). A House committee chaired by Hamilton Fish of New York had conducted an extensive investigation of New York City schools in 1930, during which the Superintendent of Schools testified that he would immediately suspend any teacher accused of being a Communist; in the 1930s, teachers' unions in New York were embroiled in controversy over Communism (Iversen 1959: 32-58, 99-118, 203-08).

[93] HUAC 1953f: 1863. Harry gave 11 January as his father's birthday; it was, in fact, 12 January.

[94] Reilly 1982: 314. Harry's manifestly false appreciation of Cooper's "courteous behavior," mentioned above, immediately follows his profession of admiration of HUAC, which may have been equally insincere.

[95] HUAC 1953f: 1863.

[96] HUAC 1953f: 1866-67.

[97] Leonard Buder, "'Refuse to Testify,' Einstein Advises Intellectuals Called In by Congress," New York Times, 12 June 1953.

[98] HUAC 1953f: 1868.

[99] HUAC, "Hearings," 84th Congress, First Session, 28 Mar. 1955 (Washington: U.S. Government Printing Office, 1955): 657-664. Uncle Al–a Harvard graduate proud to appear working-class–and Aunt Eva surprised me about 1955 by sending a book promoting CPUSA ideas.

[100] The living were Paul Zilsel, Daniel Boone Schirmer, Alan Philbrick, Lawrence S. Levy, Saul Friedberg, Wendell Furry, Louis Harap, Herbert Robbins, Paul Zilsel, Corliss Lamont, Granville Hicks, Nehemiah Sparks, Loretta Starr, Dave Grant, and Johnny Weber. Harry had heard of the ones whom he did not know personally.

[101] Donner 1961: 116.

[102] Schrecker 1986: 195.

[103] Diamond 1992: 26.

[104] Diamond 1992: 32, 128, 140, 357.

[105] Parry told the Buffalo committee "that he had been an active member of the Communist Party from 1933 to 1942, had informal relations with it while in the Army from 1942 to 1945 and quit the party in 1946" (Jennings 1988).

[106] Jennings 1988.

[107] Qtd. Cohen 1975: 17-18; *Buffalo Courier Express*, 25 May 1953.

[108] "Dr. Parry Deprived of U.B. Tenure for Red-Probe Stand," *Buffalo Evening News*, 26 June 1953 (included in Parry's FBI file).

[109] Hare 1999: 79.

[110] Qtd. Navasky 1980: xx.

[111] HUAC 1953f: 1866.

[112] HUAC 1953f: 1867 (Harry's point); Diamond 1992: 33 (National Education Association); Norman Thomas, qtd. Goodman 1968: 327; Schrecker 1986: 40, 42 (no politics in classrooms).

[113] Schlatter 1977: 56-57; Wiener 1989: 403.

[114] HJMD, 16 April 1932 ("change things"); Root 1954: 3, 7 (praise for cooperation).

[115] HUAC1955: 664 (Doyle); Navasky 1980: viii ("morality play"); Goodman 1968: 358; Iversen 1959: 313, 319.

[116] Navasky 1980: 319. Similarly, Kaplan suggests that *Kristallnacht* was a "degradation ritual" meant to convey to Jews their outlaw status (1998: 122).

[117] Schrecker, interview notes, 9 Mar. 1979.

Chapter 8

[1] HJML, 26 May 1937 (baby crying); 3 June 1937 ("noise"); Sarah (Bunny) Marks to Louis and Sophie Marks, 15 May 1937.

[2] Fritz Freyhan to HJM, 3 June 1937; HJMD, 16 Apr. 1932 (career in law), 20 July 1932 ("catastrophic").

[3] HJML, 10 Nov. 1936 (pamphlets); Alfred H. Hirschbach to HJM, 26 May 1937.

[4] HJML, 3 Jan. 1937 (Artz), 11 May 1937 (approaching WPA for job), 30 Sept. 1938 (WPA job paid $86), 28 June 1939 (still working for WPA). Since the WPA guides were presented as a collective enterprise by "representative Americans," evidence of authorship is scant (Bold 2006: 4-5). Harry worried that Congress would cut off federal funding (HJML, 28 June 1939); it did, but the state of Massachusetts assumed responsibility.

⁵ Bold 2006: 20 (fellow travelers), 65 (margins), 67 (Arts Projects).

⁶ Sarah (Bunny) Marks, note added to HJML, 10 Nov. 1936. The guests enjoyed the cookies, but it is doubtful that the invitation was any more effective than Harry's "glamorous smiles" (Bunny's addendum to HJML, 30 June 1936, and HJML, 18 Nov. 1936).

⁷ HJML, 8 March 1937 (Chicago agency), 14 Nov. 1931 (Langer's book); Papers of William L. Langer, Harvard Univ. Archives, HUG(FP) 19.9, box 5, folder Personal Correspondence 1936-41, L-P (letters of recommendation); HJML, sample letter of application dated 3 March 1937 (references evenly divided). Putting aside the newly arrived Holborn and Gerhard, Langer and Crane Brinton were "the country's two best younger European historians," and the Harvard Department of History was "one of the strongest" in the university (Keller and Keller 2001: 85). Harry must have had to repress any reaction to Langer's defense in 1936 of Germany's occupation of the Rhineland and Langer's doubt that Hitler was a militarist (Norwood 2009: 41). In a review of Norwood's book, Steven Remy suggests that "Langer's position on the Rhineland reoccupation may have been informed at least in part by his own family background and his particular take on the reverberations of the post-World War I settlement" (H-German, H-Net Reviews, July 2011, https://www.h-net.org/reviews/showrev.php?id=32995).

⁸ Langer's undated letter seems to have been written sometime in the second half of 1937; it was apparently intended for Harry's file in the Harvard Placement Office. In his 1980 interview (p. 18), Harry said he had taken all of Langer's courses available to him. Langer regularly taught History 2: Continental Europe: 1871-1914, one of the courses required of undergraduates. Harry would have taken it in 1928-29, having taken History 1 the previous year (Harvard Univ., *Announcement of the Courses of Instruction Offered by the Faculty of Arts and Sciences 1928-29*, p. 106).

⁹ The Jewish New Yorkers to whom Langer wrote on 12 Sept. 1937 were Prof. A. Broderick Cohen of Hunter College and President Paul Klapper of Queens College (William L. Langer papers, Harvard Univ. Archives, HUG(FP) 19.9, box 5, Personal Correspondence 1936-41, L-P, 19 Sept. 1937). The Romanian-born Klapper was appointed first president of Queens on 25 May 1937; the college received 3,600 applications for the initial faculty intake of 26 (Stepanchev 1987: 46-47). The generic recommendation for the American College Bureau in Chicago is dated 13 Nov. 1937; that for Sarah Lawrence, 12 April 1938.

¹⁰ Langer to Musser (13 January 1938). Hofstra had been founded in 1935 as a "feeder" school to NYU and was under its supervision until 1939. For this information, my thanks to Geri Solomon, Hofstra Archivist (email, 3 Apr. 2009). Albert N. Jorgensen, the newly appointed president

of UConn, wrote a similar recommendation for a former student, Louis T. Masson, praising his talents while warning of "one doubtful point"–"Mr. Masson is Jewish and has the characteristic trait of 'pushing' which has at times been objectionable. I suggest you check on that trait. Aside from that, I believe him to be well qualified for the position" (DRC, Papers of Albert Nels Jorgensen, correspondence, Box 1, Jorgensen to Dean Harry S. Ganders, Syracuse Univ. School of Education, 18 Nov. 1935). Masson did all right; he taught high school in the Buffalo area and published articles on science pedagogy and three books: *Chemistry Made Easy, General Science Made Easy,* and *Physics Made Easy* (see his obit, *Buffalo News,* 28 Aug. 1992).

[11] HJML, 5 May 1933 (Fay) and 30 Sept. 1938 (Miss Bouve); Barkin 1991: 154 (advice to Schorske).

[12] HJML, 28 Sept. 1938; Dietrich Gerhard had recommended Ulich to him, and after an initial talk with him Harry anticipated "many enjoyable hours," which proved too optimistic. When Klemperer, who knew Ulich in Dresden, appealed to him for help, Ulich's reply was "friendly but gloomy" (1998: 69 [13 June 1934]).

[13] HJML, 18 Oct. 1938 and 3 Jan. 1939 (teachers' examination); 26, 28, and 29 Dec. (list of candidates, oral exam). Shortly before Harry took the exam, "Dr. Louis Marks, chairman of the board of examiners" issued a report stating that 1,001 persons had taken the examination in history and civic during the past year; he speculated that the increase was due to "the emphasis on political and economic issues" in the contemporary world (*New York Times,* "History Heads List in Teachers' Favor," 23 Sept. 1938).

[14] HJML, 2 Feb. 1939 (agency in Chicago), 2 Mar. 1939 (Fieldston friends), 5 June 1939 (New Dorp job); Papers of William L. Langer, Harvard Univ. Archives, HUG(FP) 19.9, box 5, Personal Correspondence 1936-41, L-P (letter, 22 Mar. 1939); HJM 1980 ($4.50 a day); HUAC 1953f: 1856. He also taught briefly at Richmond High School and at the High School of Music and Art in Manhattan, where the pay was $6 a day (HJM 1980). While Harry was teaching in Staten Island, Congress passed a draft law; in 1940, when he was thirty-one, the age limit was 35, raised to 38 after Pearl Harbor, so he would have been eligible. Possibly the draft board considered high school teaching a sufficiently significant civilian job.

[15] HJM 1980.

[16] Stave 2006: 61-67.

[17] HJML, 30 Nov. 1932 (longer treatment); 9 Sept. 1933 ("fine gentleman"). A review of Harry's monograph concluded that despite the "excellent analysis of the forces and personalities involved," this "careful study" did not significantly challenge "generally held views" (Vandenbosch 1960: 169-70).

[18] On 8 May 1970, Schorske, the Dayton-Stockton Professor of Histo-

ry at Princeton, spoke at UConn on "Generational Conflict and Cultural Change: Vienna and the Origins of Oedipal Theory." Schorske's name appears after Harry's in Langer's list of doctoral students (Harvard Univ. Archives, papers, Teaching Materials, 1929-1967, HUGFP 19.6).

[19] Dekmejian to HJM, 5 Sept. 1970. Dekmejian, by then Associate Professor of Political Science at the State University of New York at Binghamton, reminded Harry that he was "the short, thick Armenian from Syria." Harry framed the award certificate, dated 11 Apr. 1970.

[20] HJM, undated draft, evidently 1958.

[21] HJM 1958: 364.

[22] Harry was among the faculty members interviewed by the student paper on the subject of Stalin's death; his comments were reported immediately after those of Emanuel Margolis (Richard Mautino, "University Professors Discuss Stalin's Death," *Connecticut Campus*, 9 Mar. 1953: 2).

[23] "An Historian's Art Now UConn History: Harry Marks Retires," *Willimantic Chronicle*, 1 Aug. 1978. The article is well balanced and evocatively descriptive ("Marks' taste in clothing runs toward the comfortable, wander-about-the-garden variety").

[24] Allen's book *The Nazi Seizure of Power* (1965, 1984), a study of responses to Nazism in a northern German town, shows the kind of curiosity that had animated Harry; indeed, he acknowledged Harry's "essential encouragement" (1984: xiii)

[25] Harry Marks Papers, "Preface" (dated 22 July 1951), DRC, Series I, Box 4. This box in the UConn archives contains material related to the Pivotal Period. Whether this particular Preface, which antedates his work on that book, was ever intended to accompany it is not clear. The manuscript that he sent out in 1973 has no preface.

[26] HJMD, 17 Sept. 1932.

[27] Harry Marks Papers, DRC, Series I, Box 8, Romein folder.

[28] HJML, 3 June 1937 (general-interest book); HJM 1939 (article). Selections from the article were reprinted in an anthology for upper-level history students under the heading "Revisionism and the Crisis of German Social Democracy," a section that included work by such distinguished scholars as Peter Gay, Herbert Marcuse, Joseph Schumpeter, and Gerhard Ritter (Stearns 1975).

[29] Peter V. Ritner to HJM, 9 Apr. 1962, Marks Papers, DRC, Series 1, Box 6, folder "Corresp. on Piv. Per."

[30] James to HJM, 16 Oct. 1973; Sifton to HJM, 16 Oct. 1973–both in Marks Papers, DRC, Series 1, Box 6, folder "Publishers Corresp. Aug. 1973."

[31] James L. Mairs of W.W. Norton to HJM, 9 May 1973, Harry Marks Papers, DRC, Series I, Box 6, folder "Corresp. on Piv. Per."; HJM to Herbert F. Mann of Oxford Univ. Press, 8 Aug. 1973, Marks Papers, DRC, Series 1,

Box 6, folder "Publishers Corresp. Aug. 1973." Harry continued to work on his life's project after the round of rejections in 1973. Shortly after his death, his widow, Kay Maxwell Marks–whom he married in 1964, a year after Bunny's death of breast cancer–approached a former student, Thomas R. Osborne, and invited him to edit the manuscript into a publishable work. With additional material in handwritten form, the manuscript had grown rambling and somewhat incoherent, and Osborne found "insoluble problems of documentation," grew discouraged, and ceased his labors. Reached by email in 2007, he wrote that he remained "enormously impressed with the theme and with the scholarship"; he added that he had used the concept of the Pivotal Period throughout his twenty-nine years of teaching European history (Osborne, email, 29 Aug. 2007). Osborne's effort is in the Harry Marks Papers, DRC, Series I, Box 6, Romein folder, along with Bruce Stave's letter of transmittal to Kay Marks, dated 22 Jan. 1991.

[32] HJM 1978: xx.

[33] In 1976, Harry and Kay traveled in Europe as tourists. In Berlin, although Mommsenstrasse 57 remained standing, he found much else changed: "East Berlin reminded me of the undemocratic anti-liberal Germany–drab, one-party permitted, evidence of fear, and a low level of economic revival" (HJM 1981).

[34] HJM 1978: xxxii (visa denied to Romein); Schrecker 1986: 145 (Kamen), 151 (Morrison).

[35] Schorske 1955: 340. In a telling distortion of memory, Harry told Ellen Schrecker proudly that Schorske considered his dissertation the "normative" work on the subject (interview notes, 3 July 1979). In fact, Schorske wrote that it was "somewhat weakened by the author's excessively normative approach" (1955: 340). The copy of Harry's dissertation that I borrowed from the University of California at Berkeley contains a slip from the Circulation Department indicating that it had been acquired in 1995, presumably at the request of a faculty member, and had gone out on three previous interlibrary loans, in 1995, 1997, and 2004: not bad for an unpublished work created in a bygone era. Since Harry's name carried no weight, it was the subject matter itself that attracted scholars.

[36] HJM1939: 334.

[37] HJM 1953a: 633.

[38] HJM 1937: ii.

[39] Fermi 1971: 348.

[40] HJM 1959.

[41] HJM 1953a (which demonstrates his base in German historiography, for it cites two German authorities–pp. 629 and 632n9); HJM 1953b.

[42] HJM 1966.

[43] The John Hay Fellows Program, in which Harry taught, sponsored summer programs for senior high-school teachers and public-school administrators. Harry taught "The Culture of Modern Europe" at Bennington in 1962-63 and at Oregon in 1965. His only other non-UConn teaching position after 1946 was a visiting professorship at Connecticut College in 1964-65, teaching Modern Movements in European Cultural History at a salary of $4,000 plus $450 for travel to and from New London. Apparently he was filling in when someone whom the college had expected became unavailable. Material relating to these matters is in the Harry Marks Papers, DRC, Series I, Box 14.

[44] HJM 1958a.

[45] Harry's papers in the UConn archives contain correspondence with Wesleyan University Press, his voluminous notes on Romein and on other works (in English, Dutch, and German) that he used in preparing his Introduction, and his equally voluminous corrections of fact and translation (DRC, Series I, Box 8, Romein folder). The copy that he was working from had a little more than a thousand pages, and he was comparing the translation with the original, which he owned already. A letter to the copy editor mentions thirty pages of his suggested emendations to the translation, of which he was generally admiring (HJM to Austin MacCurtain, 20 June 1977).

[46] HJM 1978: xxii-xxiii.

[47] HJM 1978: xxix-xxxi.

[48] I.e., "about." Harry is unconsciously using a German idiom, *sprechen über*, literally "to speak over."

[49] HJMD, 27 Jan. (first lecture) and 28 Jan. 1933 (second lecture).

[50] HJM 1978: xxx. The final phrases in this sentence are close to a passage in his diary for 27 Jan., except for the translation of the German words: "This evening a fine lecture by Huizinga on the Netherlands as *Vermittler* [intermediary] between West & *Mittel Europa* [Central Europe]." No doubt he refreshed his memory by rereading his diary.

[51] HJMD, 13 Apr. 1933. Mendes-Flohr quotes Huizinga—"The past must be imagined as if it were still the present"—to illustrate the point that even "individuals who were alert to the many social and political contradictions" in the Weimar Republic "could not possibly have foreseen" the horrors unleashed by the Nazis (1999: 92).

[52] HJMD, 8 June 1933. Harry misremembered the title, which is *Amerika levend en denkend*; this short book, published in 1926, was translated into English as "Life and Thought in America: Stray Remarks" (Huizinga 1972: 229-326).

Timeline

[1] Among the useful websites is the World at War Timeslines-Project; see http://www.schudak.de/timelines/germany1930-1933.html (accessed 11 Jan. 2010).

[2] Chalmers in Klemperer 1998: 486.

[3] Klemperer 1998: 249 (31 Jan. 1938).

[4] Klemperer 1998: 264 (24 Aug. 1938).

Bibliography

AAUP (American Association of University Professors). 1937. *Depression, recovery and higher education: A report by Committee Y of the American Association of University Professors.* Prepared by Malcolm M. Willey. New York: McGraw-Hill.

—. 1953. "The thirty-ninth annual meeting." *AAUP Bulletin* 39.1: 91-100.

—. 1956. "Academic freedom and tenure in the quest for national security." *AAUP Bulletin* 42.1: 49-107.

Albisetti, James C. 1988. *Schooling German girls and women: Secondary and higher education in the nineteenth century.* Princeton, NJ: Princeton Univ. Press.

Allen, William Sheridan. 1984. *The Nazi seizure of power: The experience of a single German town.* 2nd ed. Chicago: Univ. of Chicago Press.

Allert, Tilman. 2008. *The Hitler salute: On the meaning of a gesture.* Trans. Jefferson Chase. New York: Metropolitan Books.

Anderson, Mark M., ed. 1998. *Hitler's exiles: Personal stories of the flight from Nazi Germany to America.* New York: New Press.

Angress, Werner T. 1988. *Between fear & hope: Jewish youth in the Third Reich.* Trans. Werner T. Angress and Christine Granger. New York: Columbia Univ. Press.

Anon. 1936. *The yellow spot: The outlawing of half a million human beings: A collection of facts and documents relating to three years' persecution of German Jews, derived chiefly from National Socialist sources, very carefully assembled by a group of investigators.* Intro. by Herbert Hensley Henson, Bishop of Durham. London: Victor Gollancz; New York: Knight Publications. [Published in German with intro. by Lion Feuchtwanger, Paris: Editions du Carrefour, 1936.]

Arendt, Hannah, and Karl Jaspers. 1992. *Hannah Arendt/Karl Jaspers correspondence 1926-1969.* Ed. Lotte Kohler and Hans Saner. Trans. Robert and Rita Kimber. New York: Harcourt Brace Jovanovich.

Artz, Frederick B. 1934. *Reaction and Revolution 1814-1832.* New York: Harper.

Ascher, Abraham. 2007. *A community under siege: The Jews of Breslau under Nazism.* Stanford, CA: Stanford Univ. Press.

Aschheim, Steven E. 2007. *Beyond the border: The German-Jewish legacy abroad.* Princeton, NJ: Princeton Univ. Press.

Bailyn, Bernard, ed. 1986. *Glimpses of the Harvard past.* Harvard Univ. Press.

Baker, Leonard. 1984. *Brandeis and Frankfurter: A dual biography*. New York: Harper & Row.

Barkin, Kenneth D. 1991. "Émigré historians in America: The fifties, sixties, and seventies." In Lehmann and Sheehan, 149-169.

Barth, Alan. 1953. "Universities and political authority." *AAUP Bulletin* 39.1: 5-25.

Bell, Pearl K. 1986. "The Harvard Menorah Society." In N. Rosovsky, 48-50.

Bendix, Reinhard. 1986. *From Berlin to Berkeley: German-Jewish identities*. New Brunswick, NJ: Transaction.

Bentwich, Norman. 1936. *The refugees from Germany: April 1933 to December 1935*. London: G. Allen & Unwin.

—. 1953. *The rescue and achievement of refugee scholars: The story of displaced scholars and scientists 1933-1952*. Intro. by Lord Beveridge. The Hague: Martinus Nijhoff.

Berdichevski, Ivone Herz. 2001. "Adaptation." In Blumenthal, 39-57.

Berghahn, Marion. 1984. *German-Jewish refugees in England: The ambiguities of assimilation*. New York: St. Martin's Press. [Rpt. as *Continental Britons: German-Jewish refugees from Nazi Germany* (New York: Berg, 1988).]

Berghahn, Volker P. 2001. *America and the intellectual cold wars in Europe: Shepard Stone between philanthropy, academy, and diplomacy*. Princeton, NJ: Princeton Univ. Press.

Bernhard, Hannelore. 1989. "Dem Andenken jüdischer Studenten unserer Universität." *Beiträge zur Geschichte der Humboldt-Universität zu Berlin* no. 23: 68-76.

Betker, René. 1997. "Das Historische Seminar der Berliner Universität im 'Dritten Reich', unter besonderer Berücksichtigung der ordenlichen Professoren." Magisterarbeit, Technische Universität Berlin, Institut für Geschichtswissenschaft, Fachgebiet Neuere Geschichte. http://www.geschichtsredaktion.de/magisterarbeit.html, accessed 14 Dec. 2009.

Blumenthal, Gladis Wiener, comp. 2001. *In the land of the gauchos: The history of German Jewish immigration*. Trans. Hedy Lorraine Hofmann and Cláudio Walter. Porto Alegre, Rio Grande do Sul: SIBRA.

Bold, Christine. 2006. *Writers, plumbers, and anarchists: The WPA Writers' Project in Massachusetts*. Amherst: Univ. of Massachusetts Press.

Bonn, M. J. 1948. *Wandering scholar*. New York: John Day.

Brax, Ralph S. 1981. *The first student movement: Student activism in the United States during the 1930s*. Port Washington, NY: Kennikat Press.

Brenner, Arthur D. 2001. *Emil J. Gumbel: Weimar German pacifist and professor*. Boston and Leiden: Brill.

Bühnen, Matthias, and Rebecca Schaarschmidt. 2005. "Studierende als

Täter und Opfer bei der NS-Machtübernahme an der Berliner Universität." In Jahr, 143-157.

Buijnsters, Piet J. 2006. "The antiquarian book trade in the Netherlands in the Second World War." Trans. Harry Lake. *Quaerendo* 36.4: 251-292.

Burlingham, Charles C., James Byrne, Samuel Seabury, and Henry L. Stimson, eds. 1936. *Heidelberg and the universities of America*. New York: Viking Press.

Caron, Vicki. 1999. *Uneasy asylum: France and the Jewish refugee crisis, 1933-1942*. Stanford, CA: Stanford Univ Press.

Carr, Robert K. 1952. *The House Committee on Un-American Activities 1945-1950*. Ithaca, NY: Cornell Univ. Press.

Carsten, F. L. 1967. *The rise of fascism*. Berkeley: Univ. of California Press.

Caute, David. 1978. *The great fear: The anti-Communist purge under Truman and Eisenhower*. New York: Simon and Schuster.

Chalmers, Martin. 1998. "Preface." In Klemperer, vii-xxii.

Clingan, Edmund. 2006. "The German Bank Crisis of 1931: New Debates, New Interpretations." Paper presented at the Conference of the German Studies Association, Pittsburgh, Pennsylvania, 29 Sept.

Cohen, Robert. 1975. "Repression of the Left at the University of Buffalo 1949-1953." Independent study paper. Univ. of Buffalo Archives.

—. 1993. *When the Old Left was young: Student radicals and America's first mass student movement, 1929-1941*. New York: Oxford Univ. Press.

Cole, K. C. 2009. *Something incredibly wonderful happens: Frank Oppenheimer and the world he made up*. Foreword by Murray Gell-mann. Boston: Houghton Mifflin.

Committee of Five. 1953 (15 June). "Report to the Board of Trustees of the University of Connecticut by the Committee of Five investigating charges of Communism against four members of the faculty." Thomas J. Dodd Research Center, Univ. of Connecticut.

Conant, James B. 1970. *My several lives: Memoirs of a social inventor*. New York: Harper & Row.

Conradi, Peter. 2004. *Hitler's piano player: The rise and fall of Ernst Hanfstaengl, confidant of Hitler, ally of FDR*. New York: Carroll & Graf.

Coser, Lewis A. 1984. *Refugee scholars in America: Their impact and their experiences*. New Haven, CT: Yale Univ. Press.

Cosner, Shaaron, and Victoria Cosner. 1998. *Women under the Third Reich: A biographical dictionary*. Westport, CT: Greenwood Press.

Craig, Gordon A. 1999. "The Reich stuff." *New York Review of Books*, 31 Jan. 1991; rpt. *Politics and culture in modern Germany: Essays from* The New York Review of Books. Palo Alto, CA: Society for the Promotion of Science and Scholarship. 51-65.

Crossman, Richard, ed. and intro. 1963. *The god that failed*. 1949. Rpt. New York: Harper Colophon.

Curtis, Lionel. 1947. *Weltkrieg: Ursache und Verhütung (I. Teil); Krieg oder Frieden (II. Teil)*. Trans. Wilhelm Dorn. Essen-Steele Ruhr: Webels. [Translation of *World War: Its Cause and Cure* (London: Oxford Univ. Press, 1945).]

Dahlberg, Edward. 1976. *Those who perish*. 1934. Rpt. in Dahlberg, *Bottom dogs, From Flushing to Calvary, Those who perish, and hitherto unpublished and uncollected works*. New York: Thomas Y. Crowell.

Dawidowicz, Lucy S. 1975. *The war against the Jews*. New York: Holt, Rinehart and Winston.

Deutschkron, Inge. 1989. *Outcast: A Jewish girl in wartime Berlin*. Trans. Jean Steinberg. New York: Fromm.

Diamond, Sigmund. 1977. "Veritas at Harvard." *New York Review of Books*, 28 Apr.: 13-17.

—. 1982. "The arrangement: The FBI and Harvard University in the McCarthy period." In Athan G. Theoharis, ed., *Beyond the Hiss case*, 341-406. Philadelphia: Temple Univ. Press.

—. 1992. *Compromised campus: The collaboration of universities with the intelligence community, 1945-1955*. New York and Oxford: Oxford Univ. Press.

Dickinson, Donald C. 1998. *Dictionary of American antiquarian bookdealers*. Westport, CT: Greenwood Press.

Diehl, James M. 1977. *Paramilitary politics in the Weimar Republic*. Bloomington: Indiana Univ. Press.

Dodd, Martha. 1939. *Through embassy eyes*. New York: Harcourt, Brace.

Dodd, William E. 1941. *Ambassador Dodd's diary*. Ed. William E. Dodd, Jr., and Martha Dodd. Intro. Charles A. Beard. New York: Harcourt, Brace.

Donner, Frank J. 1961. *The un-Americans*. New York: Ballantine.

Dorn, Wilhelm. 1897. *Benjamin Neukirch, Sein Leben und seine Werke: Ein Beitrag zur Geschichte der zweiten Schlesischen Schule*. Litterarhistorische Forschungen vol. 4. Weimar: Verlag von Emil Felber.

—. 1904. *Meine Erfahrungen an englischen Schulen*. Beilage zum Jahresbericht der Ober-Realschule Heidelberg, 1903/1904. Heidelberg.

Draper, Hal. 1967. "The student movement of the thirties: A political history." In *As we saw the thirties*, ed. Rita James Simon, 151-189. Urbana: Univ. of Illinois Press.

Duggan, Stephen, and Betty Drury. 1948. *The rescue of science and learning: The story of the Emergency Committee in Aid of Displaced Foreign Scholars*. New York: Macmillan.

Dwork, Deborah, and Robert Jan van Pelt. 2009. *Flight from the Reich: Refugee Jews, 1939-1946*. New York: W. W. Norton.

Eagan, Eileen. 1981. *Class, culture, and the classroom: The student peace movement of the 1930s*. Philadelphia: Temple Univ. Press.

Edelheit, Abraham J., and Herschel Edelheit. 1994. *History of the Holocaust: A handbook and dictionary*. Boulder, CO: Westview Press.

Ehrenfried, Albert. 1963. *A chronicle of Boston Jewry: From the colonial settlement to 1900*. Boston, privately printed.

Emerson, William R. P. 1922. *Nutrition and growth in children*. New York: D. Appleton.

Emmanuel, Jorge. 2006. "Remembering Boone." Los Angeles: UCLA Center for Southeast Asian Studies. Retrieved from http://escholarship.org/uc/item/64v2x47b (accessed 5 Nov. 2009).

Engelberg, Achim. 2007. *Wer verloren hat, kämpfe*. Berlin: Karl Dietz Verlag.

Epstein, Catherine. 1993. *A past renewed: A catalog of German-speaking refugee historians in the United States after 1933*. Washington: German Historical Institute; New York: Cambridge Univ. Press.

Espindola, Susana Sondermann. 2001. "A story of many stories." In Blumenthal, 107-117.

"Eugene Bronstein: A tribute." 1937. *Harvard Communist* 4.1 (Nov.): 3-4.

Evans, Richard J. 2003. *The coming of the Third Reich*. New York: Penguin.

—. 2005. *The Third Reich in power: 1933-1939*. New York: Penguin.

Fermi, Laura. 1971. *Illustrious immigrants: The intellectual migration from Europe 1930-41*. 2nd ed. Chicago: Univ. of Chicago Press.

Feuer, Lewis S. 1969. *The conflict of generations: The character and significance of student movements*. New York: Basic Books.

Fowkes, Ben. 1984. *Communism in Germany under the Weimar Republic*. New York: St. Martin's Press.

Frankfurter, Felix. 1960. *Felix Frankfurter reminisces*. Recorded in talks with Dr. Harlan B. Phillips. New York: Reynal.

Freidenreich, Harriet Pass. 2002. *Female, Jewish, and educated: The lives of Central European university women*. Bloomington: Indiana Univ. Press.

Freyhan, Michael. 2003. "Hans Walter Freyhan (b Berlin, 8 December 1909; d Bedford, 7 July 1996)." Jewish Music Institute, *Suppressed Music Newsletter*, no. 5 (May). http://www.jmi.org.uk/suppressedmusic/newsletter/ifsm_news5.html#I2 (accessed 7 Dec. 2009).

Friedländer, Saul. 1997. *Nazi Germany and the Jews*. Vol 1: *The years of persecution, 1933-1939*. New York: HarperCollins.

Fromm, Bella. 1990. *Blood and banquets: A Berlin social diary*. Intro. Frederick T. Birchall. 1942. Rpt. with foreword by Judith Rossner. New York: Carol Publishing Group.

Gallin, Alice. 1986. *Midwives to Nazism: University professors in Weimar Germany*. Macon, GA: Mercer Univ. Press.

Gavroglu, Kostas. 1995. *Fritz London: A scientific biography*. Cambridge: Cambridge Univ. Press.

Gay, Peter. 1998. *My German question: Growing up in Nazi Berlin*. New Haven, CT: Yale Univ. Press.

Gerhard, Dietrich. 1970. "Hajo Holborn: Reminiscences." *Central European History* 3: 9-16.

Gilbert, Felix. 1970. "Hajo Holborn: A memoir." *Central European History* 3: 3-8.

Gittler, Margery Wurman, ed. 1953. *75th alumni roster of the Ethical Culture Schools*. New York: Fieldston-Ethical Culture Alumni Association.

Goeschel, Christian. 2007. "Suicides of German Jews in the Third Reich." *German History* 25.1: 22-45.

Goldhagen, Daniel Jonah. 1996. *Hitler's willing executioners: Ordinary Germans and the Holocaust*. New York: Alfred A. Knopf.

Goldschmidt, Dietrich. 1992. "Historical interaction between higher education in Germany and in the United States." In *German and American universities: Mutual influences–past and present*, ed. Ulrich Teichler and Henry Wasser, 11-33. Kassel: Wissenschaftliches Zentrum für Berufs- und Hochschulforschung der Gesamthochschule Kassel. Werkstattberichte, vol. 36.

Goodman, Walter. 1968. *The Committee: The extraordinary career of the House Committee on Un-American Activities*. Foreword by Richard H. Rovere. New York: Farrar, Straus and Giroux.

Gorelick, Sherry. 1981. *City College and the Jewish poor: Education in New York, 1880-1924*. New Brunswick, NJ: Rutgers Univ. Press.

Gottschalk, Paul. 1967. *Memoirs of an antiquarian bookseller*. Gainesville, FL[: Univ. of Florida].

Grüttner, Michael. 2005. "German universities under the swastika." In *Universities under dictatorship*, ed. John Connelly and Michael Grüttner, 75-111. University Park, PA: Pennsylvania Univ. State Univ. Press.

Guérin, Daniel. 1994. *The brown plague: Travels in late Weimar & early Nazi Germany*. Trans. and intro. Robert Schwarzwald. Durham, NC: Duke Univ. Press.

Gutfreind, Ieda. 2001. "Rio Grande do Sul: History and immigration." In Blumenthal, 27-35.

Haffner, Sebastian. 2002. *Defying Hitler: A memoir*. Trans. Oliver Pretzel. New York: Farrar, Straus and Giroux.

Hahn, Lili. 1974. *White flags of surrender*. Washington and New York: Robert B. Luce.

Hall, Claire M. 2009. "An army of spies? The Gestapo spy network 1933-45." *Journal of Contemporary History* 44.2: 247-265.

Hanfstaengl, Ernst S. F. 1934. "My leader." *Colliers*, 94 (4 Aug.): 7-9.

Harders, Levke. 2005. "Von Fleiss und Sachverstand: Studentinnen und Akademikerinnen an der Philosophischen Fakultät." In Jahr, 193-203.

Hare, Peter H. 1999. "Parry, William Tuthill." *American national biography.* Vol. 17. New York: Oxford Univ. Press.

Healy, David. 1998. "Pioneers in psychopharmacology." *International Journal of Neuropsychopharmacology* 1: 191-194.

Hellman, Lillian. 1976. *Scoundrel time.* Intro. by Garry Wills. Boston: Little, Brown.

Hershberg, James G. 1993. *James B. Conant: Harvard to Hiroshima and the making of the nuclear age.* New York: Alfred H. Knopf.

Hicks, Granville. 1939. "On leaving the Communist Party." *New Republic,* 4 Oct.: 244-245.

—. 1954. *Where we came out.* New York: Viking.

Hilberg, Raul. 2003. *The destruction of the European Jews.* 3 vols. 3rd ed. New Haven, CT: Yale Univ. Press.

Hill, A. V., F. Gowland Hopkins, and F. G. Kenyan. 1936. "German universities." Rpt. in Burlingham et al., 55-59. [First published in the *Times* (London), 7 Feb. 1936; and also in *Universities Review,* Apr. 1936.]

Hill, Leonidas E. 1994. "The published political memoirs of leading Nazis, 1933-45." In *Political memoir: Essays on the politics of memory,* ed. George Egerton, 224-241. London: Frank Cass.

Hirsch, Felix E. 1946. "Hermann Oncken and the end of an era." *Journal of Modern History* 18.2: 148-159.

Hirschbach, Ernest. N.d.(a). "The Borchard family: Not a saga but an affectionate tribute." Privately printed, 27 pp.

—. N.d. (b). "If there had been a choice for me." Unpublished essay written prior to 1989.

Hirschbach, Frank D. 1989. "Die Abituriententag: Die Geschichte eines Klassentreffens–fünfzig Jahre danach." *Die Zeit.* www.zeit.de/1989/25/Der-Abituriententag (accessed 21 Jan. 2010).

HUAC. 1938-44. Hearings of Dies (Special) Committee. Washington, DC: United States Government Printing Office, 1944.

HUAC. 1953a. *Hearings before the Committee on Un-American Activities House of Representatives.* Eighty-third Congress, first session. February 25, 26, and 27. Communist Methods of Infiltration (Education–Part 1). Washington, DC: United States Government Printing Office.

—. 1953b. *Hearings before the Committee on Un-American Activities House of Representatives.* Eighty-third Congress, first session. March 12, 13, 17, 18, April 14 and 16. Communist Methods of Infiltration (Education–Part 2). Washington, DC: United States Government Printing Office.

—. 1953c. *Hearings before the Committee on Un-American Activities House of Representatives.* Eighty-third Congress, first session. April 21 and 22.

Communist Methods of Infiltration (Education–Part 3). Washington, DC: United States Government Printing Office.

—. 1953d. *Hearings before the Committee on Un-American Activities House of Representatives.* Eighty-third Congress, first session. April 23 and 27. Communist Methods of Infiltration (Education–Part 4). Washington, DC: United States Government Printing Office.

—. 1953e. *Hearings before the Committee on Un-American Activities House of Representatives.* Eighty-third Congress, first session. April 29, May 19, 26, 27, and 28. Communist Methods of Infiltration (Education–Part 5). Washington, DC: United States Government Printing Office

—. 1953f. *Hearings before the Committee on Un-American Activities House of Representatives.* Eighty-third Congress, first session. June 22, 24, 29, and July 1. Communist Methods of Infiltration (Education–Part 6). Washington, DC: United States Government Printing Office.

—. 1954. *Hearings before the Committee on Un-American Activities House of Representatives.* Eighty-third Congress, first session. April 21 and June 8, 1953; and April 12, 1954. Communist Methods of Infiltration (Education–Part 8). Washington, DC: United States Government Printing Office.

—. 1955. *Hearings before the Committee on Un-American Activities House of Representatives.* Eighty-fourth Congress, first session. March 28 and 29. Investigation of Communist Activities in the Milwaukee Area–Part 1. Washington, DC: United States Government Printing Office.

—. 1958a. *Hearings before the Committee on Un-American Activities House of Representatives.* Eighty-fifth Congress, second session. March 18. Investigation of Communist Activities in the New England Area–Part 1. Washington, DC: United States Government Printing Office.

—. 1958b. *Hearings before the Committee on Un-American Activities House of Representatives.* Eighty-fifth Congress, second session. March 19. Investigation of Communist Activities in the New England Area–Part 2. Washington, DC: United States Government Printing Office.

—. 1958c. *Hearings before the Committee on Un-American Activities House of Representatives.* Eighty-fifth Congress, second session. March 14, 20, and 21. Investigation of Communist Activities in the New England Area–Part 3. Washington, DC: United States Government Printing Office.

Huizinga, Johan. 1972. *America: A Dutch historian's vision, from afar and near.* Trans. and intro. Herbert H. Rowen. New York: Harper & Row.

Iggers, Georg G. 1968. *The German conception of history: The national tradition of historical thought from Herder to the present.* Middleton, CT: Wesleyan Univ. Press.

—. 2005. "Refugee historians from Nazi Germany: Political attitudes towards democracy." Monna and Otto Weinmann Lecture Series, 14 Dec., United States Holocaust Memorial Museum. http://www.ushmm.org/research/center/publications/occasional/2006-02/paper.pdf (accessed 21 Jan. 2010).

Irwin, Elisabeth A., and Louis A. Marks. 1924. *Fitting the school to the child: An experiment in public education.* New York: Macmillan.

Isenberg, Sheila. 2001. *A hero of our own: The story of Varian Fry.* New York: Random House.

Isherwood, Christopher. 1977. *Lions and shadows: An education in the twenties.* New York: New Directions.

Iversen, Robert W. 1959. *The Communists and the schools.* New York: Harcourt, Brace.

Jacobson, Matthew Frye. 1998. *Whiteness of a different color: European immigrants and the alchemy of race.* Cambridge, MA: Harvard Univ. Press.

Jahr, Christoph, ed., with the assistance of Rebecca Schaarschmidt. 2005. *Die Berliner Universität in der NS-Zeit.* Vol. 1: *Strukturen und Personen.* Stuttgart: Franz Steiner Verlag.

Jarausch, Konrad H. 2001. "The expulsion of Jewish professors and students from the University of Berlin during the Third Reich." In *Crossing boundaries: The exclusion and inclusion of minorities in Germany and the United States,* ed. Larry Eugene Jones, 9-26. New York: Berghahn Books.

Jay, Martin. 1985. *Permanent exiles: Essays on the intellectual migration from Germany to America.* New York: Columbia Univ. Press.

—. 1996. *The dialectical imagination: A history of the Frankfurt School and the Institute of Social Research, 1923-1950.* Berkeley: Univ. of California Press.

Jennings, Irene. 1988. "UB professor William Parry dies; a target of McCarthy era probe." *Buffalo News,* 18 Aug.

Kampe, Norbert. 1993. "The Jewish arrival at higher education." In Herbert A. Strauss, ed., *Hostages of modernization: Studies on modern anti-Semitism 1870-1933/39,* 80-106. Current Research on Antisemitism, ed. Herbert A. Strauss and Werner Bergmann, vol. 3/1. Berlin and New York: Walter de Gruyter.

Kaplan, Marion A. 1998. *Between dignity and despair: Jewish life in Nazi Germany.* New York: Oxford Univ. Press.

Karabel, Jerome. 2005. *The chosen: The hidden history of admission and exclusion at Harvard, Yale, and Princeton.* Boston: Houghton Mifflin.

Kästner, Erich. 1931. *Fabian: The story of a moralist.* Trans. Cyrus Brooks. Evanston, IL: Northwestern Univ. Press, 1993.

Kater, Michael H. 1989. *Doctors under Hitler.* Chapel Hill: Univ. of North Carolina Press.

—. 1991. "Refugee historians in America: Preemigration Germany to 1939." In Lehmann and Sheehan, 73-93.

—. 1997. *The twisted muse: Musicians and their music in the Third Reich.* New York and Oxford: Oxford Univ. Press.

—. 2008. *Never sang for Hitler: The life and times of Lotte Lehmann, 1888-1976.* Cambridge: Cambridge Univ. Press.

Katz, Barry M. 1991. "German historians in the Office of Strategic Services." In Lehmann and Sheehan, 136-139.

Keller, Morton and Phyllis. 2001. *Making Harvard modern: The rise of America's university.* New York: Oxford Univ. Press.

Kennedy, A. L. 2000. The Times *and appeasement: The journals of A.L. Kennedy, 1932-1939.* Ed. Gordon Martel. Cambridge: Cambridge University Press for the Royal Historical Society.

Kershaw, Ian. 1999. *Hitler 1889-1936: Hubris.* New York: W. W. Norton.

Kessler, Harry.1999. *Berlin in lights: The diaries of Count Harry Kessler, 1918-1937.* Trans. Charles Kessler. Intro. Ian Buruma. New York: Grove Press.

Kirkbright, Suzanne. 2004. *Karl Jaspers: A biography: Navigations in truth.* New Haven, CT: Yale Univ. Press.

Klehr, Harvey. 1984. *The heyday of American Communism: The depression decade.* New York: Basic Books.

—, and John Earl Haynes. 1992. *The American Communist movement: Storming heaven itself.* New York: Twayne.

Klemperer, Victor. 1998. *I will bear witness: A diary of the Nazi years 1933-1941.* Trans. and Preface by Martin Chalmers. New York: Random House.

Klotz, Helmut, ed. 1934. *The Berlin diaries: May 30, 1932-Jan. 30, 1933.* [Trans. from *Das Berliner Tagebuch.*] Foreword by Edgar Ansel Mowrer. New York: Morrow.

Korenblat, Steven D. 2006. "A school for the Republic?: Cosmopolitans and their enemies at the Deutsche Hochschule für Politik, 1920-1933." *Central European History* 39: 394-430.

Krohn, Claus-Dieter. 1993. *Intellectuals in exile: Refugee scholars and the New School for Social Research.* Trans. Rita and Robert Kimber. Foreword by Arthur J. Vidich. Amherst: Univ. of Massachusetts Press.

Kunoff, Hugo. 1975. "Émigrés, emigration studies, and libraries." *Library Quarterly* 45.2: 141-149.

Kurshan, Virginia. 2006. "(Former) PUBLIC SCHOOL 64." Report for Landmarks Preservation Commission, New York City. June 20, Designation List 377, LP-2189. www.nyc.gov/html/lpc/downloads/pdf/reports/ps64.pdf (accessed 22 July 2006).

Küttler, Wolfgang, ed. 1999. *Das lange 19. Jahrhundert: Personen–Ereignisse–*

Ideen–Umwälzungen: Ernst Engelberg zum 90. Geburtstag. Vol. 1. Berlin: Trafo.

Ladd, Everett Carll, Jr., and Seymour Martin Lipset. 1976. *The divided academy: Professors and politics*. New York: W. W. Norton.

Laqueur, Walter. 2001. *Generation exodus: The fate of young Jewish refugees from Nazi Germany*. Hanover and London: Brandeis Univ. Press.

Large, David Clay. 2000. *Berlin*. New York: Basic Books.

Lasker-Wallfisch, Anita. 2000. *Inherit the truth: A memoir of survival and the Holocaust*. 1996. Rpt. New York: St. Martin's Press.

Latham, Earl. 1966. *The Communist controversy in Washington*. Cambridge, MA: Harvard Univ. Press.

Laub, Claudia Judite. 2001. "The Jews in Germany before emigration." In Blumenthal 2001, 15-25.

Lavin, Deborah. 1995. *From empire to international commonwealth: A biography of Lionel Curtis*. Oxford: Clarendon Press.

Leff, Laurel. 2005. *Buried by the Times: The Holocaust and America's most important newspaper*. Cambridge: Cambridge Univ. Press.

Lehmann, Hartmut. 2003. "Religious socialism, peace, and pacifism: The case of Paul Tillich." In *The shadows of total war: Europe, East Asia, and the United States, 1919-1939*, ed. Roger Chickering and Stig Förster, 85-95. Washington: German Historical Institute; Cambridge: Cambridge Univ. Press.

—, and James J. Sheehan, eds. 1991. *An interrupted past: German-speaking refugee historians in the United States after 1933*. Washington, DC: German Historical Institute; Cambridge: Cambridge Univ. Press.

Lesser, Jeffrey. 1995. *Welcoming the undesirables: Brazil and the Jewish question*. Berkeley: Univ. of California Press.

Levine, Arthur J., and Louis Marks. 1928. *Testing intelligence and achievement*. New York: Macmillan.

Levy, Hyman. 1947. *Ein Weltbild für Menschen unserer Zeit*. Trans. Wilhelm Dorn and Kurt Lütgen. Webels: Essen-Steele Ruhr. [Translation of *A Philosophy for a Modern Man* (London: Victor Gollancz, 1938).]

Lewis, Harold. 2003. *For the common good: Essays of Harold Lewis*. Ed. Michael Reisch. New York: Brunner-Routledge.

Lewis, Lionel S. 1988. *Cold War on campus: A study of the politics of organizational control*. New Brunswick: Transaction.

Liebersohn, Harry, and Dorothee Schneider. 2001. *My life in Germany before and after January 30, 1933: A guide to a manuscript collection at Houghton Library, Harvard University*. Philadelphia: American Philosophical Society.

Lipset, Seymour Martin, and David Riesman. 1975. *Education and politics at Harvard*. New York: McGraw Hill.

Lohff, Brigitte, and Hinderk Conrads. 2007. *From Berlin to New York: Life and work of the almost forgotten German-Jewish biochemist Carl Neuberg (1877-1956).* Trans. Anthony Mellor-Stapelberg. Stuttgart: Franz Steiner Verlag.

Lorenz, Werner. 2004. "Ernst J. Cohn (1904-1976)." In *Jurists unprooted: German-speaking émigré lawyers in twentieth-century Britain*, ed. Jack Beatson and Reinhard Zimmermann, 325-344. Oxford: Oxford Univ. Press.

Lowell, A. Lawrence. 1909. "President Lowell's inaugural address October 6, 1909." In *The development of Harvard University since the inauguration of President Eliot 1869-1929*, ed. Samuel Eliot Morison, lxxix-lxxxviii. Cambridge, MA: Harvard Univ. Press, 1930.

Mann, Erika. 1938. *School for barbarians.* Intro. Thomas Mann. New York: Modern Age Books.

—, and Klaus Mann. 1939. *Escape to life.* Boston: Houghton Mifflin; Cambridge: Riverside Press.

Mann, Thomas. 1982. *Diaries 1918-1939: 1918-1921, 1933-1939.* Selected by Hermann Kesten. Foreword Hermann Kesten. Trans. Richard and Clara Winston. New York: Harry N. Abrams.

Marcus, Jacob R. 1934. *The rise and destiny of the German Jew.* Cincinnati: Union of American Hebrew Congregations.

Marks, Harry J. 1931. "The Social Democratic Party of Germany, 1890-1914." Thesis (A.B., Honors), Harvard Univ. Archives.

—. 1937. "Movements of reform and revolution in the Social Democratic Party of Germany from 1890 to 1903 with an epilogue: 1903-1914." 2 vols. PhD diss., Harvard Univ.

—. 1939. "The sources of reformism in the Social Democratic Party in Germany 1890-1914." *Journal of Modern History* 9.3 (Sept.): 334-356.

—. 1953a. "Ground under our feet: Beard's relativism." *Journal of the History of Ideas* 14.4 (Oct.): 628-633.

—. 1953b. "Improved teaching in college history courses." *Social Science* 28.1: 16-24.

—. 1958a. "The first state of the cultural crisis: The pivotal period in European history." *History of Ideas Newsletter* 4.1: 2-5.

—. 1958b. "Virtue vindicated: The King vs. Mary Ann Tucker." *Connecticut Bar Journal* 32.4: 364-380.

—. 1959. *The first contest for Singapore 1819-1824.* Verhandelingen van het Koninklijk Instituut voor Taal-, Land- en Volkenkunde, vol. 27. The Hague: Martinus Nijhoff.

—. 1966. "Three notes on history or past time." In *A Guide to Reading in American History: The Unit Approach*, by Herbert Herskowitz and Bernard Marlin, 17-22. New York: New American Library.

—. [1973?] "The pivotal period in European history." Unpublished manuscript.

—. 1978. "Introduction." In Romein, xx-xxxviii.

—. 1980. "Interview with Harry Marks at his home on Eastwood Road in Storrs, by Robert Lougee, March 11, 1980." Center for Oral History Interviews Collection, Thomas J. Dodd Research Center, Univ. of Connecticut.

—. 1981. "The rise of the Nazis–a kind of personal memoir," 8 Oct. Harry Marks Papers, Box 13, Thomas J. Dodd Research Center, Univ. of Connecticut.

Marks, Louis. 1921. "A survey of Public School 64, from the standpoint of the principal." *Bulletin of the New York Society for the Experimental Study of Education* 2.5: 3.

—. 1934. "The selection, appointment, and promotion of personnel in a large city school system." PhD diss., School of Education, New York Univ.

Marrus, Michael R., and Robert O. Paxton. 1981. *Vichy France and the Jews*. New York: Basic Books.

Martinson, Deborah. 2005. *Lillian Hellman: A life with foxes and scoundrels*. New York: Counterpoint.

Mayer, Gustav. 1936. *Friedrich Engels: A biography*. Trans. Gilbert and Helen Highet. London: Chapman & Hall.

—. 1949. *Erinnerungen: Vom Journalisten zum Historiker der deutschen Arbeiterbewegung*. Munich: Verlag der Zwölf.

McAllister, Pat. 1995. "Obituary: Philip Mayer." *Anthropology Today* 11.2: 22-23.

McDonald, James G. 2007. *Advocate for the doomed: The diaries and papers of James G. McDonald 1932-1935*. Ed. Richard Breitman, Barbara McDonald Stewart, and Severin Hochberg. Bloomington: Indiana Univ. Press, in association with the United States Holocaust Memorial Museum, Washington, D.C.

Mendes-Flohr, Paul. 1988. *German Jews: A dual identity*. New Haven, CT: Yale Univ. Press.

Mertens, Lothar. 2006. *Lexikon der DDR-Historiker: Biographien und Bibliographien zu den Geschichtswissenschaftlern aus der Deutschen Demokratischen Republik*. Munich: K.G. Saur.

Meyer, Agnes E. 1953. "The attack on the intellect." *AAUP Bulletin* 39.4: 557-573.

Meyer, Gertrud Milch. 1995. "Gertrude's life story." Unpublished manuscript. 8 pp.

Minters, Arthur H. 1979. *Collecting books for fun and profit*. New York: Arco.

Mommsen, Wolfgang J. 1991. "Historiography in the Weimar Republic." In Lehmann and Sheehan, 32-66.

Moore, Bob. 1986. *Refugees from Nazi Germany in the Netherlands, 1933-1940.* Dordrecht, Boston, and Lancaster: Martinus Nijhoff.

Morison, Samuel Eliot. 1936. *Three centuries of Harvard.* Cambridge, MA: Harvard Univ. Press.

Mosse, George L. 1985. *German Jews beyond Judaism.* Bloomington: Indiana Univ. Press; Cincinatti: Hebrew Union College Press.

—. 2000. *Confronting history: A memoir.* Madison: Univ. of Wisconsin Press.

Mowrer, Edgar Ansel. 1939. *Germany puts the clock back.* 1933. Rev. ed. New York: William Morrow.

Mühlen, Patrik von zur. 1994. "Exil in Brasilien: Die deutschsprachige Emigration 1933-1945." In *Exil in Brasilien: Die deutschsprachige Emigration, 1933-1945: Eine Ausstellung des Deutschen Exilarchivs 1933-1945,* ed. Christine Hohnschopp, 11-24. Leipzig: Deutsche Bibliothek.

Müller-Enbergs, Helmut, et al. 2006. *Wer war wer in der DDR?: Ein Lexikon ostdeutscher Biographien.* Berlin: Ch. Links Verlag.

Navasky, Victor S. 1980. *Naming names.* New York: Viking.

NCC (National Coordinating Committee for Aid to Refugees and Emigrants Coming from Germany). 1937. *New York ist gross—Amerika ist groesser.* New York: NCC.

Niedhart, Gottfried. 1988. "Gustav Mayers englische Jahre: Zum Exil eines deutschen Juden und Historikers." *Exilforschung: Ein internationales Jahrbuch* 6: 98-107.

—. 1993. "Nachwort." Gustav Mayer. *Erinnerungen: Vom Journalisten zum Historiker der deutschen Arbeiterbewegung* (rpt.), 406-414. Bibliothek des deutschen Judentums, ed. Julius H. Schoeps. Hildesheim: Georg Olms Verlag.

Niewyk, Donald L. 1980. *The Jews in Weimar Germany.* Baton Rouge: Louisiana State University Press.

Noack, Karl-Heinz, comp. 1999. "Schriftenverzeichnis Ernst Engelberg." In Küttler, 309-320.

Noakes, J[eremy], and G[eoffrey] Pridham, eds. 1990. *Nazism 1919-1945: A history in documents and eyewitness accounts.* Vol. 1: *The Nazi party, state and society 1919-1939.* Vol. 2: *Foreign policy, war and racial extermination.* Rpt. of volumes published 1983-88. New York: Schocken Books.

Norwood, Stephen H. 2009. *The Third Reich in the Ivory Tower: Complicity and conflict on American campuses.* Cambridge and New York: Cambridge Univ. Press.

O'Reilly, Kenneth. 1983. *Hoover and the un-Americans: The FBI, HUAC, and the red menace.* Philadelphia: Temple Univ. Press.

Palmier, Jean Michel. 2006. *Weimar in exile: The antifascist emigration in Europe and America.* Trans. David Fernbach. London and New York: Verso.

Pflanze, Otto P. 1991. "The Americanization of Hajo Holborn." In Lehmann and Sheehan, 170-179.

Philbrick, Herbert Arthur. 1972. *I led 3 lives: Citizen, "Communist," counterspy*. 1952. Rpt. Washington: Capitol Hill Press.

Plotkin, Abraham. 2009. *An American in Hitler's Berlin: Abraham Plotkin's diary, 1932-33*. Ed. with Intro. by Catherine Collomp and Bruno Groppo. Urbana: Univ. of Illinois Press.

Popkin, Jeremy D. 2003. "Holocaust memories, historians' memoirs." *History and Memory* 15.1: 49-84.

Potter, Pitman B. 1968. "The Graduate Institute of International Studies, Geneva." *American Journal of International Law* 62. 3: 740-742.

Rader, Melvin. 1969. *False witness*. Seattle: Univ. of Washington Press.

Reisch, Michael, and Janice Andrews. 1999. "Uncovering a silent betrayal: Using oral history to explore the impact of McCarthyism on the profession of social work in the United States." *Oral History Review* 26.2: 87-106

—, and Janice Andrews. 2001. *The road not taken: A history of radical social work in the United States*. Philadelphia: Brunner-Routledge.

Reisman, Arnold. 2006. *Turkey's modernization: Refugees from Nazism and Atatürk's vision*. Washington, DC: New Academia Publishing.

Remy, Steven P. 2002. *The Heidelberg myth: The Nazification and denazification of a German university*. Cambridge, MA: Harvard Univ. Press.

Ritter, Gerhard A. 2006. "Meinecke's protegés: German émigré historians between two worlds," trans. David Lazar, *GHI Bulletin* no. 39: 23-38.

Rohe, Karl. 1966. *Das Reichsbanner Schwarz-Rot-Gold*. Düsseldorf: Droste.

Rohkramer, Thomas. 1999. "Cultural criticism in Germany 1880-1933: A typology." *History of European Ideas* 25.6 (Nov.): 321-339.

Rolfe, Edwin. 1974. *The Lincoln Battalion: The story of the Americans who fought in Spain in the International Brigades*. 1939. Rpt. New York: Haskell House.

Romein, Jan. 1978. *The watershed of two eras: Europe in 1900*. Trans. Arnold J. Pomerans. With "A Memoir of Jan Romein" by Maarten C. Brands. Intro. by Harry J. Marks. Middletown, CT: Wesleyan Univ. Press.

Root, E. Merrill. 1954. "Why the professors turned." *Faith and Freedom* 5.6 (Feb.): 3-7.

Ropp, Theodore, and David H. Pinkney. 1964. "Frederick B. Artz: The man and the teacher, the historical scholar and critic." In *A Festschrift for Frederick B. Artz*, ed. Ropp and Pinkney. Durham, NC: Duke Univ. Press.

Rosenthal, Bernard M. 1987. "The gentle invasion: Continental émigré booksellers of the thirties and forties and their impact on the antiquarian booktrade in the United States." Lecture given 15 Dec. 1986

(Second Annual Sol. M. Malkin Lecture in Bibliography). New York: Book Arts Press, School of Library Science, Columbia Univ.

Rosovsky, Harry. 1986. "From periphery to center." *Harvard Magazine*, Nov. 1979; rpt. N. Rosovsky, 53-58.

Rosovsky, Nitza. 1986. *The Jewish experience at Harvard and Radcliffe: An introduction to an exhibition presented by the Harvard Semitic Museum on the Occasion of Harvard's 350th Anniversary, September 1986*. With contributions by Pearl K. Bell and Ronald Steel. Cambridge, MA: Harvard Semitic Museum.

Rothnie, Niall. 1992. *The Baedeker Blitz: Hitler's attack on Britain's historic cities*. Shepperton, Surrey: Ian Allan.

Rudy, S. Willis. 1949. *The College of the City of New York: A history 1847-1947*. New York: City College Press.

Scheffler, Israel. 2004. *Gallery of scholars: A philosopher's recollections*. Dordrecht, The Netherlands: Kluwer.

Schlatter, Richard. 1977. In *A symposium on political activism and the academic conscience: The Harvard experience 1936-1941, Hobart and William Smith Colleges, December 5 & 6, 1975*, ed. John Lydenberg. Geneva, NY: Hobart and William Smith Colleges.

Schlemmer, Oskar. 1972. *The letters and diaries of Oskar Schlemmer*. Selected and ed. by Tut Schlemmer. Trans. Krishna Winston. Middletown, CT: Wesleyan Univ. Press.

Schlesinger, Andrew. 2005. *Veritas: Harvard College and the American experience*. Chicago: Ivan R. Dee.

Schorske, Carl E. 1955. *German social democracy 1905-1917: The development of the great schism*. Cambridge, MA: Harvard Univ. Press.

—. 1978. Obit of William L. Langer. *American Historical Review* 83.4: 1150-1152.

—. 1991. "The refugee scholar as intellectual education: A student's reflections." In Lehmann and Sheehan, 140-148.

Schrecker, Ellen W. 1986. *No ivory tower: McCarthyism and the universities*. New York and Oxford: Oxford Univ. Press.

—. 1994. *The age of McCarthyism: A brief history with documents*. Boston and New York: Bedford Books.

—. 1998. *Many are the crimes: McCarthyism in America*. Boston: Little, Brown.

Shirer, William L. 1941. *Berlin diary: The journal of a foreign correspondent, 1934-1941*. New York: Alfred A. Knopf.

Silin, Charles I. 1953. "The clear and present danger." *AAUP Bulletin* 39.4: 583-598.

Snyder, Louis L. 1984. *National Socialist Germany: Twelve years that shook the world*. Malabar, FL: Krieger.

Starr, Harry. 1986. "The affair at Harvard: What the students did." *Menorah Journal* 8 (Oct. 1922): 263-276; rpt. N. Rosovsky: 76-82.

Stave, Bruce M., et al. 2006. *Red brick in the land of steady habits: Creating the University of Connecticut, 1881-2006*. Hanover, NH: Univ. Press of New England.

Stearns, Peter N., ed. 1975. *A century for debate, 1789-1914: Problems in the interpretation of European history*. New York: Dodd, Mead.

Steel, Ronald. 1986. "Walter Lippmann's Harvard." In N. Rosovsky, 72-75.

Steinberg, Stephen. 1974. *The academic melting pot: Catholics and Jews in American higher education*. New York: McGraw Hill. 1987.

Stepanchev, Stephen. 1987. "The early years." In *The people's college on the hill: Fifty years at Queens College, 1937*, ed. Stephen Stepanchev. New York: Queens College. 46-48.

Strothmann, Dietrich. 1968. *Nationalsozialistische Literaturpolitik: Ein Beitrag zur Publizistik im Dritten Reich*. Bonn: H. Bouvier.

Supple, Barry E. 1957. "A business elite: German Jewish financiers in nineteenth-century New York." *Business History Review* 31.2: 143-178.

Swett, Pamela E. 2004. *Neighbors and enemies: The culture of radicalism in Berlin, 1929-1933*. Cambridge and New York: Cambridge Univ. Press.

Synnott, Marcia Graham. 1979. *The half-opened door: Discrimination and admissions at Harvard, Yale, and Princeton, 1900-1970*. Westport, CT: Greenwood Press.

Traub, James. 1994. *City on a hill: Testing the American dream at City College*. Reading, MA: Addison-Wesley.

Traubner, Richard. 2003. *Operetta: A theatrical history*. Rev. ed. London and New York: Routledge.

Tuttle, William M., Jr. 1979. "American higher education and the Nazis: The case of James B. Conant and Harvard University's 'Diplomatic Relations' with Germany." *American Studies* 20: 49-70.

Tyler, Kate. 2004. "A Conversation with Frank Hirschbach." *GSD Magazine* Spring: 10-12, 18. http://www.chgs.umn.edu/histories/minnesotans/andHolocaust/images/ConversationWithFrankHirschbach.pdf (accessed 21 Jan. 2010).

Vandenbosch, Amry. 1960. "The first contest for Singapore, 1819-1824 by Harry J. Marks" (review). *Journal of Modern History* 32.2: 169-170.

Veysey, Laurence R. 1965. *The emergence of the American university*. Chicago: Univ. of Chicago Press.

Walther, Peter Th. 1989. "Die nach 1933 in die USA emigrierten deutscher Neuhistoriker." PhD diss., Univ. of Buffalo.

Walton-Jordan, Ulrike. 2000. "Safeguards against tyranny: The impact of German émigré lawyers on British legal policy toward Germany, 1942-1946." *German-speaking exiles in Great Britain*, ed. Anthony Grenville. Yearbook of the Research Centre for German and Austrian Exile Studies. Vol. 2, 1ff. Amsterdam and Atlanta: Rodopi.

Wassermann, Jacob. 1933. *My life as German and Jew*. Trans. S.N. Brainin. New York, Coward-McCann.

Wechsler, James A. 1973. *Revolt on the campus*. 1935. Intro. Robert Morse Lovett. Rpt. Seattle: Univ. of Washington Press.

Weinreich, Max. 1999. *Hitler's professors: The part of scholarship in Germany's crimes against the Jewish people*. 1946. 2nd ed. Foreword by Martin Gilbert. New Haven, CT: Yale Univ. Press.

Weinstein, Allen. 1978. *Perjury: The Hiss-Chambers case*. New York: Knopf.

Weissberg, Alexander. 1951. *The Accused*. Trans. Edward Fitzgerald. Preface by Arthur Koestler. New York: Simon and Schuster.

Weitz, Eric D. 1996. *Creating German Communism, 1890-1990: From popular protests to socialist state*. Princeton, NJ: Princeton Univ. Press.

White, Theodore H. 1979. *In search of history: A personal adventure*. 1978. Rpt. New York: Warner Books.

Wiener, Jonathan M. 1989. "Radical historians and the crisis in American history, 1959-1980." *Journal of American History* 76.2: 399-434.

Williams, Bill. 2005. "'Displaced scholars': Refugees at the University of Manchester." *Melilah* 3: 1-29. http://www.mucjs.org/MELILAH/2005/3.pdf (accessed 29 Sept. 2008)

Wolman, Ruth E. 1996. *Crossing over: An oral history of refugees from Hitler's Reich*. New York: Twayne; London: Prentice Hall International.

Zuccotti, Susan. 1993. *The Holocaust, the French, and the Jews*. New York: Basic Books.

Zucker, Bat-Ami. 2001. *In search of refuge: Jews and US consuls in Nazi Germany 1933-1941*. London and Portland, OR: Vallentine Mitchell.

Index

CPSIA information can be obtained at www.ICGtesting.com
Printed in the USA
LVOW111817200212

269551LV00009B/63/P